JOURNAL FOR STAR WISDOM 2011

JOURNAL FOR STAR WISDOM

2011

Edited by Robert Powell

EDITORIAL BOARD

William Bento
Brian Gray
Lacquanna Paul
Robert Schiappacasse

SteinerBooks

Steinerbooks/Anthroposophic Press, Inc.
610 Main Street, Suite 1
Great Barrington, MA, 01230
www.steinerbooks.org

Journal for Star Wisdom 2011 © 2010 by Robert Powell. All contributions are used by permission of the authors. All rights reserved. No part of this publication may be reproduced, stored in a retrieval system, or transmitted in any form or by any means, electronic, mechanical, photocopying, recording, or otherwise without the prior written permission of the publisher. With grateful acknowledgment to Peter Treadgold (1943–2005), who wrote the Astrofire program (available from the Sophia Foundation), with which the ephemeris pages in the *Journal for Star Wisdom* are computed each year.

The star verses by Rudolf Steiner in the *Journal for Star Wisdom* were translated from the German by Robert Powell from two volumes by Rudolf Steiner (not yet published in English): *Seelenübungen mit Wort- und Sinnbild-Meditationen* ("Soul Exercises with Word and Image Meditations," CW 267), Dornach, Switzerland: Rudolf Steiner Verlag, 1997; and *Mantrische Sprüche: Seelenübungen II* ("Mantric Verses: Soul Exercises, vol. 2," CW 268), Dornach, Switzerland: Rudolf Steiner Verlag, 1999.

The views expressed in the articles published in the *Journal for Star Wisdom* are the sole responsibility of the authors of these articles and do not necessarily reflect those of the editorial board of the *Journal for Star Wisdom*.

Cover and interior design: William Jens Jensen

Printed in the United States of America

ISBN-13: 978-0-88010-728-0

ISBN-10: 0-88010-728-6

CONTENTS

PREFACE — 7

THE ROSE OF THE WORLD (*ROSA MIRA*)
Daniel Andreev — 12

EDITORIAL FOREWORD
Robert Powell — 17

WORKING WITH THE *JOURNAL FOR STAR WISDOM* — 20

THE SIGNATURE OF VENUS IN THE EVENTS OF JESUS CHRIST'S LIFE,
HISTORICAL PERSONALITIES, AND MODERN WORLD EVENTS
David Tresemer — 21

THE PLEIADES AND 2012: THE SIGNIFICANCE OF THE PLEIADES
IN NATIVE AMERICAN INDIAN CULTURE
Robert Powell — 31

PROPHECY: A CAULDRON OF CONTROVERSY
William Bento — 41

HENRY DAVID THOREAU AND THE CHRIST RHYTHM
Kevin Dann — 49

RUDOLF STEINER: THE ARTIST
Brian Gray — 54

THE HOROSCOPES OF J.F.K., GANDHI, MOZART, AND RUDOLF STEINER
IN THE LIGHT OF JACQUES DORSAN'S *CLOCKWISE HOUSE SYSTEM*
Wain Farrants — 61

EXCITEMENT OF THE POLARITIES AT 23° TO 24° OF THE FIXED SIGNS
David Tresemer — 77

WORKING WITH THE STAR CALENDER IN THE *JOURNAL FOR STAR WISDOM* — 82

COMMENTARIES AND EPHEMERIDES: JANUARY–DECEMBER 2011 — 85

CORRECTION — 150

ABOUT THE CONTRIBUTORS — 151

BOOK ANNOUNCEMENT: *THE ASTROLOGICAL REVOLUTION* — 155

ASTROSOPHY

The Sophia Foundation of North America was founded and exists to help usher in the new Age of Sophia and the corresponding Sophianic culture, the Rose of the World, prophesied by Daniel Andreev and other spiritual teachers. Part of the work of the Sophia Foundation is the cultivation of a new star wisdom, *Astro-Sophia* (Astrosophy), now arising in our time in response to the descent of Sophia, who is the bearer of Divine Wisdom, just as Christ (the Logos, or the Lamb) is the bearer of Divine Love. Like the star wisdom of antiquity, Astrosophy is sidereal, which means "of the stars." Astrosophy, inspired by Divine Sophia, descending from stellar heights, directs our consciousness toward the glory and majesty of the starry heavens, to encompass the entire celestial sphere of our cosmos and, beyond this, to the galactic realm—the realm that Daniel Andreev referred to as "the heights of our universe"—from which Sophia is descending on her path of approach into our cosmos. Sophia draws our attention not only to the star mysteries of the heights, but also to the cosmic mysteries connected with Christ's deeds of redemption wrought two thousand years ago. To penetrate these mysteries is the purpose of the yearly *Journal for Star Wisdom*.

For information about Astrosophy/Choreocosmos/Cosmic Dance workshops
Contact the Sophia Foundation of North America:
525 Gough St. #103, San Francisco, CA 94102
(415) 522-1150; sophia@sophiafoundation.org;
www.sophiafoundation.org

PREFACE

Robert Powell, Ph.D.

This is the second edition of the *Journal for Star Wisdom*. It is intended as a help to all who are interested in the new star wisdom of astrosophy and in the cosmic dimension of Christianity, which began with the star of the magi. The calendar comprises ephemeris pages for each month of the year, computed with the help of Peter Treadgold's *Astrofire* computer program, as well as monthly commentaries by Claudia McLaren Lainson with David Tresemer and Sally Nurney. The monthly commentary relates the geocentric and heliocentric planetary movements to events in the life of Jesus Christ.

Jesus Christ united the levels of the earthly personality (geocentric = Earth-centered) and the higher self (heliocentric = Sun-centered) insofar as he was the most highly evolved earthly personality (Jesus) embodying the Higher Self (Christ) of all existence, the Divine "I AM." To see the life of Jesus Christ in relation to the world of stars opens the door to a profound experience of the cosmos, giving rise to a new star wisdom (astrosophy) that is the spiritual science of Cosmic Christianity.

The *Journal for Star Wisdom* is scientific, resting on a solid mathematical–astronomical foundation and on a secure chronology of the life of Jesus Christ. At the same time, it is spiritual and aspires to the higher dimension of existence expressed outwardly in the world of stars. The scientific and the spiritual come together in the sidereal zodiac, which originated with the Babylonians and was used by the three magi who saw the star of Bethlehem and journeyed to pay homage to Jesus a few months after his birth. In continuity of spirit with the origins of Cosmic Christianity with the three magi, the sidereal zodiac is the frame of reference used to compute the geocentric and heliocentric planetary movements that are discussed in light of the life of Jesus Christ in the *Journal for Star Wisdom*.

Thus, all zodiacal longitudes indicated in the text and in shown in the following calendar are presented in terms of the *sidereal zodiac*, which should be distinguished from the *tropical zodiac* in widespread use by contemporary Western astrologers. The tropical zodiac was introduced into astrology in the mid-second century A.D. by the Greek astronomer Claudius Ptolemy. Prior to this, the astrologers used the sidereal zodiac. Such was the influence of Ptolemy upon the Western astrological tradition that the tropical zodiac eventually came to replace the sidereal zodiac used by the Babylonian, Egyptian, and early Greek astrologers. However, the astrological tradition in India remained uninfluenced by Ptolemy. Thus, the sidereal zodiac is still used today by Hindu (Vedic) astrologers.

The sidereal zodiac originated with the Babylonians in the sixth and fifth centuries B.C., and they defined it in relation to certain bright stars. For example, *Aldebaran* ("the Bull's eye") is located in the middle of the sidereal sign, or constellation, of the Bull at 15° Taurus, while *Antares* ("the Scorpion's heart") is in the middle of the sidereal sign, or constellation, of the Scorpion at 15° Scorpio. The sidereal signs, each 30° long, coincide closely with the twelve astronomical zodiacal constellations of the same name, whereas the signs of the tropical zodiac, since they are defined in relation to the vernal point, now have little or no relationship to the actual corresponding zodiacal constellations. This is because the vernal point, the zodiacal location of the sun on March 20/21, shifts slowly backward through the sidereal zodiac at a rate of 1° per 72 years; this is "the precession of the equinoxes." When Ptolemy introduced the tropical zodiac into astrology, there was an almost exact coincidence between the tropical and the sidereal zodiac, as the vernal point, which is defined to be 0° Aries in the tropical zodiac, was at 1° Aries in the sidereal zodiac in the mid-second century A.D. Thus, there was only 1° difference between the two zodiacs. So, it made little difference to Ptolemy to substitute the tropical zodiac for the sidereal zodiac. Today, however, the vernal point, having shifted backward from 1° Aries to 5° Pisces, is 25° different. Thus, there is virtually no correspondence between the two zodiacs. As shown in the three *Hermetic Astrology* volumes, the sidereal zodiac was used by the three magi, who were among the last representatives of the true star wisdom of antiquity. For this reason the sidereal zodiac is used throughout the *Journal for Star Wisdom*.

Readers interested in exploring the scientific (astronomical and chronological) foundations of Cosmic Christianity are referred to the works listed under *Literature*. The *Chronicle of the Living Christ: Foundations of Cosmic Christianity* is an indispensable reference (hereafter abbreviated "*Chron.*") for the *Journal for Star Wisdom*. The chronology of the life of Jesus Christ rests on the description of his daily life by Anne Catherine Emmerich in her four-volume work *The Life of Jesus Christ (LJC)*. Further details concerning the *Journal for Star Wisdom* and how to work with it on a daily basis are to be found in the *General Introduction to the Christian Star Calendar*. The *General Introduction* explains all the features of this journal and how to work with it on a daily basis. The 2003 edition includes sections on the megastars (stars of great luminosity) and on the 36 decans (10° subdivisions of the twelve signs of the zodiac) in relation to their planetary rulers and to the extra-zodiacal constellations—those above or below the circle of the twelve constellations, or signs, of the zodiac. Further material on the decans, including examples of historical personalities born in the various decans, and a wealth of other material on the signs of the sidereal zodiac, can be found in *Cosmic Dances of the Zodiac*. Also foundational is *History of the Zodiac*.

LITERATURE

General Introduction to the Christian Star Calendar: A Key to Understanding, 2nd ed., Palo Alto, CA: Sophia Foundation of North America, 2003.

Bento, William, Robert Schiappacasse, and David Tresemer, *Signs in the Heavens: A Message for our Time*, Boulder: StarHouse, 2000.

Emmerich, Anne Catherine, *The Life of Jesus Christ*, 4 vols., Rockford, IL: Tan Books, 2004 (cited hereafter in this *Journal* as "*LJC*").

Paul, Lacquanna, and Robert Powell, *Cosmic Dances of the Planets*. San Rafael, CA: Sophia Foundation Press, 2007.

———, *Cosmic Dances of the Zodiac*. San Rafael, CA: Sophia Foundation Press, 2007.

Smith, Edward, *The Burning Bush: An Anthroposophical Commentary on the Bible*, Great Barrington, MA: SteinerBooks, 1997.

Steiner, Rudolf, *The Spiritual Guidance of the Individual and Humanity*. Great Barrington, MA: SteinerBooks, 1992.

Sucher, Willi, *Cosmic Christianity and the Changing Countenance of Cosmology*. Great Barrington, MA: SteinerBooks, 1993. *Isis Sophia* and other works by Willi Sucher are available from the Astrosophy Research Center, PO Box 13, Meadow Vista, CA 95722.

Tidball, Charles S., and Robert Powell, *Jesus, Lazarus, and the Messiah: Unveiling Three Christian Mysteries*. Great Barrington. MA: SteinerBooks, 2005. This book offers a penetrating study of the Christ mysteries against the background of *Chronicle of the Living Christ* and contains two chapters by Robert Powell on the Apostle John and John the Evangelist (Lazarus).

Tresemer, David (with Robert Schiappacasse), *Star Wisdom & Rudolf Steiner: A Life Seen Through the Oracle of the Solar Cross*. SteinerBooks, Great Barrington. MA, 2007.

ASTROSOPHIC WORKS BY ROBERT POWELL, PH.D.

ACS Publications: These three works are in the ACS "All About Astrology" series (San Diego, CA):
History of the Houses (1997).
History of the Planets (1989).
The Zodiac: A Historical Survey (1984).
   www.acspublications.com
   or www.astrocom.com
Business Address:
Starcrafts Publishing
334 Calef Hwy.
Epping, NH 03042
Business: 603-734-4300
Fax: 603-734-4311
Contact maria@starcraftseast.com

SteinerBooks Publications:
   Orders: (703) 661-1594; www.steinerbooks.org; PO Box 960, Herndon, VA 20172.

Christian Hermetic Astrology: The Star of the Magi and the Life of Christ. Great Barrington, MA: SteinerBooks, 1998. Twenty-five discourses set in the "Temple of the Sun," where Hermes and his pupils gather to meditate on the Birth, the Miracles, and the Passion of Jesus Christ. The discourses offer a series of meditative contemplations on the deeds of Christ in relation to the mysteries of the cosmos. They are an expression of the age-old hermetic mystery wisdom of the ancient Egyptian sage, Hermes Trismegistus. This book offers a meditative approach to the cosmic correspondences between major events in the life of Christ and the heavenly configurations at that time 2,000 years ago.

Chronicle of the Living Christ: Foundations of Cosmic Christianity. Great Barrington, MA: SteinerBooks, 1996. An account of the life of Christ, day by day, throughout most of the 3½ years of his ministry, including the horoscopes of conception, birth, and death of Jesus, Mary and John the Baptist, together with a wealth of material relating to a new star wisdom focused on the life of Christ. This work provides the chronological basis for *Christian Hermetic Astrology* and the *Journal for Star Wisdom*.

The Astrological Revolution: Unveiling the Science of the Stars as a Science of Reincarnation and Karma, coauthor Kevin Dann, (Great Barrington, MA: SteinerBooks, 2010). After reestablishing the sidereal zodiac as a basis for astrology that penetrates the mystery of the stars' relationship to human destiny, the reader is invited to discover the astrological significance of the *totality* of the vast sphere of stars surrounding the Earth. This book points to the astrological significance of the *entire* celestial sphere, including all the stars and constellations beyond the twelve zodiacal signs. This discovery is revealed by the study of megastars, illustrating how they show up in an extraordinary way in Christ's healing miracles by aligning with the Sun at the time of those events. This book offers a spiritual, yet scientific, path toward a new relationship to the stars.

Journal for Star Wisdom (Great Barrington, MA: SteinerBooks, annual). Edited by Robert Powell and others in the StarFire research group: A guide to the correspondences of Christ in the stellar and etheric world. Includes articles of interest, a complete sidereal ephemeris and aspectarian, geocentric and heliocentric. Published yearly in November for the coming year. According to Rudolf Steiner, every step taken by Christ during his ministry between the baptism in the Jordan and the resurrection was in harmony with, and an expression of, the cosmos. The journal is concerned with these heavenly correspondences during the life of Christ. It is intended to help provide a foundation for Cosmic Christianity, the cosmic dimension of Christianity. It is this dimension that has been missing from Christianity in its 2,000-year history. A starting point is to contemplate the movements of the Sun, Moon, and planets against the background of the zodiacal constellations (sidereal signs) today in relation to corresponding stellar events during the life of Christ. This opens the possibility of attuning to the life of Christ in the etheric cosmos in a living way.

Sophia Foundation Press and
Sophia Academic Press Publications
PO Box 151011, San Rafael, CA 94915; (707) 789-9062; JamesWetmore@mac.com.

History of the Zodiac (San Rafael, CA: Sophia Academic Press, 2007). Book version of Robert Powell's Ph.D. thesis on the history of the zodiac. This penetrating study of the history of the zodiac restores the sidereal zodiac to its rightful place as the original zodiac, tracing it back to fifth-century B.C. Babylonians. Available in paperback and hard cover.

Hermetic Astrology, Volume 1: Astrology and Reincarnation (San Rafael, CA: Sophia Foundation Press, 2007). This book seeks to give the ancient science of the stars a scientific basis. This new foundation for astrology based on research into reincarnation and karma (destiny) is the primary focus. It includes numerous reincarnation examples, the study of which reveals the existence of certain astrological "laws" of reincarnation, on the basis of which it is evident that the ancient sidereal zodiac is the authentic astrological zodiac, and that the heliocentric movements of the planets are of great significance. Foundational for the new star wisdom of astrosophy.

Hermetic Astrology, Volume 2: Astrological Biography (San Rafael, CA: Sophia Foundation Press, 2007). Concerned with karmic relationships and the unfolding of destiny in seven-year periods through one's life. The seven-year rhythm underlies the human being's astrological biography, which can be studied in relation to the movements of the Sun, Moon, and planets around the sidereal zodiac between conception and birth. The "rule of Hermes" is used to determine the moment of conception.

Sign of the Son of Man in the Heavens: Sophia and the New Star Wisdom (San Rafael, CA: Sophia Foundation Press, 2008). Revised and expanded with new material, this edition deals with a new wisdom of stars in the light of Divine Sophia. It is intended as a help in our time, when we are called on to be extremely wakeful during the period leading up to the end of the Mayan calendar in 2012.

Cosmic Dances of the Zodiac (San Rafael, CA: Sophia Foundation Press, 2007) coauthor Lacquanna Paul. Study material describing the twelve signs of the zodiac and their forms and gestures in cosmic dance, with diagrams, including a wealth of information on the twelve signs and the 36 decans (the subdivision of the signs into decans, or 10° sectors, corresponding to constellations above and below the zodiac).

Cosmic Dances of the Planets. (San Rafael, CA: Sophia Foundation Press, 2007) coauthor Lacquanna Paul. Study material describing the seven classical planets and their forms and gestures in cosmic dance, with diagrams, including much information on the planets.

American Federation of Astrologers (AFA) Publications
PO Box 22040, Tempe, AZ 85285.

The Sidereal Zodiac, coauthor Peter Treadgold (Tempe, AZ: AFA, 1985). A history of the zodiac (sidereal, tropical, Hindu, astronomical) and a formal definition of the sidereal zodiac with the star Aldebaran ("the Bull's Eye") at 15° Taurus. This is an abbreviated version of *History of the Zodiac.*

Rudolf Steiner College Press Publications
9200 Fair Oaks Blvd., Fair Oaks, CA 95628

The Christ Mystery: Reflections on the Second Coming (Fair Oaks, CA Rudolf Steiner College Press, 1999). The fruit of many years of reflecting on the Second Coming and its cosmological aspects. Looks at the approaching trial of humanity and the challenges of living in apocalyptic times, against the background of "great signs in the heavens."

Preface

The Sophia Foundation of North America
525 Gough St. #103, San Francisco, CA 94102; distributes many of the books listed here and other works by Robert Powell.
Tel: (415) 522-1150
sophia@sophiafoundation.org
www.sophiafoundation.org

Computer Program for Charts and Ephemerides, with grateful acknowledgment to Peter Treadgold, who wrote the computer program *Astrofire* (with research module, star catalog of over 4,000 stars, and database of birth and death charts of historical personalities), capable of printing geocentric and heliocentric/hermetic sidereal charts and ephemerides throughout history. The hermetic charts, based on the astronomical system of the Danish astronomer Tycho Brahe, are called "Tychonic" charts in the program.

This program can

- compute birth charts in a large variety of systems (tropical, sidereal, geocentric, heliocentric, hermetic);
- calculate conception charts using the hermetic rule, in turn applying it for correction of the birth time;
- produce charts for the period between conception and birth;
- print out an "astrological biography" for the whole of lifework with the geocentric, heliocentric (and even lemniscatory) planetary system;
- work with the sidereal zodiac according to the definition of your choice (Babylonian sidereal, Indian sidereal, unequal-division astronomical, etc.);
- work with planetary aspects with orbs of your choice.

Includes eight house systems and a variety of chart formats. The program also includes an ephemeris

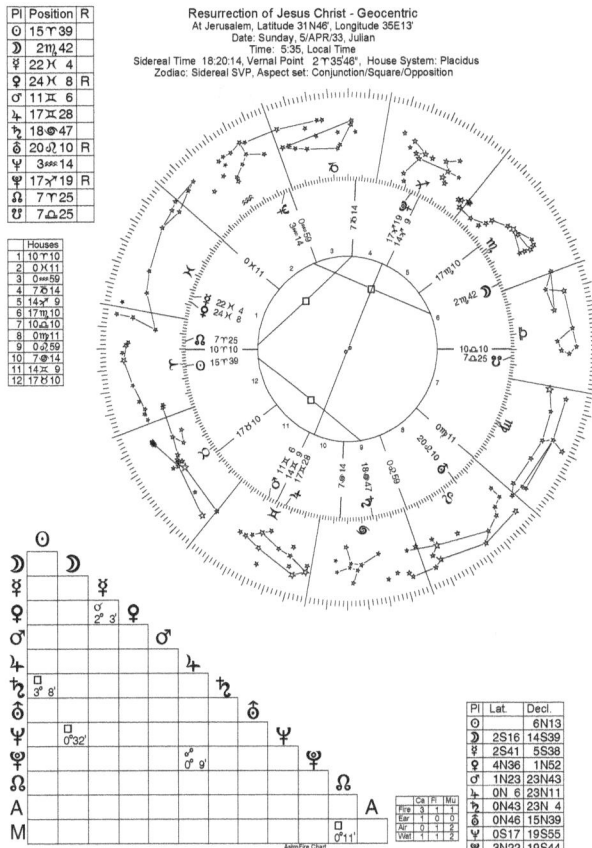

A horoscope from the Astrofire program

program with a search facility. The geocentric/heliocentric sidereal ephemeris pages in the yearly *Journal for Star Wisdom* are produced by *Astrofire*. This program runs under Microsoft Windows. Those interested in *Astrofire* may contact:

The Sophia Foundation of North America
525 Gough St. #103, San Francisco, CA 94102
Tel: (415) 522-1150
sophia@sophiafoundation.org
www.sophiafoundation.org

THE ROSE OF THE WORLD (*ROSA MIRA*)

Daniel Andreev

Daniel Andreev, 1958

By warning about the coming Antichrist, and pointing him out and unmasking him when he appears, by cultivating unshakable faith within human hearts and a grasp of the meta-historical perspectives and global spiritual prospects within human minds...[we help Sophia bring to birth the new culture of love and wisdom called by Daniel Andreev the "Rose of the World."]... [Sophia's] birth in one of the *zatomis* will be mirrored not only by the Rose of the World; feminine power and its role in contemporary life are increasing everywhere. It is that circumstance, above all, that is giving rise to worldwide peace movements, an abhorrence of bloodshed, disillusion over coercive methods of change, an increase in woman's role in society proper, an ever-growing tenderness and concern for children, and a burning hunger for beauty and love. We are entering an age when the female soul will become ever purer and broader, when an ever-greater number of women will become profound inspirers, sensitive mothers, wise counselors, and far-sighted leaders. It will be an age when the feminine in humanity will manifest with unprecedented strength, striking a perfect balance with masculine impulses. See, you who have eyes.[1]

These words are those of Daniel Andreev (1906–1959), the great prophet of the coming Age of Sophia and the corresponding Sophianic culture he called the "Rose of the World." In the this quote, *zatomis* refers to a heavenly realm within the Earth's etheric aura. Andreev refers to Sophia as *Zventa-Sventana*, "Holiest of the Holy."

> A mysterious event is taking place in the meta-history of contemporary times: new divine-creative energy is emanating into our cosmos. Since ancient times the loftiest hearts and most subtle minds have anticipated this event that is now taking place. The first link in the chain of events—events so important that they can only be compared to the incarnation of the Logos—occurred at the turn of the nineteenth century. This was an emanation of the energy of the Virgin Mother, an emanation that was not amorphous, as it had been before in human history [at Pentecost, when there was an emanation of Sophia into the Virgin Mary], but incomparably intensified by the personal aspect it assumed. A great God-born monad descended from the heights of the universe into our cosmos. (ibid., p. 356)

These words of Daniel Andreev, are prophetic. As indicated in *The Most Holy Trinosophia*,[2] he points to the descent of Sophia and the resulting Sophianic world culture, the Rose of the World, in a most inspiring way:

> She is to be born in a body of enlightened ether....There She is, our hope and joy, Light and Divine Beauty! For Her birth

---

[1] Daniel Andreev, *The Rose of the World* (Great Barrington, MA: Lindisfarne Books, 1997), p. 358. Words in brackets [ ] here and in the following text are added by Robert Powell.

[2] Powell, *The Most Holy Trinosophia: The New Revelation of the Divine Feminine* (Great Barrington, MA: SteinerBooks, 2000).

will be mirrored in our history as something that our grandchildren and great-grandchildren will witness: the founding of the Rose of the World, its spread throughout the world, and...the assumption by the Rose of the World of supreme authority over the entire Earth. (ibid., p. 357)

The Sophia Foundation of North America was founded and exists to help usher in the new Age of Sophia and the corresponding Sophianic culture, the Rose of the World, prophesied by Daniel Andreev and other spiritual teachers.

As quoted at the beginning, "Warning about the coming Antichrist, and pointing him out and unmasking him when he appears" is important. As discussed in the article "In Memory of Willi Sucher" (*Journal for Star Wisdom 2010*),

> Humanity's encounter with the Antichrist is part of the initiation trial of humanity as a whole crossing the threshold. The external aspect of this initiation trial is the meeting with the Antichrist as the embodiment of the sum-total of humanity's negative karma, *the double of humankind as a whole*. The inner aspect is the encounter with Christ or the Archangel Michael as the Guardian of the Threshold. The result of successfully passing through this initiation trial is the opening up of conscious awareness of the angelic realm. This is one aspect of the great event at the culmination of the process of humankind as a whole crossing the threshold. Another aspect of this culmination is depicted in the article on World Pentecost. (p. 24)

More than anyone else, Daniel Andreev, as prophet of the coming Sophia culture, the Rose of the World, had a visionary experience of the coming of the Antichrist. His words concerning this are not in the English edition of the *Rose of the World*. Because of the importance of Daniel Andreev's vision of the coming of the Antichrist, his words about this appear for the first time in English in this journal.

The German translation of Daniel Andreev's book *Rosa Mira: Rose of the World*, in three volumes, comprises a translation of the *whole* original Russian text, whereas the English edition corresponds to volume 1 of the three German volumes.[3]

THE PREPARATION OF HUMAN BEINGS FOR THE COMING ANTILOGOS

Certainly, humanity has not lacked warnings. Not only the *New Testament* but also the *Qur'an* and even the *Mahabharata* have warned us in the distant past. Have spiritual seers in the East and in the West not proclaimed the Antichrist as an unavoidable evil? All leaders of the Rose of the World will concentrate their forces upon the work of warning about this monster.... This bearer of a dark mission will probably not truly grasp whom he serves and for whom he prepares the way. With all his intellectual genius, his mind will be completely closed to anything of a mystical nature.... He will be greeted enthusiastically: "There he is! The one for whom we have been waiting!" He will show his true force only much later, when the "savior" holds the entire power in his hands....

Is it a matter of a human being? Yes and no. On several occasions [in *Rosa Mira*] I have indicated that this individual was incarnated as a Roman emperor and how, over the centuries and from life to life, he became enveloped in demonic substance. Concerning this monad, whom Gagtungr [Ahriman, or Satan] himself has kidnapped...enough has been said about his previous incarnation [as Stalin] in Russia.... [In that incarnation,] the forces of providence hindered [Satan's attempt] to make of him a dark, universal genius.

[Now, in 1958, he is being prepared] for the successful fulfillment of the historic role of the Antichrist. Stalin's tyrannical genius and his ability to control hypnotically the will of others is well known.... [When he reincarnates as the Antichrist,] he will have at his disposal an enormous capacity for work and a multitude of talents.... He will be uniquely and terribly beautiful. From his

---
[3] The following translation from German into English is by Robert Powell.

facial characteristics, it will be difficult to place him in any particular race or nation. Rather, he will be seen as a representative of the collective of humanity.... [At a certain point in his life, he will undergo a transformation.] His transformation will be noticed by people immediately, yet they will be unable to recognize the meaning or the "how" [of this transformation]. The external appearance of the transformed one will remain virtually unchanged. However, a terrible and frightening energy will proceed from him... Anyone who touches him will receive an electric shock. An invincible hypnotic force [will proceed from him].... The disturbing influence [on spiritually striving human beings] and upon the entire population set in motion by the transformation of the Antilogos will be extraordinary....

After a rigged vote, he—the miracle worker—will crown himself.... Humanity will be divided [into those who accept him as world ruler] and those who refuse to acknowledge the usurper.... Of course, force will be used against anyone who refuses to follow the Antichrist. Dark miracles will increasingly occur, shattering the consciousness of people to the very roots of their being. For many, Christ's miracles will pale into insignificance. Crazy enthusiasm will roll in waves across the world.... Eventually, the Antilogos will hold the sole rulership of the planet in his hands. Yet, the true and highest leaders will not subject themselves to this usurper. This will also be the case for millions, perhaps hundreds of millions, of people in every country of the world.

The age of persecution commences. From year to year, they become increasingly extensive, methodical, [and] cruel. Here, the cunning Gagtungr [Ahriman/Satan] even makes use of the heroic protest of the masses. The candidate for the Antichrist who had failed...who had taken his life at the end of World War II,[4] advances now to become the self-appointed leader of the rebels in the struggle against the world ruler.... His thoroughly dark movement will draw the hearts of many into a spiral of raging wickedness and senseless hatred.... Christ's significance will continually be weakened. Then his name will be denied—and finally enveloped in silence....

Shock and terror will take hold of many. Millions of those who had previously distanced themselves from religious matters, who occupied themselves primarily with concerns in their own little world or with artistic pursuits or scientific research, will sense that an irrevocable and very dangerous choice confronts them. In the face of this, even torture and execution pale.... Countless people will turn away from this offspring of hell... from the dark miracles and the charm of the superman, as well as from his immeasurable intelligence and frighteningly cynical wickedness.... The majority of people will fall away from God and allow themselves to be led astray by Gagtungr's protégée....

Stalin wanted not only to be feared; he also wanted to be loved. The Antichrist, however, has need of only one thing: the conviction that everyone [should hold] without exception, [to] believe in his superiority and [to] subject themselves to him without hesitation....

When [during the reign of the Antichrist] the machine civilization begins its total assault on Nature, the entire landscape of the Earth's surface will be transformed into a complete Anti-Nature.... Nature, having become inwardly empty and outwardly crippled, will no longer awaken aesthetic or pantheistic feelings....

Certainly, too, during the complete rule of the tyrant, there will be many whose innermost life will rebel against the senseless existence under the Antichrist. However, psychic control will stifle such thoughts as they arise, and only a few will succeed in acquiring a system of psychic self-defense to protect them from being physically destroyed....

All written or other testimonies that could be dangerous for the Antichrist will be destroyed....

[The suffering of human beings gives nourishment (*gavvach*) to the demons.].... No world

---

4 Daniel Andreev depicts the two main candidates for the Antichrist in their twentieth-century incarnations: Adolf Hitler and Joseph Stalin. In those incarnations, they competed with each other to become the most evil. In the following incarnation, the most evil one would become the vessel for the incarnation of the Antichrist. According to Daniel Andreev, Joseph Stalin outdid Adolf Hitler to become the chosen one, the prince of darkness. —R. POWELL

wars, revolutions, or repressions, no mass spilling of blood, could have produced *gavvach* in such amounts.... In fact, even humanity in its demonized aspect will not satisfy the Antichrist. He needs humanity as his source of *gavvach*.... [However] even in the most sinful soul, an inextinguishable spark of conscience gleams. However, despair, increasing ignorance, and sheer boredom with life will also take hold of many people, and this will lead to their rejection by the Antichrist. Of what use to him is the intellectual paralysis that sets in after such excesses of despair? Such people are hardly suited to the further development of demonic science and technology or to the conquest of the cosmos or the satanizing of the world....

[After the Antichrist's death] the world state will rapidly collapse, and only drastic measures will hinder anarchy in various parts of the world.... "And there appears a great sign in heaven: a woman clothed with the Sun" [Revelation 12:1]. Who is the *woman clothed with the Sun?* It is *Sventa-Sventana* [Sophia], embraced by the planetary Logos and chosen to give birth to the Great Spirit of the Second Aeon. The reflection of this event in world history is the Rose of the World, whose utmost striving before, during, and after the time of the Antichrist prepares humanity to become a vessel for the Great Spirit.... An unimaginable jubilation will take hold of this and other worlds as humanity passes through a great, light-filled transformation.

The prince of darkness will terrify human beings.... Christ, however, will take on as many forms as there are conscious beings on Earth to behold him. He will adapt himself to everyone and will converse with all. His forms will simultaneously yield an image in an unimaginable way: *One who appears in heaven surrounded by unspeakable glory.* There will not be a single being on Earth who will not see the Son of God and hear his Word.[5]

🙢

These words by Daniel Andreev are prophetic. They were written shortly before his death in 1959.

---

5 Daniil Andrejew, *Rosa Mira: Die Weltrose* (Frankeneck, Germany: Vega, 2009), vol. 3, pp. 202–226.

Now, more than fifty years later, not only is the encounter with the Son of God possible, but also the possibility of hearing his Word. Today, we can experience this meeting with the Son of God in the realm of life forces, also known as the *etheric realm*. This is the most important event that anyone in earthly existence can experience. This spiritual event is the initiatory aspect of human encounters with the Antichrist and the initiation trial for humanity as a whole crossing the threshold.

An example of this spiritual event is related in an account of a young woman of her initiatory experience in meeting Christ as the Greater Guardian of the threshold. She prefers to remain anonymous. This description of her meeting with Christ in the etheric realm—with the Etheric Christ, to use Rudolf Steiner's expression—can be a source of inspiration to everyone. She describes how she came to this experience of the Etheric Christ through meditating on Christ's experiences during the night prior to the Mystery of Golgotha, the night in the Garden of Gethsemane.

🙢

When a human being enters the event of Gethsemane and beholds his suffering, the light of his deed is released again into the heavens. This causes the spiritual beings to take notice of the Earth and come to her aid, but it also attracts the dark side. The light of Christ prevails over the darkness; it prevails for human beings who are willing to gaze upon the deeds of Christ (his Passion) and accept his sacrifice.

Any human being who will meditate on the event of Gethsemane and who can truly speak the words "Not my will, but Thine" radiates great light out into the cosmos. Angels come running to join with the light, and within the heart of each angel is a reflector that reflects the light out into the heavens. The angels rejoice in the opportunity to be able to send this light out. They reflect the light back to the Earth as a gift, which awakens people to the True Light. They start to feel the presence of Christ. They hear his words; they see his light. When they awake to the light, they reflect it to others. Moreover, they reflect it to nature. The light of Christ awakens and vivifies nature when human beings reflect it.

The Etheric Christ said to me, "Place your hands on my body [the body of Jesus] and allow the light to be taken in through the wounds of your hands. Let this light penetrate to your heart." I placed my hands on the shoulders of Jesus Christ, who was bleeding from every pore—bleeding light out into the cosmos. I felt the light rise in me and fill my entire being, penetrating my heart. It was indescribable!

"You Are the Light of the World."

Then, I merged with the Earth to an unfathomable degree—never before had I experienced such a merging. I became the "eye of the Earth." It was as if I became the Earth, and the Earth had become an eye. I experienced myself at the center of the eye, which was also the heart of Christ. As I looked out, I beheld the heavens from the perspective of the Earth beholding the heavens. I felt that the "eye" of the Earth could not always behold the heavens. It was as if it remains asleep until those moments when the Light awakens the Earth. Then it can behold the heavens and be *known*.

Again, I am trying to find an earthly way to describe something for which there is a lack of words. Seeing through the eye of Earth, gazing out into the heavens, I saw angels coming to grace the Earth with their presence. One of the angels came forward and placed a crystal inside of my heart. It had many facets and was a specific geometric formation. After placing it inside my heart, the angel said, "You are the light of the world!" The angels were in a state of gratitude to me for being willing to accept the light, which could come about only through great suffering. Christ spoke the same words to his disciples when he said, "You are the light of the world." He said that they were a "city on a hill." I saw how the light of the "city on the hill" shines out into the heavens and vanquishes the foe. Christ also said to me, "Your tears are the salt of the Earth. Your blood is the light, for even as your heart takes in light, it enters the blood and thus you become a living light. And the light shall not be quenched, for the angels protect and guard the heart that bears the Light of Christ."

My focus was again turned to Gethsemane. With my whole being, I entered the light of his deed in the garden and a state of ecstasy, an ineffable, unutterable ecstasy. The light of Christ in Gethsemane enveloped the Earth. Up to that point, I had never merged with such light. My heart soared in ecstasy, lifted into another realm of spirit. I exclaimed, "This is Life! This is Life eternal, the Life of the world. This is Love! This is eternal Love, which knows no boundaries, for it has penetrated everything in the Earth. It lives within the Earth as an eternal promise of redemption. His love is eternal; His love is free for all who will accept it!" Christ then gave me a message for all:

> *"Love one another and love the Earth. Send your love to your fellow beings and into the Earth that the Earth may be lifted up on wings of peace. There is a body of the Earth, which is a body of love; this is My body that I gave to the Earth. You become one with the body of love by doing works of love, by cultivating feelings of love and by thinking thoughts of love. I invite all to become one with Me in this body of love. I call you home; My arms are around you. Return to love. Remember love. For where love is there am I; and because I desire to have you in My heart, I ask you to love one another, that I may be in you and you in Me. Look for Me to come to you for I am coming and shall gather you to myself and you shall be safely folded in Me because you are precious in My sight; and My sight is ever upon you. Return to Me."*

I then gazed upon him, embracing all of the cosmos. With his arms outstretched across the expanse of Heaven, his voice penetrating the depths of my heart with these words: "I AM eternally here!"

EDITORIAL FOREWORD

Robert Powell, Ph.D.

The *Journal for Star Wisdom* (formerly *Christian Star Calendar*) has appeared every year since 1991. From the beginning the central feature has been the calendar comprising the monthly ephemeris pages together with commentaries drawing attention to the Christ events remembered by the ongoing cosmic events. The significance of following the Christ events in relation to daily astronomical events is an important foundation for the new star wisdom of Astrosophy.[1] This new star wisdom is arising in our time in response to the second coming of Christ—known as his return in the *etheric realm* of life forces—as a path of communing with Christ in his *life body* (*ether body*). It should also be mentioned that, with the onset of the second coming of Christ during the course of the twentieth century, Christ is now the Lord of Karma, and this is important to take into consideration in the development of a new relationship of humanity to the stars in our time, particularly with respect to the horoscope as an expression of human karma or destiny.

The events of Christ's life lived two thousand years ago are inscribed into his ether body, and to meditate upon these events at times when they are cosmically remembered is a way of drawing near to Christ. The recently updated version of my article "Subnature and the Second Coming," in the recent book *The Inner Life of the Earth*,[2] outlines the background to contemporary events as a confrontation between good and evil in relation to Christ's descent at this time through the sub-earthly realms and also gives an overview of the various cosmic rhythms unfolding in relation to his second coming, including the 33⅓-year rhythm of his ether body.

The *Journal for Star Wisdom* encourages the reader to engage in the practice of star-gazing. The activity of stargazing, as described on my website, astrogeographia.org (see "A Modern Path of the Magi" in the section on "The Star of the Magi"), is also fundamental to the development of the new star wisdom of Astrosophy. One of the foundations of Astrosophy lies in the science of astronomy, providing the new star wisdom with a secure scientific foundation, which moreover, can be brought into the realm of experience through the practice of stargazing. In Astrosophy there is no longer a separation between astronomy and astrology. For example, when in the *Journal for Star Wisdom* it is indicated that currently Mars in the heavens is at 15° Taurus then, assuming that Mars is visible, the red planet can be seen in conjunction with Aldebaran marking the Bull's eye at the center of the constellation of Taurus, whose longitude, as the central star in this constellation, is 15° Taurus. In Astrosophy, the astrological fact of Mars at 15° Taurus is identical with the astronomical reality of

---

[1] There are many different approaches to Astrosophy and not all use the equal-division sidereal zodiac that forms the basis of the approach followed in the *Journal for Star Wisdom*. All references to the zodiac and to planetary positions in the zodiac in the *Journal for Star Wisdom* are in terms of the sidereal zodiac as defined in my book *History of the Zodiac*. Moreover, in Astrosophy, there are different chronologies of the life of Christ, and the chronology that forms the basis of the approach followed in the *Journal for Star Wisdom* is set forth in my book *Chronicle of the Living Christ*. Thus, all references to planetary positions at the Christ events in the *Journal for Star Wisdom* are in terms of the scientifically established chronology of the life of Christ set forth in my book *Chronicle of the Living Christ*. Note: for bibliographic information for these and other books related to Astrosophy, see "Literature" (beginning page 8).

[2] O'Leary (ed.), *The Inner Life of the Earth* (Great Barrington, MA: Steiner Books, 2008), pp. 69–141.

Mars' location at the center of the constellation of Taurus. Astrosophy thus relates to sense-perceptible reality and to the Divine "background of existence" (the spiritual hierarchies)[3] underlying this reality, whereas astrology is generally practiced in such a way that there is a split between astrology and astronomy.[4] The historical background as to how this separation between astronomy and astrology arose is described in my book *History of the Zodiac*.[5]

The present issue of the *Journal for Star Wisdom* is the twenty-first, but is the second published under the new title, as all previous issues were published under the title *Christian Star Calendar*. By way of explanation concerning the new title: this publication is intended as an outreach from the StarFire research group (an Astrosophy group) that meets yearly in Boulder and occasionally in Fair Oaks, California.[6] The *Journal for Star Wisdom* is intended as an organ for the development of the new star wisdom of Astrosophy. This was also the purpose of the *Christian Star Calendar*. However, there the focus, at least, initially, was primarily on the calendar—the monthly ephemeris and commentaries. In the course of time, more and more research articles on the new star wisdom of Astrosophy came to be published in the *Christian Star Calendar*. A point was reached where it became clear that the publication is more of a journal than a calendar, although the calendar continues to play an important role. It is therefore a natural transition from the *Christian Star Calendar* to the *Journal for Star Wisdom*.

Another important reason for the change of title is that the editorial board of the *Journal for Star Wisdom*, drawn from members of the StarFire research group, acknowledge their debt to the pioneer of the new star wisdom of Astrosophy, Willi Sucher (1902–1985), who from 1965 to 1972 published his research findings in the regularly appearing *Star Journal*. The change of name emphasizes the line of continuity from the *Star Journal* to the *Mercury Star Journal*, which I edited from 1974 to 1981. The *Christian Star Calendar* (1991–2009) was also in this same line of continuation from Willi Sucher's original *Star Journal*, but without the line of continuity being explicitly indicated by way of the title.

A major change is that the *Journal for Star Wisdom* is published by SteinerBooks, our new publisher. From 2006 to 2009, issues of the *Christian Star Calendar* were published by the Sophia Foundation Press. Another major change is that whereas I compiled the monthly commentaries for all nineteen issues of the *Christian Star Calendar*, the monthly commentaries for the *Journal for Star Wisdom* are compiled by a team of contributors: Claudia McLaren Lainson together with David Tresemer and Sally Nurney.

Astrosophically, 2011 is an extraordinary year. This year, Pluto retrogrades back to 9°59' Sagittarius in September, where it was located at the miracle of the changing of water into wine at the wedding at Cana, after having moved forward to 12½° Sagittarius in March to April, where Pluto was at the healing of the paralyzed man, then to return back to 12½° Sagittarius at the end of the year. In this region of the zodiac between 10° and 12½° Sagittarius, Pluto was located at several of Christ's most significant miracles during the early part of his ministry: raising of the youth of Nain (10°21' Sagittarius), raising of Jairus' daughter (11° Sagittarius), death of John the Baptist (12°09' Sagittarius), healing of the paralyzed man (12½° Sagittarius). Then, on December 28–29, 2011, the

---

3 According to Rudolf Steiner, constellations are the abodes of the first hierarchy, called *seraphim, cherubim,* and *thrones*. The movement of the planets takes place against the background of the zodiacal constellations, which—considered the abode of the first hierarchy—form the Divine "background of existence" in the heavens. "Suppose you wanted to point to some particular [group of] thrones, cherubim, and seraphim, one denotes them by a particular constellation. It is like a signpost. In that direction over there are the [group of] thrones, cherubim, and seraphim known as the Twins; over there [the group of thrones, cherubim and seraphim known as] the Lion, etc." (Steiner, *The Spiritual Hierarchies and the Physical World* (Great Barrington, MA: SteinerBooks, 2008), p. 99 (words in brackets [] added by RP).

4 In this example, modern astrology, which uses the tropical zodiac (rather than the equal-division sidereal zodiac used in Astrosophy) would say that Mars is "in Gemini."

5 Powell, *History of the Zodiac*.

6 See the website StarWisdom.org. Other websites concerned with the new star wisdom of Astrosophy are sophiafoundation.org and astrogeographia.org.

conjunction of the Sun and Pluto takes place at 12°19' Sagittarius.[7] By way of analogy, the Sun represents Christ together with the forces of light in his service, and Pluto, at least in its manifestation as Pluto-Hades,[8] is a symbol for the dark forces of opposition to Christ. It is a matter of focusing upon "the light shining in the darkness" (John 1:5) as the primary focus, whereas the darkness itself—one has to be aware of its existence, otherwise one would be living in illusion—is secondary, simply a counterpart to the light.

Where does the light come from? William Bento in his article takes up the very important theme of prophecy. Perhaps the greatest prophecy of our time—one that is little known, but which is the reason for the existence of this journal, and is a source of tremendous spiritual light—is Rudolf Steiner's prophecy from 1910, just one hundred years ago. On January 12, 1910, he prophesied the second coming of Christ, which he referred to as *Christ's appearance in the etheric realm*—not a return in a physical body, but in an *etheric (life) body*, in the realm of life forces. Here is my translation of Marie Steiner's notes from this important, hitherto unpublished lecture:

- 3000 B.C. Kali Yuga commenced and lasted until 1899. Time of transition.
- 1933—human beings will appear with clairvoyant faculties, which they will develop naturally. At this time, which we are approaching, the newly beginning clairvoyant faculties have to be satisfied, to experience what they [human beings] should do with them.
- I am with you always, even unto the end of the world.

- Christ will appear in an etheric form. The physical Christ became the Spirit of the Earth—this was the midpoint, the balance, of Earth evolution.
- Fifth Letter of the Apocalypse: I will come again; however, take heed that you do not fail to recognize me.
- 2,500 years is the time which humanity has to develop again the gifts of clairvoyance. Around 1933 the Gospels must be recognized in their spiritual meaning such that they have worked preparing for Christ. Otherwise untold confusion of the soul will be caused.
- Around 1933, there will be some representatives of black magical schools, who will falsely proclaim a physical Christ.
- Each time that he becomes perceptible, Christ is perceptible for other faculties.

(Translated from the first page of Marie Steiner's notes, which were recently published in German for the first time in *Der Europäer*, vol. 14, December 2009–January 2010, p. 3).

This was Rudolf Steiner's greatest prophecy: the second coming of Christ, which he referred to as the *appearance of Christ in the etheric realm*, beginning in 1933. It is this event, the presence of the *Etheric Christ*, lasting from 1933 for 2,500 years (until 4433), that is the *raison d'être* of the *Journal for Star Wisdom*.

In conclusion, I would like to express gratitude to our publisher, Gene Gollogly of SteinerBooks, and to the able assistance of Jens Jensen of SteinerBooks, for making this second issue of the *Journal for Star Wisdom* available. I would also like to thank all those who have contributed to make this issue possible, in particular to our authors for presenting their research articles as contributions to the foundations of the new star wisdom of Astrosophy. And, finally, we express our gratitude to all our readers, who, ultimately, are the reason for the existence of the *Journal for Star Wisdom*.

---

7 Powell and Dann, *Christ & the Maya Calendar: 2012 and the Coming of the Antichrist* (SteinerBooks: Great Barrington, 2009), pp. 230–234 discusses the significance of the third temptation of Christ in the wilderness in relation to the Sun–Pluto conjunction.

8 Powell, "Pluto–Hades and Pluto–Phanes": sophiafoundation.org/articles; this article, written with the help of Krista Kösters, describes the dark and the light sides of Pluto.

WORKING WITH THE JOURNAL FOR STAR WISDOM

The listing of major planetary events each month is intended as a stimulus toward attunement with the Universal Christ, the Logos, whose being encompasses the entire galaxy. The deeds of the historical Christ wrought two thousand years ago are of eternal significance—inscribed into the cosmos—and they resonate with the movements of the heavenly bodies, especially when certain alignments or planetary configurations occur bearing a resemblance with those prevailing at the time of events in the life of Jesus Christ. With the rare astronomical event of the transit of Venus across the face of the Sun that took place June 8, 2004, at exactly the zodiacal degree (23° Taurus), where the Sun stood at Christ's Ascension, a new impulse was given from divine-spiritual realms for the further unfolding of star wisdom, *Astro-Sophia*.

Toward the end of the journal, the calendar is to be found, comprising ephemeris pages for the twelve months of the year and accompanying monthly commentaries on the astronomical events listed on the ephemeris pages. Indications regarding the similarity of contemporary planetary configurations with those at events in the life of Christ are given in the lower part of the monthly commentaries, and the upper part gives a commentary on the notable astronomical occurrences each month. Unless otherwise stated, all astronomical indications regarding visibility mean "visible to the naked eye." See the note concerning time on the page preceding the monthly commentaries.

With this calendar, astronomy and astrology, which were a unity in the ancient star wisdom of the Egyptians and Babylonians, are reunited and provide a foundation for astrosophy, the all-encompassing star wisdom, *Astro-Sophia*, an expression of Sophia and referred to in the Revelation of John as the "Bride of the Lamb."

THE SIGNATURE OF VENUS
IN THE EVENTS OF JESUS CHRIST'S LIFE, HISTORICAL PERSONALITIES, AND MODERN WORLD EVENTS

David Tresemer, Ph.D.

Venus crosses the face of the Sun in 2012, perhaps the most important astronomical event of the year. From the perspective of Earth, Venus normally conjuncts the Sun either above or below the ½° diameter of the Sun. Approximately every 125 years, Venus crosses twice in front of the Sun, those two times separated by eight years. This particular transit is an *occultation*, or *eclipse*.[1] How can we call it an eclipse when Venus is one-thirtieth the diameter of the Sun? I prefer this term because the event has an energetic effect.

An eclipse of the Sun by Venus did not happen during the lifetime of Jesus Christ. Nevertheless, we can correlate the event in 2012 to those times during Jesus' life when Venus was conjunct the Sun, both inferior (Venus between the Sun and Earth, closest to the phenomenon of the eclipse) and superior (Venus behind the Sun). During an inferior conjunction, Venus seems to move very swiftly in a retrograde direction, about one day within 1° of exact conjunction. During a superior conjunction, Venus travels with the Sun from the Earth's point of view, and can seem to be in a 1° orb for many days, in one instance cited here, for nine days.

Rudolf Steiner suggested that Venus in inferior conjunction stimulates the "head pole"—that is, the nervous system and the organism of thinking, concepts, and illusions. By contrast, the superior conjunction, with Venus farther away than the Sun is (behind the Sun), stimulates the limbs—that is, the "will pole," the initiator of action.[2]

During the lifetime of Jesus Christ, Venus crossed three times between the Sun and the Earth—that is, in inferior conjunction (most like the eclipse that will occur June 6, 2012), and three times in superior conjunction. I have arranged these into short vignettes, followed by commentaries, as we have done with other planets.[3] We will build an understanding of Venus as we go through these vignettes, organized by theme.

As research on Venus unfolded, I realized that another Venus position proved important. The conjunction with the Sun was supplemented in many themes by Venus along the Aldebaran–Antares axis, running from 15° Taurus for the Life Star (*Aldebaran*) to 15° Scorpio, for the Star of Death and Rebirth (*Antares*), the two main Royal Stars of Persia, exactly opposite each other, and the basis for the divisions of the zodiac.[4]

---

1 The term *transit* normally means any angular relation between moving celestial bodies. Thus it is confusing when it also refers to something quite specific.

2 From a close reading of Rudolf Steiner's *Man in the Light of Occultism, Theosophy, and Philosophy* (Blauvelt NY: Spiritual Science, 1989; original lectures 1912) pp. 165–167. The issues of illusion and phantasms accentuated in the eclipse (inferior conjunction) by Venus of the Sun in 2004 are described in "Lifting the Darkness into the Air and Light: The Solar Cross Image at 23 Degrees Scorpio," at StarWisdom.org (under "Current Research") and its follow-up in this journal, "The Excitement of the Polarities at 23° to 24° of the Fixed Signs." The realm of feeling is especially stimulated when Venus lies furthest from the Sun as viewed from the Earth, a location that we do not have space to investigate here.

3 The methodology of this approach is discussed in "Signature of Saturn..." and "Signature of Jupiter...", in previous issues of the *Journal for Star Wisdom* (or its predecessor, *Christian Star Calendar*). The methodology is also available at StarWisdom.org. More about the spiritual side of Venus can be found in Lacquanna Paul and Robert Powell, *Cosmic Dances of the Planets*, pp. 133–161.

4 On the use of the Aldebaran-Antares axis to set out the zodiac, see Powell, *History of the Zodiac*. On the qualities of Aldebaran and Antares, see Tresemer and Schiappacasse, *Star Wisdom & Rudolf Steiner*.

1. Theme of Destiny, the Divine Plan, and Listening

1A: Imagination: Inferior Conjunction in the Goat: Listening to the Past and to the Future

A month earlier, the Teacher had come down from his time alone in the desert mountains and his encounter with demons and the Father God. He spoke to no one about this, but his mother knew of his retreat to the wilderness. She could feel his movements—both outer and inner—where he had traveled, and what he felt. She tried to understand what he intended, where it was all going. At the great wedding, where friends and relatives gathered at Cana, he had done something magical. She had helped by instructing the servants to heed his commands. He had challenged her, saying, "Woman, what relationship is there between you and me?" She had remembered this comment and wondered about it, because something extraordinary had happened. All agreed on that, though none could agree on what had actually happened. Who was this man, her son?

On this day, after traveling with his students, the Teacher came to meet and speak with his mother long into the evening. He told her about what he had experienced in the mountains and what he was going to experience in the coming few years—a time that would end in a bloody way. He spoke of events in the world of men and women, as well as within his own soul.

A few months earlier, he had spoken to her about the abandonment of humanity by the spiritual forces that had been such strong supports in the past. What remained were empty rituals. The Essenes had succeeded in keeping demons and distractions out of their community, but those demons then attacked the rest of humanity even more strongly. He suffered immensely from the realization of what humanity had become, and it motivated him to seek his own destiny. He mixed his words with sounds unknown to Mary, sounds that she could not identify though she understood their meaning. In this conversation, Mary felt herself expand in light and in communion with the Mother of the world.

This evening he spoke of his future and the future of humanity. It was an immense story, containing horror and bliss, ending with a sword piercing her heart so that it would open more fully to others. The vast tapestry of the story linked Earth's depths with the heavens' heights, all interwoven with human actions and words. She knew that she would not be able to speak to others about what he told her that night. She knew she would knit together the followers her son had attracted, both the poor and the rich, the vital and the limping, the stragglers and the scholars, the men and the women, into a strong community with her strength as its core. Then, after everything he told her had unfolded, and after the followers had all fled in terror, she would pull them together again and rebuild.

Comment: The first intimate sharing occurred just before Jesus decided to seek the water initiation offered by John the Baptist. Venus was conjunct Antares, the Star of Death and Rebirth.[5] With his mother, Jesus used unusual words and sounds that they both understood.[6] Rudolf Steiner admired this conversation between mother and son (technically, the Solomon Mary and her stepson[7]) as intimate sharing between the Sun God, the Christ light, and the bearer of the divine feminine, Sophia.[8]

The second intimate sharing occurred during the short span of time when Venus was in inferior conjunction to the Sun, just five weeks after the "forty days in the wilderness," and ten days after turning water into something precious at the wedding at Cana.[9] Although on many occasions Jesus had given little hints to his disciples and audiences about his expected trials, this account

---

5 Venus 15 Scorpio, Sun at 0° Libra 50, thus also a maximum distance from the Sun (from the Earth's point of view), putting this event also in the heart realm.
6 Peter Selg, *Rudolf Steiner and the Fifth Gospel* (SteinerBooks, 2010), p. 142.
7 The story of the two Jesus children and their mothers named Mary can be found in Robert McDermott's introduction to Rudolf Steiner, *According to Luke* (Anthroposophic Press, 2001), Powell's *Chronicle of the Living Christ* and my own *Star Wisdom & Rudolf Steiner* (SteinerBooks, 2007).
8 Selg, op. cit., pp. 56, 73, 74, 145.
9 This sharing occurred on January 8, A.D. 30, Sun and Venus at 20° Capricorn 36. One degree either way, that is, from 19° Capricorn 36 to 21° Capricorn 36 goes from noon on January 8 to 5:40 p.m. January 9, not quite 30 hours. Emmerich, *LJC* II, p. 62.

to the bearer of Sophia-Wisdom herself was the most comprehensive. Where the Sun stood at the Mystery of Golgotha, Venus stood at the event of Pentecost, when Mother Mary assumed the central role of mediator of the spirit of love to humankind.[10] In this fragment, we see her central importance in fulfilling the life mission of Jesus Christ.

The planet and sphere of Venus creates the deep inner spaces of the soul to embrace all that is beloved. Here we have a summary of the past when Venus lies conjunct the distant powerful star Antares. When it lies conjunct the Sun, it becomes more immediate and oriented to the future. Prophecy pours forth, not fearful predictions, but rather ones that engage the will to look courageously at what unfolds. The key to this kind of prophecy is the quality of listening, soul opening to soul. Then, both are able to participate in destiny unfolding, sharing the sense of responsibility that prophecy can bring. When prophecy flows, one becomes larger than the usual: Christ light and Divine Wisdom, Sophia.[11]

Venus in the head pole stimulates pictures of the future that ask one, "Will you engage in this destiny for the good of all?" Here we have the best example of an important trait of Venus—Venus listens[12]—which we could amend and explain: "In the realm of Venus, listening, speaking, listening." If we understand Venus the planet, Venus as Aphrodite, Venus as Sophia or the divine feminine, Lucifer as the Illusionist, and Lucifer as Christ's brother in light interconnected,[13] then we can see that here we have the best of relationship between Venus/Lucifer and the light of Christ expressing on the human plane.

Summary: Prophecy listened to becomes intimate sharing in destiny. The destiny links male and female, heavenly destiny and earthly story. Venus listens.

1B: Related Event: Inferior Conjunction in the Twins: Death of the Solomon Jesus

On June 5 A.D.12, the Solomon Jesus passed over the threshold, with Venus (15° Gemini 54) very close to the Sun (14° Gemini 12).[14] This body was the vehicle for the great being Zarathustra, the wisest, who, a few months earlier on April 3, had transferred his wisdom to the one we think of as Jesus.[15]

Summary: Once the gifting of wisdom has been conferred, the bearer of wisdom departs. Duty to one's group (in this case all humanity) ends, and one affiliates again with one's celestial group.

1C: Event: Superior Conjunction in the Lion: "I Have a Dream"

On August 28, 1963, Martin Luther King Jr. delivered a speech that has echoed ever since as a poetical clarion call to social justice. He imagined in public how the different streams of brothers and sisters in the Venus sphere could come together: "I have a dream that one day on the red hills of Georgia, the sons of former slaves and the sons of former slave owners will be able to sit down together at the table of brotherhood."[16] One could see this in the head pole or the will pole, for King worked both ends. Whenever possible, he exhorted people to action, and this speech works with Venus at the will pole.[17]

Summary: A remarkable man sets out a grand vision of the common destiny of humanity, where

---

10 Sun at Mystery, 15° Aries 40; Venus at Pentecost, 17° Aries 2. These two events are joined in Sun-Venus conjunction.

11 See William Bento, "Prophecy: The Cauldron of Controversy," in this journal.

12 Paul and Powell, *Cosmic Dances of the Planets*, op. cit., p. 145.

13 Concerning Aphrodite as the origin of illusion, refer to the classical scholar, Peter Kingsley, *Reality* (Golden Sufi Center, 2004). Rudolf Steiner (*Man in the Light of Occultism, Theosophy, and Philosophy*, 165, 168) speaks of Lucifer as the same as Venus, thus connecting the seductive feminine with the master illusionist.

14 *Chronicle*, 88, a reasoned estimate based on little evidence, and thus to be held lightly. Also, Mars was conjunct at 16 Gemini 16, and Neptune opposed at 16 Sagittarius 11.

15 The story of the two Jesuses can be found in my *Star Wisdom & Rudolf Steiner* (SteinerBooks, 2007), with many other references there.

16 Venus at 10° Leo 1, Sun at 10° Leo 24.

17 King's birth Venus, at 16° Aquarius 49, lay square to the Aldebaran–Antares axis in Taurus-Scorpio. Another event that laid out an entirely new vision for humanity occurred in a superior Venus–Sun conjunction—the signing of the Magna Carta, giving rights outside of nobility, June 15, 1215, Venus at 16° Gemini 55 and Sun at 16° Gemini 24.

all gather as brothers and sisters. Venus listens and speaks; many listen.

1D: Event: Inferior Conjunction in the Water Carrier: Birth of The Mother

Mirra Alfassa, who became The Mother to Aurobindo's ashram at Pondicherry in India was born in an inferior conjunction of Venus and the Sun.[18] In her, the power of the feminine, the divine Mother, and thinking about the true destiny of the human body connect her to the event of sharing between Christ Light and Mother Mary. Her major work had to do with a close listening to the human body, indeed an intensely intimate love of each cell of the human body. Venus listens and speaks.[19]

2. THEME OF JOINING TO ANCIENT TRADITIONS

2A: Imagination: Inferior Conjunction in the Ram: Anointing for the Burial

Mary Magdalene enjoyed a special relationship to the Teacher, which the other students did not understand. Some of them resented her special position. When she brought one of her exotic perfumes to anoint the Teacher, the men grumbled about the meaning of such treatment, especially Judas. They wondered that the Teacher tolerated this kind of treatment. The day before, she had brought a bowl and washed his feet, drying them with a towel thrown over her shoulder and then putting a new ointment, a new smell, on the Teacher's head. On this day, she went further. She met him at the gate and unfurled her hair, wiping his dusty sandals with her hair. The men could not contain their grunts of disapproval, but said nothing as the Teacher accepted the treatment, and then went in to the house. The men settled in the room, and Mary Magdalene entered with a new ointment, rubbed it into the Teacher's scalp and onto his feet, and then unfurled her hair again, wiping off the excess oil with her hair. The men spoke among themselves, agreeing that this was inappropriate and scandalous.

Comment: This inferior conjunction of Venus occurred on March 21 A.D. 33. In the last weeks of the Teacher's ministry, Mary Magdalene used seven ointments in all. The two ointments spoken of during this conjunction with Venus were second and third in the series. She used three vials at the Last Supper, where her behavior was questioned aloud—by Judas—and defended by the Teacher. Use of various ointments, indeed of seven or fourteen, formed part of the Egyptian system of preparation for death. Mary had been trained in that system. Here we see a snippet of a connection to the goddess traditions, fired by the relation to Venus. As we see the theme of Venus and one's karmic or spiritual group, we can see that Mary Magdalene declares Jesus as belonging, at least in part, to the great initiation traditions of Egypt.[20]

The sign of the Ram in this Sun-Venus conjunction evokes the virtuous quality of devotion as a power of sacrifice. Sacrifice is on behalf of the group, in service to which several groups are joined: Egyptian priest craft through this priestess, the simple untrained folk who follow Jesus. This deep gesture of serving shows a chasm full of feeling. Directly across from the Goddess star, Spica, Mary Magdalene stands in for Sophia herself. Many have assumed that the connection between Magdalene and Jesus was sexual—an aspect of Venus—the unfurling of the hair, the familiarity with perfumes and potions, her capacity of sensual experience of the world. However, more accurately Magdalene's capacities were a refinement of Eros, expressed here as sensual devotion. One cannot understand the depth of the meeting between Magdalene and the risen Christ without understanding this sense of devotion, active and fired in the head.

---

18 Born February 21, 1878, Venus 9° Aquarius 18, Sun 9° Aquarius 43.
19 The Mother's thirteen volumes of writing are summarized in Satprem, *The Mind of the Cells, or Willed Mutation of the Human Species* (Institute for Evolutionary Research, 1982).

20 The "day before" is March 19, and the day of the unfurling of the hair March 20, A.D. 33, Venus and Sun at 1° Aries 28, opposite Spica, the Goddess Star at the end of Virgo. The 1° orb goes from late at night on March 20 to dawn on March 22. The understanding of Magdalene as a priestess in the tradition of Isis is presented by David Tresemer, in the preface to Jean-Yves Leloup, *The Gospel of Mary Magdalene* (Inner Traditions, 2002).

Summary: Linking groups through intimate sharing of secrets. Eros becomes devotion.

2B: Event: Birth of Amedeo Modigliani, artist of the divine feminine

Modigliani's interpretive paintings of women are astonishingly potent, deserving his birth mention in this recognition of the feminine power of Mary Magdalene.[21]

2C: Imagination: Inferior Conjunction in the Ram: Cursing of the Fig Tree

Walking with his students, the Teacher stopped at a fig tree. It had leaves but no fruit. Jesus cursed it, saying that the fig tree would no longer bear fruit. The next day the students passed that way again and were surprised to see the tree was entirely barren of fruit and leaves, and that its branches had withered, becoming dry and brittle, some broken.

Comment: Many commentators have wondered about the significance of cursing the fig tree, especially so close to the Mystery of Golgotha.[22] It has been suggested that the fig represented the old religion, and that the Teacher was announcing—and demonstrating—a new relationship with Divinity.[23] Speaking in terms of the Venus connection with karmic groups, the demonstration communicated the severance of connection with the old group and an announcement of the new. One does not affiliate with all ancient traditions but only with the ones to which one is connected by destiny.

3. THEME OF RELATIONSHIP BEYOND HUMAN TO THE DIVINE

3A: Imagination: Inferior Conjunction in the Ram: Theophany

In the last days of his teaching, Jesus entered the temple, and said, "This day my soul is troubled. Shall I say, 'Father, save me from this hour?' No, it is my destiny to come to this hour. Father! Father! Glorify your name!" Immediately, the sky thundered, from which many heard the words, "I have glorified it, and I will glorify it again!" When the thunder calmed, Jesus explained, "This voice has come for your sake, not for mine. When I am lifted from the Earth, I will draw all people to myself." The people swooned with the impact of this demonstration of unity and the promise of the resolution of time. From the room rose a unified exhalation, "Ah!"

Comment: Here Jesus affirms the importance of human destiny and the affiliation with one's true group of belonging, represented by his own being. The *theophany* (meaning appearance of deity) affirms these truths through thunder and words.[24] In the Ram, we again find the sense of one's self-sacrifice to what is greater. Sun and Venus lie directly opposite *Spica,* the Goddess star, the star of Sophia. This alignment looks like this: Beginning of the Ram (Aries)–Sun–Venus–Earth–Spica–end of Virgo. The vowel "ah" is thought to arise from the planet Venus, and could be uttered at every one of the theophanies, as well at most of the events mentioned in this paper.

Summary: Ultimate group identification, the all with the All. Venus listens—to the voice of Divinity.

3B: Events: Superior Conjunctions: Divinity Speaks

At the two previous times that Divinity spoke which we have recorded, Venus lay in relation not to the Sun but to a powerful polarity in the cosmos, Aldebaran-Antares, 15° Taurus and 15° Scorpio, dividing the heavens into halves. On September 23 A.D. 29, Venus lay at 15° Scorpio 3, at the event of the Water Initiation (Baptism), conjunct Antares. On March 28 A.D. 31, Venus lay at 14° Taurus 1, conjunct Aldebaran, the Life Star, when Divinity spoke in words that people could hear. Not only does the Sun magnify a planet, but also major stars in the cosmos can magnify a planet, these two in particular being very powerful in our experience. Thus, the event of the speaking of Divinity is shown to relate to strong positions of

---

21 Amedeo Modigliani, born July 12, 1884, Venus (26° Gemini 47) in inferior conjunction to the Sun (27° Gemini 11).
22 March 20 A.D. 33. Venus at 2° Aries 10 and the Sun at 0° Aries 23. Mark 11. See also Luke 13:6–9.
23 Among others, Adriana Koulias, in *The Secret Gospel* (forthcoming), develops the notion of the Fig School as the older religion, rejected by Jesus in this conjunction of Venus and Sun.
24 John 12:27–32 and Emmerich, *LJC* IV, pp. 20–22, Venus 2° Aries 4, Sun 0° Aries 33.

Venus, where she is empowered by the Sun or by great stars. Venus listens.

3C: Event: Inferior Conjunction in the Crab: Historical Event: The Entry of the First Crusaders into Jerusalem

On July 15, 1099, heeding a call to reclaim their connection with the life and vitality of Jesus Christ, the first Crusaders accomplished the goal set many months earlier: They entered Jerusalem. This rejoined the imagination of Christendom with its home in the Middle East, a profound reconnection with one's karmic group and karmic geography—karma, here, meaning the influence that destiny has on one's life beyond this day and even this lifetime. Was it karmic necessity to have Western influence in this multi-cultural center? The Crusaders were, like Judas (see below), propelled by a vision (head pole) of what they wanted. Rather than taking the experience into their heart and negotiating truces along the way, they wanted exclusive possession and murdered to achieve their goal.[25]

Summary: Christian culture yearned to lay claim to the geography of the Christ events, feeling a need to reunite with the spiritual ancestry. Zeal to connect with one's destiny group leads to extreme acts.

3D: Event: Superior Conjunction in the Bull: The discovery by Johannes Kepler of the Third Law of Planetary Dynamics.

At a superior conjunction of Venus and the Sun, and thus interestingly connected with the will pole of the human being, Johannes Kepler discovered the way in which the heavens were ordered according to musical harmonies.[26] Here a daring human being looked out beyond the thought forms of the day, peering into the hidden dynamics of the heavens, and perceiving its innate harmonic order. The theophany appeared to Kepler as the square of the period of rotation of a planet around the Sun in proportion to the cube of its distance from the Sun. To introduce this third law, Kepler wrote in *Harmonices mundi*, book 5, "I have stolen the golden vessels of the Egyptians from which to furnish for my God a holy shrine far from Egypt's confines." He thus connects the spirit/karma stream of the Egyptian initiates (see again imagination 2) with the present. Kepler continued, "But now, Urania, there is need for a louder sound while I climb along the harmonic scale of the celestial movements to higher things, where the true archetype of the world fabric is kept hidden."[27] One could say that Kepler felt he was lifting the veil of Isis–Sophia–Venus–Divine-Feminine. The accomplishment is less a feat of the mind and more one of climbing a celestial ladder, stealing the golden vessels, sharing with humanity.

Summary: The Divine expresses as harmonious musical order and a person can perceive this beauty.

3E: Events: Other Theophanies

The first man thrown into space might be a modern scientific and materialist world version of this connection of the community of humanity with the All: Yuri Gagarin pressed through the atmosphere into the heavens, April 12, 1961, with Venus (26° Pisces 0) in inferior conjunction to the Sun (27° Pisces 42). It is interesting to conceive of this as more related to the head pole, to how we think about ourselves, rather than an act of will.

Second, the first explosion of an atom bomb occurred on July 16, 1945, whereupon the head of the project to develop this penetration of the atom's secrets, the physicist Robert Oppenheimer, felt the

---

25 July 15, 1099, Venus 16° Cancer 27 in inferior conjunction to the Sun 15° Cancer 33. At another dramatic battle where displaced people came in force to reclaim a connection to their land—namely on D-Day, June 6, 1944—Venus (at 15° Taurus 55) lay conjunct Aldebaran, the Life Star, an influence very powerful in the heavens. This all has a shadow side, too. The beginning of World War II was related, as was its end, to a Venus event: Germany invaded Poland because it was claimed to belong to the Fatherland September 1, 1939, Venus 12° Leo 38, Sun 13° Leo 55.

26 May 15, 1618 (Venus 6° Taurus 35, Sun 4° Taurus 59). We have this date from Nick Kollerstrom's historical research in *The Eureka Effect*, book and website.

27 Kepler invokes Urania, the muse of astronomy. However, one could ask where Uranus might have been on the day of discovery, even though it had not yet been identified in the heavens. On the day of Kepler's discovery of the third law, December 27, 1571, Uranus (26° Gemini 37) lay directly opposite Kepler's Birth-Sun (26° Sagittarius 41) and Venus (29° Sagittarius 48).

revelation of Krishna as ten thousand suns, recorded in the *Mahabharata*. Peering into the immensity of light, Oppenheimer heard and spoke the words, "I am become Death, destroyer of worlds."[28]

Thirdly, the invention of the particle accelerator by Ernest Walton—permitting a look into the insides of the atomic world—occurred when Venus lay conjunct the Life Star, Aldebaran.[29]

4. THEME OF THE PERSONAL CALL TO ONE'S KARMIC GROUP

4A: *Imagination: The Call to Join the Brotherhood, Inferior Conjunction in the Goat*

The Teacher walked purposefully, and his students walked swiftly to keep up, close by each other for each wished to stay close, to hear every word that the Teacher might speak. They had traveled over many kinds of terrain and through many kinds of weather, and the students felt intimate with the Teacher. As they passed boats on the shore of the great lake, one of them said, "Teacher, look there. Many fishermen are caring for their boats. We know them! They should come join us and help spread the words of your teaching. Master, shall I go beckon them to join us?"

The Teacher paused and observed the scene—the boats, the piles of nets, the huts for equipment needed for repairs, and all the activity of men, women, and children to support the task of catching fish on the great lake. "I have not yet called them, though I will do so. What they do supports many people, and until they are needed they must perform that service."

Comment: This occurred at an inferior conjunction of Venus to the Sun on January 8 A.D. 30, with Sun and Venus at 20° Capricorn 36. It demonstrates the Venus connection with belonging to groups, with who will be in or not, and, in this instance, who belongs in the group but not quite yet. The fishermen they observed included Peter and Andrew.

---

28 Venus at 15° Taurus 14, conjunct Aldebaran, the Life Star. Conjunctions with the fixed stars are always inferior conjunctions.
29 April 13, 1932, Venus at 15° Taurus 7, conjunct Aldebaran.

Summary: Who belongs to the group, and when is the right time to admit them?

4B: *Imagination: The Call to Judas and Thomas, Superior Conjunction in the Scorpion.*

Bartholomew pointed toward a man in the distance and said to the Teacher, "Look, there is a man who is earnest in his seeking, a hard worker, modest in appearance, trained in his uncle's business of tanning hides, and good with numbers. His name is Judas from Iscariot—though his mother has a bad reputation, and his father is not known."

Another student spoke up sharply, "His mother is an exotic dancer who has had many men." He waited for the expected mumbles of concern among the other students. "When her child was an infant, she abandoned him near a waterhole where wild animals were known to come." More mumbles. "She has no idea who the father was." This was too much—not knowing your parentage and therefore your blood group. Several students exclaimed their amazement that such a person would even be considered.

Bartholomew defended Judas. "I know him. He has talents and good qualities. His uncle raised him and can vouch for him. Teacher, looking at the man himself, do you not think that he would make a good student and be helpful to us?"

The Teacher sighed and said, "Yes, but not yet, not just yet."

Two days later, the Teacher and Judas met. Judas asked to become a student, to study the teachings diligently. The Teacher said, "You can join, or you can decide to leave this position for another." Judas insisted that he would join, for he wanted to be part of the most exciting movement of his time.

A week later, the Teacher met with Thomas, another young man who had been recommended. He was a student of law, trained to doubt anything based only on hearsay and without evidence. Thomas asked to join the group and, more than that, the close community of brothers and sisters who had gathered around the Teacher. The Teacher agreed.

Comment: These calls occurred during a superior conjunction. On October 24 A.D. 30, with

Venus at 2° Scorpio 19 and Sun at 1° Scorpio 50, the Teacher gave Judas the choice to come on the path that the Teacher saw lay ahead.[30] The Teacher summoned Thomas, the student of law, the doubter, on October 29, with Venus at 8° Scorpio 31 and Sun at 6° Scorpio 49 (a bit greater than our usual orb, but clearly relevant to being called to a group to which one belongs). The other disciples (those we know of) were chosen in connection with other planets.[31]

Choosing of both Judas and Thomas brought two of the most willful of the lot into the group—a sense of the superior conjunction relating to the will pole of the human being. These men were responsible for deeds; they neither furthered nor laid out thoughts. The choice of Judas was for an act necessary to the Teacher's unfolding story. Thomas played the role of demanding physical proof, needing to put his fingers (extension of the will pole of the arms) into the wounds of the risen Christ.

Summary: Call to one's karma or destiny group.

4C: Imagination: Judas Shifts Allegiances, Inferior Conjunction in the Ram

Judas had returned with the students and the Teacher through the Golden Gate in a triumphant procession. Nevertheless, he was dissatisfied, and while the others were busy with meals and plans to distribute goods to the poor, he slipped out and ran to the house of Caiaphas, the high priest of Jerusalem, and agreed to identify which of their band was the leader Jesus.

Comment: Judas takes "the first definite step in his treacherous course," that of exposing the Teacher to force his hand to a miracle of overthrowing the Roman government.[32] In this act, Judas disaffiliates himself with one group and affiliates with another, continuing the theme of calling and belonging. He is propelled by his vision of what Jesus *should* be, thus a relationship to the head-man pole of the inferior conjunction.

Summary: Trying to force one's destiny group to change based on one's own ideas and illusions.

4D: Imagination: The Call to Zacchaeus, Superior Conjunction in the Twins

The Teacher led a band of several hundred as they entered the city of Jericho. Crowds pressed in from both sides of the street cheering, both the healthy and the sick. The latter have gathered to see the healer, knowing that they would have a good chance to see him later to be healed of their afflictions. Approaching the town square, the Teacher stopped and turned to face one of the great sycamore trees that lined the road into the town. He held up his hands, and the crowd grew silent. He shouted up to the tree, "Zacchaeus!" There was complete silence. "Zacchaeus!" Some leaves shook and out stuck the head of little Zacchaeus, the greatly feared tax collector and agent of the Romans. The crowd gasped. The Teacher held up his hands again. "Zacchaeus, come down. Prepare your house, for today I shall enter." The Teacher then turned and waved for all to follow him to the town square. The entire populace cheered and fell in behind him, knowing that there they would find the healing that they so earnestly sought. Later, Zacchaeus changed his allegiance from the tax collecting and the occupying Roman forces to the fellowship of Jesus.

Comment: This encounter is developed in a story for Mars, as there is a significant aspect with Mars here, too.[33] In terms of the superior conjunction of Sun and Venus on May 30 A.D. 32, with Venus and the Sun at 8° Gemini 8, the call to Zaccheus joins these other calls to join the community of destiny.

---

30 At this meeting, the Sun lay on the great circle (perpendicular to the ecliptic) that included Algol. This meeting is discussed in those terms in Bento, Schiappacasse, and Tresemer, *Signs in the Heavens*.

31 Andrew was chosen at a moment where the Sun lay opposed to Saturn and conjunct to Pluto; Matthew was chosen with Sun square Mars; Peter was chosen with Sun square Spica; Philip was chosen with Sun conjunct Mercury and square Spica. The timing gives each of these students a particular celestial imprimatur that colors their participation in the Teacher's community. Recall that Andrew and Peter had been among the fishermen when they were considered in the Venus-Sun conjunction of Part One, but not found ready quite yet.

32 March 20 A.D. 33, inferior conjunction. Emmerich, *LJC* IV p. 22.

33 We feature this story in our presentation of the signature of Mars (forthcoming).

Summary: In the sphere of Venus, one hears a call to join a new group, affiliations and relationships related to one's destiny.

5. THEME: THE QUEST OF PARSIFAL

5A: *Event: Superior Conjunction in the Crab: The Tale of Parsifal #1, First Visit*

The tale of Parsifal tells of the Grail King's wound that will not heal and the young man who would solve the enigma and heal the old king. Parsifal, the young innocent, chances upon the Grail Castle, where he meets the Grail King and observes a ceremony of profound meaning, to which he feels drawn. Confused, young, and trained to hold his tongue, Parsifal says nothing. He listens. He does not ask about what is going on. Specifically, he does not ask the question for which the king and all the court have awaited. After he leaves the next day, Parsifal learns of his inadequate behavior from Cundrie. She is a counterpart to Mary Magdalene, both of whom are in the role of the divine feminine, Venus, in relation to world events. Parsifal wanders for years before he is finally able to find the Grail Castle again and ask the special question that heals the wounded king.[34]

Summary: In the aura of Venus, individuals can observe their destined group as a mysterious stranger, and then be lost from it. One listens but does not speak. "In this learning to ask questions lies the ascending stream of humanity's evolution."[35]

5B: *Event: Superior Conjunction in the Bull: The Tale of Parsifal #2, Completion*

After five years of wandering and learning through life experience, Parsifal is ready to return. He earns the role of Grail King near Easter, a deed that is sealed and profoundly healed at Pentecost fifty days later, another Venus–Sun conjunction.[36] In the Bull, this completion at Pentecost refers to the deeper cosmological significance of that constellation in relation to Earth evolution—the foundation of the "I." It opens up the new mystery schooling from an esoteric Christian perspective—the new gathering of souls in disciplined devotion to the center, the Grail, is in an important way the new yoga.[37]

Summary: In Venus, one finds completion of one's destiny in leadership of a group of others to find their destiny.

5C: *Event: Superior Conjunction in the Ram: The Tale of Parsifal #3: Birth of Mani*

The philosopher Mani, founder of Manichaeism, was born with Venus in superior conjunction to the Sun.[38] He has been considered a previous incarnation of Parsifal.[39] His philosophy linked together many of the karmic streams governed by the sphere of Venus. Manichaeism can be found in the Templar Knights (cf. the entry to Jerusalem already mentioned), in the life and accomplishments of Parsifal, and in the Cathars and other mystical spiritual streams that emphasize the development of the individual's relationship to

---

34 The first visit of Parsifal occurs July 15, 828 (Julian), with Venus at 15° Cancer 57 and the Sun at 17° Cancer 57. The dating has been worked out by Joachim Schmidt in a 1947 article, "Parsifal and the Stellar Script," published by Suso Vetter in the 1987/88 edition of the *Sternkalendar* (Star Calendar, Philosophisch-Anthroposophisch Verlag, Dornach). William Bento works with this event and date in "Saturn in the Crab and the Mysteries of the Holy Grail," *Christian Star Calendar*, 2006. At the event in 828, other planets were conjunct to Venus and the Sun: the Moon at 14° Cancer 24, Mercury at 21° Cancer 45, Jupiter at 13° Cancer 52, and Saturn at 22° Cancer 51. The Sun in 828 lay at the place where Saturn lay at the Mystery of Golgotha (18° Cancer 45). Much more on Parsifal is in "Lifting the Darkness," op. cit. More about this can be found in the wonderful publication by Robert J. Kelder (ed.) *Werner Greub: Wolfram's Grail Astronomy* (Willehalm Institute for Grail Research, 1999; also available from www.StarWisdom.org).

35 Rudolf Steiner, *The Fifth Gospel*, cited in Selg, op. cit., pp. 113–114.
36 May 15, 833, Venus at 19° Taurus 51, Sun at 19° Taurus 30.
37 Much more is said about Parsifal in my "Lifting the Dark" paper, op. cit., as well as in Walter Johannes Stein, *The Ninth Century: World History in Light of the Holy Grail* (London: Temple Lodge, 1991).
38 Mani, born April 14, 216, Venus 24 Aries 0 and Sun 23 Aries 12. Richard Seddon, *Mani, His Life and Work, Transforming Evil* (London: Temple Lodge, 1996); L. J. R. Ort, *Mani: A Religio-Historical Description of his Personality* (The Netherlands: E. J. Brill, 1967), p. 156.
39 Seddon, ibid., chapter 9.

Divinity, and the sense of uniting in the light to confront the dark with strength.

Summary: In the sphere of Venus, brothers and sisters find each other. Different expressions of the same individuality link up across time.

5D: Event: Superior Conjunction in the Bull: The Tale of Parsifal #4: Birth of Richard Wagner

The great composer Richard Wagner was born with Venus conjunct the Sun.[40] His music was felt as the most powerful expression of the German, and indeed European, folk soul. It united millions of people in this sense of karmic group. Wagner's last opera, *Parsifal*, links him with the theme of Parsifal. It pictured groups of men and women, some lost, some ill, some enchanted, all finding one another again through alignment to their higher purposes in life—namely, through affirming the Holy Grail.

Thus, we find some suggestions about the character of the sphere of Venus from those individuals and their expression of its vivifying influence. Pondering these signatures of Venus may assist us in preparing for the Venus eclipse of June 2012.

---

40 May 22, 1813, Venus at 7° Taurus 33, Sun at 8° Taurus 26.

> *He said there was something called the Grail,*
> *whose name—how it is known—he had read clearly in the stars.*
> *A [heavenly] host left it upon the Earth,*
> *and then flew up above the stars on high.*
>
> —Wolfram von Eschenbach, *Parsifal* 454, 21–25

The Russian poet and mystic Daniel Andreev also had a vision of the Holy Grail in the starry heavens and revealed its name:

> "I remember seeing a glowing mist of stunning majesty, as though the creative heart of our universe had revealed itself to me in visible form for the first time. It was Astrofire, the great center of our galaxy."
>
> —Daniel Andreev, *The Rose of the World*, p.198

THE PLEIADES AND 2010
THE SIGNIFICANCE OF THE PLEIADES IN NATIVE AMERICAN INDIAN CULTURE

Robert Powell, Ph.D.

This article appears in honor of the original people of this continent, the Native Americans, or First Nations, who were guided by the starry constellations and created ancient star maps. According to Native American legend, Turtle Island is the name for the North American Continent. In this mythology, North America rests on the back of a large turtle. The tortoise volunteered itself so that its shell would serve as a home for all creatures on the land. In Native American lore, there was a time when the Earth was in a watery condition. Consequently, there was no place for human beings and animals to live on this world of water. Then, arising from the water, a giant turtle offered its shell. According to this myth, North America came to live on the back of this turtle, one of whose hind legs is Florida, while the other is Baja California, with Mexico the tail.

Some Native Americans believe that all tribes in North America originated from the Pleiades. In this view, Native Americans are actually descended from that star cluster and have the task, given by the Pleiades, to tend and care for Mother Earth.

It would be necessary to write an entire book to cover all the myths, legends, and esoteric teachings related to the Pleiades. This short article provides some background on the Pleiades and indicates some of the Native American beliefs about this star cluster.[1]

A central theme of the Pleiades is the impulse for community. The seven main stars stand in community, appearing to the naked eye as a

The Dance of the Pleiades *by Elihu Vedder in an engraving by F. E. Fillebrown*

well-defined cluster. Traditionally, the star cluster known as the Pleiades represents seven sisters, the daughters of Atlas and Pleione. In Hindu mythology, they are the seven wives of the Seven Holy Rishis, represented by the Big Dipper, which are the seven most prominent stars in the constellation of the Great Bear (Ursa Major). In fact, the appearance of the Pleiades, as we can see in the following image ("The two parents, left, and the Seven Sisters of the Pleiades") resembles a Small Dipper. Tradition holds that the Seven Holy Rishis revealed the Vedas, the holy scriptures of India. In some schools of esoteric thought, the Pleiades are one of three stellar configurations (along with the Big Dipper and Sirius) most important to our solar system as animators and inspiration to earthly and human evolution.

The Pleiades also appear in ancient Jewish lore. The Book of Job, the oldest book of the Bible, mentions them. "[He] maketh the Great Bear, Orion, the Pleiades, and the chambers of the south" (Job 9:9). "Canst thou bind the sweet influences of the Pleiades, or loose the bands of Orion?" (Job 38:31). The Old Testament names the Pleiades *Kimah*.

---

1 This short introduction does not include references and notes to guide the reader to further investigation. However, it is this author's hope to write a more extensive and complete treatise on the Pleiades.

Cave painting of Taurus, with the Pleiades above, from 16,500 years ago in Lascaux, France

They are associated with the story of Noah and with the biblical flood in the set of Jewish scriptures known as the Babylonian Talmud: "When the Holy One decided to bring the Deluge on the Earth, He took two stars from Kimah and brought the Deluge on the Earth."

The Pleiades are featured in the star lore of many ancient cultures. For example, at Lascaux in central France, a cave painting from 16,500 years ago shows the Pleiades in their usual place in the constellation of Taurus the Bull.

A Chinese text from around 2357 B.C. mentions the Pleiades. Ancient Mesopotamians depicted them as the place of exaltation (most powerful location) of the Moon. It is interesting that Pope John Paul II, who, according to Lakota spiritual leader Chanupa Wambdi Wicasa (Deer Man), was a Pipe Carrier in the eyes of the Lakota, was born with both the Sun and Moon in conjunction with the Pleiades. Moreover, the only male U.S. citizen, hitherto, to have been pronounced a saint, John Neumann, Bishop of Philadelphia and the founder of the first Catholic diocesan school system in the United States, was born when the Moon was exalted—that is, when the Moon was in conjunction with the Pleiades. In addition, the English Romantic poet John Keats was born when the Moon was at exaltation in conjunction with the Pleiades. The poet Algernon Swinburne called Keats's poem "Ode to a Nightingale" "one of the final masterpieces of human work in all time and for all ages." It has also been described as one of the poems in the English language that comes closest to being perfect. The following lines from "Ode to a Nightingale" seem to allude to the Moon's exalted position (as in Keats' birth horoscope):

*Already with thee! tender is the night,
And haply the Queen-Moon is on her throne,
Cluster'd around by all her starry Fays...*
                                        (lines 35–37)

In 1846 Johann von Mädler of the Estonian Dorpat Observatory postulated that the Pleiades are located at the center of the galaxy. Some 440 light years away, the stars in the Pleiades cluster are thought to have been formed together around 100 million years ago. Viewed from the Northern Hemisphere, the Pleiades reach their highest point in the sky around midnight November 21, six months after the conjunction of the Sun with the Pleiades (at 5 degrees Taurus) on May 20. During May, the Sun is drawing close to its conjunction with this beautiful star cluster, and so the Pleiades are not visible. One of the best months for viewing them is November, when they are opposite the Sun in the heavens. December and the following winter months are also very good times for viewing the Pleiades, when the star cluster can be seen in the evening sky after sunset.

In the teachings of Rudolf Steiner's spiritual science, the Pleiades are significant, being "the region where the whole solar system entered the universe." Steiner also stated, "The next solar system will take place in the Pleiades. The whole solar system is moving toward the Pleiades."

Alcyone, the brightest star of the Pleiades is more than 800 times more luminous than our Sun.

*... the great and burning star,
Immeasurably old, immeasurably far,
Surging forth its silver flame
Through eternity,... Alcyone!*
—ARCHIBALD LAMPMAN, "Alcyone"

In connection with the Pleiades and the year 2012, it is worth noting that May 20 is the date of an annular solar eclipse (May 21, 2012, for local time in the Eastern Hemisphere). A solar eclipse occurs when the Moon passes between Earth and the Sun, totally or partially obscuring the Sun from Earth. An annular solar eclipse occurs when the Moon's apparent diameter is smaller than the Sun, causing the Sun to look like an annulus (ring), blocking most of the Sun's light. An annular eclipse appears as a partial eclipse over a region thousands of miles wide. The annular solar eclipse on May 20, 2012, is in conjunction with the Pleiades. In other words, as seen from the Earth, the annular eclipse occurs against the background of the Pleiades. The annular phase is visible from the Chinese coast, the south of Japan, and the western part of the U.S. Tokyo is on the central path. Its maximum occurs in the North Pacific, south of the Aleutian islands, for 5 minutes and 46 seconds, and finishes in the western U.S. It is the first central eclipse of the twenty-first century in the continental U.S. In Sacramento, California, the Moon obscures about 87% of the Sun; in San Francisco about 84%; and in Los Angeles about 78%. The illustrations on page 35 show the significance of the annular solar eclipse on May 20, 2012, in conjunction with the Pleiades.

The two parents, left, and the seven sisters of the Pleiades

The Pleiades cluster is not always easy to see in the heavens. At first glance, it appears as a fuzzy haze. The appearance of the Pleiades in the night sky changes nightly throughout the year, depending on viewing conditions. If conditions are excellent, one can see with the naked eye all seven stars in the Pleiades, the Seven Sisters. To ensure seeing all of them, however, it is best to view these stars with binoculars. The easiest way to locate them is to begin by finding Orion's Belt—the three stars in the middle of Orion—which appear close together in a straight line. In the northern hemisphere, one then extends the line of these three stars up diagonally to the right. As a stargazer in the northern hemisphere, if one then follows the imaginary line of Orion's belt down diagonally to the left, the bright star Sirius comes into view. If, however, one follows the line up, away from Sirius, the extended line passes a little below the bright star Aldebaran (15° Taurus), marking the eye of the Bull in Taurus, until one comes to the Pleiades. The three stars in the belt of Orion serve as a pointer to locate the Pleiades, with Aldebaran as a marker on the way: Aldebaran on the tip of the left arm of a distinctive tilted V-shape of stars that form the cluster known as the Hyades (the half-sisters of the Pleiades). In the Southern Hemisphere, simply reverse this description, so that one follows the line extending from the belt of Orion down to the Pleiades.

Because the Pleiades are located in the neck of the Bull, at 5° in the sign of Taurus, they are too close to the Sun to be visible during May, when the Sun is also in Taurus (the Sun is in the sidereal sign of Taurus from May 15 to June 15). After the conjunction of the Sun with the Pleiades on about May 20, they first become visible again in the night sky before sunrise on the eastern horizon in the second half of June. This first viewing in the East, before sunrise, is the heliacal rising of the Pleiades. For the Maori of New Zealand, the heliacal rising of the Pleiades denoted the beginning of the year. After the day of their heliacal rising, they begin to rise a little earlier each morning, becoming visible each night for a longer period before dawn. They are clearly visible in November, when they rise as the Sun is setting and set at sunrise, making them visible throughout the night around November 21. Around this date, six months after the Sun's conjunction with the star cluster around May 20, the

Pleiades are in opposition to the Sun. This signifies the rising of the Pleiades simultaneously with the setting of the Sun, which is the acronychal rising of the Pleiades. This was important to the Pawnee tribe of Native Americans. On a clear winter night, the unaided eye might be able to see the six brightest stars in the cluster, and if conditions are excellent, all seven, together with the two stars marking the parents of the Seven Sisters: Atlas and Pleione. However, as mentioned, it is generally advisable to use binoculars. As winter progresses, the time of their setting gradually draws closer to sunset. By mid-April, one can see them for only a short time after sunset as they set in the West. Then, in May, they are no longer visible, as they approach their conjunction with the Sun on May 20.

It is interesting that Rudolf Steiner spoke of the conjunction of the Sun with the Pleiades as significant for the impulse of freedom.

> The Moon is set,
> And the Pleiades.
> Night's half gone,
> Time's passing.
> I sleep alone now.
> —Sappho

To realize the impulse of freedom, it was necessary for a time that human beings should forget their relationship not only to the Pleiades but also with all the stars in the heavens. The Sun and Moon uniting in the Pleiades, in the crucial year of 2012, announces that this time of "forgetting the stars" may be over.

In the ancient Egyptian mysteries, we hear how Osiris was slain by Typhon/Seth and how Isis made the priests keep the whereabouts of his grave a secret. She instituted a great cult to honor Osiris. The cult maintained sacredness of the memory of Osiris, whereby the spiritual perception that once existed in humanity lived on. According to Rudolf Steiner, the time that Typhon/Seth slew Osiris was in November, when the Sun sets in Scorpio and the full Moon appears in the Pleiades. It was during the Egyptian cultural epoch that Christ, in his gradual descent toward the Earth, began to work down from the Sun into the sphere of the Moon. This Egyptian myth indicates the full Moon in the Pleiades. The "death of Osiris," which took place at this time, was symbolically a "departure" of Osiris from the Sun; or, rather, it denoted a new phase of activity of Osiris, who, while still inwardly united with the Sun, was now working into the sphere of the Moon and, through the Moon's phases, was radiating down upon the Earth.

In images, Isis often wears a crown of cow horns that have solar disk between them. Legend tells us that she lost her original crown because, after Typhon–Seth was imprisoned, she had the imprudence to set him free, and that her enraged son Horus tore off her crown, which Hermes then replaced with cow horns. Rudolf Steiner speaks of "lifting the veil" of Isis Sophia by transforming the cow horns through the power of the living Word. As the Pleiades are located at 5° in the neck of the Bull and the horns rise from the center of this constellation, marked by the star Aldebaran at 15° Taurus, it is easy to imagine that on the human level it is the Eustachian tubes rising from the larynx which are represented here. Contemplating human physiology in the region of the throat, on a corresponding heavenly level an image of cosmic listening arises whereby the horns of the Bull serve as antennae to bring in from the Pleiades and other special stellar locations the cosmic forces that resurrect the living Word.[2]

Through receiving the living Word, humanity transforms the will. The living Word sounding from the Pleiades, as mentioned by Steiner, marks the origin of our solar system—the beginning of life brought forth through the Word. With the annular solar eclipse of May 20, 2012, in the Pleiades, just sixteen days before the astronomically rare event of the Venus transit across the face of the Sun on June 5/6, 2012, we are called to contemplate Isis Sophia, to the work of lifting the veil of the Divine Feminine—also with the Venus transit, when the disk of the Sun, united with transiting Venus, appears in the latter part of Taurus between the horns of the Bull. As Steiner describes

---

2 For further indications regarding the Word and the constellation of the Bull, see the description of Taurus in Paul and Powell, *Cosmic Dances of the Zodiac*.

it, the veil of Isis Sophia is lifted by transforming the lower will forces through the power of the living Word, an image that corresponds to the Sun

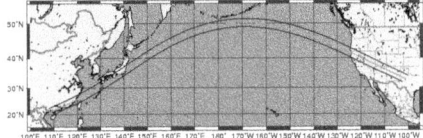

Path of the annular solar eclipse, May 20, 2012 (www.hermit.org/Eclipse/2012-05-20/)

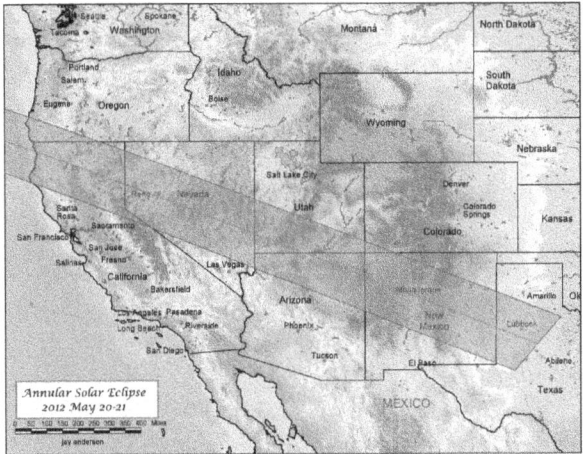

Path of the May 20, 2012, eclipse across the U.S. (home.cc.umanitoba.ca/~jander/ase2012/usa1.png)

in Taurus between the Bull's horns, as at Christ's Ascension, when the power of the Word united Heaven and Earth.

As this eclipse path crosses the U.S., it passes over Mt. Shasta, the great power center of the North American continent, sacred to Native Americans and spoken of by the poet Joaquin Miller: "Lonely as God, and white as a winter moon, Mount Shasta starts up sudden and solitary." The path also passes over Los Alamos, where the explosion of the first atomic bomb took place on July 16, 1945, a line of development arising because of the extreme materialism that gained a stronghold in the United States. Materialism is thwarting the true mission of Turtle Island. As expressed by the "signs in the heavens," the Great Mother is calling to her children. Connecting to the Cosmic Word, the Great Spirit, by awakening us to Isis Sophia, who speaks to us through the signs in the heavens, can help awaken us to the true mission of Turtle Island. This is what the ancients knew. White Buffalo Calf Woman, a manifestation of an aspect of Sophia, brought the sacred peace pipe to Native Americans. Pipe Carriers lift her veil by making peace. When we lift the veil of Isis Sophia, we see the stars and learn again to read the heavenly script. The picture language of Egypt that died into the abstract intellect is rising again, but in a new way. Above and below are reuniting. Hermes stands ready to renew the crown of Isis Sophia, wisdom of God.

In 2012, the annular eclipse of the Sun in the Pleiades on May 20, the Venus transit across the Sun 16 days later (June 5/6), and the Sun at the winter solstice (December 21) crossing the Galactic Equator, marking the end of the Maya calendar, are heavenly signs along the way that we need to change our ways. We are called to remember the Great Mother clothed in the mantle of Nature. Moreover, we are inspired to behold Sophia in the Sun, Moon, and stars as the promise of America's true mission. This is one aspect of the message from the heavens expressed through these great events in the year 2012, signifying that this time of "forgetting the stars" is over and that we are to reestablish our connection with the Pleiades and all the other wonderful stars and star clusters in the heavens. Another aspect of this message calls us to dance together as do the seven sisters, in peace and harmony with all creation.

※

Native Americans, the "Children of the Pleiades," issued a call in 1996 for the protection of Mother Earth.

Standing Elk, a spiritual leader of the Lakota Sioux and, for them, the Keeper of the Six-Pointed Star-Nation Altar, was led through a vision to organize a conference that would gather the "star knowledge" of tribal cultures. "The Star Knowledge Conference and Sun Dance" took place on the Yankton Sioux Reservation in South Dakota in June 1996. The unprecedented gathering brought together indigenous tribal leaders from across the Americas and from as far away as Australia. Interested people from nontribal cultures also attended—one being Richard J. Boylan, Ph.D., who offers tapes of the discussion and a published summary online (www.v-j-enterprises.com/skcrichb.html), which forms the basis for the following text.

In announcing the conference, Standing Elk stated that his vision told him that Native American spiritual knowledge about the Star Nations was "to be shared with our brothers of the four directions." He meant among the tribes and with the other races of Earth. His Lakota people are among the American tribes who proudly trace their origins to the Pleiades, but the star connection encompasses all according to Standing Elk. "The Way of the Stars is in every culture."

Steve Red Buffalo, also of the Lakota, discussed the Star People coming to Earth from the Pleiades. He said that the Pleiades are connected with the *chanupa,* the sacred pipe. He said the *chanupa* symbolizes the union of the Earth, represented by the pipe's stone, with the sky, represented by the hollow stem through which smoke is drawn and sent heavenward. Further, the bowl of the pipe, with its hole for accepting the pipe stem, represents the woman; the stem represents the man. Joining the pipe symbolizes a union and balance between male and female aspects of the world.

According to the conference report, in keeping with the theme of sharing wisdom among cultures, "Lakota spiritual leader Chanupa Wambdi Wicasa (Deer Man) startled those listening by stating that Pope John Paul II was a Pipe Carrier." This indicates a person who keeps the traditions of Native American spirituality. "The Pope fasted and entered a sweat lodge ceremony with the Lakota while visiting in Canada, and congratulated the Lakota for keeping their traditions and ceremonies," Deer Man told the conference.

Deer Man then spoke of the dangers of pollutants such as herbicides, acid rain, and nuclear tests, by which he said humanity has unbalanced the Earth. "We have to help the Earth come back into balance," he said. "Time as you know it is coming to an end, sooner than you think." The shift and the danger, he said, accompanies our crossing from the Fourth World to the Fifth, a teaching also held by the Hopi people.

The end of the Fourth World and beginning of the Fifth takes place in 2012 or 2013, according to the ancient Maya calendar. In addition to tracing their origins to the Pleiades, the Maya also speak of the Pleiades as the seven great powers of the Cosmos, the seven Suns that are the brothers of our Sun. The period called "the end times" of the Fourth World began in 1987, according to Don Alejandro Wandering Wolf of Guatemala, who promoted the Maya message of the Pleiades through lectures, both before and after the Yankton Star Conference. Now the dawn of the Maya new age is quickly approaching.

Wandering Wolf said in a 1999 speech in Santa Fe:

> There will be huge problems. Catastrophes and cataclysms will befall us. So I have been asked to speak to you, and all over the world, of these prophesies. We speak in defense of the natural world. No more pollution of the planet. It cannot survive it, and then we will not be able to survive without our Mother Earth. There is no more distinction between races and colors and creeds. Your sadness and loneliness is the same as mine. We have the same feelings of love. Why? We have the same Sun, one breath, all the Earth is fed by the one Sun, air, water—Mother Earth—and we return here.

This call for a new level of togetherness among the people of the Earth reminds us all to take care of this special planet, to which the Maya say we return. It is the heart and soul of the modern message emerging from the star lore of today. This message is entirely in keeping with another aspect of the Pleiades celebrated by tribal people. Throughout all of known time, the little family cluster of the Pleiades has stayed together, its stars small but united in glittering splendor. In their Hako ceremony, the people of the Pawnee Nation of indigenous peoples sing a prayer of hope to the Pleiades in November as they rise across the eastern horizon shortly after sunset.

Look as they rise, rise up

Over the line where sky meets the earth;
Pleiades!
Lo! They, ascending, come to guide us,
Leading us safely, keeping us one;
Pleiades, teach us to be, like you, united.
—*Ha-ko Ceremony*
(trans. Alice C. Fletcher, 1904)

The Pleiades star cluster represents an underlying unity. A communal nature holds them invisibly together. Gazing up at these special stars, one can contemplate down through the ages those who, like Native Americans, have looked up to their light for inspiration. As the poet Alfred Lord Tennyson wrote, the Pleiades glitter "like a swarm of fireflies tangled in a silver braid." Powerful modern telescopes confirm his words; they show that the cluster of seven stars shines within a group of more than one thousand stars "tangled in a silver braid."

Further notes concerning the Pleiades and Native Americans:[3]

The Native American tribe, the Kiowa, have a story that explains the creation of the Pleiades. According to the Kiowa, seven young maidens went out to play and were spotted by several giant bears. The bears saw the young women and began to chase them. In trying to escape the bears, the women climbed onto a rock and prayed to the spirit of the rock to save them. Hearing their prayers the rock began to rise from the ground toward the heavens so that the bears could not reach the maidens. The seven women reached the sky, where they turned into the star constellation we know today as the Pleiades. The bears, in an effort to climb the rock, left deep claw marks in its sides, which had become too steep to climb. That rock is Devil's Tower, located in the state of Wyoming.

The Lakota tribe also have a legend that links the origin of the Pleiades to Devil's Tower.

Early Dakota stories speak of the *Tiyami* home of the ancestors as being the Pleiades. They say

---

[3] The primary source for these further notes is the Wikipedia article "The Pleiades in Folklore and Literature of Indigenous Peoples of the Americas": en.wikipedia.org/wiki/Pleiades_in_folklore_and_literature.

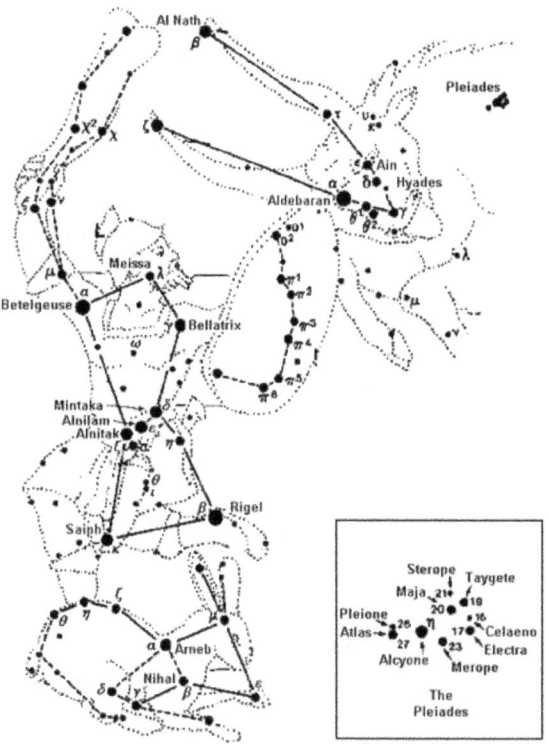

Constellation map of Orion, Taurus, and the Pleiades

that the Pleiades rise with the Sun in May and that, when someone dies, that person's spirit returns south to the seven sisters.

The Hopis called the Pleiades the *Chuhukon*, meaning those who cling together. They consider themselves direct descendents of the Pleiades.

The Navajos named the Pleiades the "Sparkling Suns," or the *Delyahey*, the home of the "Black God."

The Iroquois pray to them for happiness.

The Cree say that they first came to Earth from the stars in spirit form and then became flesh and blood.

According to the Seris (of northwestern Mexico), these stars are seven women giving birth. The constellation, known to them as *Cmaamc*, is apparently an archaic plural of the noun *cmaam*, or woman.

It was common among the indigenous peoples of the Americas to measure keenness of vision by the number of stars one sees in the Pleiades, a practice also used historically in Europe, especially in Greece.

In the ancient Andes, the Pleiades were associated with abundance, because they return to the Southern Hemisphere sky each year at harvest time. In Quechua, they are called *collca,* or storehouse.

Paul Goble, a Native American storyteller, tells a Blackfoot legend that he says other tribes also tell. In this story, the Pleiades are orphans neglected by the people, which led them to become Stars. Mistreatment of the children angered Sun Man, who punishes the people with a drought until the dogs, the only friends of the orphans, intercede on behalf of the people.

The Hopis built their underground *kivas* for various utilitarian uses, the most important of which is for ceremonial meetings. The access is a ladder through a small hole in the roof of the round hole in the ground. During certain ceremonies, the night passage of the Pleiades over the center of the entrance opening provides a direct signal to begin the ceremony. Most of the cultures use the angle of the Pleiades in the night sky as a time-telling device.

A Cheyenne myth, "The Girl Who Married a Dog," tells us that the group of seven stars known as the Pleiades originated from seven puppies, to which a Cheyenne chief's daughter gave birth after being visited mysteriously by a dog in human form, to whom she vowed, "Wherever you go, I go."

The early Monte Alto Culture and others in Guatemala, such as Ujuxte and Takalik Abaj, made its early observatories, using as a reference the star Eta Draconis and the Pleiades, which they called the seven sisters, believing them to be their people's place of origin.

The ancient Aztecs of Mexico and Central America based their calendar on the Pleiades. Their calendar year began when priests first remarked the asterism rising heliacally in the east, immediately before the Sun's dawn light obliterated the view of the stars. Aztecs called the Pleiades *Tianquiztli,* or marketplace.

The Pleiades and 2012

This article refers to the annular eclipse of the Sun on May 20, 2012, which is aligned with the Pleiades. As Rudolf Steiner mentioned, the conjunction of the Sun with the Pleiades is an indicator of freedom. Thus, the eclipse of the Sun in the Pleiades, though not a total eclipse, can be seen as indicating a force of opposition to the impulse of freedom, or it may be thought of as a sign of the heavens supporting the development of freedom for humanity.

This will be a critical time for the world. The push toward a global government will assert itself powerfully as part of the events leading up to the galactic alignment of December 21, 2012 (the end of the Maya calendar), referred to in the article "World Pentecost" in the previous issue of this journal. In this connection, it is important to realize that there are always two levels in relation to all cosmic events: first, as an expression of the forces of the light; and second, as signs of efforts by the dark forces to invert the good impulses streaming from the heavens. Because the Pleiades represent both freedom and community, it is important that true community develops in complete freedom, motivated by love, as expressed in the words of Christ: "Where two or three are gathered in my name, there am I in their midst" (Matthew 18:16).

The push toward global government can be seen as an inversion of the good impulses—those streaming from the Pleiades (May 20, 2012), having to do with freedom and community; those connected with the Venus transit (June 5–6, 2012), having to do with the Christ impulse of the Holy Grail and the awakening of unconditional love, and those emanating from the galactic alignment (December 18–21, 2012), connected with the great wave of Divine Love, as discussed in the previous journal article, "World Pentecost." An essential question arises: Is the push toward global government taking place while respecting individual freedom, or is it is forcing "world community" without the Christ impulse and drawing its motivation by creating a great wave of fear (the global "war on terrorism"), rather than in alignment with the great wave of Divine Love? In relation to the forces of light, the heavenly intention for humanity is World Pentecost. Regarding the forces of darkness, the counter-impulse is the drive toward global government under a single leader (see Daniel Andreev, "The Rose of the World," in this issue of the journal).

In keeping with the community impulse of the Pleiades, the Rose of the World is the name for the true global community of the future, which will arise through the inspiration of Divine Sophia in the sixth cultural epoch (to use Steiner's term for this future culture of brotherly and sisterly love destined to arise during the Age of Aquarius). The task of humanity is to work gradually toward the Rose of the World by living the Christ impulse and by aligning with Sophia, the Holy Wisdom of creation, who holds the Divine Plan for the Earth and humankind. As the true global community of the future, the Rose of the World will arise only through freedom and love. The inversion of the Rose of the World (as discussed in *Christ and the Maya Calendar*), is the one-world government ruled by the Antichrist. Although the push toward the one-world government is taking place now, so also the Rose of the World is already taking shape on a higher level in preparation for its cultural manifestation in the Age of Aquarius. Now in an embryonic form, it is called "Sophia's Beehive." The Pleiades may be thought of as a star portal that crowns Sophia's Beehive—a portal open to the influx of freedom and love.

Sophia's Beehive

This article will conclude with the text of a vision from the young woman. (See also the text of this woman's vision at the conclusion of Daniel Andreev's "Rose of the World (Rosa Mira)" in this issue.) This vision came to her in relation to beholding a Choreocosmos workshop, in which the participants engaged in the community-building activity of cosmic dance, which is very much in the spirit of the Pleiades, the seven sisters who loved to dance.

> I then saw a dome of light appear that remained fixed over the location of a Sophia community. It resembles a beehive of violet light, whose top is a crown of stars and a portal into the spiritual dimension.... Inside the dome of light were astonishing honeycomb light formations rising in a spiral. Inside the "honeycombs of light," I saw numberless angelic beings at work. They were constructing a spiritual edifice that will descend to the physical realm in the future—a place where spiritual honey shall flow freely. The nectar of life will flow in the Sophia community....
>
> I then began to hear the hum of angelic beings above, like that of honeybees, only it was the music of the spheres being sung from above. Beyond any earthly sound, it was the sound of "AUM" (if one can imagine heavenly beings making that sound), pouring it into the dome of light. I saw everyone spiritually present within the dome receive these musical vibratory currents; it is how each person's heart is tuned to this music, the music of Sophia's heart.
>
> I was then taken into the Heart of Sophia, passing through in rays of violet light. Within her Heart were the hearts of all of humanity. All of humanity was in her Heart. Each human being is a light within Her Heart and has her light within each one's heart—rays of every color and intensity—so many shades of light! Sophia loves all human beings. I was imbued with the fragrance of roses given off by the light of her beholding us. We are all flowers in her glorious garden.
>
> From Sophia's Heart....
>
> Love thy neighbor: Again, I say, Love thy neighbor, for all are one in the Heart of Sophia—we are all one. Sophia loves all alike, and all are known by her. She gazes upon each and every face; She recognizes you, each and every one. The warmth

around you is her embrace; she holds you in her arms; you are her Heaven—and she is yours. You are the Heaven that she knows. As she smiles upon you, her sweet breath caresses your face—the dew that falls upon you is her kiss. You are her star; she sent you to Earth to become an Earthstar.... Wherever human beings have become stars, the ground around them becomes holy ground. They become saints in the eyes of Sophia and the ground where they live and work become their temples.

Meditate upon entering the beehive of Sophia, where Sophia's work is being done and where all of her workers are nourished by the nectar of truth, beauty, and goodness. You do not have to live anywhere in particular. Wherever you are, you may enter the spiritual beehive of Sophia.

(Excerpted from "Choreocosmos and Sophia's Beehive Vision (June 10, 2009)," published in the Advent 2009 Starlight *newsletter of the Sophia Foundation of North America. This vision of Sophia's Beehive was bestowed upon a young woman who is very dedicated to Sophia and who wishes to remain anonymous.)*

As I stood before Christ in the Etheric, He lifted me up so that we were hovering just above the Earth. He was like a fire, a purifying fire. He was glowing like the Sun. Upon His chest was a brilliant cross of light, with rays of blue-violet light emanating out from it. He spoke to me:

O child of light, I came to Earth that I might illuminate it with My love, and My love knows no bounds. I love all, and the light of My love shines upon all beings, both good and evil. And all those whom I love, who receive My love, receive illumination to their souls. And this illumination calls forth the darkness from their souls. The darkness is there because of pain. Those who let go of their darkness in My light receive the light of My love into their souls. And My light emanates from their souls and then illuminates others' souls. In this way, others awaken to My love, and also awaken to their darkness. I hold their darkness in My love, and call it forth that their hearts may be purified and prepared to receive Me. I am the light that shall lead you out of your darkness. Keep your eyes on Me.

From the *Journal for Star Wisdom 2010* (pp. 25–26). This vision of the Etheric Christ was experienced by a young woman who wishes to remain anonymous.

PROPHECY
A CAULDRON OF CONTROVERSY

William Bento, Ph.D.

The *Journal for Star Wisdom 2010* contained articles that conveyed declarations about possible events to occur in the near future. This author concluded his article "Contemplations on the Jupiter–Uranus Conjunction" with what one might expect to meet and the possibilities of how to live consciously through the Jupiter–Uranus conjunctions of 2010. Robert Powell's article "World Pentecost" specifically mentioned the winter solstice of 2012 "as a possible time of fulfillment through which humanity as a whole will receive a great wave of Divine Love—and this is precisely the event prophesied by Rudolf Steiner as the *World Pentecost*." In the article "Sun on the Galactic Center," David Tresemer points out that the alignment of the Sun on the Galactic Center does not take place at the winter solstice 2012 once and for all, as many have assumed, but at every winter solstice from 1980 to 2245. This "marks the time when our solstice season interacts with the Galactic Center in a dynamic way" wrote Tresemer.

If these writings did not trigger a surge of wonder and will in readers, then they failed. For some, they may have even provoked consternation and doubt. The aim of these articles was not merely to impart information, but also to instigate thoughtfulness about the times in which we live. Yet, in retrospect, there were also portions of the journal expressed in a way that could be easily misunderstood or simply regarded as dramatic embellishments.

Sensationalism surrounding issues of prophecy are all too prevalent in these days, particularly with the long-awaited Maya prophecy of 2012 being featured in various media. Those of us who feel responsible for the content and quality of this journal do not wish to be considered purveyors of sensationalism. My own observations of the impact of prophetic declarations on the public, as well as on my circle of friends, have revealed to me that a cardinal element of a prophecy is its tendency to polarize. Aside from the primary polarization between true believers and skeptics, provocations of fear and cynicism underlie the debates and controversies that arise from the subject of prophecy. It is my contention that the polarization phenomenon is an unfortunate, blind veiling the true significance and value of prophecy. In this article, I explore the polarization phenomenon, advocate an understanding of prophecies from both spiritual and psychological points of view, and place prophecy in a context of relevancy for our *post*-postmodern time.

Polarization

The polarization phenomenon is a fundamental principle in evolutionary processes. It can be seen as a response to an initial movement to introduce a new factor into any setting or situation. Otto Scharmer addresses this principle in his book, *Theory U* (2007), as the debate phase. The polarization prompts an awakening to aspects of a situation that have either been ignored or marginalized. It helps the parties involved in the debate to a wider scope of issues than his/her own point of view. The danger occurs when polarization is fixed and unable to move forward with new insights.

It is this latter aspect of polarization—the fixed and intractable views that create unbearable tension—that captures most people's attention. When this becomes the only way to experience polarization, it becomes a negative phenomenon, and, as such, people often avoid or dismiss both sides of the polarity as having no value. In my experience, the cauldron of controversy that arises with prophecy is stirred far more by the dynamic swirling around fixed polarities than by a search for new insights.

True believers are quick to latch onto prophecies that confirm their fears or bolster their hopes and beliefs. Skeptics are equally quick to reject prophecies based on their seeming absurdity or the preconception that seeing into the future is simply impossible. In both cases, we witness the power of an unchecked feeling life. Sympathies and antipathies seep into prospective judgments and color the tone of the debate. When we allow feelings to dominate, there is little opportunity, if any, to consider seriously the realm of possibilities. Rather than being a catalyst for opening minds, emotional reactivity becomes a lock on the gate of the collective mind, rendering all conversation a futile enterprise.

Such polarization is not only an outer affair; it also has internal dimensions. Prophecy sets in motion a conflict between what has been, what is, and what might become. Each individual is compelled to wrestle with this riddle as prophecy presents itself. Questioning the source of the prophecy, the veracity of its message, the context it addresses, and the potential outcomes of a prophecy requires an open mind and rigorous discernment. It is not unusual to find one's self split on the matter or to realize that, at some level, one may be of two minds on the issue. This is part of the polarization phenomenon as it emerges in the interior landscape of every psyche.

Denying the internal aspects of polarization engendered by a prophetic declaration usually leads to either an emotive reaction or to an entrenchment of one's blind spot. Becoming aware and feeling responsible for the inner polarization is the first step toward resolution. This is a key psychological concept advanced by Carl Jung in his *Two Essays on Analytical Psychology* (1953). Accepting the inner tension and living with the paradox that both responses to the declared prophecy may be correct is vital to escaping the mental clamp of duality that feeds doubt and fear. In this inner movement of thinking we can find the wellspring of freedom. From attention upon the paradox to concentrating on the possibilities of both prospects of the prophecy we create the conditions for a genuine meditative activity. We move from the conceived mental pictures to a sense-free thinking, unbiased by judgments and prejudices.

The practice of Rudolf Steiner's method of cognition as stated in his book *Intuitive Thinking as a Spiritual Path: A Philosophy of Freedom* (1994), guides us to further steps for resolution. Once we have developed a sense-free thinking with regard to the matter of the prophecy, we can contemplate it not as a *fait accompli*, but as a process streaming into exceptional states of consciousness with a specific purpose. Scharmer describes this state of consciousness as *presencing*. It is the only place that we can truly understand prophecy. The past has already had its results, and the future remains a virgin realm. Only the present state of one's consciousness can enter a dialogue with the being behind the prophecy. To be quite clear, it is not the prophet I refer to here, but the spiritual being who has entered the consciousness of the prophet. To do this, we must behold the image that is being evoked out of the content of the prophecy.

Beholding the image evoked from the contents of the prophecy requires both an objective discernment and courage to bear all things and all possibilities. This phenomenon is not a fantasy-rich picture charged with strong emotions. It is what Steiner calls "moral imagination." It arises as a result of uniting one's thinking with the angels, archangels and archai (third spiritual hierarchy). Prophecy is to these beings a language of the complexity of time as it engages the consciousness of humanity. It is with these beings we should seek to converse about the purpose of any specific prophecy. Out of such inner conversation, we transcend the polarities of debate and move into generative dialogue that ignites not only our thinking, but also fires our heart's sensibility. We open ourselves up for inspiration. The heart (not one's head) then becomes the organ for understanding the meaning of a prophecy. Forces of compassion and empathy become the new wings of thought, the thinking of the heart. The forms such a prophecy may manifest in time, the movements it is bound to provoke in humanity, and the return to sources of wisdom are all part of this cognitional phase of inspirational cognition.

With the open heart receiving inspirations issuing from across the threshold the will can also experience an opening... an opening to experience what *moral technique* demands and what *moral intuition* has revealed. This is the source of resolution, for working with and through the riddles of prophecy. Without the effort to practice a spiritual path of cognition the phenomenon of polarization will persist and wreak havoc wherever prophecy is being talked about.

The Nature and Mission of Prophecy

One the most useful resources for coming to terms with the nature and mission of prophecy is a lecture by Rudolf Steiner in Berlin, Germany on November 9, 1911, "Prophecy: Its Nature and Meaning" (2009).

> Interest in prophecy is connected not only with curiosity in the ordinary sense but also with curiosity concerning very intimate regions of the human soul. The search for knowledge concerning the deeper interests of the human soul has met with so many disappointments that earnest, serious science nowadays is unwilling to listen to such matters. (p. 16)

Priestess of Delphi *by John Collier (1891)*

This sentiment holds just as true for the position of today's science. Despite the growing trend of new holistic sciences, there remains a widespread attempt to debunk any public assertion of prophecy. The grip of the materialistic worldview of modern science has taken such an ironclad hold on contemporary consciousness that any reflection on the nature and meaning of prophecy is considered superstition or pure heresy. The exclusion of any serious review of the historical role of prophecy in humankind's evolution has had the effect of perpetuating a certain ignorance and fear of prophecy.

Only four and a half centuries ago, "very distinguished and influential scholars engaged in prognostication and prophecy." Included in this group is one of science's most outstanding representatives, Johannes Kepler. He practiced the fine art and science of astrology, a prevailing view based on the "real connection between the world of the stars, the movements and positions of the stars, and human life." This form of prophecy differed from the method of the Greek seers in the great oracles such as Delphi or methods of the ancient Hebrew prophets. It was nevertheless a continuation of the role of prophecy in the human evolutionary journey to read once again the formative messages flowing from the future.

Except for a few modern scientific advances and some relatively new techniques, the contributors to this journal abide by and practice the same art of prognostication that Kepler employed. Voices from the scientific and intelligentsia sectors of cultural life continue to dismiss Kepler's devoted pursuit of astrological wisdom and resist entertaining any notion that the course of the planets and the position of the constellations have any measurable influence on the course of earthly events or in the individual and collective lives of people. Yet, millions of people throughout the world regard the connection between the movements of Heaven and

Nostradamus

the events on the Earth as relevant and significant, as evidenced by the increasing interest in astrology and horoscope predictions. Although some may see the latter as capitalizing on human egoism and the unsettling anxieties that most human beings have about the future, the desire for predictions nevertheless points to symptomatic efforts to know more about very intimate regions of the human soul and their relationship to the cosmos.

Rudolf Steiner describes the progression of prophetic capacities, from Nostradamus to Tycho Brahe and Kepler, in his lecture. He reveals that Nostradamus was a soul who retained something of the somnambulant qualities of the Greek seers. Nostradamus did not base his approach on mathematical calculations of the heavens (as was the case with Kepler), but more on deep contemplation and gazing into the stars with a sense of wonder and awe. His predictions remain some of the most astonishing presentations and accurate prognostications of modern history. Tycho Brahe based his approach on a conviction that human spiritual experiences are connected with events in the great cosmos. His interpretation of individual horoscopes demonstrates a comprehensive understanding of the nature of the planets, their rhythmic patterns, and their corresponding influences on issues of the human soul's intimate regions.

Steiner's offers a guiding principle for the art of prognostication, based on the conviction that

Tycho Brahe in his laboratory

"human life on the Earth is not a chaotic flow of events.... Just as celestial events are governed by cyclical law, so, too, a certain cyclic law, a certain rhythm, is manifest in human and earthly conditions" (2009, p. 28). Astrological tradition views this as the natural correspondence of planetary rhythms with human developmental themes, either by progressions or by transits. Critics of astrology, whether scientists or others, are apt to refute this guiding principle of cyclic law and correspondence by stating that such a principle contradicts human freedom of will. Yet this opinion, as Steiner affirms, is unfounded and a clear indication of superficial thinking. He explicates the lack of logic in such an argument and concludes that we do not deprive ourselves of freedom "by anticipating that causes will have their effects later on. This principle has nothing directly to do with freedom in life" (2009, p. 30).

Movements in the heavens correspond to rhythms in human life. This premise does not arise from some ancient theory; it is the result of centuries of diligent and intelligent observation of the correspondences. It is a phenomenological reality, subject only to a willingness to observe those correspondences for ourselves. Areas where this tenet is projected into the subtle, as when Steiner extends this tenet into a law of reincarnation, sets off controversy of a different nature. This is akin to debates over prophecy. Steiner addresses this kinship of reincarnation and prophecy:

> Just as knowledge of the workings of karma (the law of destiny) arises from insight into how causes lie in the womb of time and appear again in transformation, so, too, this insight was present in all those who have taken prophecy seriously or have actually engaged in it; they have been convinced that laws prevail in the course taken by human life and that the soul can awaken the forces whereby these laws may be fathomed. But the soul needs points of focus. (2009, pp. 32–33)

Key words and phrases to take into contemplation from the this quote are: law of destiny; womb of time; transformation; laws prevail in the course taken by human life; soul can awaken forces; and soul needs points of focus. In this writer's view, if we can penetrate these words and phrases, insights into the correspondences between cosmic and human rhythms will lead to a greater appreciation for the acceptance of laws active in our experiences, though not always perceptible to our ordinary senses or faculties. To grasp these ideas, we must come to terms with the need for observation and reflective thought. Without the point of focus provided by spiritual scientific tenets, the modern soul is subject to the postmodern relativistic mind-set, which continues to feed the disposition of cynicism and dismissive attitudes.

To advance in our understanding of the nature and value of prophecy we must also bring into our reflective activity a mood of devotion and reverence to the great truths of cosmic and human existence presented by spiritual science. Steiner's lecture on prophecy articulates a wonderful example of the need for these qualities of soul. He describes how Nostradamus faced the stars in purity and freedom, and as a result his soul was subject to pictures and images that revealed themselves as prophecies.

> He completely put away all cares and anxieties, all concerns of the outer world. In utter forgetfulness of self, with no feeling of his own personality, his soul knew the truth of the axiom he always quoted: It is God Who utters through my mouth. If anything I am able to tell touches your concerns, take it as spoken to you by the grace of your God. Without such reverence, there is no genuine seership. (2009, p. 36)

Steiner's lecture on the nature and meaning of prophecy contains in it a four-stage method of developing the faculties for understanding and receiving prophetic visions of the future. Thus far, I have described three of these stages: 1) observation of the phenomenon, (the context to which the prophecy refers); 2) reflective thought on the tenets of spiritual science as we discern the formulation of the prophecy and its plausibility or relevancy, thus confronting the dynamics of polarization; 3) devotion and reverence of soul toward the great truths of cosmic and human existence. The fourth stage I call "the urge to take up initiative." Steiner expresses the fourth stage of this method in his passionate and moving closing words in his lecture. It is beneficial to read these words with the mood of devotion and reverence required in stage three of this method.

> The gift of seership is directly connected with the urge to action in men, with the transformation of surplus forces in the soul.
>
> Seership is therefore by no means an incomprehensible faculty; it can be reconciled with the kind of thinking pursued in natural science itself. But it is obvious, too, that the gift of seership leads beyond the immediate present. What is the way, the only way, of reaching out beyond the present? It is to have ideals. Ideals, however, are usually abstract: people set them before themselves and believe that they conform with the realities of the present. But, instead of setting up abstract ideals, those who desire to work in line with aims of the suprasensory try to discover causes lying in the womb of the ages, asking themselves: How do these causes express themselves in the flow of time? They approach this problem not with the intellect but with the

deeper faculty of seership. True knowledge of the past—when this is acquired by the operations of deeper forces and not by way of intellect—calls up before the soul pictures of the future, which conform more or less to fact.... Humankind is standing at the threshold of transition; certain forces hitherto concealed in darkness are becoming more and more apparent. And just as today people are familiar with intellect and with imagination, so, in a future by no means distant, a new faculty of soul will be there to meet the urge for knowledge of the suprasensory world.

The dawn of this new power of soul can already be perceived. When such glimpses of the future astonish us, our attitude will not be that of the fanatic, neither will it be that of the pure realist, but we shall know why we do this or that for the sake of spiritual evolution. This, fundamentally, is the purpose of all true prophecy. We realize that this purpose is achieved even when the pictures of the future outlined by the seer may not be absolutely accurate.... What matters is that impulses connected with evolution as it moves on toward the future shall work upon and awaken slumbering powers in the human being. These prophecies may or may not be accurate in every detail; what matters is that powers shall be awakened in the human being.

Prophecy, therefore, is to be conceived less as a means of satisfying curiosity by prediction of the future than as a stimulating realization that the gift of seership is within one's grasp....

The unwillingness to be really objective about prophecy today is due to the fact that our age sets too high a value on purely intellectual knowledge—which does not kindle impulses of will. But spiritual science will bring the recognition that, although there have been many shadow sides in the realm of ancient and modern prophecy, nevertheless in this striving for consciousness of the future, a seed has formed, not for the appeasement of cravings for knowledge or curiosity, but as fire for our will....

Progress in life must be made in the light of a kind of knowledge that reveals that, at the beginning, the middle, and the end, everything turns upon human activity, human deeds. (2009, pp. 39–42)

Although a century old, these words remain as relevant today as then. Not only are Rudolf Steiner's words kindling for the "fire of our will," his life's work also stands as a bulwark of prophecy for the century we are now living in.

Prophecy Revisited for the Twenty-first Century

Given the continual external upheavals of natural disasters, a global culture whose landscape is dominated by technology, a rampant politics of power and mediocrity, and a collapse of the world economy, there is a sense of urgency and no shortage of angst in our collective psyche. The war of terrorism—punctuated by the strikes on the World Trade Center in New York City on September 11, 2001—is not only an outer phenomenon, but is also now a fear-driven inner dynamic for all peoples on the planet. Whether we like it or not, fear is fertile soil for the uprising of prophetic declarations. Discerning the source, nature, and meaning of such declarations shall become the affair of many. However, guidelines by which to conduct a considered evaluation are still lacking. Hence, we are justified in our need to create a provisional set of criteria for testing the veracity and validity of prophetic statements.

Another factor in revisiting the topic of prophecy in the twenty-first century is the transition humanity is going through in the arc of evolution. Steiner's prophetic statements about humanity crossing the threshold between the sensory and suprasensory worlds are no longer just possibilities, but have become actualities. From near-death experiences to the many accounts of unexpected extrasensory experiences, evidence is growing steadily for the acceptance of suprasensory realities, once unquestioned by our ancestors and today rejected by the intellect as superstition. The pronouncement made by Steiner in 1911 that "certain forces hitherto concealed in darkness are becoming more and more apparent" has begun to manifest in paranormal experiences and interests. "And just as today people are familiar with intellect and with imagination, so in a future by no means distant, a new faculty of soul will be there to meet the urge for knowledge of the suprasensory world" (2009, p. 40). The future Steiner refers to is here and now.

There is little doubt in most minds that humanity is facing a crucial juncture in its history. As in most such exigencies of real concern, prophets appear and petition humanity to be ever more diligent about the unfolding events in their midst. As has always been the case, such moments in history are replete with both true and false prophets. For this reason, it is important to revisit the role of prophecy in our time and outline a means to evaluate its relevancy and significance. Prophecies do not render the future a *fait accompli;* they are invitations to create a better future.

Just as fears can give rise to a hotbed of doomsday scenarios, so hopes can become naïve projections of subjective wishes. To safeguard against both natural tendencies, discerning individuals are best served by reaffirming *faith in the good powers of wisdom*, which are ever-present in the stream of evolution, and by examining prophetic declarations based on *love for the truth*. These two dispositions of soul are key prerequisites for developing the "new faculty of soul" needed to grasp and assimilate "knowledge of the suprasensory world," which is often embedded in genuine prophecy. This process is not only an inward-looking reflection, but also requires one to look into the world and survey the field of human activities to which such prophecies refer. When we look through eyes of faith and love rather than a compulsion to see the negation and destruction implied by so many prophetic warnings, we can apprehend an objective perception of what the world needs. In this way, we can view prophecy as a lens through which to perceive a different kind of hope—not based on wishful thinking but on the power of conviction in which *hope can spring eternally*. This is the first criterion for examining the prophecies of our time. The question we must carry into this process is: *What does the objective phenomena reveal to me about the need to take this prophecy seriously?* This is the first stage of the previously mentioned method for assessing prophecy. It is the exercise of our ability to observe and read the signs of the time.

By carrying this question into meditative activity, we engage ourselves in a dialogue with the good powers of wisdom; we enter an inner conversation with the spiritual beings across the threshold of the suprasensory world. The language needed is contained in the perennial wisdom of the ages and in the advance of spiritual-scientific knowledge as it pertains to the evolution of humankind. Out of this interest, spiritual beings make their presence felt and may become more available to inspire our contemplations of discernment. The question to hold before our soul at this stage is: *Who wishes to speak through this prophecy?* This refers to the second stage of our methodology, in which we practice reflective thinking on the formulation of the prophecy and the credibility of the one who prophecies. Discerning the intention and probable consequences of a prophecy in the cauldron of controversy helps prepare us to discuss with others without succumbing to the subliminal messages and sensational dramas that prophecy so often provokes.

Comprehending the nature and meaning of any prophecy involves immersion in a mood bearing the quality of devotion for truth and reverence to sustain a sacred inner dialogue with spiritual beings who earnestly seek to awaken us to the pressing needs of the future. Understanding emerges as a heartfelt recognition that we are just as responsible for the outcome of prophecies as are those who disseminate them. The result at this third stage of discernment is being accountable for knowing the interrelationship between the cosmos and humanity on Earth. The cardinal question to live with at this stage is: *Why am I bearing this knowledge at this time in human evolution?*

From an understanding of the prophecy and a true sense of accountability, discerning individuals can then inaugurate the final stage of the method of discernment. This stage involves the resolve to act on what the prophecy means. This is required of seekers of truth in our age. Knowing aspects of truth about the suprasensory world and its influence on the shaping of events on the Earth carries a spiritual mandate: to take up initiatives in cooperation with the angels, archangels, and archai, who await our active participation in co-creating the future; they impart flashes of revelation to all prophets. This final act of discernment arises from the sincere soul-searching question: *How should I act in response to what I now know about the nature and meaning of this prophecy?*

The entire matter of discerning prophecy has its urgency in the following words of Karl König, who wrote the following inspiring epistle to the Camphill coworkers of the last century. It sounds as true today as it did then. May we all take it to heart and find in it the wellspring for all our actions.

KNIGHTHOOD OF THE TWENTY-FIRST CENTURY

There is a knighthood of the twenty-first century
Whose riders do not ride through the darkness
    of physical forests,
As of old, but through the forest
    of darkened minds.

They are armed with a spiritual armor,
And an inner sun makes them radiant.

Out of them shines healing,
Healing that flows from the knowledge
    of the human being
As a spiritual being.

They must create inner order, inner justice,
Peace, and conviction in the darkness of our time.

They must learn to work side by side
    with angels.

(additional last line from William Bento;
revised by Leslie Loy)

REFERENCES:

Jung, C. G., (1953). *Two Essays on Analytical Psychology*. New York, NY: Pantheon Books.

Powell, Robert, (Editor) (2010). *Journal for Star Wisdom 2010*. Great Barrington, MA: SteinerBooks.

Scharmer, C. Otto, (2007). *Theory U: Leading from the Future as It Emerges*. Cambridge, MA: Society for Organizational Learning.

Steiner, Rudolf, (1994). *Intuitive Thinking as a Spiritual Path: A Philosophy of Freedom*. Great Barrington, MA: SteinerBooks.

———, (2009). *Astronomy and Astrology: Finding a Relationship to the Cosmos* (lecture of Nov. 9, 1911). London: Rudolf Steiner Press.

My head bears
The being of the resting stars.
My breast harbors
The life of the wandering stars.
My body lives and moves
Amidst the elements—
This am I.
—RUDOLF STEINER

HENRY DAVID THOREAU AND THE CHRIST RHYTHM

Kevin Dann, Ph.D.

Admired in the United States and around the world for his resolute individualism, his insight into and celebration of nature, and his piercing social criticism, Henry David Thoreau (1817–1862) is also usually remembered as being fervently anti-Christian, at least in his criticism of the established churches of New England. Nevertheless, Thoreau's repugnance for the church never affected his devotion to Christ. In *A Week on the Concord and Merrimac Rivers,* he said, "Christ was a sublime actor on the stage of the world. He knew what he was thinking when he said, 'Heaven and earth shall pass away, but my words shall not pass away.' I draw close to him at such a time"; and "It is necessary not to be a Christian, to appreciate the beauty and significance of the life of Christ."

Thoreau identified with Christ the fellow heretic not only as a historical figure, but as a living presence whom he had experienced intensely in the dark of winter in his Walden cabin. In *Walden*—a sacred book whose every word was scrutinized seven times over and has not a single sentence out of its painstakingly chosen place—in a chapter called "Winter Visitors," Thoreau vividly describes a pair of visitors, one a "poet" and the other "one of the last of the philosophers." Critics assume Ellery Channing to be the unnamed poet, and Bronson Alcott the philosopher, and indeed, if one compares Thoreau's journal notes about Alcott to the passage in *Walden,* they are nearly identical in some places. This philosopher was given to the world by Connecticut and "peddled her wares" (Alcott was from Connecticut, where he had worked as a peddler). The entry "When Alcott's day comes Laws unsuspected by most will take effect" becomes, in *Walden,* "But though comparatively disregarded now, when his day comes, laws unsuspected by most will take effect, and masters of families and rulers will come to him for advice." *Walden* is a book in which almost nothing is quite as it meets the eye. In this book, as in all his writing, Thoreau loved to hide his deepest spiritual convictions in plain sight. This unnamed philosopher is "a true friend of man"; "an Old Mortality, say rather an Immortality"; "the sanest man...the same yesterday and tomorrow." This last phrase, taken from the Christian Testament (Hebrews 13:8), gives away the philosopher's identity as Christ. "I do not see how he can ever die; Nature cannot spare him," Thoreau declares.[1]

But there is a place in Thoreau's life where Christ's presence was hidden even from him. Ironically, the man who perhaps was America's most profound student of nature's rhythms, could not see the most important rhythm in his own nature, a rhythm that broke into his life on November 16, 1850. No one wishing to chronicle Thoreau's daily thoughts and actions before November 16, 1850, can rely on his journal; missing pages and dates outnumber the remaining dated journal leaves. Prior to this date, Thoreau rarely gave date headings to his entries; in 1850, only seven journal entries are headed by dates before November 16. For those eleven months of the year, just another dozen or so dates occur at all in the body of the journal entries. After November 16, Thoreau almost never missed a daily entry, and assumed the habitual practice of heading each day's journal entry with the date.

Beginning with this November 16 entry, Thoreau's journaling practice transforms entirely,

---

1 *Walden,* 268; P *Jl* 2: 225; *Walden,* 268, 269; 270

Henry David Thoreau (1856)

becoming a laboratory for phenomenological perception and description. Whereas previously he had on dated days typically taken up individual questions, told single discrete stories, or noted particular places or people, and in undated entries separated subjects from one another slightly, now a single day's reflections would come cascading one upon another, alternating between diurnal or seasonal arcana and perennial philosophical discussions. November 16 opens with Thoreau's report that he had found three arrowheads while out walking. He then declares that he regards the tiniest tributary brook with the same awe he would feel for the Orinoco or Mississippi. His next paragraph claims it is always the wild element in literature that is most compelling. He discovers that cranberries are fine fare as one crosses meadows; wonders what alarm a blue jay is sounding in some birch grove; muses on how he chooses his bearing when setting out on a walk; wrestles with his antipathy and sympathy toward friends; confesses that the scream of a cat whose tail was caught by a closing door drove off celestial thoughts; asks why shrub oaks keep their leaves all winter; observes black walnut trees heavy with nuts, and birches bare but for their catkins; notes the late autumn burst of blossoming by spring herbs; hears cows running scared in the woods; asks what salvation there might be for men who are afraid of the dark, since "God is silent and mysterious"; discovers that some of our brightest days are ones when the sun is not shining; comments that land where trees have been cut off and are rejuvenating is called "sprout land"; questions whether the partridge-berry should not be called "checker-berry"; and laments the loss of wild apple trees. He closes with this extraordinary, though for Thoreau altogether ordinary, declaration:

> My Journal should be a record of my love. I would write in it only the things I love, my affection for any aspect of the world, what I love to think of. I have no more distinctness or pointedness in my yearnings than an expanding bud, which does indeed point to flower and fruit, to summer and autumn, but is aware of the warm sun and spring influences only. I feel ripe for something, yet do nothing, can't discover what that thing is. I feel fertile merely. It is seedtime with me. I have lain fallow long enough
>
> Notwithstanding a sense of unworthiness which possesses me, not without reason, notwithstanding that I regard myself as a good deal of a scamp, yet for the most part the spirit of the universe is unaccountably kind to me, and I enjoy perhaps an unusual share of happiness. Yet I question sometimes if there is not some settlement to come.

With this entry, he had already begun practicing his intended goal for his journal: the string of reflections is punctuated with "I love to pause in mid-passage" (crossing fences); "I love my friends"; "I love nature, I love the landscape." "I love" hereafter becomes one of the journal's most characteristic expressions.[2]

Thoreau always had a keen sense of seasonality, of turning points in time marking transformation and change, but after November 16, 1850, it becomes the main *leitmotif* of his journal. The following day, November 17, he finds in a field of winter rye what he first takes to be a smooth white pebble, but as he picks it up it breaks and he finds

---

2 *Journal* 2: 96-101.

it is a snapping turtle egg. "The little turtle was perfectly formed, even to the dorsal ridge, which was distinctly visible." Seeing into biological form as it unfolds in time becomes the central quest of Thoreau's life after this November, and the daily logging of observations in his journal is his main method for accomplishing that quest. Two days later, he breaks off a shrub oak leaf, and finds the cambium layer still green, inspiring a diligent search for life in warm, south-facing places. This marks the beginning of his search for precise moments in the stages of plant growth, when time stands still for an instant as what for weeks or months had been stem and leaf suddenly erupts into flower, or for days had been flower metamorphoses into seed. A parallel mystery struck him as he watched wheeling flocks of migrant birds: "Now...you will see flocks of small birds forming compact and distinct masses, as if they were not only animated by one spirit but actually held together by some invisible fluid or film, and will hear the sound of their wings rippling or fanning the air as they flow through it, flying, the whole mass, ricochet like a single bird,—or as they flow over the fence." What was the "invisible fluid" that allowed the flock to act as one body? What invisible agent guided so precisely the embryonic form of the snapping turtle or signaled plants when to leaf out, flower, and fruit?[3]

Though he criticized himself for lying fallow, his life was actually unfolding in complete harmony with the etheric forces, which were, in their holding of memory, the carriers of destiny as well as of life. Up until November 16, 1850, Thoreau's destiny had been to craft an authentic life in the face of a society growing less and less authentic, and he did this principally by attending to the divinity within and around human nature. Now, almost at a single stroke, he would become America's premier chronicler of Nature.

November 16, 1850, was three years, four months and four days after Henry David Thoreau's thirtieth birthday, almost to the day the exact length of the Christ rhythm of 33 1/3 years, which was the length of life from the birth of Jesus on December 6, 2 B.C. to the resurrection on April 5, A.D. 33.[4] Unlike the planetary and solar rhythms pulsing eternally through time, this rhythm was "won" for humanity by a god becoming a human being, and was forever after inscribed into the cosmos only after Christ's death and resurrection. While the planetary rhythms manifest in space as the orbital periods moving against the background of the zodiac, the Christ rhythm does not have a spatial significance, being a purely temporal rhythm, measured out by the duration of the life of Jesus Christ. Since 33 A.D., three times each century that pulse has echoed through human history, rippling into the nineteenth century.

Since Rudolf Steiner's identification of this rhythm in 1917, a number of authors have deepened our understanding of the Christ rhythm and its role in human biography.[5] It seems altogether fitting that in Henry Thoreau's biography, the Christ rhythm manifested so precisely, as a vocational turning point whereby Thoreau began to practice systematically the study of rhythm in the natural world. There is the unmistakable stamp of the unique "I" in this event, a reminder that for every one of us, since the Mystery of Golgotha, Christ's deed of sacrifice offers us the potential to express fully our individualism as an echoed offering to the human community.

According to Robert Powell's research into this rhythm, 56 cycles of 33⅓ years were completed in 1899, the date—according to Rudolf Steiner—of the end of the Dark Age (Kali Yuga) and the start of the New Age (Satya Yuga). Steiner's indications point to the New Age as the age of Christ's second coming.[6] In the nineteenth century, beginning in 1799, as Christ's etheric body entered the Moon sphere[7]—the realm of the Angels—the Christ

---

3 *Journal* 2: 102; 103–104.

4 Powell, *Chronicle of the Living Christ*.

5 Rudolf Steiner, lecture of December 23, 1917, entitled "Et Incarnatus est—the time cycle in historical events"; William A. Bryant, *A Journey Through Time: Biographical Rhythms* (Fair Oaks, California: Rudolf Steiner College Press, 2006), pp. 47–54. See also, Powell, *Chronicle of the Living Christ*, pp. 415–423.

6 Robert Powell, *The Christ Mystery: Reflections on the Second Coming* (Fair Oaks, California: Rudolf Steiner College Press, 1999).

7 O'Leary (ed.), *The Inner Life of the Earth*; see

rhythm of 33⅓ years was particularly manifested in individuals who had destinies closely allied with the spiritual beings doing battle under the Archangel Michael. Henry Thoreau left his home in the stars with a sure eye for his place and time on Earth, having chosen to ally himself with a cohort of Grail knights—Emerson, Alcott, Fuller, Brownson and their fellow Transcendentalists—who could only dimly recall the pact they made before birth. Having crossed the Lethean river of forgetfulness, there was no guarantee that they would carry out their missions. These individuals, between the ages of thirty and thirty-three, chose to follow or forget their spiritual patrimony. At the culmination of his Christ period, Thoreau still considered himself blessed, his only reservation being that he had not accomplished some as yet undefined task. Even as he expressed this thought in his journal—which as of this moment became his true life's work—he was embarking upon that task, which would see him indefatigably, over the next twelve years, chronicle the life history of the plants of Concord.

A couple of weeks before this November 16 turning point, Thoreau had had a long discussion with Ralph Waldo Emerson during which Emerson maintained that America, unlike England, was not yet prepared to realize its destiny, as it "want[ed] a fortnight's more sun." Thoreau disagreed, saying that the English were "mere soldiers ... in the world," whose role in world history was "winding up." America, Thoreau believed, to be a "pioneer ... unwinding his lines." Within the body of that pioneering republic, Thoreau was a pioneer unwinding the lines of his destiny in a rhythm that could only be seen long after his last waves had beat upon the shore.[8]

POSTSCRIPT: THE 33⅓-YEAR RHYTHM IN AMERICAN HISTORY

Knowing from Rudolf Steiner's spiritual-scientific research that a century is three times the Christ rhythm of 33⅓ years—a threefold rhythm that brings historical impulses to a certain culmination and fulfillment—and from the spiritual research of Robert Powell that 1775 was the year in which Sophia, in her journey toward the Earth from the Galactic Center, entered our local arm of the galaxy,[9] what manifestation of the Christ rhythm can one find in American history since the nation's founding?

As the modern nation, which in both its exoteric history and in its esoteric, etheric characteristics distinguishes itself through a Promethean power of the will, America has struggled throughout its history with the most varied spiritual impulses. In 1809, 33⅓ years on from the start of the American Revolution, the newly created Illinois Territory was the "West," soon to change when Lewis and Clark returned from their great adventure. In just three years, America would fight a second war against Great Britain, while the whole of Europe was wracked by the Napoleonic Wars. Robert Fulton's patenting of the steamboat in 1809 heralded the liberation of machine power from the fetters of waterpower and draft animals. The immense telluric forces of magnetism that Rudolf Steiner would a century later point to as so determinative of American destiny were already working upon the first two generations of Americans.

Transcendentalism clearly represents a Michaelic stream, and one finds in the years around 1842 (the second pulse of the 33⅓-year rhythm), the apex of Transcendentalist activity and influence. The nineteenth century's most well-known spiritual stream, the Theosophical Society, was founded in New York City in September 1875, at the culmination of three 33⅓-year periods from 1775. The year 1909—marking the fourth rhythm of 33⅓ years since America's birth in 1776—was truly an *annus mirabilis* for Sophia's growing presence in the world, particularly as it was heralded by Rudolf Steiner's Christological revelations. 1909/1910 was also the time in which Theosophical Society President Annie Besant was publicly proclaiming young Jiddu Krishnamurti as

---

"Postscript" to Robert Powell's article "Subnature and the Second Coming," pp. 125–141.

8 *Emerson Journal* 8: 135-6, Riverside 1905 ed., October 26, 1850

9 See sophiafoundation.org/articles; "Sophia and the Rose of the World," p. 8.

the reincarnated Christ and new World Teacher; indeed, one can expect that at the time of each of these expressions of the Christ rhythm in American history, there will also be manifestations of anti-Christian activity, often in the form of new religious movements.

The year 2009 marked the completion of seven 33⅓-year rhythms from 1775 and 1776, and along with the survival and continued spread of a variety of occult schools, American popular culture now throws up new occult schools seemingly every season. From the "Oneness Movement," at the center of which is the *deeksha* blessing ritual to dozens of schools based in the teachings of Agni Yoga, eastern "mahatmas," and channeled "masters"; to the explosion of "remote viewing" institutes and instructional sites, America is awash in occult schools, none of them any longer "occult," in the sense of being hidden from public view. Indeed, the very public nature of so many of these magical schools suggests that in a way, America has already seen the realization of Rudolf Steiner's 1919 prophecy: "When Ahriman incarnates in the West at the appointed time, he will establish a great occult school for the practice of magic arts of the greatest grandeur, and what otherwise can be acquired only by strenuous effort will be poured over humankind."[10]

---

10 Steiner, *The Incarnation of Ahriman: The Embodiment of Evil on Earth* (London: Rudolf Steiner Press, 2006), lecture of November 15, 1919.

"*The starry sky painted by night, actually under a gas jet. The sky is aquamarine, the water is royal blue, the ground is mauve. The town is blue and purple. The gas is yellow and the reflections are russet gold descending down to green-bronze. On the aquamarine field of the sky the Great Bear is a sparkling green and pink, whose discreet paleness contrasts with the brutal gold of the gas. Two colourful figurines of lovers in the foreground.*"
—Vincent van Gogh (from his brother Theo)

RUDOLF STEINER, THE ARTIST

Brian Gray

An article featuring Rudolf Steiner's artistic work appeared in *The New York Times Style Magazine for Sunday* (April 11, 2010). "Soul Man," written by Douglas Brenner (a former Waldorf School student), called attention to Rudolf Steiner's contributions to world of the arts through a traveling exhibit that opened in May 2010 in Wofsburg, Germany. "Rudolf Steiner—Die Alchemie des Alltags" ("Rudolf Steiner: Alchemy of the Everyday") was organized by the Vitra Design Museum in collaboration with the Kunstmuseums of Wolfsburg and Stuttgart. Nearly a century after his creative artistic outpouring, Rudolf Steiner is being recognized by world culture as a significant artist in his own right.

The article and the traveling exhibit of Rudolf Steiner's artistic work (sponsored by museums outside of anthroposophic circles) offer clear evidence of Rudolf Steiner "speaking" artistically through his natal fifth house Sun position. At his birth on February 25, 1861, the Sun was in Aquarius, the water bearer, and at the exact moment of his birth, the Sun stood in the fifth house of Rudolf Steiner's birth chart (see birth horoscope of Rudolf Steiner.) The fifth house of the birth chart (roughly equivalent to the five o'clock position on a clock face) is the region of a birth chart where the "I" can choose to unfold its creative activities through the arts, through creativity and love for creating, through children, and through child-like spontaneous, loving creative deeds.

Rudolf Steiner stated that the human being must learn to "speak to the stars." How did he "speak" artistically through his fifth house Sun in Aquarius during his life? Rudolf Steiner's entire life is a work of art, and he developed it in ways that could be compared with the growth of a plant. We will explore three matters in this article: first, the fifth house Sun position in Rudolf Steiner's birth chart and how he spoke through it as an artist; second, the plant-like stages of Rudolf Steiner's lifework creatively unfolding; and third, the Moon node rhythms in Rudolf Steiner's biography.

The Moon Node Rhythms in Biography and Human History

First, note that Rudolf Steiner was born in 1861, 18.61 centuries after the birth of Jesus "at the turning point of time." It takes 18.61 years for the Moon's nodes—the line of intersection between the Sun–Earth plane (plane of the ecliptic) and the Moon's orbital plane around the Earth (Moon's plane being tilted 5° off that of the ecliptic) to cycle through the entire Zodiac and return to its initial nodal position. Rudolf Steiner pointed to this recurring rhythm of 18.61 years as marking significant turning points in the biography of a human being. That is, at key moments in every human biography—around 18.61 years of age, and again at 37.2 years, 55.8 years, 74.4 years, and 93.0 years of age—a person may experience moments of deep spiritual insight. It might seem as if a window briefly opens into the spiritual world, allowing one to glimpse back at her/his "prenatal intentions."[1] In examining biography, the deeper significance of these insightful 'Moon node return' events begins to emerge.

Another important rhythm shines light into the mysteries of human history—the rhythm of one hundred years (three times 33.3 years). Rudolf Steiner remarked that one can look at

---

1 See Steiner, *Mystery of the Universe: The Human Being, Model of Creation*, (London: Rudolf Steiner Press, 2001), lecture 4.

Rudolf Steiner, the Artist

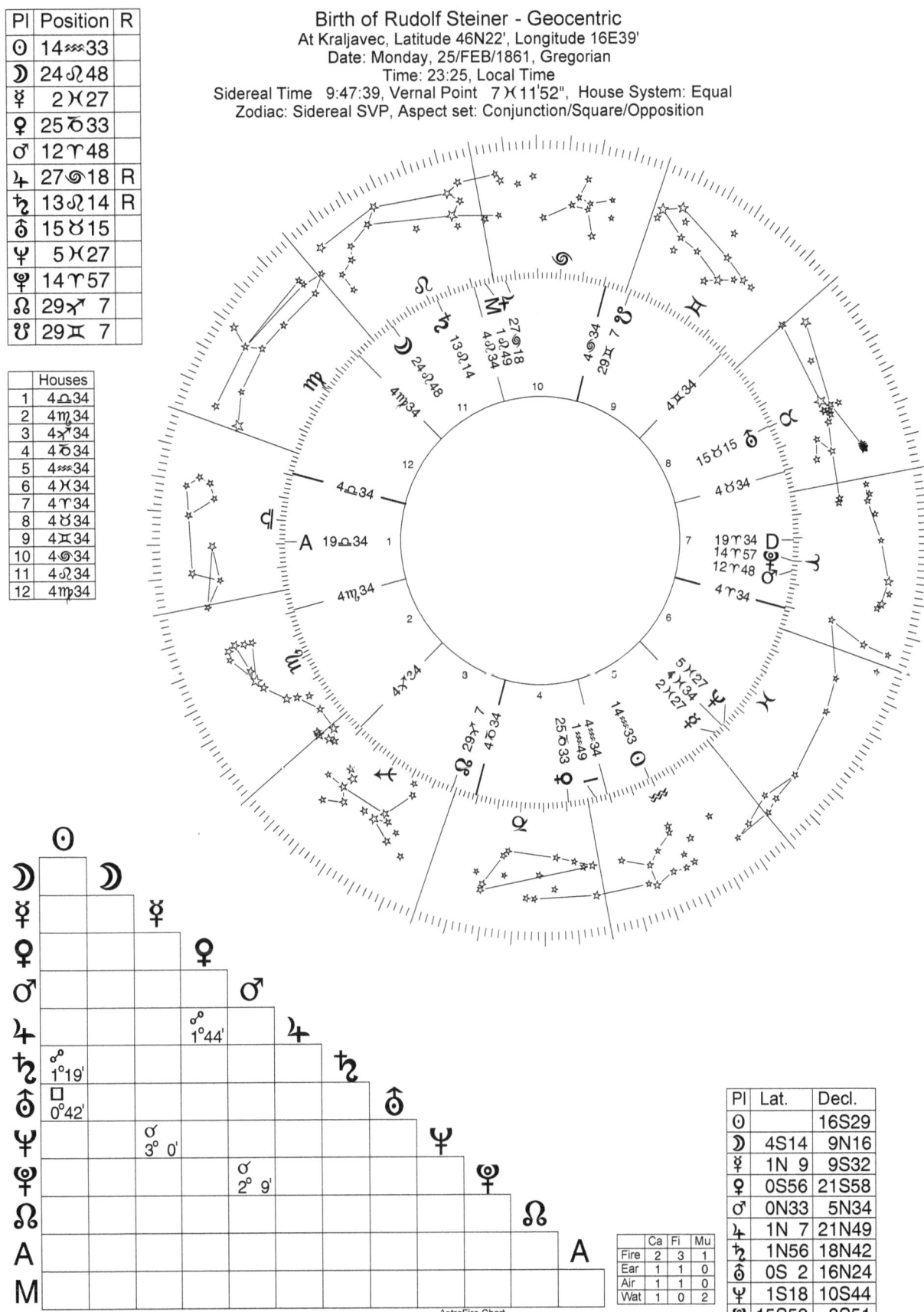

each century since the time of Christ as being roughly equivalent to one year in the biography of a human being. When the cosmic Christ united with humanity and earth evolution, new mysteries of time were birthed. "History" and "human biography" began to unfold their meaning more clearly within cycles of time. A new hundred-year cycle of humanity's biography started to unfold at the time of Christ, and this cyclic unfolding continues throughout history.

For example, one can begin to imagine events in the fourth century A.D. as comparable to humanity's fourth year of life. In the ninth and tenth centuries A.D., humanity was undergoing its 'nine-year change.' With the Renaissance that began in the fifteenth century, humanity blossomed into its adolescence. Now, in the twenty-first century, humanity as a whole is slowly approaching age twenty-one. We are still not quite fully come-of-age. The human race will not achieve age 21 until the beginning of the twenty-second century. We fully experience how adversarial beings are working very hard to distract all of us—humanity at large—from awakening to our divine nature. When humanity becomes twenty-one centuries old, we might have more clarity and spiritual maturity available to us than is apparent right now, in 2011.

Coming back to Rudolf Steiner's year of birth—1861—we can see that Rudolf Steiner was born at the centenary "Moon-node return of humanity," 18.61 centuries since the Christ began to incarnate and planted the seed of the "I Am" in all of humanity. Rudolf Steiner's incarnating in 1861 could signify the birth of an initiate intending to awaken all of humanity to the vital significance of the "I Am" bestowed by the Christ to each human being, and to exemplify through his own biography what a spiritually awakened human being can creatively accomplish—in freedom and love. We can begin to view Rudolf Steiner's entire life unfolding organically and creatively through the cycles of time—artistically.

First Moon Node Return, 1879

The spirit seed of Rudolf Steiner's intended lifework rooted in fertile soil through his meeting two helpers: the great teacher Karl Julius Schröer (1825–1890) and the clairvoyant herb gatherer Felix Koguzki (1833–1909). This took place in Vienna at Rudolf Steiner's first Moon node return at the age of 18.61 years in the autumn of 1879. His relationship to the Solar Archangel Michael is also apparent here, as the Archangel Michael became the ruling spirit of the time (*Zeitgeist*) in the autumn of 1879, exactly the moment of Rudolf Steiner's first Moon node return. The new reign of Michael over history brought forth Sun-like clarity and strength to Rudolf Steiner's world historic mission as he unfolded the artistry of his life beginning in 1879.

In 1882, at the age of twenty-one, Rudolf Steiner's lifework broke forth organically through the soil, forming "dicotyledons" through his meeting with the Master M (thought by some to have been Christian Rosenkreutz,[2] and by others to be both Rosenkreutz and the Master Jesus[3]). Felix Koguzki arranged this meeting. Responding to Rudolf Steiner's questions, the Master directed him to study Fichte's thought, to *transform the dragon of materialism that had overtaken natural science* and *to take the bull of public opinion by the horns*. At the same time, Schröer handed the young Rudolf Steiner (recognized as a genius at 21) the task of editing all of Goethe's scientific work. As he penetrated Goethe's discovery of plant metamorphosis and the creative artistry of mother nature, Rudolf Steiner's artistic appreciation grew, while his spiritual insights deepened.

His lifework developed healthy stem and leaves over the next twelve years, culminating in his book *The Philosophy of Freedom* at the age of thirty-three in 1894. This brief but monumental work not only established an individually experienced basis for the scientific art of knowing, it also clearly revealed the spiritual wellspring of all human creativity.

---

2 See Bamford, "Rudolf Steiner and Rosicrucianism," in *The Secret Stream: Christian Rosenkreutz & Rosicrucianism*, (Great Barrington, MA: SteinerBooks, 2000), pp. 248–249.

3 See Meyer, *Rudolf Steiner's Core Mission: The Birth and Development of Spiritual-Scientific Karma Research*, (London: Temple Lodge, 2010), pp. 111–113.

Human beings can become free and creative in three stages of activity: first, by quickening our capacity to grasp individual "moral intuitions" through the practice of living thinking; second, by loving one's moral ideas and artistically transforming them into "moral imaginations," so that those ideas might come to live and thrive in earthly reality; and third, by performing actions that translate these moral imaginations into creative acts of love, making them realities on Earth through "moral technique." At the age of thirty-three, Rudolf Steiner was already living his life as a free human being, demonstrating the power of human artistic creativity enlivened by spiritual insight and love for what he was doing.

Second Moon Node Return, 1898

Rudolf Steiner's second Moon node return in the spring of 1898 (at 37.2 years of age) occurred during a time of deep inner conflicts and personal struggles. His lifework contracted into the "calyx" stage, during which severe personal trials and deep suffering led him to seek firsthand insight into the "Mystery of Golgotha," the crucial events in the life of Jesus Christ and in the evolution of Earth and humanity. He encountered great difficulties while penetrating the deep veils shrouding the Christ event from the seer's spiritual perception. He finally broke through those intense struggles at the end of 1899. In his *Autobiography*, Rudolf Steiner expresses his spiritual breakthrough in this way:

> During the period when my statements about Christianity seemingly contradict my later ones, a conscious knowledge of true Christianity began to dawn within me. Around the turn of the century this knowledge grew deeper. The inner test described above occurred shortly before the turn of the century. *This experience culminated in my standing in the spiritual presence of the Mystery of Golgotha in a most profound and solemn festival of knowledge.*"[4]

Model for the columns and capitals for the 1st Goetheanum

Rudolf Steiner was thirty-eight years old when he achieved this new Christ revelation, just as the new Age of Light began to dawn in 1900. He was fully awake, prepared, and fired with creative potential. From 1900 until his death in 1925, Rudolf Steiner's lifework blossomed artistically; his creativity poured into every lecture, article, book, gesture, social activity, and new artistic impulse that he touched. Moreover, the fruit of his efforts were not only spiritually *true* and morally *good;* they were also essentially *beautiful* and artistic in every way.

In 1907, at the Munich Congress of the Theosophical Society, Rudolf Steiner declared, "Never more will spiritual research be separated from the arts."[5] His artistic lifework bore tangible fruits. Rudolf Steiner decorated the hall in Munich with the seven capitals of planetary evolution and paintings of the seven apocalyptic seals, all of them truly original. He illustrated the program for the Munich Congress with metamorphic planetary seals he designed for each day of the week.

In the following years, Rudolf Steiner developed new art forms of speech and the movement art of eurythmy. He wrote and directed performances of four major mystery dramas, which depict individual trials, interpersonal crises, and karmic relationships among the leading characters as experienced over the spans of several

---

4 Rudolf Steiner, *Autobiography: Chapters in the Course of My Life, 1861–1907* (Great Barrington, MA: SteinerBooks, 2005), p. 188.

5 For more on this important event, see *Rosicrucianism Renewed: The Unity of Art, Science & Religion: The Theosophical Congress of Whitsun 1907* (Great Barrington, MA: SteinerBooks, 2007).

The 1st Goetheanum

incarnations. In addition, he began to conceive the sculptural and architectural forms for a modern mystery temple. The "Foundation Stone" of the new building he designed, the Goetheanum, was laid in the earth in Dornach, Switzerland, September 20, 1913.

The Goetheanum was envisioned and built as the complete mystery temple embodying the seven main arts: architecture; sculpture; painting; music; poetry, speech, and drama; eurythmy movement; and human community. This modern mystery temple arose from Rudolf Steiner's creative genius. The spiritual world did not dictate the artistic forms to him, as was case for ancient mystery temples in earlier times. During the present age of the consciousness soul (1413–3573), and with the dawning of the new Age of Light that began in 1899, modern initiates must strive creatively on their own.

The Goetheanum was truly an artistic "open secret." It awakened insights into mystery wisdom for anyone with eyes to see and ears to hear and the good will to become active inwardly while contemplating the artistic forms Rudolf Steiner created. The culminating artistic focus of the building was to be a hand-carved, thirty-foot-tall statue, "The Representative of Humanity," a remarkable work of art that he never quite finished. Its purpose was to stand on the main stage as backdrop for the entire Goetheanum.[6]

---

6 This statue could be compared with the "Brazen Sea" that Hiram Abiff attempted to forge for Solomon's Temple. See Steiner's descriptions of that event in *The*

Rudolf Steiner working on the upper portion of "The Representative of Humanity"

Rudolf Steiner's third Moon node return, 1916

In the fall of 1916, at the age of 55.8 years, Rudolf Steiner experienced his third Moon node return. World War I, which had been raging for two years, took a severe turn, and many worried about the outcome. What would become of Central Europe, and how could true balance be reestablished in the world? Rudolf Steiner turned his spiritual activity toward practical solutions to the problems facing humanity. He quietly began to cultivate an idea that first occurred to him three decades earlier: the threefold nature of the human form and its relationship to thinking (truth), feeling (beauty), and willing (goodness). Rudolf Steiner perceived that the human being—the greatest work of art created by the spiritual world—if properly understood artistically in form and function, could be a blueprint for restructuring and healing the human social order.

Continuing his work in the fields of cognition, art, and the social formation, he made remarkable discoveries about the artistry of the human form and functioning. In the summer of 1916, he had given lectures detailing (for the first time) the twelve senses and the seven life processes of the human being. Whenever he could be in Dornach, he worked on the Goetheanum and (with Edith Maryon, an English sculptor) "The Representative

---

Temple Legend (London, Rudolf Steiner Press, 2002).

of Humanity." On July 20 1916, part of Rudolf Steiner's greeting to his collaborators working on the Goetheanum included these words:

> If one endeavors to become familiar with the cravings, the artistic cravings of our time, it will be discovered everywhere that there is an obscure striving but that people do not know within this obscure striving whither they wish to go. It will be seen that, even in this obscure way, the search is really for what we are striving toward here. It will be seen that it is necessary to find one's way into the artistic forms which are here developing out of the bosom of spiritual science. However surprising very much in our architectural forms may be, no long time will pass before this will be felt to be the self-evident result of the sensitivity and the feeling of the present age and the immediate future.[7]

In October 1916, Rudolf Steiner began nine lectures on the history of art. He would gradually show lanternslides of more than 700 works of art, bringing new insights about the evolutionary stages of human consciousness that each artwork revealed. He began to write essays, which he published as *Riddles of the Soul* in 1917, including a clear exposition of the threefold nature of the human being in an appendix. He gradually developed this seed into the "threefold social organism" in 1917 and 1918, which led in 1919 to founding the first Waldorf school. In a notebook of 1918, Rudolf Steiner wrote of the spiritual role that the arts play in fostering aesthetic experiences of *beauty* needed by the human spirit to incarnate properly into the human body:

> Our connection with the spirit is broken if it is not sustained through the medium of beauty. Beauty connects the "I" to the body.[8]

The world did not readily accept Rudolf Steiner's work and the new artistic impulses that he was shaping into the Goetheanum. The spiritual

The second Goetheanum

and artistic seed of the Goetheanum went through a sacrificial fire process during New Year's Eve of 1922. An arsonist burned the unfinished wooden temple to the ground, tragically robbing humanity of that artistic embodiment of mystery wisdom. The event also took a tremendous toll on Rudolf Steiner's health. Nevertheless, he did not give up. He artistically metamorphosed the fire-sacrificed temple into "The Foundation Stone," a mantra-like verse, a year later at the "Christmas Conference" of 1923.[9] The Foundation Stone is a contemplative mystery poem that human beings can lay into their hearts as a seed to create the highest art form of human community, spiritually aligned with the mission of humanity—to become Spirits of Freedom and Love.

Rudolf Steiner also artistically metamorphosed the forms of that wooden temple (the Goetheanum) into the second Goetheanum, this one built with reinforced concrete and standing in Dornach on the original site. In 1924, the last active year of his life, Rudolf Steiner traveled widely, pouring forth enough lectures on karma to fill eight volumes.[10] Rudolf Steiner heroically continued outpouring his creative gifts and performing healing deeds to assist his brothers and sisters, even as his own health was rapidly failing. In his

---

7 Quoted in Wachsmuth, *The Life and Work of Rudolf Steiner* (Blauvelt, NY: Spiritual Science Library, 1989), p. 288.

8 Steiner, notebook of 1918, Das Goetheanum, vol. XII, no. 14.

9 For more on that conference and "The Foundation Stone" verse, see Steiner, *The Christmas Conference for the Foundation of the General Anthroposophical Society* (Hudson, NY: Anthroposophic Press, 1990).

10 Steiner, *Karmic Relationships: Esoteric Studies,* 8 vols. (London: Rudolf Steiner Press).

"Last Address," on September 28, 1924, Rudolf Steiner pointed to the artist Raphael and the poet Novalis as representing a stream that would guide humanity spiritually at the turn of the twentieth and twenty-first centuries. The Raphael–Novalis being is connected with the arts and with healing and transforming the Earth.

Now, in the twenty-first century, we face daily the great question foreseen by Rudolf Steiner: Will we actively and creatively turn our attention toward the spirit, or will we become more deeply immersed in materialism? Performing the arts rhythmically, and striving toward spiritual insight through study and meditation is a key to overcoming materialism. Living an artistic life incarnates us properly and helps make us more truly human. The arts mediate between and assist human beings in bridging science and religion, which today are polarized.

During his lifetime, Rudolf Steiner—the great scientist of spirit—became "the artist." He surrounded himself with artists in Vienna, Berlin, and Dornach, and they in turn drew inspiration from him. Rudolf Steiner dressed as an artist, walked, spoke, and gestured as an artist. He performed his lifework as an artist. His lectures, books, and meditative verses are thoroughly artistic in their conception, structure, and detail. Participating in the fruits of his creative efforts as fellow human beings, our own souls become artistically ennobled, our loving creativity becomes fired, our spiritual intentions become brighter and more clear.

Rudolf Steiner lived his life in continual artistic activity. Acting as a lawful spiritual creation, his lifework inspires his human brothers and sisters to become freer and more creatively active. Lifting his creativity toward the spirit in all that he did, Rudolf Steiner demonstrated the task that human beings have in becoming co-creators with spiritual beings: to create seeds for a new Heaven and new Earth while living fully in the present. He lived his life artistically as a creative and loving human being. Perhaps this is how Rudolf Steiner spoke through his fifth house Sun in the Water Bearer.

"A composer works on the basis of compositional theory, which is a sum of all that one needs to know before one can compose. In composing, the laws of composition serve life, serve reality. In just the same way, philosophy is an *art*. All real philosophers have been *artists in concepts*. For them, human ideas have become artistic materials and scientific methods have become artistic technique. Thereby, abstract thinking attains concrete, individual life. Ideas become powers of life. Then we not merely know *about* things, but have made knowing into a real, self-governing organism. Our active, real consciousness has lifted itself above mere passive reception of truths.

How philosophy as an art relates to human *freedom*, what freedom is, and whether we do, or can, participate in it—this is the principal theme of my book. All other scientific discussions are included only because, in the end, they throw light on these (in my view) most immediate human questions. These pages are meant to offer *a philosophy of freedom*."
—RUDOLF STEINER (*Intuitive Thinking as a Spiritual Path*, pp. 256–257)

I would like to kindle every human being out of the spirit of the cosmos
   that they all become flames and unfold in fire their being's very being.
Others—they would wish to draw from cosmic waters that which quenches flame,
   and drenching, cripple true being in them.
O joy, when human flames burns brightly, even when at rest;
O bitterness, when they become beings in bonds, when they would active be.
            —RUDOLF STEINER (from his notebooks of the early 1920s)

THE HOROSCOPES OF J.F.K, GANDHI, MOZART, AND RUDOLF STEINER
In the Light of Jacques Dorsan's *Clockwise House System*

Wain Farrants

Robert Powell, the principal editor of the *Journal for Star Wisdom,* like me, considers *The Clockwise House System* by Jacques Dorsan to embody one of the most important discoveries of twentieth-century astrology. The following brief description portrays the essence of his discovery. It has to do with the twelve houses in astrology, normally viewed in a counterclockwise direction, the direction of the zodiac signs. According to Jacques Dorsan, however, we should view them in a clockwise direction. What led him to consider this reversal of the houses?

Jacques Dorsan (1912–2005) was the pioneer of sidereal astrology in France. Sidereal astrology, in contrast to the usual tropical astrology applied in the West, views the twelve signs of the zodiac, each 30° long, as embedded in the corresponding zodiacal constellation. For example, in sidereal astrology if a planet is seen in conjunction with Antares, the red supergiant star marking the heart of the Scorpion, it is said to be at 15° Scorpio (the center or heart of the sign of Scorpio), whereas in tropical astrology it is said to be at 10° Sagittarius. Today's astrologers in India employ the ancient sidereal zodiac, which maintains the relationship between astronomical observation and astrological interpretation. We see from the foregoing example that, when using the tropical zodiac, we lose this relationship. The reintroduction of the ancient sidereal zodiac in our time reestablishes astrology on the solid foundation of observational astronomy and heals the disconnect between astronomy and astrology created by the introduction of the tropical zodiac into astrology.

Robert Powell's Ph.D. thesis, *History of the Zodiac,* traces the sidereal zodiac back to ancient Babylon. From there it was transmitted to Egypt, Greece, Rome, and India. Except in India, the tropical zodiac introduced by Greek astronomers subsequently replaced this system. The Greek astronomer Ptolemy (second century A.D.) unwittingly introduced the tropical zodiac into astrology through his astrological textbook, *The Tetrabiblos,* as described in detail in *History of the Zodiac.* Early in his career as an astrologer, Jacques Dorsan recognized the ancient sidereal zodiac to be the authentic astrological zodiac, as described in several of his books (available in French). He went on to recognize the clockwise house system as the authentic system of the astrological houses, as described in the book mentioned here. Hitherto, his book, *The Clockwise House System*, has been available only in French, so it is with great joy that we are able to announce here the forthcoming publication of an English translation of Dorsan's book on the houses by Lindisfarne Books.

In the Northern Hemisphere, we look primarily toward the south to see the Zodiac. Most geographical maps show north at the top, south at the bottom, east on the right and west on the left. Compared to a geographical map, a horoscope is "upside down" so that everything seems reversed. The zodiac signs circle the horoscope in a counterclockwise direction, in an order extending from west to east. This is the view of the zodiac in the Northern Hemisphere (in the Southern Hemisphere it is reversed).

When viewed at the same time every night against the background of the signs of the sidereal zodiac, we see that the Moon moves some 12° to 15° to the east each night, entering into a new zodiac sign approximately every 2⅓ to 2½ days. This progression of the Moon in a counterclockwise direction, from west to east, also takes place for the Sun in relation to the zodiac. In general, this also takes place for the planets, except at certain times when one or the other planet appears to move retrograde, in a clockwise direction (east to west) against the background of the stars comprising the signs of the zodiac. However, this retrograde movement of the planets is relatively infrequent in contrast to the usual movement of the planets, seen to move in a counterclockwise direction through the zodiac, as do the Sun and Moon.

In contrast to the counterclockwise motion of the Sun, Moon, and planets against the background of the zodiac signs, each day they rise in the east, cross the sky in a clockwise direction, disappear in the west, and reappear in the east on average twelve hours later. Again, this daily movement (the diurnal motion) is the perspective from the Northern Hemisphere; the Southern Hemisphere sees the Sun, Moon, and planets rise in the east and move in a counterclockwise direction toward the western horizon. Dorsan sees this daily clockwise motion of the Sun, Moon, and planets as the background for the twelve astrological houses. In his *History of the Houses*, Robert Powell describes how the house system originated in ancient Egypt and may have been based on the Egyptian "star clocks," originally clockwise, which were based on observation of the diurnal motion of the heavenly bodies. He also mentions that Rudolf Steiner referred to this clockwise direction for the presentation of the zodiac in eurythmy. Powell points out that Steiner indicated this clockwise perspective based on the daily cycle (diurnal motion) of the Sun.

In traditional astrology, there are three fundamental ways of interpreting a person's character and circumstances through a horoscope. These interpretations arise by examining three astrological aspects: 1) the planets in relation to the fixed stars (in particular, the planets as seen against the background of the twelve sidereal signs of the zodiac); 2) the planets in the twelve houses; and 3) the angles between the planets (known as the aspects). A relationship exists between the planets and the signs of the zodiac by virtue of the astrological tradition that links the various planets with different signs according to the teaching that each planet "rules" a zodiac sign. In his lecture of January 8, 1918,[1] this teaching was confirmed as authentic by Rudolf Steiner (at least, in the classical form of this teaching). At the same time, in looking at a horoscope, the planets occupy the twelve different houses, as we will see in the horoscope of Rudolf Steiner's birth. In it, the Sun is in the sign of Aquarius in the ninth house according to the clockwise house system.[2]

Traditional Western astrologers interpret the houses as if they were rotating in the same direction as the zodiac signs—that is, in a counterclockwise direction. This counterclockwise tradition of houses came about as Egyptian astronomers, in two-hour "watches," observed the region of the heavens that rises following the moment of birth, with each portion crossing the ascendant, known as the *horo-scope* (meaning "watcher of the hour").[3] According to Jacques Dorsan, however, we should enumerate the houses in a clockwise direction, following the diurnal motion (of the Sun, for example) that we see each day. Of the twelve houses, the first and most important house, is said to relate to the personality and physical appearance of the person and should start at the Ascendant, marked by the zodiacal degree rising on the eastern horizon at the moment of birth.[4] Dorsan agrees with the traditional perspective that the circle of twelve houses begins at the Ascendant. However, whereas traditional astrology counts the houses in a counterclockwise direction, usually starting with the Ascendant, Dorsan's revolutionary approach

---

1 Rudolf Steiner, *Ancient Myths and the New Isis Mystery* (Hudson, NY: Anthroposophic Press, 1994).

2 Note that in Brian Gray's article in this issue of the journal, where Brian uses a modified form of the traditional counterclockwise system, the Sun's zodiacal location in Aquarius remains unchanged, but its house position is in the fifth house rather than in the ninth house according to the clockwise perspective.

3 Deborah Houlding, *The Houses: Temples of the Sky* (Bournemouth, UK: The Wessex Astrologer, 2006), p. 19.

4 Note that Brian Gray (in this journal) uses a modified counterclockwise house system in which the Ascendant is placed in the center—not at the beginning—of the first house, and that all houses are shown as equal in size. This is a very different approach to house division, which Brian will describe in a future article.

commences with counting the houses at the Ascendant and proceeds in a clockwise direction around the horoscope. What does this signify in practice?

If the moment of birth coincides with sunrise (a condition rarely achieved, one might add), then the first house in traditional Western astrology would cover, on average, the last two hours of darkness prior to sunrise (roughly 4 to 6 a.m.). This region of the heavens, which would rise in the two hours following the moment of birth, is traditionally considered the first house. However, in the clockwise house system presented by Dorsan, the first house relates to the the portion of the heavens already visible above the horizon at the moment of birth, which, theoretically, would be traversed during the first two hours of daylight following sunrise (more or less 6 to 8 a.m.). For Dorsan, the most important house in the circle of twelve houses, the first, pertains to emergence into the light rather than the darkness preceding the emergence of light. Similarly, in traditional astrology the second house (said to indicate a person's finances and relationship to money) would cover the early hours of the morning (approximately 2 to 4 a.m.). It would be beneath the horizon in the traditional horoscope, and this portion of the heavens would rise and cross the ascendant *(horo-scope)* during the two hours following the two-hour period as the first house rises. In Dorsan's view, it makes more sense for the house of money to be located above the horizon in the "daylight sector" of the horoscope, which is visible at the moment of birth. The second house ("house of money"), in Dorsan's system, relates to the morning period when people start to earn money (8 to 10 a.m.).

Following the houses in this way around the circle of the horoscope, the twelfth house in traditional astrology would cover the first two hours of daylight after sunrise (around 6 to 8 a.m.). That is, the portion of the heavens visible above the ascendant will be the last, or twelfth, portion to rise across the ascendant following the moment of birth. However, as Dorsan points out, traditionally the twelfth house is interpreted as the house of confinement, indicating a person's enemies. In Dorsan's view, it makes more sense for the twelfth house to be located beneath the eastern horizon, corresponding to the two hours prior to sunrise (around 4 to 6 a.m.), thus connected with the darkness lurking beneath normal daytime consciousness.

In the view of Robert Powell (and this is also my experience), when we use the clockwise house system with the sidereal zodiac, everything suddenly falls into place astrologically when looking at a horoscope. It is a key that unlocks the mystery of the horoscope. Thanks to Jacques Dorsan, a true form of astrology based on the sidereal zodiac and utilizing the clockwise house system has finally come to the light of day, enabling a giant leap forward in the practice of astrology. I say "come to the light of day," since the ancient Babylonians already practiced astrology based on the positions of the planets against the background of the signs of the sidereal zodiac. Moreover, the ancient Egyptians viewed the clockwise diurnal motion of the Sun, Moon, and planets, as significant cosmic indicators—this experience of the "star clocks" of the Egyptians, as documented in Powell's *History of the Houses*, may have subsequently been translated into the astrological house system. Thus, it is a matter of recovering the original astrology. This is possible today with the help of Rudolf Steiner's indications mentioned earlier. The research of Michel Gauquelin, who investigated hundreds of thousands of horoscopes statistically, supports the idea that the astrological houses may run in a clockwise direction.[5] As stated by Michel Gauquelin's wife and collaborator, Françoise Gauquelin, "The favorable zones should have been progressively expanded to 30° after the rise and culmination of the planets, i.e., Houses XII and IX. Instead, the 30° before the rise and culmination of the planets were adapted as more essential for knowing the native's character and social status. When will the astrological community admit that this was an error?"[6]

The following horoscopes are cast in both the counterclockwise and clockwise sidereal zodiac house systems. The clockwise descriptions come from a manuscript copy of Jacques Dorsan's book.

---

5 Michel Gauquelin, *Neo-Astrology: A Copernican Revolution* (London: Arkana Books, 1992).
6 Françoise Gauquelin. *Psychology of the Planets* (Epping, NH: ACS Publications, 1982).

The counterclockwise descriptions come from a traditional textbook, *The Manual of Astrology* by Sepharial.[7] Both house systems are determined using the Placidus method of house division.[8]

John F. Kennedy

There is a stellium of five planets in the clockwise fifth house or the counterclockwise eighth House (see next page). First, we will look at the traditional counterclockwise eighth house. The Sun: steady fortunes after marriage (*true*); chance of fame or honors at death (*true*); danger of death in midlife (*true*). Mercury: inconstant fortunes; troubles of a minor character in financial affairs after marriage (*untrue*). Venus: chance of favors from deceased women (uncertain); the partner will be fond of pleasures, jewels and pretty things (*true*); success in finance comes after marriage (*untrue*). Mars: the marriage partner spends the substance of the native (uncertain); strife concerning the property of deceased persons (*uncertain*); danger of a violent death (*true*); losses by fire and theft (*untrue*). Jupiter: marriage brings prosperity; the partner is or will be rich (*true*); gain by legacy (*true*); a happy death (*untrue*).

Now we look at the clockwise fifth house (see page 66). Sun: increases the vital energy and prolongs dynamism into the following generation; promises satisfaction in pleasures, theater, general entertainment and all that touches education and the fine arts (*true*); success is promised in personal business ventures and initiatives that make him stand out and even put him into the limelight (*more or less true*); a flattering liaison will be worth a certain degree of prestige, few children, an only child is more likely to be a boy (*he had a son and a daughter*); tendency toward pride and jealousy in love (*uncertain*); takes care that excesses do not harm the reputation or strike a blow against one's esteem (*true*). Jupiter: this brings good fortune, both in matters of the heart and materially; tends to be excessive in the pursuit of pleasure (*true*); sociable, loves parlor games, community entertainment, going out on the town; he smiles at life and life in turn smiles down on him (*true*); he will enjoy loving relationships with good, rich and honorable people; lucky in love; the children will be essentially good and grateful (*true*).

The Moon is in the eleventh counterclockwise house: unreliable friends; patronage of women; many acquaintances, but few lasting attachments. (*While he had affairs, it seems he also had many deep friendships.*) Moon in the second clockwise house: This position creates a sensitivity toward all that concerns money and finance (*more or less correct*); financial success will frequently depend on the public rather than on a small number of people or on one employer (*uncertain*).

Saturn and Neptune are in the tenth counterclockwise house. Saturn shows a rise in life, followed by a downfall, in government, defeat; danger of the ruin or loss of a parent in early life; public affairs fail or bring loss and discredit (*On the one hand, the Bay of Pigs affair was a failure, but, on the other hand, the Cuban Missile Crisis was a success.*) Neptune gives a strange and eventful career; chance of honors in some artistic field; a highly inspirational nature capable of attaining honors through some unique achievement; he does so under curious circumstances, either using an assumed name or some covert means (*not true*).

Saturn in the third clockwise house: it favors all serious mental pursuits, in which tact and diplomacy must predominate (*true*); there is an aptitude for methodical reflection and tireless pursuits (*he was a voracious reader*); displays an aptitude for works requiring time and concentration, discretion and secrecy (*true*). This is one of the surest indications of great ambition, especially if it is at the end of the house close to the M.C. (*true*); serious accidents or delays of great consequence during travels are to be dreaded (*JFK assassinated on a trip to Dallas and when the motor cavalcade slowed down*). Neptune in the third clockwise house is one of the best configurations for being inspired, having a boundless imagination; his ideal is often very different from that of those around

---

7 Sepharial, *The Manual of Astrology* (Berkshire, UK: Foulsham, 1962).
8 As stated, a future article by Brian Gray will explore another system of equal-house division, with the ascendant placed in the center of the first house.

The Horoscopes of J.F.K, Gandhi, Mozart, and Rudolf Steiner

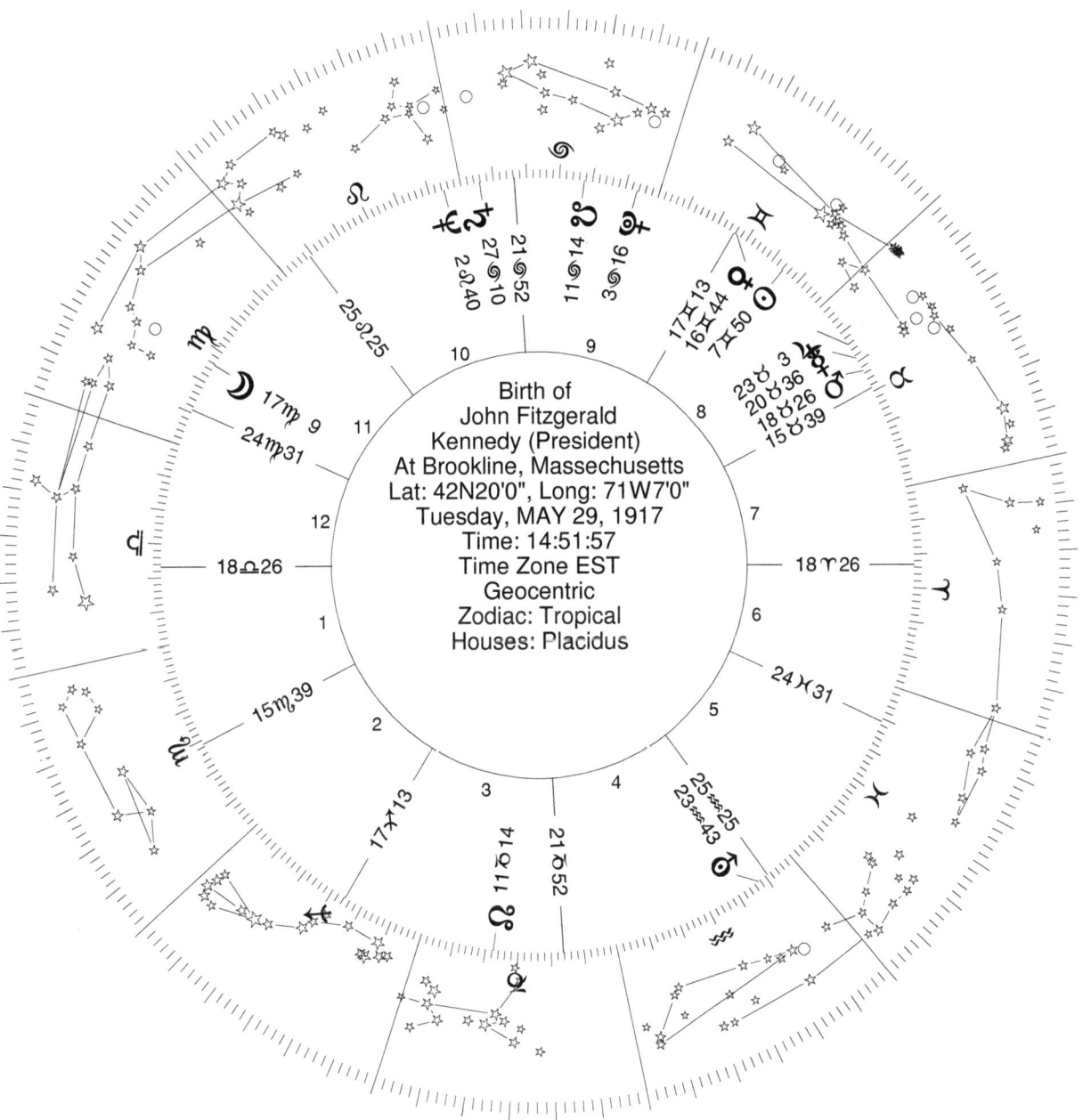

him (*true*); professional success in maritime navigation (*he famously commanded a PT boat while in the navy during World War II*).

Uranus in the fourth counterclockwise house suggests many changes of house; misfortune in the place of birth; trouble through the parents (*uncertain*); danger of paralysis or other incurable infirmity in old age (*he suffered from a war injury, Addison's disease, and other serious medical conditions*); a sudden end to life (*true*).

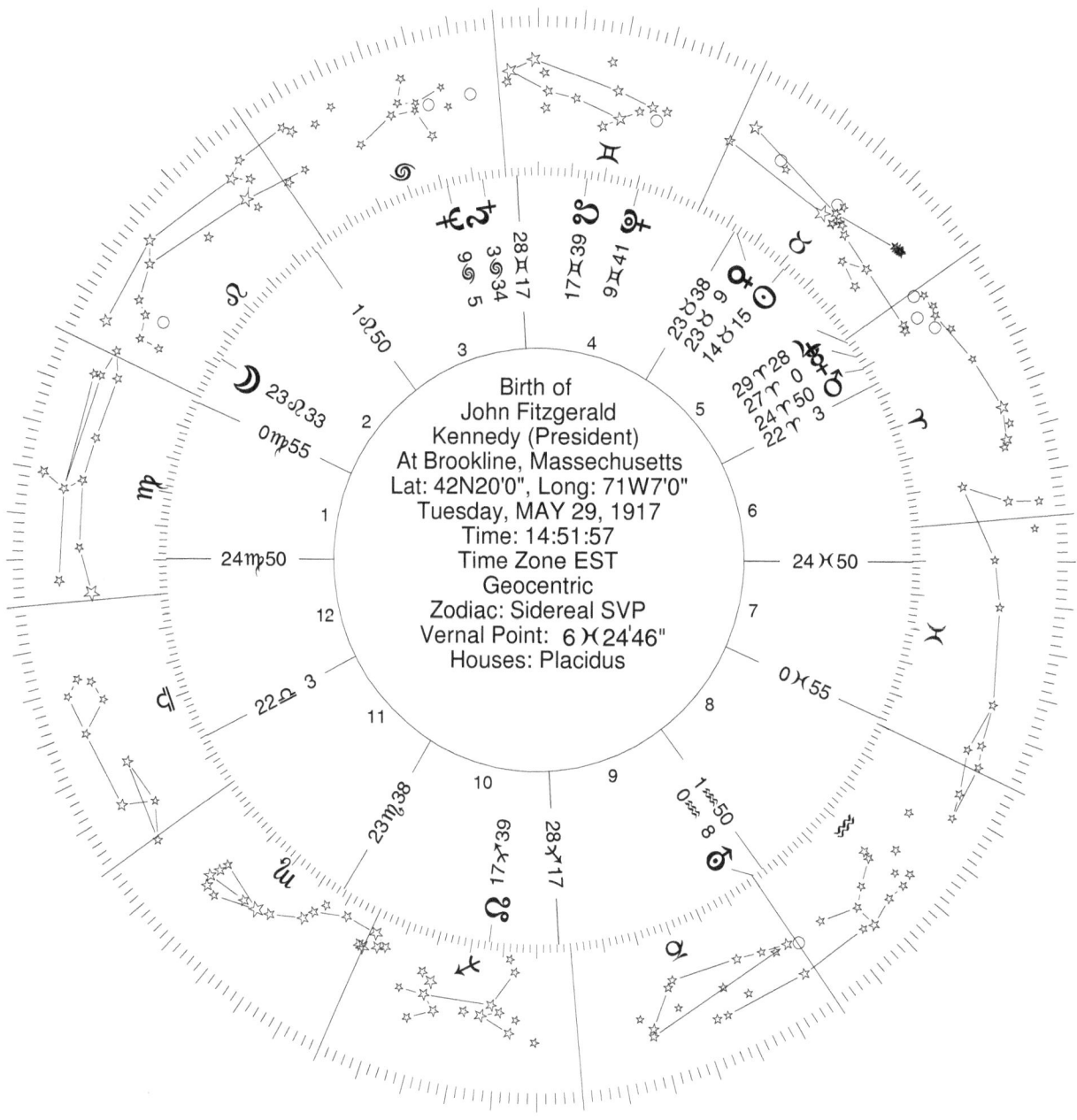

Uranus in the ninth clockwise house is in a position that suits it perfectly. It grants exceptionally rare intellectual aptitudes. She will get the best from his sensitivity, receptivity, and intuition. He will be very interested in the happiness of humankind and in his own spiritual elevation. He should take special note of his early-morning dreams. Overall, his satisfactions will be more on a spiritual plane than of a material nature. (*All of this appears to be true and, despite his*

many shortcomings and human flaws, made him a much-loved President.)

Pluto in the ninth counterclockwise house will give an interest in unorthodox forms of religion and a refusal to adhere to orthodoxy (*he seemed to be a staunch Catholic*); shows a strong desire for travel (*true*); sometimes shows conditions of exile (*never happened*); is associated with interest in space travel (*he launched the project that landed a person on the Moon*). Pluto in the fourth clockwise house: the subject believes that he ought to accomplish his mission; he will be the object of envy in his professional situation, which will bristle with strange circumstances; he will suffer great periods of upset in life, crises, and extraordinary turning points (*all true*); he will come out unharmed from dangers and adversities, against which he would seem to be immune (*untrue*).

MOHANDAS K. GANDHI

Sun in the clockwise first house (see next pages, sidereal chart on page 68) gives a strong-willed, authoritative personality, conscious of his own value; has untold confidence in himself; is noble, dignified and truly magnanimous (*true*).

Sun in the counterclockwise twelfth house gives danger of exile, or life apart from kindred; enmity of great men; life in far-off lands; he vanquishes his enemies (*more or less true*).

Mercury in the clockwise twelfth house gives the impression of being a discreet, secret or mysterious person. He has a tendency to be introspective; has an aptitude for work carried out in a quiet, calm and isolated location; should not utter careless words; he should take great care as to what he writes down, as there could be secret enemies who seek to harm him (*true*). Mercury in the counterclockwise first house is a restless person, given to ceaseless inquiry and concern; many journeys, quick, nervous speech; taste for literature (*probably untrue*).

Venus in the clockwise twelfth house is devoted and compassionate toward the sick, those suffering from an infirmity, and those who are nature's outcasts. He is capable of acts of sacrifice and abnegation (*true*). Venus in the counterclockwise first house has a fondness for poetry, music, singing, dancing, the drama, fine arts, and so on (*not true beyond what his culture demanded of him, at least not an obvious delineation of his character*).

Mars in the clockwise twelfth house is a serious warning for if he acts unwisely and impulsively under the influence of passion or anger, grave consequences are to be feared. He could provoke hostile feelings, which are all the more serious as they are carried out undercover (*true*). Mars in the counterclockwise first house gives danger of cuts, burns, scalds and abrasions; makes him bold, free and independent, fond of competition and strife and reckless of danger (*some true, some less so*).

Jupiter in the clockwise sixth house grants an element of protection in health. He helps the sick and needy. The marriage partner will have a jovial and optimistic character. He will benefit from his partner's presence (*more or less correct*). Jupiter in the counterclockwise seventh house gives a faithful and well-disposed partner, happy associations, and gain by marriage; enemies become friends, or friendships and benefits arise from strikes (*does not ring true*).

Pluto in the clockwise sixth house is tenacious at work, to the point of being fanatical. The marriage partner will be an eccentric. (*He married when he and his wife were very young and, at times, he did not treat her well. This is reflected in his horoscope by the oppositions of Jupiter and Pluto with Venus and Mars.*) Pluto in the counterclockwise seventh house signifies that marriage can mean leaving familiar surroundings; if badly aspected, shows a danger of the disappearance of the marriage partner (*he left her*).

Uranus in the clockwise fourth house is a strange personality who will suffer and strongly benefit from the environment. He will experience problems with superiors and will aspire to professional independence. Difficulties will arise when dealing with public servants, the established order and narrow-minded people. Generally, he rises in fits and starts, rather abruptly as a result of unexpected and even extraordinary circumstances (*true*). Uranus in

Birth of (Mahatma) Mohandas K. Gandhi – Geocentric
At Porbandar, India, Latitude 21N38'0", Longitude 69E37'0"
Date: Saturday, OCT 2, 1869, Gregorian
Time: 7:37:45, Local Time
Sidereal Time 8:21:15, House System: Placidus
Zodiac: Tropical, Aspect set: Major Variable Orbed

the counterclockwise ninth house indicates misadventures in foreign lands (*South Africa, perhaps*), legal difficulties (*the British considered his salt march illegal*), and a taste for occult and eccentric knowledge (*uncertain*).

Neptune in the clockwise seventh house could indicate a union, which goes against his nature. He is not adapted to married life (*true*). Neptune in the counterclockwise sixth house gives psychic faculties, a visionary nature, danger of mental

The Horoscopes of J.F.K, Gandhi, Mozart, and Rudolf Steiner

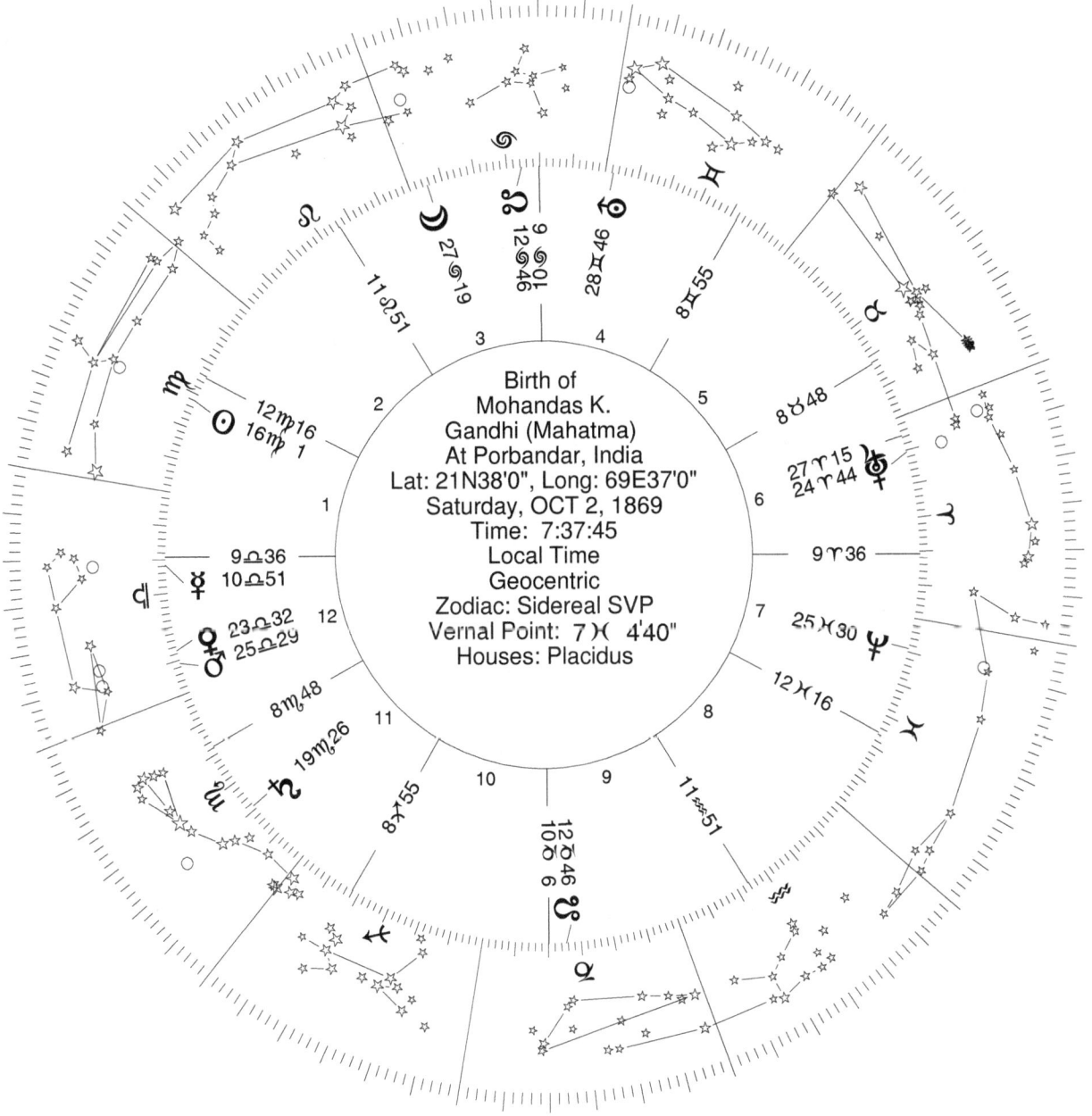

troubles, a chaotic religious mania, legal suits (*more or less incorrect*).

Saturn in the clockwise eleventh house warns of trouble from false friends. Success or defeat in the social and professional life will depend upon the assistance of friends and relations (*uncertain*). Saturn in the counterclockwise second house indicates business losses, a thrifty nature, hard work for little gain and sometimes poverty (*not true*).

Moon in the clockwise third house has a thirst for knowledge in the most varied subjects. Success through intellectual occupations, especially through works of imagination and through popularity. Attraction to sea cruises. (*He was certainly well educated and went to South Africa and the United Kingdom by sea.*) Moon in the counterclockwise tenth house means that women influence the position; changes in occupation and a rise in life, followed by a reversal of popularity (*not true, except at the end of his life, when many objected to his desire to prevent India and Pakistan from separating*).

Wolfgang Amadeus Mozart

Neptune in clockwise second house may cause the person to forsake the idea of earning money through normal channels (traditional chart page 70; sidereal chart, page 71). He will be interested only in the exploitation of inspired ideas or speculative combinations. (*He rejected a secure income in Salzburg, in favor of Vienna, where he often lacked money.*)

Neptune in the counterclockwise eleventh house gives seductive friends and alliances, unreliable advisers; treachery among supposed friends; the wife or husband is liable to moral delinquency (*certainly not true*).

Jupiter in clockwise eleventh house grants a sociable, jovial, and charitable disposition. The more he cultivates his relations, the greater his success. Among his friends, he can count a good number of wealthy, influential, and high-ranking people, officials, people of the law, and clerics (*true*).

Jupiter in counterclockwise second house is the best position for wealth, increase of property, gain and greater prosperity (*Mozart was buried in a pauper's grave*).

Moon in clockwise ninth house gives a lively imagination favoring creativity, an aptitude for the study of metaphysics, philosophy, law, religion, and occultism (*for example,* The Magic Flute, *his Masonic opera*). He is unstable, in search of newness, and will study profoundly and at great length before forming an opinion. Success will depend greatly on all that is outside the immediate environment. Promised recognition of his talents. Success and popularity is announced far from his native land (*Mozart never left this part of the world but his music is played everywhere*).

Moon in counterclockwise fourth house gives an uncertainty of position, some chance of inheritance, frequent changes of residence, some popularity at the end of life, and favors from women (*this does not do Mozart justice*).

Pluto in clockwise ninth house seeks the truth, has elevated ideals, pursues a superior quest, loves adventure, and travels afar. Vicissitudes in far-off lands with voluntary exile (*partially correct*). Note that the counterclockwise third house of short journeys is below the Ascendant whereas the ninth house of long journeys is above the Descendant. However, when you see someone off on a cruise liner or an airplane, the person disappears over the horizon, whereas if you make a short trip, you can look back and see where you came from if there were no buildings or trees blocking your view. Hence, it makes more sense that short journeys should be ruled the clockwise third house, which is above the horizon and long journeys ruled by the clockwise ninth house, which is invisible below the horizon.

Pluto in counterclockwise fourth house often signifies someone who has lived in an orphanage or shows a destruction of early home life because the parents part or die; and loneliness at the end of life (*not true*).

Mars in the clockwise third house favors mental activity; expresses himself easily, frankly and forcefully (*true*). Mars in the counterclockwise tenth house gives success in military life; in other fields of work, danger of discredit; he suffers from slander and his life is filled with turmoil and strife (*not true*).

Sun in the clockwise eighth house gives an impetus to create light where there is darkness, which leads to an interest in mysterious things. Vitality will decrease owing to heart problems. (*The first part is true; health problems are uncertain.*) Sun in the counterclockwise fifth house makes for success in relation to children, schools, theaters, all

The Horoscopes of J.F.K, Gandhi, Mozart, and Rudolf Steiner

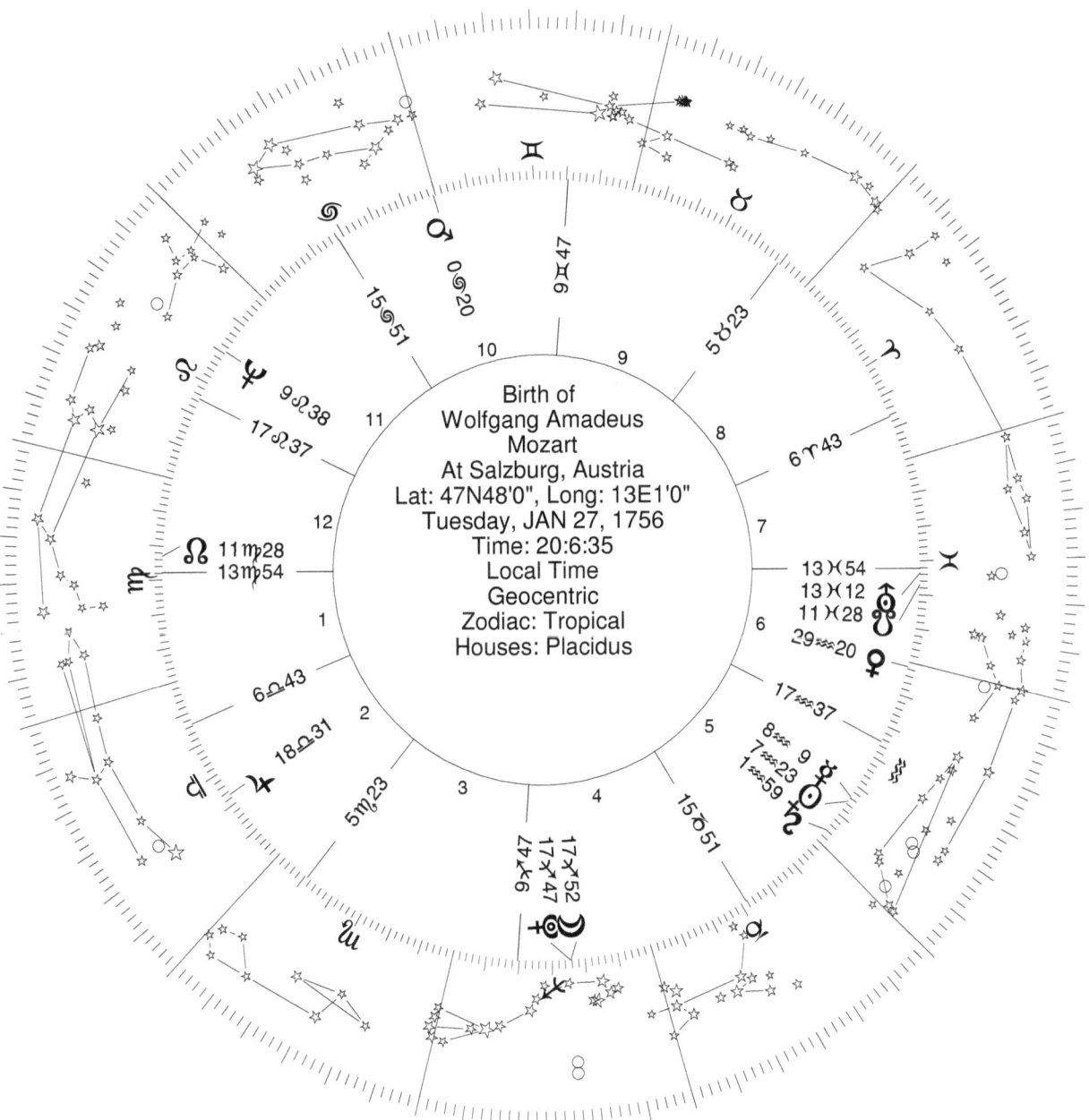

sorts of amusements and love affairs. (*This could fit the silly American film version.*)

Mercury in the clockwise eighth house is often subject to melancholia when thinking deeply about death. It favors studies, profound investigations, history, and occultism. There is a possibility of a serious illness during the course of a trip or toward the end of life while far from home. There could be money worries after marriage (*more or less correct*). Mercury in the counterclockwise fifth house leads to many little worries and concerns with speculative affairs and inconstancy in love (*not true*).

Journal for Star Wisdom 2011

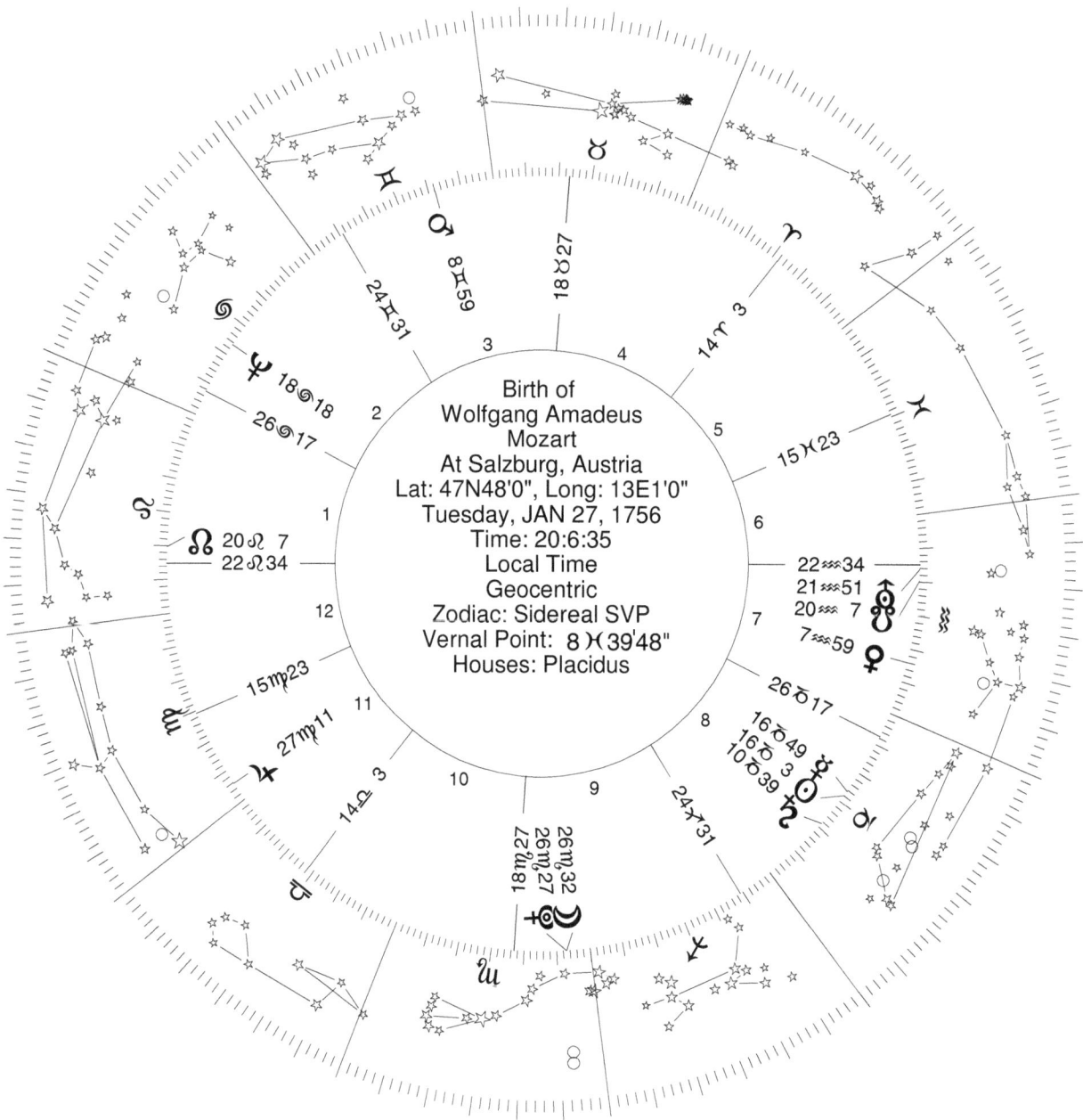

Saturn in the clockwise eighth house attracts one to the occult (*true*). He is predisposed toward catching chills (*uncertain*), suffering from rheumatism (*uncertain*), or falls from high places (*untrue*). Frequently, wealth will be elusive owing to uncontrollable circumstances; the financial situation will often worsen after marriage (*true*). Saturn in the counterclockwise fifth house leads to disappointment in early love affairs, loss of a child, losses through speculations and games of chance;

danger of heart problems and drowning. (*Only the loss of children through stillbirths is correct*.)

Venus in the seventh clockwise house gives protection against adversity and open hostilities. It is one of the best configurations for human contacts in married life (*true*). Venus in the counterclockwise sixth house gives a love of fine dress, a delicate appetite, fondness for pretty adornments and improvements in health after marriage (*uncertain*).

Uranus in the seventh clockwise house warns of the difficulties encountered when endeavoring to obtain harmony and lasting agreement in associations. This configuration bodes ill in matters affecting the public or in relationships with others. An impulsive marriage may take place, which is out of the ordinary (*true*). Uranus in the sixth counterclockwise house causes nervous diseases, losses and anxieties through servants and changes that interfere with health and comfort (*uncertain*).

RUDOLF STEINER

I am assuming that most readers will know enough about Rudolf Steiner to decide which system is preferable. Counterclockwise comments are by Sepharial (S) and Bill Herbst (BH).[9]

Counterclockwise House System

Venus (third house) gives a strong inclination to the fine arts, pleasant travels; success in writing, speaking, poetry, music, singing and painting (S). (See counterclockwise chart opposite.) Things do not interest him as much as people do (BH). Sun (fourth house) gives a small chance of honors or dignities until the very end of life (S). He maintains essential privacy as a way of guarding his importance. His life goal is to achieve and maintain security, to define what family means, and to experience the fulfillment of social safety for himself and complete acceptance by those he emotionally values (BH). Mercury (fourth house) is here today and gone tomorrow, changing residence through matters concerned with business (S). What he knows is often kept secret, and though it is certainly natural that he be conservative with his information, this can occasionally work to his disadvantage (BH). Neptune (fifth house) indicates illicit amours, love of pleasures of a sensuous nature, and leads to trouble in love affairs (S). Creativity tends to be spiritual rather than material, intangible rather than concrete (BH). Mars (sixth house) leads to quarrels and thefts among servants, extravagance in food and dress, and inflammatory complaints in the bowels and the neck (Mars in tropical Taurus) or head (Mars in Sidereal Aries) (S). Fights with others over inequality and struggle with others over authority. Thinking is passionate and direct, sometimes glossing over an important step (BH). Pluto (sixth house) emphasizes the liability to industrial forms of sickness (S). At times, he probes beyond appearances, revealing the hidden links that unify life. Other times, he is ineffective, almost blind to what is happening. Only by seeing the whole and that the parts merge will his analyses become so deep and accurate that others marvel at his vision (BH). Uranus (seventh house) leads to impulsive attachments, a hasty marriage followed by estrangement, many open enemies and public contests (S). Commitment is hardly the tenor of this placement (BH). Jupiter (ninth house) gives success in religious and philosophical pursuits, legal matters and foreign affairs or in foreign countries (S). Philosophy, ethics, religion, or law are synthesized in an endless search for the perfect generalization (BH). Saturn (tenth house) is a rise in life, followed by a downfall; patience and firmness of purpose; in business, financial ruin, in professional life, dishonor and failure. A fatality hangs over the native from his birth (S). Ambition is immensely powerful; life is a struggle, survival of the fittest; the challenge is to wield power with the dignity his role demands and to treat others with the respect they deserve (BH). Moon (tenth house) has a desire for public life; many changes and voyages; changes in occupation; women influence the position for good or evil (S). Taking care of others is a deep imprint, to be responsive and nurturing in ways that foster strength (BH)

Clockwise House System

Moon (third house) is mentally active and curious (see page 74); thirst for knowledge in the

---

9 Bill Herbst, *Houses of the Horoscope* (Epping, NH: ACS Publications, 1988).

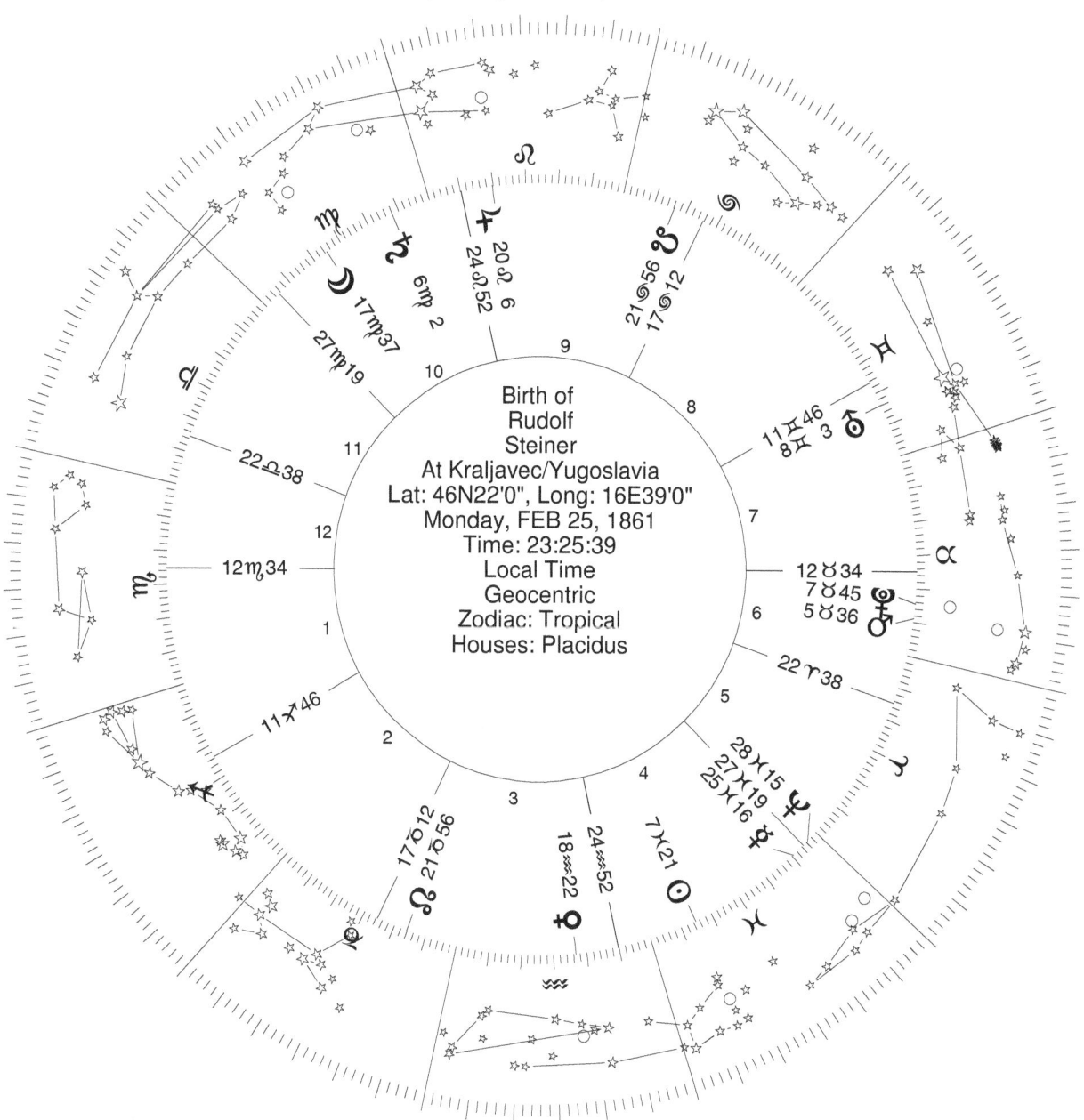

most varied subjects; flees monotony; changes of educational establishments during youth; numerous voyages, preferably with the family or as part of a group. Saturn (third house) favors all mental pursuits in which tact and diplomacy must be predominant, but warns that certain tribulations will affect studies or mental capacities. He seems more mature than his actual age when he is young but will grow old slowly. He will have to keep a watch over his pen and avoid sarcastic

The Horoscopes of J.F.K, Gandhi, Mozart, and Rudolf Steiner

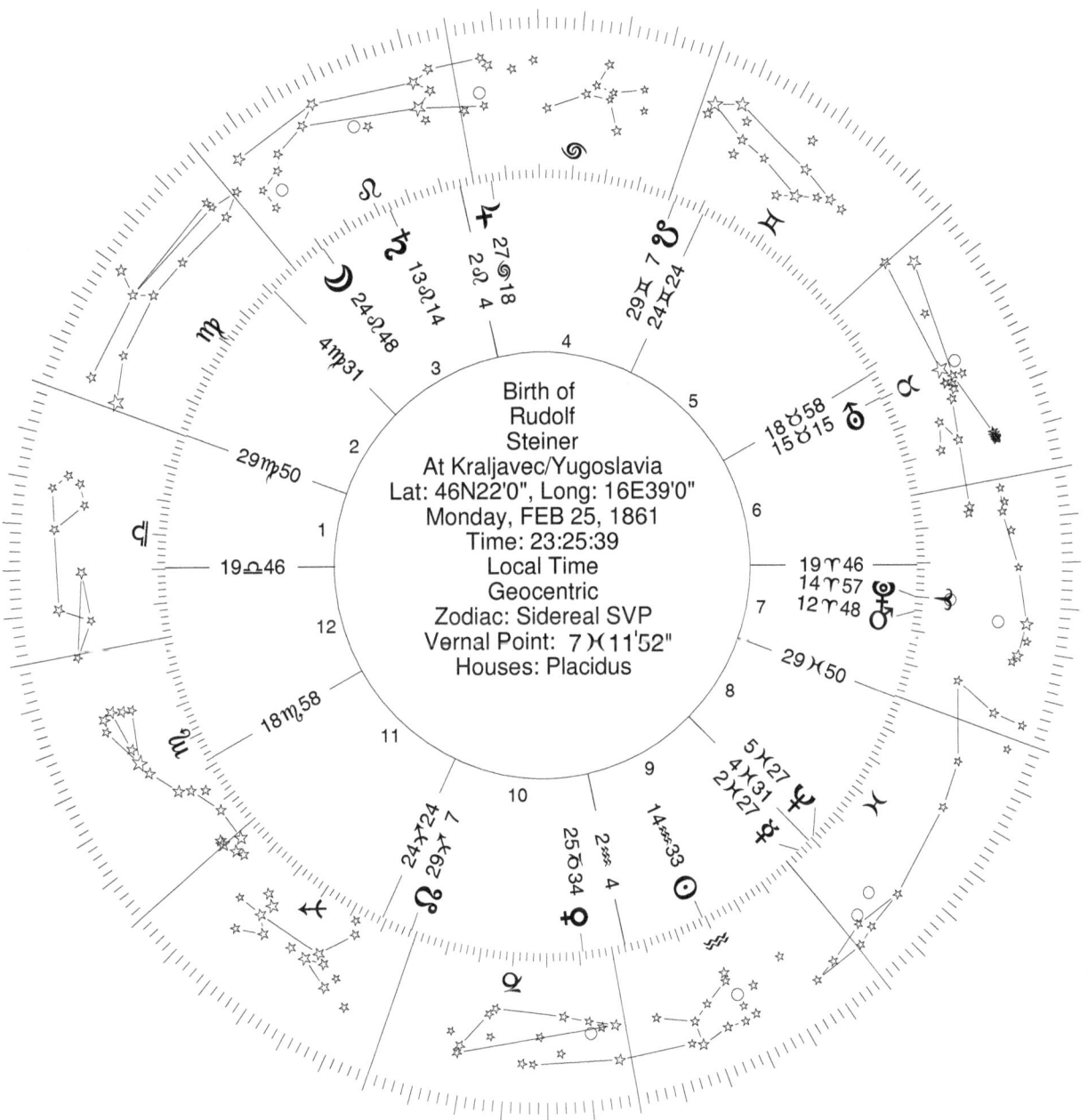

comments. Jupiter (fourth house) gives an acute sense of justice and an optimistic, honest and generous nature. This configuration is the surest indication of success in life.[10] Uranus (sixth house) gives exceptional psychic faculties and receptivity; predisposed toward sudden irregularities in the natural functions; he should lead a healthy life and exercise regularly; marriage partner could

---

10 Michel Gauquelin discovered that the sector clockwise from the Midheaven is a strong career indicator.

be rather eccentric and a reciprocal liberty must be accorded. Pluto (seventh) seeks contacts with the world's great people; marriage will bring the unexpected into his life; destiny will depend upon the results, rivalries and obstacles against which he will continually stand up and fight. Mars (seventh house) indicates success through collaboration with others; marriage later in life, more to satisfy his sexual instincts or through his need for an energetic partner by his side, than through any genuine (romantic) feelings. Neptune (eighth house) can facilitate astral travel, the vision of auras and other metaphysical gifts. Death often takes place in rather strange circumstances. Mercury (ninth house) engenders a great thirst for knowledge and provokes overwhelming mental activity; the main areas of interest could be law, the sciences, philosophy, religion, occultism, and metaphysics; ideas are expressed easily and clearly; favors writing or teaching. Sun (ninth house) here is an excellent configuration for intellectual and scientific pursuits and speculations of the mind; he has a high sense of ideals and a sense of prophecy; numerous voyages over long distances will be advantageous; success, honors, and prestige probable in foreign lands. Venus (tenth house) indicates a pleasant, easy, and comfortable early life and a happy old age, satisfied that projects have come to fruition and that he has lived a full life.

The Clockwise House System, by Jacques Dorsan and edited by Wain Farrantes, is to be published by Lindisfarne Books in spring 2011.

The Clockwise House System contains more than eighty horoscopes cast in the sidereal zodiac, including most of those from the French edition along with many more added to this English edition. As editor, I have checked each horoscope for accuracy to the best of my ability, rectified each by the hermetic rule and compared the result with events in the person's life. I am grateful to Robert Powell for his help in editing and proofreading the manuscript.

Since my discovery of this system of counting houses, I have used it successfully to describe my clients and as an aid in rectifying horoscopes closer to their true time of birth. While I am open to equal house-division and centering houses on the Ascendant and Midheaven, I still prefer Placidus house-division, because I have often found significant events taking place as planets cross the house cusps. It also works well with the tropical zodiac.

We are only at the beginning, and when master astrologers discover the clockwise house system, I have no doubt that their more psychological approaches will enhance its effectiveness.

Every earthly condition during a certain period of time is to be explained as a weaving and interplay of those forces that come into flower and those that die away, those that belong to the rising and those that belong to the falling line—sunrise and sunset—and in between, the zenith at noon, where the two forces unite and become one. Seen from one's horizon, a person beholds the stars in the sky, rising in the east and climbing ever higher until they reach their highest point in the south. From then onward, they sink until they set in the west. And though the stars disappear from sight in the west, one must nevertheless say to oneself: The real place of setting lies in the south and coincides with the zenith, just as the true place of rising is in the north and coincides with the nadir. The rising starts from the nadir. Through that, a circular motion is described that can be divided into two halves by a vertical line running south to north. In the part containing the eastern point, the rising forces are active. In the part containing the western point, the sinking forces are present. The eastern and western points cut the semicircle through the center. They are the two points in which, for our physical eye, vision of the forces begins and ends. They are one's horizon.

—Rudolf Steiner, *"Freemasonry" and Ritual Work*
(SteinerBooks, 2007), p. 387

EXCITEMENT OF THE POLARITIES AT 23° TO 24° OF THE FIXED SIGNS

David Tresemer, Ph.D.

The full moon and total lunar eclipse of December 10, 2011, occurs with the Sun at 23° of Scorpio and the Moon at 23° Taurus, reminding us that Venus, in her dance and with the Sun in June of 2004, had a special relationship with exactly that degree of Taurus, The Bull.

Normally, Venus lies either above or below the Sun when she crosses in front of the Sun (inferior conjunction) or behind (superior conjunction). On rare occasions, Venus passes directly in front of the Sun, a phenomenon astronomically called a "transit," though I prefer the word "eclipse" as it suggests a dramatic energetic connection between Sun and Venus.[1] These Sun–Venus eclipses occur in pairs separated by eight years, those pairs being more than a hundred years apart from each other.[2] The last pair of Sun–Venus eclipses took place in 1874 and 1882. The first of the present pair took place on June 8, 2004, at 23°5' of The Bull (Taurus), directly opposite to 23°5' of Scorpio. Its pair-mate will take place on June 5 to 6, 2012, at the twenty-first degree of Taurus.

When the full moon undergoes its total lunar eclipse on December 10, 2011, at 23°16' of The Bull, the darkened Moon is moving through this same degree of the Bull that was stimulated during the Venus eclipse of 2004, and prepares us for the Venus eclipse of 2012, the most astrologically interesting feature of that year.[3]

What lives right at 23° to 24° of the fixed signs? The answer to this question involves a personal story as introduction. At the first Venus eclipse in 2004, I was deeply involved in understanding the different qualities of each of the 360 gates of the heavens, the degrees of the zodiac. I did this by examining the Christ events that occurred at a particular degree, expanding my knowledge of the event through research into that time, and then taking the whole matter into repeated meditations. The result was the Images and commentaries of the Oracle of the Solar Cross, inaugurated with the book *Star Wisdom and Rudolf Steiner: A Life Seen Through the Oracle of the Solar Cross*.[4] Since that time, I have continued to revise the images and commentaries, a task I have nearly completed. The text has now expanded to 1,500 pages and is growing. I have learned from readings with individuals that the most important personages are not those who were born through the same "gate" (the zodiacal degree of the Sun at birth), but rather the powerful individualities who died into that gate, often separated by many years, whose influences remained in that gate for the one passing through at birth. I would like to include this information in future versions of that work.

In assigning a Solar Cross to someone, I rely on the birth time to tell me what degree—that is, through what gate—that individual came into this material world with the first breath (technically enlivening the astral body at that breath). When I

---

1 Eclipse, from *ek* (out) and *leipein* (to leave), with the sense of forsaking or failing to appear or ceasing to exist.
2 This pattern is true for many centuries but does not hold for ancient times. More about the June 2012 "transit" or eclipse, also called occultation, may be included in the *Journal for Star Wisdom 2012*.
3 The location of Venus and Sun on June 5, 2012, will be 20° Taurus 50.

4 The authors introduce the Oracle of the Solar Cross in *Star Wisdom & Rudolf Steiner* and at www.starwisdom.org; readings can be arranged through the website. Note that the celestial address is based on sidereal reckoning—that is, the actual location of the Sun in relation to the constellations.

review historical personalities, however, since we often do not know the exact time of birth or death, I have felt that I must look a bit into the next degree, ten minutes or 1/6 of a degree. For example, if the client was born with Sun at 23°30' Taurus (the midpoint of that degree), I would examine relationships with historical personalities between 22°50' Taurus and 24°10' Taurus, thus spanning 23° to 24° and adding ten minutes at either end.

When examining the ephemeris for 2011, I saw that the full moon in December occurs at 23°16' Taurus, with the Sun at 23°16' Scorpio. I realized that this would reinvigorate the celestial address already stimulated by the Venus eclipse of 2004 at 23°5' Taurus, a mere six months before the second Venus eclipse of 2012 at 20° Taurus 50°. My attention first went to the location of the Sun at the full moon, and the Solar Cross Image in Scorpio for 23° to 24° (the twenty-fourth degree). I realized that this relates intimately to the Image that preceded it, at 22° to 23° Scorpio. I researched that degree in great detail and wrote an article about what it could teach us, which I feel is an important precursor to meeting the second Venus eclipse in 2012.

Let us review the positions of the planets in these two events, in the polarity of Taurus and Scorpio:

23° TO 24° TAURUS	23° TO 24° SCORPIO
Venus 2004	
Sun 2004	
Moon, December 2011	Sun, December 2011

Every position of a planet activates the heavens directly behind it, as well as the position directly opposed. We should place our attention on the twenty-fourth degree of Taurus, with reference to the twenty-fourth degree of Scorpio, and, even though these events occur at the very beginning of the twenty-fourth degree, very near the twenty-third degree, we should focus on the twenty-fourth degree.

Foundations

The best way to understand the polarities in the twenty-fourth degree and its relation to the Venus 2004 eclipse seems to come from what we observe in the twenty-third degree of Scorpio. There, we find the raising from death of "the youth of Nain," the twelve-year old Martialis, who would go on in subsequent incarnations to become the teacher Mani in the third century, and then the hero Parsifal in the ninth century. I shall summarize that event, and then we will come to the twenty-fourth degree that the Venus 2004 eclipse has enlivened and that the December 10, 2011, total lunar eclipse will enliven.[5]

In the story of raising the youth of Nain, we receive the picture of townspeople in a funeral procession, carrying a dead youth to the place of his burial. A wise man—Jesus Christ—visits and asks the procession to stop. He asks for a sprig of hyssop. From his cloak, he pulls a small bowl and a container of special water. Using the sprig, he flicks out water over the crowd. From all of them rise dark figures, vague, restless, black, to be absorbed into the air and light. They all sigh deeply and the child breathes. He had been suffocated by the dark forms of the community. When these had been lifted, he can breathe again, and he stands with renewed life force and cheerfulness.

What are these dark forms? The Romanian philosopher Ioan Couliano realized that the Renaissance philosopher Giordano Bruno understood the role of mental phantasms in culture, what H. P. Blavatasky, Alice Bailey, and Rudolf Steiner would later call "thought forms."[6] The Avatar technique has trained people for twenty-five years to identify thought forms as having size, shape, texture, quality of movement, and so on before dealing with them.[7] Usually these phantasms lie unseen within our mental and emotional worlds, organizing our experience yet remaining invisible and transparent. We can understand those dark

---

5 See "Lifting the Darkness into the Light," www.starwisdom.org.

6 For example, Rudolf Steiner, *Approaches to Anthroposophy*, "The Mission of Spiritual Science and of its Building at Dornach" (London: Rudolf Steiner Press, 1992); and Ioan Couliano, *Eros and Magic in the Renaissance* (Chicago: University of Chicago, 1987). Though he concentrated on Bruno, he also organized the writing of Marsilio Ficino on this topic.

7 Online at www.avatarepc.com.

forms rising from the townspeople as thought forms, or phantasms, made visible. In the sixteenth century, Bruno explained clearly that the foundation for mental phantasms is Eros, life force, the power of love applied to matter, which creates the phenomena of our world. Eros pours into us and spills over in abundance to affect our thinking, feeling, and willing.

Eros awakens and stimulates not only overt sexuality and self-involved fascination with pornography, but also every kind of desire, such as celebrity worship, propaganda, corporate branding, and patriotism. On a personal level, Eros enters thought forms as craving for chocolate, rage over a wrong, fetishes, movie scenes repeating over and over, compulsions, yearning for comfort, addictions, stories about others (gossip, grudges, judgments, crushes, and infatuations) stories about ourselves (rationalizations and justifications), concern over one's identity and appearance (cosmetic surgery and cosmetics), and many other patterns of behavior and thought. Bruno instructed how magicians can manipulate others through the power of erotic phantasms. His text, four centuries old, reads like a primer for today's politicians and merchants. Bruno's work "deserves to have the real and unique place of honor among theories of manipulation of the masses."[8] In this picture of the suffocation and revivification of the young boy, we are dealing with a mass phenomenon, with erotic mental phantasms of the community that have lifted off from the souls of the populace as dark forms for all to see. Only after we deal with these dark forms can the future Grail King breathe again.

This story understands the source of these erotic phantasms. In our longing (Eros) for spirit, we pour out our selfhood into our sensory perceptions, seeking sensory satisfaction in the material world. Longing and yearning for certain sensations and feelings affect the way we think about matter, and our desires for satisfaction permeate the concepts we form when thinking about matter, thereby hardening them into dense thought forms attached to specific mental images of matter—erotic mental phantasms. People carry these hardened mental images, charged with desires, within their souls as a source of erotic fantasies or phantasms, as Bruno called them.

There are several aspects to these erotic phantasms; specific *concepts* have been attached to *memory images* of earlier *sensations*, and permeated with *longing or desire for further satisfaction*. For example, if I have a yearning (Eros) for an ice cream cone, I can picture it. I may think that the concept is the same as my picture of an ice cream cone, because that is what arises whenever I think of it. I feel the desire or craving for what is pictured. The picture is only the facade of a motive force—a movement of Eros within my being—that I do not see. Every picture (phantasm) of things in the world has such dynamism of Eros moving behind it. For example, a jingle in itself is silly but it stays in the mind because a magician (advertiser) has understood how the jingle will engage Eros working in us. Eros is the fuel, and the phantasm the vehicle.[9] We do not see the fuel of Eros driving us toward satisfaction; we see only the vehicle—the image of the thing desired, the hardened phantasm lodged in our soul.

In this story, we see the erotic powers at work *behind* the phantasms of individuals and the community at large. We see the dynamic activity of Eros that has attached itself to matter, creating dark figures. At the end of the story, we have a hint of the Being of Love who can absorb all the dark forms and transform them into air and light. The darkness does not take over, but, squirming, it is absorbed into the great, quiet, powerful, and original being of Love. In his next incarnation as Mani, the youth of Nain will be able to transform evil into goodness—not by rejecting or avoiding evil, but by embracing it and returning it to its source in Eros, divine Love.

In ancient Greece, Aphrodite (in Latin, Venus) was known as the origin of illusion, linking the Illusionist Lucifer, the planet Venus, the focus of Eros through Venus, the connection of Venus to

---

8 Couliano, op. cit., p. 89, about Bruno's *De Vinculis in Genere* ("Of Chains in General"), a study of what binds us and our life force.

9 Freudians have studied this dynamic from the view of the libido (Eros, vital force) moving through the ego (structure of the personality) to *cathect* (attach) to objects.

the groups and initiatives to which one connects through destiny, and the illusions affecting the community.[10] This preparatory degree shows the workshop of Lucifer, the Illusionist.

Wrestling with Phantasms

It took months of observation of others, self-introspection, and research to come to terms with the true nature of erotic phantasms. So many pieces fell into place, pointing to this as the most important concept for the Venus 2004 eclipse: Wagner's opera *Parsifal* premiered in 1882, the year of the last Venus eclipse. At the end of that first performance, the Moon was at 23° Scorpio. At Wagner's birth, Neptune lay exactly at this same degree. The dark magician Klingsor paralleled the dark magic of Megiddo. In Wolfram von Eschenbach's version, Parsifal first entered the Grail Castle when Venus was conjunct the Sun. Wagner was born when Venus was conjunct the Sun—and so on. I wrestled with the themes and wrote my research in many drafts, which my colleagues generously read, struggled over, and offered streams of comment.

It all seemed so perfect—a rare celestial event pointing to dark powers that cripple individuals and the whole community, the young people overcome and suffocated, with a clear picture of what to do to heal this ailment. I had entered an erotic phantasm of high drama. I felt that the best I could do is to point out how one can create *positive* erotic phantasms, not ones that cripple and suffocate.

I now feel that all these details join in a prologue, not untrue, yet also not the true picture accentuated by the Venus 2004 eclipse and the total lunar eclipse of December 2011. This prologue prepares one for the twenty-fourth degree of the fixed signs.

---

10 Concerning Aphrodite as the origin of illusion, refer to the classical scholar, Peter Kingsley, *Reality* (Point Reyes, CA: Golden Sufi Center, 2004). Rudolf Steiner (*Man in the Light of Occultism, Theosophy, and Philosophy*, [Blauvelt, NY: Garber, 1989], pp. 165, 168) speaks of Lucifer as the same as Venus, thus connecting the seductive feminine with the master illusionist. Finally, Giordano Bruno names the chief mistress of phantasms: "The strongest chain is that of Venus…all bonds relate to the bond of love, either because they depend on it or because they are reduced to it…. The chain of chains is love" (cited in Couliano, op. cit., p. 97).

Twenty-fourth Degree of the Scorpion

In the next degree, the Solar Cross Image has to do with the visit by Jesus Christ to Megiddo, the fortress atop the small mountain (Har) of Megiddo, thus called Har Megiddo, abbreviated as "Armageddon," the site of the prophesied last battle between good and evil at the end of time. The fortress Megiddo ruled the passage through the valley, the best route from the North (Damascus, Greece, Asia Minor) to the South (Egypt). Megiddo was an important military site for many hundreds of years. When I visited there, I could feel wisps of very old magical spells, heavy and invasive.[11] Magic had been used for military purposes in those days as well as in ours, as leaked documents from military commands repeatedly prove.

In this degree, Jesus Christ set foot for the only time at the place of black magic and the place pointed to by John in the book of Revelation as the site of the end of time.

Twenty-fourth Degree of the Bull

In contrast, the main event that took place during the time of Christ's ministry—with the Sun between 23° and 24° of Taurus—was the Ascension of Jesus Christ, the lifting into increasingly brilliant light of this great avatar. After the death and resurrection—such mysteries, hardly comprehensible!—the being of Christ taught for some weeks before becoming so transparent and full of light that he completely disappeared into the etheric world of clouds. The light of Christ was so bright that none except Mother Mary could look upon it.

Twenty-fourth Degree of the Lion and the Waterbearer

Before exclaiming how extraordinary that polarity is, consider other aspects of this degree. At the twenty-fourth degree of the Lion, Mother Mary was assumed into heaven, in her own version of ascension. At the twenty-fourth degree of

---

11 Confirmed by Anastacia Nutt, whose specialty includes the perception of such energy patterns. See her excellent book, *Unseen Worlds and Practical Aspects of Spiritual Discernment* (Arcata, CA: R. J. Stewart Books, 2008).

the Waterbearer (Aquarius), Jesus Christ visited the source of the Jordan River, the most astonishing phenomenon at Banias, near Dan in the north of Israel, where water that melts from the snows of Mount Hermon and travels underground down to the arid lower lands suddenly bursts out of a hillside—a demonstration of beginnings.

The Solar Cross at the Twenty-fourth Degree of the Fixed Signs

The exact wording of the Solar Cross Images gives more information, more poetically. However, we do not have the space for that here. To summarize these events, we can note that there are beginnings from unseen creators—as expressed through the waters gushing out of a hillside at 23° to 24° Aquarius—contrasted with the place of endings, where the last battle will be fought at the end of time, as expressed at Megiddo at 23° to 24° Scorpio. Beginning beyond time and ending beyond time. The ascension into light of Jesus Christ at 23° to 24° Taurus parallels the ascension into light of Mother Mary at 23° to 24° Leo, the divine masculine and divine feminine linking in this 1°.

The work with erotic phantasms in the degree leading up to this degree gives the key to one's interpretation of these upcoming star events. A true appreciation for the beginning (Aquarius) and for the end (Scorpio), and the ascension into light of Mary (Leo) and Jesus Christ (Taurus)—with a focus on the ascension at Taurus, to which the 2004 Venus eclipse (Venus and Sun) and the Moon at the December 2011 lunar eclipse both point—goes beyond phantasms. There are no pictures that can accurately represent these events. It is not about finding a more positive phantasm to paper over the power of Eros. It is not about getting a better concept or picture. There is no great evil to encounter, no specific directions about what to do.

These events deserve the title "mysteries," not in a way that turns us away with dullness, but asks us to be even more awake. Those present at the ascension of Christ at 23° to 24° Taurus found the light that consumes all the forms was too bright to see anything. Some turned away; some continued their attempt to look into the light, unseeing and realizing that light surrounded and permeated them. None could make out pictures. Only Mother Mary could gaze calmly, because she knew the territory of Eros without phantasm. We can perceive in this extraordinary cross at the twenty-fourth degree of the fixed signs the revelation of Eros in its highest, most refined, and most powerful divine emanation, as life force itself, before and beyond form. The polarities dissolve each other into a celebration of being, without picture or concept.

To prepare for such an encounter, we can identify our own dark forms of habits and addictions—those that have all-too-familiar pictures or phantasms on top—the training we get from the twenty-third degree of Scorpio—and lift them into the light. Then we attend to the wonder of pre-form and post-form—what the ancient seers called *arupa*—which indeed lies behind and under all form and, in the end, does not require these preparations.

Coming to this twenty-fourth degree through the passageway of the previous twenty-third degree has helped me eschew forms in favor of the mysteries of the twenty-fourth degree, which the Venus 2004 eclipse and the December 2011 total lunar eclipse excite. The Venus 2012 eclipse will come with its own teaching about true leadership for humanity. For now, we can lift the dark forms of our phantasms into the air and light and participate in the power of life force itself, Eros.

&

WORKING WITH THE STAR CALENDER
IN THE *JOURNAL FOR STAR WISDOM*

In taking note of the astronomical events listed in the Star Calendar of the *Journal for Star Wisdom* (*JSW*), it is important to distinguish between long- and short-term astronomical events. Long-term astronomical events—for example, Pluto transiting a particular degree of the zodiac—will have a longer period of meditation than would the five days advocated for short-term astronomical events such as the new and full moon. The following describes, in relation to meditating on the full moon, a meditative process extending over a five-day period.

Sanctification of the full moon

As a preliminary remark, let us remind ourselves that the great sacrifice of Christ on the Cross—the Mystery of Golgotha—took place at full moon. As Christ's sacrifice took place when the Moon was full in the middle of the sidereal sign of Libra, the Libra full moon assumes special significance in the sequence of twelve (or thirteen) full moons taking place during the cycle of the year. In following this sequence, the Mystery of Golgotha serves as an archetype for *every* full moon, since each full moon imparts a particular spiritual blessing. Hence the practice described here of *Sanctification of the full moon* applies to every full moon. Similarly, there is also the practice of *Sanctification of the new moon*, as described in *Hermetic Astrology, Volume 2: Astrological Biography*, chapter 10.

During the two days prior to the full moon, we can consider the focus of one's meditation to extend over these two days as *preparatory days* immediately preceding the day of the full moon. These two days can be dedicated to spiritual reflection and detachment from everyday concerns, as one prepares to become a vessel for the in-streaming light and love one will receive at the full moon, something that one can then impart further—for example, to help people in need, or to support Mother Earth in times of catastrophe. During these two days, it is helpful to hold an attitude of dedication and service and try to assume an attitude of receptivity that opens to what one's soul will receive and subsequently impart—an attitude conducive to making one a true *servant of the spirit*.

The day of the full moon is itself a day of *holding the sacred space*. In doing so, one endeavors to cultivate inner peace and silence, during which one attempts to contact and consciously hold the in-streaming blessing of the full moon for the rest of humanity. One can heighten this silent meditation by visualizing the zodiacal constellation/sidereal sign in which the Moon becomes full, since the Moon serves to reflect the starry background against which it appears.

If the Moon is full in Virgo, for example, it reminds us of the night of the birth of the Jesus child visited by the three magi, as described in the Gospel of St. Matthew. That birth occurred at the full moon in the middle of the sidereal sign of Virgo, and the three magi, who gazed up that evening to behold the full moon against the background of the stars of the Virgin, witnessed the soul of Jesus emerge from the disk of the full moon and descend toward Earth. They participated from afar, via the starry heavens, in the Grail Mystery of the holy birth.

In meditating upon the full moon and opening oneself to receive the in-streaming blessing from the starry heavens, we can exercise restraint by avoiding the formulation of what will happen or what one might receive from the full moon. Moreover, we can also refrain from seeking tangible results or effects connected with our attunement to the full moon. Even if we observe only the date but not the exact moment when the Moon is full, it is helpful to find quiet time to reflect alone or to use the opportunity for deep meditation on the day of the full moon.

We can think of the two days following the full moon as a *time of imparting* what we have received from the in-streaming of the full disk of the Moon against the background of the stars. It is now possible to turn our attention toward humanity and the world and endeavor to pass on any spiritual blessing we have received from the starry heavens. Thereby we can assist in the work of the spiritual world by transforming what we have received into goodwill and allowing it to flow wherever the greatest need exists.

It is a matter of *holding a sacred space* throughout the day of the full moon. This is an important time to still the mind and maintain inner peace. It is a time of spiritual retreat and contact with the spiritual world, of holding in one's consciousness the archetype of the Mystery of Golgotha as a great outpouring of Divine Love that bridges Heaven and Earth. Prior to the day of the full moon, the two preceding days prepare the sacred space as a vessel to receive the heavenly blessing. The two days following the day of the full moon are a time to assimilate and distribute the spiritual transmission received into the sacred space we have prepared.

One can apply the process described here as a meditative practice in relation to the full moon to any of the astronomical events listed in the *JSW*, especially as most of these *remember* significant Christ Events. Take note, however, whether an event is long-term or short-term and adjust the period of meditative practice accordingly.

Symbols Used in Charts

	Planets		Zodiacal Signs		Aspects
⊕	Earth	♈	Aries (Ram)	☌	Conjunction 0°
☉	Sun	♉	Taurus (Bull)	✶	Sextile 60°
☽	Moon	♊	Gemini (Twins)	☐	Square 90°
☿	Mercury	♋	Cancer (Crab)	△	Trine 120°
♀	Venus	♌	Leo (Lion)	☍	Opposition 180°
♂	Mars	♍	Virgo (Virgin)		
♃	Jupiter	♎	Libra (Scales)		
♄	Saturn	♏	Scorpio (Scorpion)		
♅	Uranus	♐	Sagittarius (Archer)		
♆	Neptune	♑	Capricorn (Goat)		
♇	Pluto	♒	Aquarius (Water Carrier)		
		♓	Pisces (Fishes)		

Other

☊	Ascending (North) Node	☌⊙	Sun Eclipse
☋	Descending (South) Node	☍☽	Moon Eclipse
P	Perihelion/Perigee		Inferior Conjunction
A	Aphelion/Apogee		Superior Conjunction
	Maximum Latitude	⚷	Chiron
	Minimum Latitude		

TIME[1]

The information relating to daily geocentric and heliocentric planetary positions in the sidereal zodiac is tabulated in the form of an ephemeris for each month, where the planetary positions are given at 0 hours universal time (UT) each day. Beneath the geocentric and heliocentric ephemeris for each month, the information relating to planetary aspects is given in the form of an aspectarian, listing the most important aspects—geocentric and heliocentric/hermetic—between the planets for the month in question. The day and the time of occurrence of the aspect on that day are indicated, all times being given in universal time, which is identical to Greenwich mean time. For example, 0 hours universal time is midnight Greenwich time. This time system applies in Britain; however, when summer time is in use, one hour has to be added to all times.

In other countries, the time has to be adjusted according to whether it is ahead of or behind Britain. For example, in Germany, where the time is one hour ahead of British time, one hour has to be added and, when summer time is in use in Germany, two hours have to be added to all times. On the other hand, in California, where the time is eight hours behind that of London, eight hours have to be subtracted and, for daylight saving time in California, seven hours have to be subtracted from all times.[1] This subtraction will often change the date of an astronomical occurrence, shifting it back one day. On this account, since most of the readers of this calendar live on the American Continent, astronomical occurrences during the early hours of day x are listed as occurring on days x-1/x. For example, an eclipse occurring at 03:00 UT on the 12th is listed as occurring on the 11/12th since in America it takes place on the 11th.

---

1. See *General Introduction to the Christian Star Calendar: A Key to Understanding*, new edition (Palo Alto, CA: Sophia Foundation of North America, 2003) for an in-depth clarification of the features of the calendar in the *Journal for Star Wisdom,* including indications as to how to work with it. Using the calendar in the USA, do the following subtraction from all time indications according to time zone: Pacific time subtract 8 hours (7 hours when daylight saving time is in use); mountain time subtract 7 hours (6 hours when daylight saving time is in use); central time subtract 6 hours (5 hours when daylight saving time is in use); eastern time subtract 5 hours (4 hours when daylight saving time is in use).

COMMENTARIES AND EPHEMERIDES: JANUARY–DECEMBER 2011

The commentaries to the ephemerides of the *Journal for Star Wisdom* bring a deeper understanding of Astrosophy. Though we refer to specific events in *time*, through the movement of the stars, the Christ's teachings in the commentaries are *timeless*. The stars above and the events on Earth below are in continual resonance. The hermetic maxim "as above so below" is the essence of Star Wisdom. Christ was in continual connection with the stars throughout his ministry. The etheric sphere surrounding the Earth holds the memories of Christ's perfect biography. We can see these biographical memories as portals through which above and below communicate. Materialistic thinking creates another sphere around the Earth. We can liken that sphere to the thorn hedge around Sleeping Beauty's castle. It strives to prevent humanity from accessing the Christological memories of the perfect biography. Sophia, as the world of stars, is the Sleeping Beauty who awakens from behind the thorn hedge when human beings awake to the memories of Christ's life. Awakened human beings stand on the threshold to the spiritual world (as did the triumphant prince in the story of Sleeping Beauty) as witness to the hermetic revelations entering into the stream of time.

The following commentaries take us through the movement of the Stars as they align with the events of Christ's life. Christ is teaching through these events now, just as he taught through them during the forty days after the Resurrection. These images offer us an understanding of world events. This is part of the teachings in the school of the Greater Guardian—Christ in His Second Coming. As every move by Christ was in union with the beings of the stars, the events and the star locations are of great significance. Events in the life of Christ at his Second Coming are in reverse to events of the First Coming. The first event is the World Pentecost, a theme addressed by Valentin Tomberg in the appendix ("The Four Sacrifices of Christ") of his book, *Christ and Sophia*.[1]

World Pentecost is a time when the light of spiritual truth enlightens the Earth. It is related to 2012. We can liken this to living in a room with a ten-watt bulb that suddenly becomes a thousand-watt bulb. In the dim light, we cannot see much. As the watts increase, we see more of what is in the room. There comes a critical point when the light strikes directly through the windows of the room, causing immediate illumination. Some things in the room may be difficult to bear, but this is our time, and the changes that come with this period of illumination are spiritual gifts.

We live in a wilderness of materialism. The more we understand Christ and the beings of the stars, the greater will be the infusion of healing and transformation from the Archangel Michael and the wisdom of Sophia. These commentaries are offered to help us understand the planets and constellations (the beings of the stars) and to deepen our understanding of the life of Christ. In his three-and-a-half years on Earth, he brought the possibility of healing to every aspect of the Fall. The need for healing, of both the Earth and humanity, becomes more certain each year.

We encourage readers to take these commentaries in the spirit in which they are offered—as glimpses into the mysteries of spiritual causality behind world events. To unite with the mysteries

---

1 Valentin Tomberg, *Christ and Sophia: Anthroposophic Meditations on the Old Testament, New Testament, and Apocalypse* (Great Barrington, MA: SteinerBooks, 2006).

of Christ's biography helps us to unite with the presence of Christ in the etheric realm.

Three people contributed to the entries in the ephemeris. Sally Nurney wrote the summary of where to see planets in the sky. David Tresemer's initials (DT) follow his entries. Claudia McLaren Lainson wrote all other entries. We are deeply grateful to Richard Bloedon, who served as copyeditor for the commentaries.

Full and new moons last longer than the moment of the exact alignment. Some traditions honor them for seven days—three days before, the day of the alignment, and three days after. Thus, the themes for the day of alignment are magnified for at least that period, with effects rippling through the month. We give a range of days for the full moons as a reminder of this span of time. The same can be said of the new moons. David Tresemer draws from his work in the Oracle of the Solar Cross (described in *Star Wisdom & Rudolf Steiner*, from www.starwisdom.org) to elucidate the themes operative during the moon periods. As in the Solar Cross work, David tends to refer to Jesus Christ as the *Healer* or the *Teacher*.

We are unable to include everything for every date. We recommend that you collate these entries with past issues of the *Journal for Star Wisdom* to see what other events are resonant on the dates of the year. For the aspects, we emphasize those that are rare and usually involve Venus conjunctions. One of the main phenomena of 2012 is the very rare event on June 5/6, of Venus transiting across the face of the Sun, which occurs in pairs every 121.5 or 105.5 years, this being the second in a pair (the first occurred on June 8, 2004). More on that phenomenon will be in the 2012 *Journal for Star Wisdom*. Although they are usually too numerous to mention, we can look at some of the Venus conjunctions for this year, noting how they relate to the theme for Venus of gathering oneself to the group of brothers and sisters with whom one has the most serious destiny—one's "karmic group."

Themes are emphasized that can be taken into meditation for a day or a week or for the entire month.

The closing words of Rudolf Steiner's Foundation Stone Meditation are words through which the human being turns to the Etheric Christ for his light in one's mind, his love in one's heart, and his goodness in one's will:

O Light Divine,

O Sun of Christ,

Warm thou our hearts,

Enlighten thou our heads,

That good may become

What, from our hearts, we found

And, from our heads, direct

With single purpose.

—*this is the essence of all that comes to expression in these commentaries for the* Journal for Star Wisdom.

JANUARY

We begin the year with the Sun in the middle of the Archer (Sagittarius), hiding Mars in its light. This is an invitation for daytime stargazing, using capacities of the heart, rather than the physical eyes! We have many opportunities during this (and every) year to open to the planets invisible by day. Knowing what planets are hidden in the radiant light of the Sun opens a connection by day that carries into the night.

The 4th is a new moon and partial solar eclipse that includes Mars, still close to the Sun. Also, Jupiter is visible after sunset to the southwest in the Fishes (Pisces) and the Quandrantids meteor shower peaks this day. Look to the northeast, below the Big Dipper after dark.

Venus begins 2011 as brilliant morning star in the first degrees of Scorpio and continues to rise before the Sun until August of this year. The Sun enters into Capricorn on the 15th. The Moon appears full on the 19th. Late-nighters on the 25th can enjoy the waning half moon conjoined with Saturn in Virgo, near the star Spica (29° Virgo), rising to the east just after midnight. Two days later, Saturn stations Retrograde, and will appear to move backward against the Zodiac until it stations Direct in mid-June.

January 1: Sun 16° Sagittarius: birth of the Nathan Jesus. The year begins with the commemoration of this Holy birth. Still today, the archangelic Nathan being is our shepherd and our mediator to Christ and Sophia. How do we find him now, and where? We find him as our heart matures into an open chalice. In this state of humble receptivity we become more concerned with the needs of others than with our own egoistic selves. In the process of gradually opening, the archangelic shepherd can draw near from spirit realms. Blessed are the peacekeepers, for they are the humble servants of the shepherd and they strive to regulate human communities on Earth with the same harmony and love that regulates the community of stars in the heavens. The peacekeepers are forming a new leadership.

The seeds for new leadership were planted at the beginning of the twenty-first century, in 2000, when Jupiter and Saturn came into conjunction in the constellation of the Ram (Aries). Saturn and Jupiter come together approximately every twenty years. This meeting marks one of the rhythmical spiritual "touches" of divine guidance. Saturn calls for the renewal of form, Jupiter calls for the renewal of wisdom in communities. Into this union, between Saturn and Jupiter, between form and community, spiritual guidance finds its footing.

Midway through a Saturn–Jupiter conjunction is the opposition. This year of 2011 marks the final of three oppositions between Jupiter and Saturn (March 28, 2011). The conjunction in 2000 was the beginning of a spiritual awakening in nature.[1] Peace and harmony between all beings, including the beings of nature, were the seeds then sown. Now, more than ten years later, this new leadership and nature's awakening are being tested for the third and final time. The tension mounts as to the nature of the leadership that humanity will choose—or the leadership that will instead be chosen for us! The Second Coming of Christ is creating a stream of leadership founded on love and collaboration.

In preparation for the First Coming of Christ, the Rachel being, the wife of Jacob, tended the children of Israel, nourishing them with the milk and honey of grace and love. The Bible tells us that Rachel wept for her children, her tears creating a mirror in the group soul of Israel, into which divine guidance could find its reflection. The John being came into this prepared stream as witness to the birth of Christ. Now, in the time of the Second Coming, the John being is here again, working, as was Rachel before the First Coming, to guide human beings seeking Christ and Sophia. Again we live in a time of choosing. One choice leads us toward the New Jerusalem, the other to the Antichrist. The New Jerusalem can be seen as the rarefied state of consciousness belonging to future humanity.

A sacrificing angel, who united with the Nathan Jesus being, watches over human beings. This angel has sacrificed its lower sheaths so that Christ might work into humanity on Earth (see

---

[1] See Robert Powell's article in the *Christian Star Calendar 2000*.

SIDEREAL GEOCENTRIC LONGITUDES : JANUARY 2011 Gregorian at 0 hours UT

DAY	☉	☽	☊	☿	♀	♂	♃	♄	♅	♆	♇
1 SA	15 ♐ 19	4 ♏ 21	7 ♐ 52	24 ♏ 57	28 ♎ 41	23 ♐ 29	1 ♓ 40	21 ♍ 46	2 ♓ 4	1 ♒ 51	10 ♐ 27
2 SU	16 20	17 46	7 52	25 16	29 38	24 16	1 48	21 49	2 5	1 53	10 29
3 MO	17 21	0 ♐ 57	7 53	25 42	0 ♏ 37	25 2	1 56	21 51	2 7	1 55	10 31
4 TU	18 22	13 56	7 53R	26 14	1 36	25 49	2 5	21 54	2 8	1 56	10 33
5 WE	19 24	26 41	7 52	26 53	2 35	26 35	2 13	21 56	2 10	1 58	10 35
6 TH	20 25	9 ♑ 12	7 51	27 37	3 35	27 22	2 22	21 58	2 11	2 0	10 37
7 FR	21 26	21 31	7 49	28 26	4 35	28 9	2 31	22 0	2 13	2 2	10 39
8 SA	22 27	3 ♒ 38	7 47	29 19	5 36	28 55	2 40	22 2	2 14	2 4	10 42
9 SU	23 28	15 37	7 44	0 ♐ 16	6 37	29 42	2 49	22 4	2 16	2 5	10 44
10 MO	24 29	27 30	7 42	1 16	7 38	0 ♑ 29	2 58	22 6	2 18	2 7	10 46
11 TU	25 31	9 ♓ 22	7 40	2 19	8 40	1 15	3 7	22 8	2 20	2 9	10 48
12 WE	26 32	21 16	7 40	3 25	9 42	2 2	3 17	22 9	2 21	2 11	10 50
13 TH	27 33	3 ♈ 17	7 40D	4 34	10 45	2 49	3 27	22 11	2 23	2 13	10 52
14 FR	28 34	15 30	7 41	5 44	11 48	3 36	3 36	22 12	2 25	2 15	10 54
15 SA	29 35	28 0	7 42	6 57	12 51	4 23	3 46	22 13	2 27	2 17	10 56
16 SU	0 ♑ 36	10 ♉ 50	7 44	8 11	13 54	5 10	3 56	22 14	2 29	2 19	10 58
17 MO	1 37	24 4	7 45	9 27	14 58	5 57	4 6	22 15	2 31	2 21	11 0
18 TU	2 38	7 ♊ 43	7 46R	10 44	16 2	6 43	4 17	22 16	2 33	2 23	11 2
19 WE	3 39	21 46	7 45	12 3	17 7	7 30	4 27	22 17	2 35	2 25	11 4
20 TH	4 41	6 ♋ 10	7 43	13 23	18 11	8 17	4 38	22 18	2 37	2 27	11 6
21 FR	5 42	20 50	7 40	14 44	19 16	9 4	4 48	22 18	2 40	2 29	11 8
22 SA	6 43	5 ♌ 38	7 36	16 6	20 22	9 51	4 59	22 19	2 42	2 31	11 10
23 SU	7 44	20 26	7 31	17 29	21 27	10 39	5 10	22 19	2 44	2 33	11 12
24 MO	8 45	5 ♍ 8	7 27	18 54	22 33	11 26	5 21	22 20	2 46	2 36	11 14
25 TU	9 46	19 36	7 24	20 19	23 39	12 13	5 32	22 20	2 49	2 38	11 16
26 WE	10 47	3 ♎ 48	7 22	21 45	24 45	13 0	5 43	22 20	2 51	2 40	11 18
27 TH	11 48	17 41	7 22D	23 11	25 51	13 47	5 54	22 20R	2 53	2 42	11 20
28 FR	12 49	1 ♏ 15	7 23	24 39	26 58	14 34	6 6	22 20	2 56	2 44	11 22
29 SA	13 50	14 33	7 25	26 7	28 5	15 21	6 17	22 20	2 58	2 46	11 24
30 SU	14 51	27 35	7 26	27 37	29 12	16 9	6 29	22 19	3 1	2 49	11 26
31 MO	15 52	10 ♐ 23	7 27R	29 7	0 ♐ 19	16 56	6 40	22 19	3 3	2 51	11 28

INGRESSES :

2 ♀ → ♏ 8:54
☽ → ♐ 22:14
5 ☽ → ♑ 6:19
7 ☽ → ♒ 16:46
8 ☿ → ♐ 17:28
9 ♂ → ♑ 9:16
10 ☽ → ♓ 5: 2
12 ☽ → ♈ 17:28
15 ☽ → ♉ 3:46
☉ → ♑ 9:46
17 ☽ → ♊ 10:31
19 ☽ → ♋ 13:47
21 ☽ → ♌ 14:53
23 ☽ → ♍ 15:35
25 ☽ → ♎ 17:31
27 ☽ → ♏ 21:45
30 ☽ → ♐ 4:30
♀ → ♐ 17:10
31 ☿ → ♑ 14: 9

ASPECTS & ECLIPSES :

2 ☽ ☌ ☿ 14: 1
3 ☽ ☌ ☊ 12:45
☽ ☌ ♇ 17:41
4 ♀ □ ♆ 8:36
☉ ● P 8:50
☉ ☌ ☽ 9: 2
♃ ☌ ♅ 12:19
☽ ☌ ♂ 23:49
7 ☉ □ ♄ 13:53
☽ ☌ ♆ 20:51
10 ☽ ☌ A 5:41
☽ ☌ ♅ 9:42
☽ ☌ ♃ 11:11
☽ N ☊ 20:34
11 ☿ □ ♅ 0: 6
☿ □ ♃ 20:33
12 ☽ ☍ ♄ 1:46
☉ □ ☽ 11:31
15 ☿ ☌ ☊ 15: 4
16 ☽ ☍ ♀ 6: 7
18 ☽ ☌ ☋ 0: 4
☿ ☌ ♇ 5:44
☽ ☍ ♇ 5:45
☽ ☍ ☿ 5:45
19 ☉ ☍ ☽ 21:21
20 ☽ ☍ ♂ 3:41
21 ☽ ☍ ♆ 18:57
22 ☽ ☌ P 0:17
23 ☽ ☍ ♅ 20: 7
24 ☽ ☍ ♃ 0:21
☽ S ☊ 3:48
25 ☽ ☌ ♄ 4:34
26 ☿ □ ♄ 9:46
☉ □ ☽ 12:57
30 ☽ ☌ ♀ 3:17
☽ ☌ ☊ 18:26
31 ☽ ☌ ♇ 2: 1

SIDEREAL HELIOCENTRIC LONGITUDES : JANUARY 2011 Gregorian at 0 hours UT

DAY	Sid. Time	☿	♀	⊕	♂	♃	♄	♅	♆	♇	Vernal Point
1 SA	6:41:12	10 ♌ 47	23 ♋ 51	15 ♊ 19	29 ♐ 10	12 ♓ 47	15 ♍ 55	4 ♓ 48	3 ♒ 13	10 ♐ 17	5 ♓ 6'24"
2 SU	6:45: 8	15 29	25 29	16 20	29 46	12 53	15 56	4 48	3 13	10 18	5 ♓ 6'24"
3 MO	6:49: 5	20 2	27 6	17 21	0 ♑ 23	12 58	15 58	4 49	3 13	10 18	5 ♓ 6'23"
4 TU	6:53: 1	24 26	28 44	18 22	0 59	13 4	16 0	4 49	3 14	10 18	5 ♓ 6'23"
5 WE	6:56:58	28 42	0 ♌ 21	19 23	1 36	13 9	16 2	4 50	3 14	10 19	5 ♓ 6'23"
6 TH	7: 0:55	2 ♍ 50	1 59	20 25	2 13	13 15	16 4	4 51	3 14	10 19	5 ♓ 6'23"
7 FR	7: 4:51	6 51	3 36	21 26	2 49	13 20	16 6	4 51	3 15	10 19	5 ♓ 6'23"
8 SA	7: 8:48	10 44	5 14	22 27	3 26	13 26	16 8	4 52	3 15	10 20	5 ♓ 6'23"
9 SU	7:12:44	14 31	6 51	23 28	4 3	13 31	16 10	4 53	3 15	10 20	5 ♓ 6'23"
10 MO	7:16:41	18 11	8 29	24 29	4 40	13 37	16 12	4 53	3 16	10 20	5 ♓ 6'22"
11 TU	7:20:37	21 46	10 6	25 30	5 16	13 42	16 14	4 54	3 16	10 21	5 ♓ 6'22"
12 WE	7:24:34	25 15	11 44	26 31	5 53	13 48	16 16	4 55	3 17	10 21	5 ♓ 6'22"
13 TH	7:28:30	28 39	13 21	27 33	6 30	13 53	16 18	4 55	3 17	10 21	5 ♓ 6'22"
14 FR	7:32:27	1 ♎ 59	14 59	28 34	7 7	13 59	16 20	4 56	3 17	10 22	5 ♓ 6'22"
15 SA	7:36:24	5 14	16 36	29 35	7 44	14 4	16 22	4 57	3 18	10 22	5 ♓ 6'22"
16 SU	7:40:20	8 25	18 14	0 ♋ 36	8 21	14 10	16 24	4 57	3 18	10 22	5 ♓ 6'22"
17 MO	7:44:17	11 33	19 51	1 37	8 58	14 15	16 26	4 58	3 18	10 23	5 ♓ 6'21"
18 TU	7:48:13	14 38	21 28	2 38	9 35	14 21	16 28	4 58	3 19	10 23	5 ♓ 6'21"
19 WE	7:52:10	17 39	23 6	3 39	10 13	14 26	16 30	4 59	3 19	10 23	5 ♓ 6'21"
20 TH	7:56: 6	20 38	24 43	4 40	10 50	14 32	16 32	5 0	3 19	10 24	5 ♓ 6'21"
21 FR	8: 0: 3	23 34	26 20	5 41	11 27	14 37	16 34	5 0	3 20	10 24	5 ♓ 6'21"
22 SA	8: 3:59	26 28	27 58	6 42	12 4	14 43	16 36	5 1	3 20	10 24	5 ♓ 6'21"
23 SU	8: 7:56	29 20	29 35	7 43	12 42	14 49	16 38	5 2	3 20	10 25	5 ♓ 6'21"
24 MO	8:11:53	2 ♏ 10	1 ♍ 12	8 44	13 19	14 54	16 40	5 2	3 21	10 25	5 ♓ 6'21"
25 TU	8:15:49	4 59	2 49	9 45	13 56	15 0	16 42	5 3	3 21	10 25	5 ♓ 6'20"
26 WE	8:19:46	7 47	4 27	10 46	14 34	15 5	16 44	5 4	3 22	10 26	5 ♓ 6'20"
27 TH	8:23:42	10 33	6 4	11 47	15 11	15 11	16 46	5 4	3 22	10 26	5 ♓ 6'20"
28 FR	8:27:39	13 19	7 41	12 48	15 49	15 16	16 48	5 5	3 22	10 26	5 ♓ 6'20"
29 SA	8:31:35	16 4	9 18	13 49	16 26	15 22	16 50	5 6	3 23	10 27	5 ♓ 6'20"
30 SU	8:35:32	18 49	10 55	14 50	17 3	15 27	16 52	5 6	3 23	10 27	5 ♓ 6'20"
31 MO	8:39:28	21 34	12 32	15 51	17 41	15 33	16 54	5 7	3 23	10 27	5 ♓ 6'20"

INGRESSES :

2 ♂ → ♑ 8:54
4 ♀ → ♌ 18:47
5 ☿ → ♍ 7:27
13 ☿ → ♎ 9:38
15 ⊕ → ♋ 9:53
23 ☿ → ♏ 5:39
♀ → ♍ 6:11

ASPECTS (HELIOCENTRIC +MOON(TYCHONIC)) :

1 ⊕ □ ♄ 14:31
2 ☿ ⚹ ⊕ 5:41
3 ☽ ☌ ♇ 17:14
⊕ ☌ P 20:47
5 ☽ ☌ ♂ 9:52
☿ △ ♂ 19:40
6 ☿ ☍ ♅ 11:58
♀ ☍ ♆ 18:41
7 ☿ □ ♇ 21:27
☽ ☌ ♆ 23:13
8 ☽ ☍ ♀ 3:40
☿ ☍ ♃ 17:30
9 ☿ ☌ ♄ 10:51
10 ♂ ⚹ ♅ 9: 6
☽ ☌ ♅ 14:57
11 ♀ △ ♇ 3:32
☽ ☌ ♃ 8:50
☽ ☍ ♄ 13:55
12 ☽ ☍ ☿ 11:10
☿ □ ⊕ 12:42
14 ☿ △ ♆ 9:35
15 ☿ □ ♂ 23:20
16 ☿ ⚹ ♇ 14:54
18 ☽ ☍ ♇ 4:36
♀ N ☊ 6: 7
20 ⊕ △ ♅ 7:46
☽ ☍ ♂ 8: 0
21 ☿ ☌ ☋ 0: 3
☽ ☍ ♆ 20:17
23 ☿ ⚹ ♀ 4:56
☽ ☌ ♀ 16:45
☽ ☍ ♅ 23:51
24 ☿ □ ♆ 10: 3
☽ ☍ ♃ 16:15
☽ ☌ ♄ 19: 8
25 ☿ △ ♅ 0:34
26 ♀ ☍ ♅ 9:13
♂ ⚹ ♃ 23:36
27 ☿ △ ⊕ 16:57
28 ☿ △ ♃ 17:34
29 ☽ ☌ ☿ 3:31
☿ ⚹ ♂ 4: 6
☿ ⚹ ♄ 6:45
♂ △ ♄ 16:14
♀ □ ♇ 17: 4
30 ⊕ △ ♃ 15:55
31 ☽ ☌ ♇ 0: 7
☿ ☌ A 10:15

Rudolf Steiner, *The Four Sacrifices of Christ*). Now this angel is in its fifth sacrifice and has sacrificed the ability to gaze into the mighty vistas of the spiritual world. This has caused a kind of swooning in its own being.[2] Yet through the open chalice of the selfless servants of Christ and Sophia, this being can awaken into the consciousness of awakened human hearts, thereby shepherding forward individuals and groups choosing to serve the reappearance of Christ in the etheric realm. Christ's etheric nature is feminine, thus the Second Coming is a great empowerment of the Divine Feminine. Saturn and Jupiter conjoining in Aries, the constellation of self-sacrifice, is an imagination of the Second Coming. The spiritual world then asked human beings to form communities (Jupiter), into which the forming power (Saturn) of Christ and Sophia could work. In this final opposition (March 2011), Saturn stands in Virgo (the Virgin), bringing form to the streams of Divine Wisdom (Sophia). Jupiter stands in Pisces, the constellation of Love.

May the commemoration of this holy birth, in these times of blatant opposition to what is truly human, remind us that there is a choice to be made. An angel has sacrificed spiritual sight, so that *we* may see the way forward in spite of the distractions by those who follow a different leader—a shepherd who leads his sheep more deeply into materialism and who grows more desperate as time inches toward the world change of World Pentecost (see Robert Powell's article in the 2010 *Journal*).

We begin our year with this angelic human, who awakens in us as we awake to others. May we serve the good, name what is evil, and be blessed to know the difference.

January 2: Mercury conjunct Moon 25° Scorpio. Mercury stood at this very degree on December 6, 2 B.C., when the Nathan Jesus was born, as well as at the conception of the Virgin Mary. This moment of communion between the Moon and Mercury remembers the hermetic undertaking ("as above, so below," or Mercury) of Jesus Christ and the Virgin Mary, who brought the light of understanding through the gateway of the Moon into the Scorpionic realms of the underworld. This was Christ's three-day descent into Hell. It was the Virgin Mary who spiritually bore witness to Christ's mighty trial. Mercury in Scorpio reveals the hidden dynamics behind the world of the senses. It can plumb the depths and/or soar to the heights, as exemplified through both Judas and John. Judas received the sting of the scorpion, and he met death. John received the wings of the eagle, and he wrote the Book of Revelation. Today and for the next seven days (Mercury in Scorpio), our thinking has penetrating insight, and we may ask: What lies hidden beneath and above the interactions we may witness or be a party to?

January 4: New moon and partial solar eclipse, 19° Sagittarius (DT): Fruitfulness. In a fruit-growing region, Jesus spoke about fruit trees that wave about, drawing much attention to themselves, and yet produce little fruit. He invites us to ask: How much flurry am I making in my life and community, and how much actual fruit am I bearing, for myself and for my community? An important connection is with the new moon on March 4 (more there): the Healer visits the daughter of Jairus after she has been cured; at this point, we find her strong and happy.

ASPECT (DT): Jupiter conjunct Uranus. This is the third and final pass of Jupiter over the position of Uranus at 2° Pisces, the prior ones having occurred on June 8 and September 19, 2010. William Bento wrote at length about this aspect in the *Journal for Star Wisdom, 2010*. In short, big (Jupiter) unexpected (Uranus) occurrences can occur, or be seeded, in this period from December 26 to January 13. In this aspect Max Planck (1858–1947) proposed that vibrating atoms that emit light do so in discrete amounts, that is, in *quanta*. This was the beginning of all the uses of *quantum* that we see today, as in "quantum shift," "quantum health" and "quantum of solace."

This new moon recalls the conception of the Virgin Mary, when Sun, Jupiter, and Moon all stood close together—also during a new moon at 18° to 19° Sagittarius. The Virgin Mary is the

---

2 See Robert Powell's article "Valentin Tomberg: A Platonic Soul," at sophiafoundation.org/articles.

individuality who walked the Earth as the Queen of the South:

> The queen of the South will rise at the judgment with this generation and condemn it, for she came from the ends of the Earth to hear the wisdom of Solomon, and behold, something greater than Solomon is here. (Matt. 12:42)

Ultimately, it is the content of our speech that the Queen from the South will judge: "Out of the abundance of the heart the mouth speaks" (Matt. 12:34). With this new moon in Sagittarius (control of speech), it is a powerful time to reflect on the moral content of our speech. Our speech reveals the degree to which one's "I" governs the lower passions and desires.

ASPECT: Jupiter conjunct Uranus, 2° Pisces. Today is a clarion call for the "Fools of Christ," who are choosing to form visionary communities (Jupiter–Uranus) born of free and moral goodwill. Those who are truly free have the wisdom (Jupiter) to become the fools. When Christ descended into the underworld, he was powerless against Ahriman, and Ahriman is powerless in the face of powerlessness. When we have nothing to defend and no need to convince, we become the "Fool"—free human beings standing as a uniting force between opposites. Free human beings are open to receive the illuminating imaginations coming from the future (Uranus). This final of three conjunctions between Jupiter and Uranus in Pisces asks us to free ourselves from binding conventions, so that we may find the magnanimity (Pisces) to perceive new possibilities, new paradigms in social wellness. By contrast, destructive, though brilliant, ideas (negative Uranus) enslave communities through the agendas of tyrannical (negative Jupiter) power mongers. We can ask: Where does my conventional thinking block my receptivity for the new?

January 15: Sun enters Capricorn. Courage becomes the power of redemption, the power to develop conscience and the insight to know what is right. On this day last year, Pluto crossed 8° 55 Sagittarius, exactly where it was at the third temptation of Christ. Just three days before this major event[3] a 7.0 earthquake struck Haiti. This was the country's worst earthquake in more than 200 years.

January 18: ASPECT: Mercury conjunct Pluto, 11° Sagittarius. Mercury and Pluto were conjunct at 11° Sagittarius at the second conversion of Mary Magdalene (December 26, 30). The healing forces of Mercury moved through Christ from the realm of the Father (higher Pluto–Phanes) as he freed Magdalene of possession (lower Pluto–Hades). "The influences that entered us over the course of our incarnations are still at work. They are still present and remain effective throughout our lives, though we know nothing about them. This is what the great Buddha realized."[4] Buddha brought the teachings of the eightfold path as remedy to these parasitic forces that we carry from one incarnation to another. These were the forces that Christ freed from Magdalene. The ten-petal lotus flower is the Mercury chakra. It is always awake and holds all memories from our current incarnation. If one does not decide definitively to serve the good, one may unwittingly serve evil, for such parasites are clever. Acute vigilance is needed today in memory of the healing of Magdalene from possessing forces. This is a propitious day to meditate on the higher aspect of Pluto (Divine Love) and to take inventory of our ability to discern what is true and what is not true (Mercury). We may ask: How free is my thinking? A demon is an autonomous being that possesses a mental life of its own. Demons work against the intentions of the human individual. What lives in me that has not been chosen freely? Am I free from desiring and coveting?

January 19 (16-19-22): Full moon, 4° Capricorn (DT). Complicated intertwined human dynamics. A servant of a wealthy man approaches the Healer to ask in desperation for healing of the wealthy man's son. The Healer can see immediately that the servant is the actual father, though revealing this would be dangerous for many people. The Healer

---

3   See *Journal for Star Wisdom 2010*.

4   Steiner, *According to Luke: The Gospel of Compassion and Love Revealed* (Great Barrington, MA: SteinerBooks, 2001), p. 66.

recommends that the public father, the wealthy man, lie upon the boy, eye-to-eye and heart-to-heart, and speak certain prayers. Then the servant lies upon the boy, eye-to-eye and heart-to-heart, and breathes into the boy's mouth, whereupon a dark blue vapor exits the boy's mouth and he is made whole. How do the hidden complications of our socio-sexual lives affect those around us? How was the boy affected by the intrigues taking place between the adults? How can we sort out these complications and make everyone whole?

This full moon remembers the July 21, 2009 solar eclipse, two years ago, at 4° Cancer, where the Moon is today. This was the longest solar eclipse of the twenty-first century, with Pluto standing so very close to *exactly* where it was at the Baptism of Jesus, when the Light of the World entered earthly existence. The lengthy solar eclipse of 2009 was an inversion of the Baptism; it was the darkening of the light. Principalities striving against Christ are empowered during an eclipse. Today, the full moon illumines the darkness of that eclipse as it shines forth in Cancer. The beings of the constellation of Cancer work through catharsis to bring human breathing into harmony with cosmic breathing (Cancer forms the rib cage, which shelters the lungs).

The process of catharsis frees human beings into harmony with cosmic respiration. Catharsis releases false attachments of egoism. Today's full moon asks us to connect with our inner work of transformation, which leads to catharsis. In catharsis, the small house of the ego unfolds into the larger house of the "I," but only after having passed through the "still point"—the eye of the needle between inhalation and exhalation. This still point stands between the karmic past and future destiny. Catharsis can be experienced as the fusion of time and space, collapsed into a still point, where all that has played out in time is experienced in a single condensed, timeless moment. It requires selflessness to endure this transformative and cathartic timeless space of the still point. Lack of selflessness is egoism, which prevents catharsis. Enduring the still point allows us to emerge from our enclosed crab shells into greater oneness with cosmic respiration. Whatever the nature of the eclipse two years ago, the antidote to any darkness is to breathe in light. The light gained through catharsis awakens us to any intrigues that may be afoot as a result of that 2009 eclipse. We may ask: What forces strive against the principles of peace and harmony among all beings? The Sun was at this degree when Philip was summoned to be a disciple. And we can look to the nature of Philip for inspiration; he was modest and humble. The Moon was here at the birth of John the Baptist. This witness to the true light was uncompromising in the face of the hardened Pharisaic teachings. This full moon asks us to courageously face truth with humility so that we may find catharsis. This work is a signature of the next few years.

January 21: Sun 6° Capricorn. The Adoration of the Magi (December 26, 6 B.C.). The magi were those who continued the Chaldean astrological tradition inaugurated in Babylon by Zarathustra in the sixth century B.C. The Jupiter and Saturn conjunction in 7 B.C., in Pisces, could be viewed as the onset of the magi's star, as this conjunction marked the beginning of the revelations of their teacher "Radiant Star" (Zarathustra), whose rebirth as the Solomon Jesus this conjunction foretold. At the birth of the Solomon Jesus, the magi spiritually beheld a joyous image:

> From the womb of Mary, in her house in Bethlehem, the newborn child emerged to begin a new incarnation upon the Earth. And at this very moment the magi beheld an awe-inspiring vision in the heavens. They saw the full moon in the Virgin, whereby the Virgin appeared standing on the Moon. In her right hand she was holding a sheaf of wheat, at the tip of which was the ear of corn (Spica), and on her left side was a vine. Encircling the Moon they saw a magnificent halo, a rainbow of light, upon which the Virgin was enthroned. Issuing forth from the Virgin they beheld a chalice—the sacred vessel of the Grail—from which there arose a child. Above the child's head was a disc, like the Blessed Sacrament, from which rays of light streamed forth. The child was radiant with light, and

proceeded from the Virgin toward them; and they knew that they were to follow it. And it was this child of radiant light, the incarnating soul of "Radiant Star" himself, which was the star that later guided them to the place of the birth.[5]

The soul of their teacher went before them, guiding them as a star, to the place of his birth. This was not an outwardly perceptible star. This belongs to the mysteries of the Holy Grail. The magi lose sight of the star as they near Jerusalem. Herod's realm has become dark and starless. It is not until they leave Jerusalem and draw near Bethlehem that the star of this great soul shines forth again, leading them forward. The position of today's Sun reminds us that there is a star above our heads just as there was a star leading the magi. This star leads us toward our true destiny. Christ is this star! We are to remember how easily we can lose our way in the overcast skies of materialism. We are emerging from the depths of winter's night filled with the gift of Christmas. This gift is the light of the Christ child born anew in human hearts each Christmastide. The magi, as representatives of the soul of humanity, remind us to cherish this gift—for it represents our future spiritual potential for the coming year. Thus we are encouraged to follow our star no matter how strongly the forces of materialism press upon us. We may ask: Am I tending faithfully the germinal new beginnings stirring from the depths of my being? Am I following the star above my head?

Also at this Sun degree, the second conversion of Mary Magdalene is remembered (see January 18 above). She stands as representative of all human souls. Today's Sun remembers this profound transformation of the human astral body, when Jesus addressed those gathered and offered to drive the forces of possession from those longing to be freed, and he told those willing to keep this bondage to leave. Today the Adoration and the Conversion stand witness to both the victory over materialism (the star that leads us out of materialism) and to victory over its consequence in the human soul (Magdalene's conversion). We may ask: Will we stay, and hear Christ, or will we leave?

Of Note: In 2010, Sun 6° Capricorn, the Supreme Court ruled that corporations are entities that may spend money without limit in political campaigns. Here we can see the inversion of the adoration of the magi. The magi bowed before the One who would sacrifice himself for others. Corporations tend to be kings who would sacrifice others for themselves. The twenty-first century will ask us to actively choose whom we adore, lest the choice will be made for us.

January 29: Sun 14° Capricorn: Beheading of John the Baptist. John the Baptist is the great individuality whom Rudolf Steiner foretold would be with us again at the end of the twentieth century, to lead humanity past the great crisis it would then be facing. As John was there to behold the Light at the First Coming, so is this being here again to meet those witnessing the true Light of the Second Coming. John was united with Lazarus when Lazarus was raised from the dead. The John being in collaboration with the Lazarus being are initiates now preparing us to meet our individual shadow natures in preparation for meeting and withstanding the encounter with the collective shadow nature of humanity.[6] As John, after his beheading, became the guardian of the circle of disciples of Christ, so now does John serve as guardian for the community of disciples working with Michael and Sophia in the name of Christ during this time of the Second Coming. John was beheaded. We may ask: Can I cast off the limitations of brain-bound thinking, so that I may think with the heart? Capricorn works to transform darkness into light—to steadfastly meet resistance from rigid thought forms holding on to the past. We are not to fear resistance; we are to meet it with equanimity. We are to overcome the limitations of ordinary reality as did John the Baptist. May our heads serve our hearts!

---

5 Powell, *Christian Hermetic Astrology*, p. 33.

6 See Powell, "World Pentecost," *Journal for Star Wisdom 2010*.

FEBRUARY

The Sun begins in Capricorn (the Sea Goat) and moves into Aquarius (the Water Carrier) on the 14th. The new moon on the 3rd involves Sun, Moon and Mars, as in January, but now in front of the Sea Goat. The full moon is on the 18th with Sun in the Water Carrier and Moon in Leo (the Lion).

Uranus (not visible to the naked eye) and Jupiter (easily visible) are in the southwest at sunset in front of the Fishes (Pisces) until the beginning days of March, when Jupiter disappears into the Sun's glow. The waxing moon on the 6th joins Jupiter, visible to the west in the evening sky.

On the 21st, early risers can again catch the waning half moon meeting with Saturn near the star Spica (29° Virgo) in the southwestern sky.

February 3: new moon, 19° Capricorn (DT): The knowing glance. The crazy and possessed are presented to the Healer. With a knowing glance, the Healer sees the soul within each, beset by concepts, patterns, and foreign intelligences. This glance releases them from possession. The people emerge as if coming out of a dream, and recall nothing of what they had said or done or thought while in the previous state of possession. Though possession is not popular to speak about, one can see it in every direction, and in oneself—possession by habits and desires and compulsions to behave in certain ways. The "knowing glance" does not study the negative pattern; rather it simply names it, and thus it affirms the greater power of selfhood temporarily squashed by the weight of the distractions. How can we develop the knowing glance for ourselves and for others?

February 4: ASPECT: Sun conjunct Mars 20° Capricorn. John the Baptist stands out as a stunning example of the power of Sun and Mars working together. The radiance of Sun forces working through the individuality of John, combined with his fiery ability to speak the living Word, made him a threat to his enemies and an inspiration to the faithful. When Sun and Mars come together, both the highest and lowest expressions are possible. This aspect grants us the opportunity to meditate on the radiance of our "I" and its command over our words. The opposite of the John being's example is when egoism sparks words of conflict, deceit, and harm. What fire stands behind our words? Can we stand in our truth?

ASPECT: Today through the 17th, Neptune is passing through the exact degrees of the zodiac that it did during the period from the Passion of Christ through the Ascension.

February 10: Sun 26° Capricorn. The Presentation in the Temple (January 15, 1 B.C.). According to traditional Jewish law, sanctification of the firstborn should take place on the fortieth day after birth. This was also a naming day for the infant. The Holy Family traveled to Jerusalem and stayed on the outskirts of town. The following day, they set off for the temple. It was still dark when Mary and Joseph arrived with their infant son. Simeon, the old priest of the temple, had been told in a dream the previous night that the first child presented that morning would be the Messiah. When Simeon saw the infant Jesus, he was taken up in rapturous joy. Rudolf Steiner tells us that Simeon was the reincarnation of Asita, who was a sage during the time of the Buddha. Asita wept when he saw the little Bodhisattva who would become Buddha, for he knew he would not live to see the day when the Bodhisattva would walk the Earth as the Buddha. But now, in his incarnation as Simeon, he was granted witness to the Buddha. The astral sheath of the Nathan Jesus was filled with the presence of the Buddha:

> When the Buddha appeared to the shepherds in the image of the "heavenly hosts," he was present not in a physical body, but in an astral body through which he continued to influence the Earth.[1]

Thus, Simeon saw further stages of development of the beloved little Bodhisattva when he blessed the Jesus child in the temple. The next day, Simeon died in peace. On this naming day in 1 B.C., the name of the one who would bear the Christ was pronounced. Now this name lives in each of us: Christ is in us. "Hallowed be your

---
1 Steiner, *According to Luke,* p. 77.

SIDEREAL GEOCENTRIC LONGITUDES : FEBRUARY 2011 Gregorian at 0 hours UT

DAY	☉	☽	☊	☿	♀	♂	♃	♄	♅	♆	♇
1 TU	16 ♑ 52	23 ♐ 0	7 ♐ 25R	0 ♑ 37	1 ♐ 27	17 ♑ 43	6 ♓ 52	22 ♍ 18R	3 ♓ 6	2 ♒ 53	11 ♐ 30
2 WE	17 53	5 ♑ 27	7 22	2 9	2 34	18 30	7 4	22 17	3 9	2 55	11 31
3 TH	18 54	17 44	7 16	3 41	3 42	19 18	7 16	22 17	3 11	2 57	11 33
4 FR	19 55	29 53	7 9	5 14	4 50	20 5	7 28	22 16	3 14	3 0	11 35
5 SA	20 56	11 ♒ 55	7 0	6 47	5 58	20 52	7 40	22 15	3 17	3 2	11 37
6 SU	21 57	23 51	6 51	8 22	7 6	21 40	7 52	22 14	3 19	3 4	11 39
7 MO	22 58	5 ♓ 44	6 43	9 57	8 14	22 27	8 4	22 12	3 22	3 6	11 40
8 TU	23 58	17 34	6 36	11 33	9 23	23 14	8 17	22 11	3 25	3 9	11 42
9 WE	24 59	29 27	6 30	13 9	10 32	24 2	8 29	22 10	3 28	3 11	11 44
10 TH	26 0	11 ♈ 26	6 27	14 47	11 40	24 49	8 42	22 8	3 31	3 13	11 45
11 FR	27 1	23 35	6 26	16 25	12 49	25 36	8 54	22 7	3 34	3 15	11 47
12 SA	28 1	5 ♉ 59	6 26D	18 4	13 58	26 24	9 7	22 5	3 37	3 18	11 49
13 SU	29 2	18 43	6 27	19 44	15 7	27 11	9 20	22 3	3 40	3 20	11 50
14 MO	0 ♒ 3	1 ♊ 52	6 28	21 24	16 17	27 58	9 32	22 1	3 42	3 22	11 52
15 TU	1 3	15 28	6 27R	23 6	17 26	28 46	9 45	21 59	3 45	3 24	11 53
16 WE	2 4	29 34	6 25	24 48	18 36	29 33	9 58	21 57	3 48	3 27	11 55
17 TH	3 5	14 ♋ 7	6 20	26 31	19 45	0 ♒ 20	10 11	21 55	3 52	3 29	11 56
18 FR	4 5	29 2	6 13	28 16	20 55	1 8	10 24	21 53	3 55	3 31	11 58
19 SA	5 6	14 ♌ 12	6 4	0 ♒ 1	22 5	1 55	10 37	21 50	3 58	3 34	11 59
20 SU	6 6	29 25	5 55	1 47	23 15	2 43	10 51	21 48	4 1	3 36	12 1
21 MO	7 7	14 ♍ 31	5 46	3 33	24 25	3 30	11 4	21 45	4 4	3 38	12 2
22 TU	8 7	29 21	5 38	5 21	25 35	4 17	11 17	21 42	4 7	3 40	12 4
23 WE	9 7	13 ♎ 49	5 33	7 10	26 45	5 5	11 31	21 40	4 10	3 43	12 5
24 TH	10 8	27 50	5 30	9 0	27 55	5 52	11 44	21 37	4 13	3 45	12 6
25 FR	11 8	11 ♏ 26	5 30	10 50	29 6	6 40	11 57	21 34	4 17	3 47	12 8
26 SA	12 9	24 38	5 30D	12 42	0 ♑ 16	7 27	12 11	21 31	4 20	3 49	12 9
27 SU	13 9	7 ♐ 29	5 31R	14 34	1 27	8 14	12 25	21 28	4 23	3 52	12 10
28 MO	14 9	20 4	5 30	16 27	2 37	9 2	12 38	21 25	4 26	3 54	12 11

INGRESSES :

1 ☽ → ♑ 13:27
4 ☽ → ♒ 0:13
6 ☽ → ♓ 12:24
9 ☽ → ♈ 1: 6
11 ☽ → ♉ 12:30
13 ☽ → ♊ 20:38
☉ → ♒ 22:54
16 ☽ → ♋ 0:43
♂ → ♒ 13:37
18 ☽ → ♌ 1:31
☿ → ♒ 23:51
20 ☽ → ♍ 0:54
22 ☽ → ♎ 1: 3
24 ☽ → ♏ 3:46
25 ♀ → ♑ 18:29
26 ☽ → ♐ 9:57
28 ☽ → ♑ 19:14

ASPECTS & ECLIPSES :

1 ☽ ☌ ☿ 16:42
2 ♀ □ ♅ 12:44
3 ♃ □ ☊ 0:41
☉ ☌ ☽ 2:30
☽ ☌ ♂ 3:16
4 ☽ ☌ ♆ 6:11
☉ ☌ ♂ 17:13
5 ♀ ☌ ☊ 19:24
6 ☽ ☌ ♅ 19:12
♀ □ ♃ 19:39
☽ ☌ A 23: 2
7 ☽ ☐N ☊ 1:58
☽ ☌ ♃ 4:50
8 ☽ ☍ ♄ 9:18
10 ♀ ☌ ♇ 1:46
11 ☉ □ ☽ 7:18
14 ☽ ☌ ☋ 8:12
☽ ☍ ♇ 17:45
15 ☽ ☍ ♀ 3:41
17 ☉ ☌ ♆ 10: 4
☽ ☍ ☿ 22:35
18 ☽ ☍ ♂ 3:30
☽ ☍ ♆ 7: 8
☉ ☍ ☽ 8:35
♀ □ ♄ 19:10
19 ☽ ☌ P 7:38
20 ☽ ☍ ♅ 7:17
☽ ☐S ☊ 10:10
☽ ☍ ♃ 18:23
☿ ☌ ♂ 22:38
21 ☿ ☌ ♆ 1: 4
♂ ☌ ♆ 4:18
☽ ☌ ♄ 11:35
24 ☉ □ ☽ 23:26
25 ☉ S☌ ☿ 8:31
♃ □ ♇ 19:54
26 ☽ ☌ ☊ 20:16
27 ☽ ☌ ♇ 8:53

SIDEREAL HELIOCENTRIC LONGITUDES : FEBRUARY 2011 Gregorian at 0 hours UT

DAY	Sid. Time	☿	♀	⊕	♂	♃	♄	♅	♆	♇	Vernal Point
1 TU	8:43:25	24 ♏ 18	14 ♍ 9	16 ♋ 52	18 ♑ 19	15 ♓ 38	16 ♍ 56	5 ♓ 7	3 ♒ 24	10 ♐ 28	5 ♓ 6'19"
2 WE	8:47:22	27 3	15 46	17 53	18 56	15 44	16 58	5 8	3 24	10 28	5 ♓ 6'19"
3 TH	8:51:18	29 49	17 23	18 54	19 34	15 49	17 0	5 9	3 24	10 28	5 ♓ 6'19"
4 FR	8:55:15	2 ♐ 35	19 0	19 55	20 11	15 55	17 2	5 9	3 25	10 29	5 ♓ 6'19"
5 SA	8:59:11	5 21	20 36	20 56	20 49	16 0	17 4	5 10	3 25	10 29	5 ♓ 6'19"
6 SU	9: 3: 8	8 9	22 13	21 57	21 27	16 6	17 6	5 11	3 26	10 29	5 ♓ 6'19"
7 MO	9: 7: 4	10 59	23 50	22 57	22 5	16 11	17 8	5 11	3 26	10 30	5 ♓ 6'19"
8 TU	9:11: 1	13 49	25 27	23 58	22 42	16 17	17 10	5 12	3 26	10 30	5 ♓ 6'18"
9 WE	9:14:57	16 42	27 3	24 59	23 20	16 22	17 12	5 13	3 27	10 30	5 ♓ 6'18"
10 TH	9:18:54	19 36	28 40	26 0	23 58	16 28	17 14	5 13	3 27	10 31	5 ♓ 6'18"
11 FR	9:22:51	22 32	0 ♎ 17	27 0	24 36	16 33	17 16	5 14	3 27	10 31	5 ♓ 6'18"
12 SA	9:26:47	25 31	1 53	28 1	25 14	16 39	17 18	5 15	3 28	10 31	5 ♓ 6'18"
13 SU	9:30:44	28 33	3 30	29 2	25 51	16 44	17 20	5 15	3 28	10 32	5 ♓ 6'18"
14 MO	9:34:40	1 ♑ 37	5 6	0 ♌ 2	26 29	16 50	17 22	5 16	3 28	10 32	5 ♓ 6'18"
15 TU	9:38:37	4 45	6 42	1 3	27 7	16 55	17 24	5 16	3 29	10 32	5 ♓ 6'17"
16 WE	9:42:33	7 56	8 19	2 4	27 45	17 1	17 26	5 17	3 29	10 33	5 ♓ 6'17"
17 TH	9:46:30	11 11	9 55	3 4	28 23	17 6	17 28	5 18	3 29	10 33	5 ♓ 6'17"
18 FR	9:50:26	14 29	11 31	4 5	29 1	17 12	17 30	5 18	3 30	10 33	5 ♓ 6'17"
19 SA	9:54:23	17 53	13 7	5 5	29 39	17 17	17 32	5 19	3 30	10 34	5 ♓ 6'17"
20 SU	9:58:20	21 21	14 44	6 6	0 ♒ 17	17 23	17 34	5 20	3 31	10 34	5 ♓ 6'17"
21 MO	10: 2:16	24 54	16 20	7 6	0 55	17 28	17 36	5 20	3 31	10 34	5 ♓ 6'17"
22 TU	10: 6:13	28 32	17 56	8 7	1 33	17 34	17 38	5 21	3 31	10 35	5 ♓ 6'17"
23 WE	10:10: 9	2 ♒ 16	19 32	9 7	2 11	17 39	17 40	5 22	3 32	10 35	5 ♓ 6'16"
24 TH	10:14: 6	6 7	21 8	10 7	2 49	17 45	17 42	5 22	3 32	10 36	5 ♓ 6'16"
25 FR	10:18: 2	10 4	22 44	11 8	3 27	17 50	17 43	5 23	3 32	10 36	5 ♓ 6'16"
26 SA	10:21:59	14 7	24 20	12 8	4 5	17 56	17 45	5 24	3 33	10 36	5 ♓ 6'16"
27 SU	10:25:55	18 18	25 55	13 9	4 43	18 1	17 47	5 24	3 33	10 37	5 ♓ 6'16"
28 MO	10:29:52	22 37	27 31	14 9	5 21	18 7	17 49	5 25	3 33	10 37	5 ♓ 6'16"

INGRESSES :

3 ☿ → ♐ 1:38
10 ♀ → ♎ 19:53
13 ☿ → ♑ 11:25
⊕ → ♌ 23: 1
19 ♂ → ♒ 13:18
22 ☿ → ♒ 9:28

ASPECTS (HELIOCENTRIC +MOON(TYCHONIC)) :

1 ⊕ ⚹ ♄ 1:33
♃ ☐S ☊ 12:46
♀ ☍ ♃ 23:23
2 ♀ ☌ ♄ 18:13
3 ☽ ☌ ♂ 3:47
4 ☽ ☌ ♆ 7: 1
☿ ⚹ ♆ 7:14
⊕ ☍ ♂ 17:13
☿ □ ♅ 22:21
5 ♀ △ ♂ 5: 9
♀ ⚹ ⊕ 12:51
6 ☿ ☌ ♇ 19:55
☽ ☌ ♅ 22:54
7 ☽ ☌ ♃ 21:21
☽ ☍ ♄ 23:10
8 ☽ ☍ ♀ 18:24
☿ □ ♃ 21:13
9 ☿ □ ♄ 4:14
11 ♂ ☐S ☊ 5:50
12 ♀ △ ♆ 23:37
14 ☽ ☍ ♇ 15:23
15 ☿ ⚹ ♅ 4: 2
16 ☿ □ ♀ 5:40
☽ ☍ ☿ 17:49
17 ♀ ⚹ ♇ 9:32
⊕ ☍ ♆ 10: 4
☽ ☍ ♂ 23:57
18 ☽ ☍ ♆ 7: 5
☿ ⚹ ♃ 19:43
☿ △ ♄ 21:30
20 ☽ ☍ ♅ 9:21
☿ ☐S ☊ 15: 5
21 ☽ ☍ ♃ 4:45
☽ ☌ ♄ 4:55
22 ☿ ☌ ♂ 23:18
23 ♃ ☍ ♄ 2:26
☿ ☌ ♆ 7:55
☽ ☌ ♀ 10:56
24 ⊕ △ ♇ 11:11
25 ☿ ⚹ ♇ 3:13
♂ ☌ ♆ 3:25
☿ ☍ ⊕ 8:31
27 ☽ ☌ ♇ 5:54

name." May this serve as a reminder to hold respectfully each name in the community and see the Christ in each other.

February 14: Sun enters Aquarius: Discretion becomes silence, becomes meditative force, and becomes power.

Sun 1° Aquarius: Healing of the Paralyzed Man.[2] This is a story revealing the paralyzing effects of egoism. This can manifest physically or emotionally. One can suffer the binding power of rigidified movement in body, mind, or soul. Where do we tether ourselves to paralyzing beliefs?

February 17: Sun conjunct Neptune 3° Aquarius: Neptune in Aquarius remembers much of the life of Christ, from the death of Lazarus (July 15, 32) to the death of the Blessed Virgin Mary (August 15, 44). Today, Sun and Neptune come together near the exact location of Neptune at the Ascension and Pentecost. Neptune, called "Night" in Orphic cosmogony, arose from the primal will as the cosmic harmony of the World Soul, Sophia. This realm is the source of the higher stage of consciousness known as *Inspiration,* the source of devotion and religious awakening born of inner hearing, whereby the cosmic soul inspires through the human soul. This is a state engendering harmony and love for all beings.

The negative side of Neptune is a wall of hatred for all that is good, noble, charitable, loving, and kind. It engenders a "sucking" force of attraction toward all that is egoistic. When the feeling life rules the soul, one is being "sucked in," resulting in illusion. When the soul is independent of its feelings it rises to receive Inspiration, it is being "lifted" into the harmony of the spheres. Through the constant use of electronic devices and the cultivation of virtual relationships, the human soul is drifting further from the realms of Inspiration. This is an attack, long planned and patiently carried forward. Our mechanistic world is inciting a spiritual emptiness in which deaf human beings succumb to inspirations of war, fear, and terror. Yet, with Neptune now in Aquarius, there is a memory of the perfect biography of the One, which serves as an antidote to opposing forces. If we listen, we hear the sound of peace, trust, and love. This is a good day to walk in nature and listen to her sounds. May we practice the art of listening so compromised in our time!

February 18 (15-18-21): Full moon, 4° Aquarius (DT): Living water. The Teacher sits by an ancient well in a foreign place. A woman comes and offers to send a bucket (locked in a nearby building) down into the well and bring some water up for him. He says, "Everyone who drinks of this water will be thirsty again, but whoever drinks of the water that I will give will never be thirsty again" (John 4:13–14). He tells the woman intimate details about herself. She runs into town to bring the townspeople. They gather to receive the true living water. In the light of the full moon, doorway to the watery realm, what is the nature of water—physical water for a thirsty body, and spirit water for a thirsty soul? Can we participate in both during these days?

The raising of Lazarus occurred with the Moon at 4° Leo. As Lazarus had been dead for more than three days, his etheric body had already dissolved into the collective etheric sphere. Therefore, when he was raised from the dead, he was given an etheric body (the living waters) by Christ himself. During his time between death and being raised, Lazarus was in the underworld. At his rebirth, he rose with knowledge that is now opening for all of us. The seeds of redemption then placed into Lazarus by Christ guide us now, as we are all collectively crossing the threshold into the spiritual world. Why are we crossing the threshold?

> Because it is no longer the soul's task to enter the body fully, which is beginning to crumble away, the soul's task is instead to prepare for what will happen on Jupiter [the next incarnation of the Earth]. Our souls are even now making preparations for the future.[3]

Human beings are gradually becoming either more spiritual or more material, either rising with

---

2 See *Journal for Star Wisdom 2010.*

3 Rudolf Steiner, *The Fall of the Spirits of Darkness* (London: Rudolf Steiner Press, 1993), p. 77.

evolution or becoming victims of the second "fall" (the fall into subnature). Whether rising or falling, souls will increasingly encounter spiritual beings and spiritual worlds of one kind or another. Lazarus did this before us. He went through the portal of the Moon into the subterranean realms and was raised by Christ. The compassion (Leo) of Christ fills us with protection, guiding us toward future Jupiter evolution as we align with him. At this full moon, we can contemplate the Moon in Leo shining forth with Christ's compassion and the Aquarian Sun pouring healing waters. Spiritual nourishment is needed to counter the "crumbling" of the material body at this stage of humanity's evolution. Spiritual nourishment comes from unadulterated seeds, the living Word, and through capacity for imagination. World headlines provide ample evidence that, where spiritual nourishment is lacking, other influences enter to fill the void. Genetically manipulated seeds, constant noise pollution, and the onslaught of virtual images work against humanity's capacity to receive spiritual nourishment. We may ask: Are we are drinking enough from the living waters?

February 21: Mars conjunct Neptune 4° Aquarius: Healing the Official's Son (John 4:46–54). At the Healing of the Official's Son, Mars and Neptune were conjunct. The power of Inspiration (Neptune) worked directly through the living Word (Mars) as a healing force. In this second miracle of Christ, He healed the stream of heredity: The present worked back onto the past. Selathiel came to Christ to beg that his son Joel be healed. Joel had been adopted by the nobleman Zorobabel; even fatherhood had been given away. This meant Selathiel had to suppress his own "I" to serve his master's "I." This suppression weakens the "I." The weakness of the father's "I" created a physical weakness in the son's body. The boy's blood was too weak to carry an "I," therefore his blood became inflamed.

In his illness, the boy constantly repeated: "Jesus, the prophet of Nazareth, alone can help me!" In desperation Selathiel rode to find Jesus. Jesus spoke: "Go; your son will live." When Selathiel asked if this was really true, Jesus responded: "Believe me, in this very hour he has been cured." The nobleman's faith in Christ restored his "I" to uprightness, and healed his son. Jesus Christ gave the nobleman a new name. Instead of *basilikos* (belonging to a king) he was called *pater* (father); he became "father of the house." This fatherhood involves not only responsibility in the physical world, but also the appointment of being a spiritual authority in the home. This story teaches the absolute necessity of fathering children with spiritual authority. This healing reveals the *fact* of the power of the vertically aligned, Christ centered "I" over any horizontal influence in the hereditary stream. We may contemplate today where we may be compromising our true self to gain favor with any powers of this world. Have we become a satellite of any person or collective body of thought? There is a great deal of reality being created by "human satellites." Are we moons, or suns? Do we create, or are we puppets of another's creation? Are we taking up the responsibility of spiritually fathering our children?

February 24: Sun 10° Aquarius: Feeding of the Five Thousand and the Walking on Water. These two miracles comprise a day side (feeding of the five thousand) and a night side (walking on water). Christ feeds five thousand with moral sensory impressions, and these impressions echo in the night for the twelve disciples.

Rudolf Steiner frequently spoke of spiritualizing sensory impressions; "moral impressions" was the term he gave to sensory impressions of moral and spiritual phenomena. Christ, whose heart was connected with the twelve constellations of the zodiac, filled the twelve senses[4] of the multitude with moral impressions. This satisfied their hunger. They sought to crown him king in this world, whereby they could continue to passively receive spiritual nourishment. His disciples, on the other hand, bear witness to his spiritual kingliness when, later that *night,* he approaches their boat

---

[4] On the twelve senses, see Rudolf Steiner, *Anthroposophy (A Fragment): A New Foundation for the Study of Human Nature* (Hudson, NY: Anthroposophic Press, 1996), chapter 2, "The Human Being as a Sensory Organism."

walking on water, saying, "It is I; do not be afraid" (John 6:20). These words contain the revelation of Christ's kingly nature.

> It does not call the Christ to govern (as the five thousand wished), but bestows on human beings the spiritual force of self-determination. The kingly nature of the Christ is his capacity not only to give humankind freedom, but also to give the needed strength to assert that freedom. In the spiritual moral sense, it would be proper to say that the royal nature of Christ involves giving kingly dignity to human beings.[5]

In the night is the recognition of the kingly dignity Christ gives to human beings. His words "It is I; do not be afraid" remind us of who brings us certainty when the winds of change and the waves of uncertainty threaten our equilibrium. We are also reminded of the different natures of sensory impressions. Moral impressions echo into the higher hierarchies by night, strengthening the human "I." Immoral impressions, synthetic impressions, made to *imitate* creation, echo into the sphere of materialism by night, weakening the "I." What is taken in by day determines which school we enter at night. This is a good day to ponder the quality of impressions we place before our senses and, more important, the quality of impressions we allow to enter the senses of our children. For the nature of these impressions by day will determine who it is they will meet in the night.

February 25: ASPECT: Superior conjunction of Sun and Mercury, 11° Aquarius. At both the conception of the Nathan Mary and the Transfiguration of Christ, Mercury and Sun were very close to conjunction. Both of these events represent the potential purity of every human soul as it fulfills the hermetic law: As above, so below. In conjunction, the hermetic messaging from Mercury has direct access to the individuality (Sun), giving birth to spiritualized thinking (Imagination). Mercury heals when receiving messages from supranature, and it is a thief when receiving messages from subnature. If the majority of human beings are receiving their imaginations from subnature, the social order becomes ill. Judith von Halle writes of the connection between human thinking (Mercury) and disease:

> Today, likewise, illnesses are caused by the conditions and circumstances which human beings themselves create: not just our actions but also our feelings and thoughts.... The arrival of new diseases that have not yet been wholly explained and for which no remedy has yet been found, is also connected with the appearance of that third, dark power which stands in complete opposition to Christianity and thus also to the Christian impulse for healing. With the end of the twentieth century—for the third time since the Mystery of Golgotha—it is mustering its forces against humanity's spiritual awakening.[6]

Mercury represents the power of healing. The profundity of the fact that adversarial forces are striving to rob human thinking of its spiritual capacities is sobering. The effect of materialistic thinking is disease, war, fear, and terror. Mercury governs the lungs. The two lobes of the lungs are called into movement through Mercury and serve as minister and chancellor to the heart. If Mercury, the planet closest to the Sun, listens to the anti-sun rather than the true Son, thinking seeks to dominate nature rather than collaborate with her. This is the thinking behind everything from resource exploitation to genetic manipulations. The Transfiguration and the Nathan Mary are living examples of Mercury's power to unite human beings with heavenly beings.

In today's conjunction in Aquarius we work with Mercury through the power of *pneumatism*, or "spiritual airwaves." The adversaries compete for dominion over these airwaves through saturating the free air with electronic noise. This noise contaminates inner silence (Aquarius). Because of the ubiquitous presence of this noise, we can

---

5 Tomberg, *Christ and Sophia*, p. 254.

6 Judith von Halle, *Illness and Healing: And the Mystery Language of the Gospels* (London: Temple Lodge, 2008), pp. 156, 160.

see a plan to destroy the human ability to receive spiritual thoughts. We may wish to remember that imagination comes from two sources: one serves the Christ, and the other the Antichrist. We can ask: Is our thinking a thief, or is it a messenger of the gods? The stronger our spirit is, the healthier our social organism will be, and a healthy social organism restores health to our Mother. We restore the Earth when we love her creation and all her beings. May our Sun hearts receive spiritual messages that create harmonious airwaves!

ASPECT: Jupiter square Pluto (DT). In this aspect, cures were invented for the world, as in the wise teacher in Jupiter wresting from the dark world of disease something of the secret of the cure. These include the discovery of the polio vaccine by Jonas Salk in March 1953 and the practical development of penicillin by Howard Florey and Ernst Chain in May 1940. Note that both arenas are still rife with dark side effects. The polio vaccine sometimes leads to the disease it was designed to prevent, while the antibiotic (anti-life) substance penicillin can also have serious side effects.

February 28: Sun 14° Aquarius: Jesus teaches on the same theme as the Sermon on the Mount: the Beatitudes and the Lord's Prayer (Matt. 5:3–12; 6:9–13). Both Rudolf Steiner and Valentin Tomberg gave close attention to the Lord's Prayer and the Beatitudes. It is significant that both of these great teachers of humanity were born with the Sun at exactly 14½° Aquarius. This is a star language worth hearing. Both were masters of reading the occult script. This is a good day to find inner silence in which meditative force becomes the power to see freely the signs of the times.

Aquarius is future-oriented and brings something new into the present. Aquarian teachers bear witness to the true light. Aquarius is leading us into the next cultural epoch, the Slavic cultural epoch that will begin around 2375. We are on the doorstep to this Aquarian Age, which calls for freedom from the past, all the while remaining faithful to its tradition. This is the rule of law for changing times. This law is expressed in the fifth commandment given Moses: "Honor your father and your mother" (Exodus 20:12). This is the law of continuity, or the life of tradition. Continuity is movement, and movement is change. Without change tradition becomes "good in the wrong time" (one of Rudolf Steiner's descriptions of evil). Both of these great teachers can be found through prayer and meditation.

It became clearer and clearer to me—as the outcome of many years of research—that in our epoch there is really something like a resurrection of the Astrology of the third epoch [the Egyptian–Babylonian period], but permeated now with the Christ Impulse. Today, we must search among the stars in a way different from the old ways. The stellar script must once more become something that speaks to us.
—RUDOLF STEINER (*Christ and the Spiritual World and the Search for the Holy Grail*, p. 106)

In Palestine during the time that Jesus of Nazareth walked on Earth as Jesus Christ—during the three years of his life, from his thirtieth to his thirty-third year—the entire being of the cosmic Christ was acting uninterruptedly upon him, and was working into him. The Christ stood always under the influence of the entire cosmos; he made no step without this working of the cosmic forces into and in him.... It was always in accordance with the collective being of the whole universe with whom the Earth is in harmony, that all which Jesus Christ did took place.
—RUDOLF STEINER (*Spiritual Guidance of Man and Humanity*, p. 66)

MARCH

On the 1st, the waning sliver of the Moon and Venus are visible just before sunrise, to the east in the Sea Goat (Capricorn). The Sun is in Aquarius, moving into Pisces on the 16th. We will need capacities other than physical sight to experience Venus, Mars, Uranus, Jupiter and Mercury clustered within the Sun's glow this month, leaving the evening sky empty with the exception of the Moon and Saturn. The new moon on the 3rd is in Capricorn, and the Moon will grow to fullness by the 18th. Saturn will appear on the eastern horizon about three hours after sunset March 1st, and about one hour after sunset by month's end. Moon and Saturn join just past full moon on the 20th.

March 4: new moon, 19° Aquarius (DT): What is the value of life? Jairus, a man who attained a high rank for his accomplishments among the Essenes, has a daughter whom he loves more than anything. The daughter neither loves nor respects him. In the background is a complicated mother who urges her daughter into vain, superficial activities. The daughter has fallen ill, and has died. Overcoming his own vanity that he should have been able to heal her, Jairus contacts the Healer, who lifts the daughter from seeming death, warning the daughter and mother to change their ways. What do we do that is superficial and vain and leads us astray, even to death? How do we understand the mother's complicated motivations and the father's hesitation and embarrassment?

March 9: ASPECT: Mercury conjunct Uranus, 5° Pisces. The Moon stood at 5 Pisces when Jesus came again to the River Jordan, some five weeks after His Baptism, and John the Baptist beheld Jesus on the opposite side of the river and spoke, "Behold the Lamb of God" (John 1:29; December 1, 29; *Chron.*,[1] p. 208). Mercury, the wing-footed messenger, and Uranus (lightning bolts of imagination), when in conjunction can brighten perception and illumine ordinary thinking. This conjunction remembers the witness to the True Light (John) and the beginning of Christ's ministry. Inversely, forces of egoistic thinking tend to behold false lambs: puppets of beasts. The bombardment of virtual thoughts is weakening the "muscles" of free thinking (Mercury). This is a good day to find concentrated stillness. Mercury can receive mighty thoughts when personal thoughts are quieted. We can ask ourselves if we may find a moment to see what thoughts are striving to find us.

March 13: ASPECT: Mercury square Pluto, 12°25' Sagittarius. Human thinking (Mercury) in tension with Divine Love or Divine Wrath (Pluto). It is noteworthy that this aspect occurred with the first eruption of Iceland's Eyjafjallajökull Volcano March 20, 2010. Divine love or divine wrath? Sagittarius is the constellation of the centaur. This is the imagination of the human being mastering animal forces. Perhaps one of our questions would be: Is the centaur (Sagittarius) riding the horse, or is the horse riding the centaur? The former finds divine thought; the latter is eventually overcome by subversive thoughts. This aspect brings out the relationship between human thinking and divine will.

Noteworthy: April 20, 2010, one month after the eruption of the volcano, marks the explosion of the BP Deepwater Horizon oil platform. At the time of this writing, it is possible that that oil well tapped into an oil reserve similar to an inverted, underwater volcano. The sixth subearthly sphere is the *Fire Earth*. Rudolf Steiner refers to that layer as the realm of unharnessed passions, a layer that reacts strongly to excesses of human will. It can push through into physical forces such as earthquakes, tsunamis, and volcanic eruptions. Ahriman predominates in the sphere of Fire Earth.

March 14: Sun 28° Aquarius: Jupiter stood here through the last three temptations of Christ in the wilderness and on the fortieth day, when angels came to minister to him. The Sun today remembers the ministering waters of the Holy Spirit that poured from the urns of Aquarius during these trials of God incarnate. This water continues to pour upon humanity as part of a world awakening,

---

[1] "*Chron.*"= Robert Powell, *Chronicle of the Living Christ: The Life and Ministry of Jesus Christ : Foundations of Cosmic Christianity* (Hudson, NY: Anthroposophic Press, 1996),

SIDEREAL GEOCENTRIC LONGITUDES : MARCH 2011 Gregorian at 0 hours UT

DAY	☉	☽	☊	☿	♀	♂	♃	♄	♅	♆	♇
1 TU	15 ♒ 9	2 ♑ 26	5 ♐ 27R	18 ♒ 21	3 ♑ 48	9 ♒ 49	12 ♓ 52	21 ♍ 21R	4 ♓ 30	3 ♒ 56	12 ♐ 13
2 WE	16 10	14 38	5 20	20 15	4 59	10 36	13 6	21 18	4 33	3 58	12 14
3 TH	17 10	26 43	5 11	22 10	6 10	11 24	13 19	21 15	4 36	4 1	12 15
4 FR	18 10	8 ♒ 43	5 0	24 5	7 21	12 11	13 33	21 11	4 40	4 3	12 16
5 SA	19 10	20 38	4 46	26 1	8 32	12 59	13 47	21 8	4 43	4 5	12 17
6 SU	20 10	2 ♓ 32	4 32	27 57	9 43	13 46	14 1	21 4	4 46	4 7	12 18
7 MO	21 10	14 23	4 18	29 53	10 54	14 33	14 15	21 0	4 50	4 10	12 19
8 TU	22 11	26 15	4 6	1 ♓ 48	12 5	15 21	14 29	20 57	4 53	4 12	12 20
9 WE	23 11	8 ♈ 10	3 56	3 43	13 16	16 8	14 43	20 53	4 56	4 14	12 21
10 TH	24 11	20 9	3 49	5 36	14 27	16 55	14 57	20 49	5 0	4 16	12 22
11 FR	25 11	2 ♉ 18	3 45	7 29	15 39	17 42	15 11	20 45	5 3	4 18	12 23
12 SA	26 10	14 39	3 43	9 20	16 50	18 30	15 25	20 41	5 6	4 20	12 24
13 SU	27 10	27 18	3 43	11 8	18 2	19 17	15 39	20 37	5 10	4 23	12 25
14 MO	28 10	10 ♊ 19	3 43	12 55	19 13	20 4	15 54	20 33	5 13	4 25	12 26
15 TU	29 10	23 47	3 42	14 38	20 25	20 51	16 8	20 29	5 17	4 27	12 27
16 WE	0 ♓ 10	7 ♋ 44	3 39	16 17	21 36	21 39	16 22	20 25	5 20	4 29	12 27
17 TH	1 10	22 11	3 33	17 53	22 48	22 26	16 36	20 20	5 24	4 31	12 28
18 FR	2 9	7 ♌ 4	3 25	19 24	23 59	23 13	16 51	20 16	5 27	4 33	12 29
19 SA	3 9	22 17	3 14	20 50	25 11	24 0	17 5	20 12	5 30	4 35	12 29
20 SU	4 9	7 ♍ 39	3 3	22 10	26 23	24 47	17 19	20 7	5 34	4 37	12 30
21 MO	5 8	22 58	2 52	23 25	27 35	25 34	17 34	20 3	5 37	4 39	12 31
22 TU	6 8	8 ♎ 3	2 42	24 34	28 46	26 21	17 48	19 59	5 41	4 41	12 31
23 WE	7 7	22 46	2 35	25 36	29 58	27 8	18 2	19 54	5 44	4 43	12 32
24 TH	8 7	7 ♏ 1	2 31	26 31	1 ♒ 10	27 55	18 17	19 50	5 47	4 45	12 32
25 FR	9 6	20 46	2 29	27 18	2 22	28 42	18 31	19 45	5 51	4 47	12 33
26 SA	10 6	4 ♐ 3	2 29	27 59	3 34	29 29	18 46	19 41	5 54	4 49	12 33
27 SU	11 5	16 55	2 29	28 32	4 46	0 ♓ 16	19 0	19 36	5 58	4 51	12 34
28 MO	12 5	29 28	2 28	28 57	5 58	1 3	19 15	19 31	6 1	4 53	12 34
29 TU	13 4	11 ♑ 44	2 25	29 15	7 10	1 50	19 29	19 27	6 5	4 55	12 35
30 WE	14 3	23 49	2 19	29 25	8 22	2 37	19 44	19 22	6 8	4 57	12 35
31 TH	15 3	5 ♒ 47	2 11	29 28R	9 34	3 24	19 58	19 17	6 11	4 59	12 35

INGRESSES :

3 ☽ → ♒ 6:32	23 ♀ → ♒ 0:34
5 ☽ → ♓ 18:53	☽ → ♏ 12: 5
7 ☿ → ♓ 1:32	25 ☽ → ♐ 16:36
8 ☽ → ♈ 7:33	26 ♂ → ♓ 15:42
10 ☽ → ♉ 19:29	28 ☽ → ♑ 1: 2
13 ☽ → ♊ 5: 2	30 ☽ → ♒ 12:21
15 ☽ → ♋ 10:47	
☉ → ♓ 20: 2	
17 ☽ → ♌ 12:41	
19 ☽ → ♍ 12: 4	
21 ☽ → ♎ 11: 7	

ASPECTS & ECLIPSES :

1 ☽ ☌ ♀ 2:57	9 ☿ □ ☊ 2:37	☽ ☍ ♂ 2:50	☽ ☌ ♇ 15:47
3 ☽ ☌ ♆ 14:37	☿ ☌ ♅ 15:58	☽ S☊ 16:54	27 ♀ ☌ ♆ 1:41
4 ☽ ☌ ♂ 7:28	12 ☉ □ ☽ 23:44	☉ ☍ ☽ 18: 9	28 ☉ □ ♇ 12: 0
☉ ☌ ☽ 20:45	13 ☽ ☌ ☋ 11:56	☽ ☌ P 19:16	♃ ☍ ♄ 20:59
5 ♅ □ ☊ 4:42	☿ □ ♇ 17:21	☽ ☍ ♅ 20:44	29 ♂ □ ☊ 16: 7
☽ ☌ ☿ 12:57	14 ☽ ☍ ♇ 3:49	20 ☽ ☍ ♃ 15:22	30 ☽ ☌ ♆ 22:21
6 ☽ N☊ 3:58	16 ☿ ☌ ♃ 1:23	☽ ☌ ♄ 19:26	31 ☽ ☌ ♀ 8:29
☽ ☌ ♅ 4:33	17 ☽ ☍ ♀ 1: 5	21 ☽ ☍ ☿ 0:46	
☽ ☌ A 7:50	☽ ☍ ♆ 19:58	☉ ☌ ♅ 12:23	
☽ ☌ ♃ 23:42	18 ☿ ☍ ♄ 13:42	25 ☽ ☌ ☊ 21: 7	
7 ☽ ☍ ♄ 13:19	19 ☉ □ ☊ 1:42	26 ☉ □ ☽ 12: 7	

SIDEREAL HELIOCENTRIC LONGITUDES . MARCH 2011 Gregorian at 0 hours UT

DAY	Sid. Time	☿	♀	⊕	♂	♃	♄	♅	♆	♇	Vernal Point
1 TU	10:33:49	27 ♒ 3	29 ♎ 7	15 ♌ 9	5 ♒ 59	18 ♓ 12	17 ♍ 51	5 ♓ 25	3 ♒ 34	10 ♐ 37	5 ♓ 6'16"
2 WE	10:37:45	1 ♓ 38	0 ♏ 43	16 9	6 37	18 18	17 53	5 26	3 34	10 38	5 ♓ 6'15"
3 TH	10:41:42	6 21	2 18	17 10	7 15	18 23	17 55	5 27	3 35	10 38	5 ♓ 6'15"
4 FR	10:45:38	11 13	3 54	18 10	7 53	18 29	17 57	5 27	3 35	10 38	5 ♓ 6'15"
5 SA	10:49:35	16 15	5 30	19 10	8 32	18 34	17 59	5 28	3 35	10 39	5 ♓ 6'15"
6 SU	10:53:31	21 25	7 5	20 10	9 10	18 40	18 1	5 29	3 36	10 39	5 ♓ 6'15"
7 MO	10:57:28	26 44	8 41	21 10	9 48	18 45	18 3	5 29	3 36	10 39	5 ♓ 6'15"
8 TU	11: 1:24	2 ♈ 13	10 16	22 10	10 26	18 51	18 5	5 30	3 36	10 40	5 ♓ 6'15"
9 WE	11: 5:21	7 50	11 52	23 10	11 4	18 56	18 7	5 31	3 37	10 40	5 ♓ 6'14"
10 TH	11: 9:18	13 36	13 27	24 10	11 42	19 2	18 9	5 31	3 37	10 40	5 ♓ 6'14"
11 FR	11:13:14	19 29	15 3	25 10	12 20	19 7	18 11	5 32	3 37	10 41	5 ♓ 6'14"
12 SA	11:17:11	25 30	16 38	26 10	12 58	19 13	18 13	5 33	3 38	10 41	5 ♓ 6'14"
13 SU	11:21: 7	1 ♉ 36	18 13	27 10	13 36	19 18	18 15	5 33	3 38	10 41	5 ♓ 6'14"
14 MO	11:25: 4	7 48	19 48	28 10	14 14	19 24	18 17	5 34	3 39	10 42	5 ♓ 6'14"
15 TU	11:29: 0	14 4	21 24	29 10	14 53	19 29	18 19	5 34	3 39	10 42	5 ♓ 6'14"
16 WE	11:32:57	20 22	22 59	0 ♍ 10	15 31	19 35	18 21	5 35	3 39	10 42	5 ♓ 6'13"
17 TH	11:36:53	26 42	24 34	1 9	16 9	19 40	18 23	5 36	3 40	10 43	5 ♓ 6'13"
18 FR	11:40:50	3 ♊ 0	26 9	2 9	16 47	19 46	18 25	5 36	3 40	10 43	5 ♓ 6'13"
19 SA	11:44:47	9 17	27 44	3 9	17 25	19 51	18 27	5 37	3 40	10 43	5 ♓ 6'13"
20 SU	11:48:43	15 31	29 20	4 8	18 3	19 57	18 29	5 38	3 41	10 44	5 ♓ 6'13"
21 MO	11:52:40	21 39	0 ♐ 55	5 8	18 41	20 2	18 31	5 38	3 41	10 44	5 ♓ 6'13"
22 TU	11:56:36	27 42	2 30	6 8	19 19	20 8	18 33	5 39	3 41	10 44	5 ♓ 6'13"
23 WE	12: 0:33	3 ♋ 37	4 5	7 7	19 57	20 13	18 35	5 40	3 42	10 45	5 ♓ 6'13"
24 TH	12: 4:29	9 25	5 40	8 7	20 35	20 19	18 37	5 40	3 42	10 45	5 ♓ 6'12"
25 FR	12: 8:26	15 4	7 15	9 6	21 13	20 24	18 39	5 41	3 42	10 45	5 ♓ 6'12"
26 SA	12:12:22	20 33	8 50	10 6	21 51	20 30	18 41	5 42	3 43	10 46	5 ♓ 6'12"
27 SU	12:16:19	25 53	10 25	11 5	22 29	20 35	18 43	5 42	3 43	10 46	5 ♓ 6'12"
28 MO	12:20:16	1 ♌ 4	12 0	12 4	23 7	20 41	18 45	5 43	3 44	10 46	5 ♓ 6'12"
29 TU	12:24:12	6 4	13 35	13 4	23 45	20 46	18 47	5 43	3 44	10 47	5 ♓ 6'12"
30 WE	12:28: 9	10 56	15 10	14 3	24 23	20 52	18 49	5 44	3 44	10 47	5 ♓ 6'12"
31 TH	12:32: 5	15 37	16 44	15 2	25 1	20 57	18 51	5 45	3 45	10 47	5 ♓ 6'11"

INGRESSES :

1 ♀ → ♏ 13:16
☿ → ♓ 15:31
7 ☿ → ♈ 14:22
12 ☿ → ♉ 17:43
15 ⊕ → ♍ 20: 9
17 ☿ → ♊ 12:33
20 ♀ → ♐ 10:13
22 ☿ → ♋ 9:16
27 ☿ → ♌ 19: 1

ASPECTS (HELIOCENTRIC +MOON(TYCHONIC)) :

1 ☿ △ ♀ 16:43	☽ ☌ ♃ 8:54	13 ♀ ⚹ ♄ 0:30	☿ ☍ ♀ 13:14	☿ □ ♃ 17:33	☿ N☊ 13:28
2 ☿ ☌ ♅ 19:25	8 ♀ □ ♂ 4: 1	☿ □ ♆ 7:53	17 ☽ ☍ ♆ 18:34	☽ ☍ ♃ 19:22	⊕ □ ♇ 16:18
3 ☽ ☌ ♆ 13:42	☿ ⚹ ♆ 6: 0	☿ ⚹ ♅ 15:20	☿ □ ⊕ 20: 7	21 ⊕ ☍ ♅ 12:23	27 ♀ ☌ ♇ 5:24
♀ □ ♆ 19: 9	♂ ⚹ ♇ 8:41	♀ △ ♃ 17:24	18 ☿ △ ♆ 2:30	22 ♀ ⚹ ♆ 18:10	28 ♀ □ ⊕ 3: 9
☿ □ ♇ 21: 8	☽ ☌ ☿ 22:44	14 ☽ ☍ ♇ 0:40	☿ □ ♅ 9:56	23 ☿ △ ♅ 8:24	☿ ☍ ♆ 12:41
☽ ☌ ♂ 22:15	9 ♂ ☌ P 11:28	15 ☿ □ ♂ 3:26	☽ ☍ ♂ 16: 2	☿ ⚹ ⊕ 17:24	29 ☿ △ ♇ 23:17
4 ♀ △ ♅ 23:35	☿ △ ♇ 11:52	♀ ☌ ☋ 7:24	19 ☿ ☍ ♇ 5:30	24 ♀ □ ♅ 0: 8	30 ☽ ☌ ♆ 19:52
5 ☿ ☍ ♄ 8:13	☿ ⚹ ♂ 15:12	☿ △ ♄ 16:16	☽ ☍ ♅ 20:51	25 ☿ ⚹ ♄ 15:41	31 ☿ △ ♀ 8:54
☿ ☌ ♃ 11: 4	11 ☿ ☌ ☊ 16:21	☿ ⚹ ♃ 20:56	20 ☿ △ ♂ 11: 0	☿ △ ♃ 23:45	
6 ☽ ☌ ♅ 5:58	12 ☿ △ ⊕ 3:11	16 ☿ ☌ P 8:58	☿ □ ♄ 11:37	26 ☽ ☌ ♀ 10: 3	
7 ☽ ☍ ♄ 7:26	☽ ☍ ♀ 4:21	♃ ☌ P 9:21	☽ ☌ ♄ 16:59	☽ ☌ ♇ 12:25	

World Pentecost. This awakening is in concert with Wisdom Sophia (Jupiter). As She tended to the trials of Christ in his First Coming, so, too, she tends humanity in its trials at his Second Coming. Though trials may intensify, the healing waters still flow. We are urged not to be distracted by the clamor of adversaries, but rather attend the wisdom and love, *of* creation and *in* creation. The God incarnate goes before us. Through the practice of inner silence (Aquarius) wisdom can find us.

March 15: Sun enters Pisces: Magnanimity becomes love. The challenge is to stay grounded in reality in the inclination toward the mystical.

March 16: ASPECT: Mercury conjunct Jupiter, 16° Pisces. The conception of the Nathan Jesus occurred with the Sun at this degree. This was the first incarnation of this pure being who bore the immaculate soul of the first Adam, the portion held back and guarded by the cherubim at the time of the Fall. Today the mental clarity of Mercury is quickened by wisdom as it meets with Jupiter in Pisces, an influence full of love and creativity (Pisces). This is a good day to remain flexible to change (Pisces), carefully attending to surrounding conditions. Pure thoughts are awaiting an invitation into our hearts. This immaculate conception lives eternally as a source of healing.

March 18: ASPECT: Mercury opposite Saturn, 20° Pisces. Mercury was here at the Crucifixion and the Descent into Hell. Cosmic thoughts are continually and increasingly coming into time, seeking human minds to work *with* them. We can open to cosmic thinking, or we can distract ourselves to death.

Mercury opposite Saturn provides an opportunity for intellectual precision: "This is an appeal for the reason of light rather than the light of reason," a recommendation brought to expression by Marsilio Ficino (1433–1499), the Renaissance "astro-musicologist" whom Thomas Moore called a "Physician of the Soul."[2] Ficino describes the "reason of light" as the "crowning element" of the psyche and its prime spiritual nourishment. "Light comes first, then our intelligence, because our powers of reasoning are only a participation in a higher intelligence."[3] The reason of light (Saturn) and the light of reason (Mercury). This is a good day for inner reflection. Are we seeking the crowning element (Saturn) so that we may practice the art of participation in higher intelligence? This requires stilling the distracted mind. Meditate!

March 19 (16-19-22): Full moon, 4° Pisces (DT): Paralysis and its cure. Twelve men stand in a line, with arms paralyzed from work-related accidents. Others have paralyzed hands. The Healer strokes the limbs over and over, returning life force into the limbs. In the division of thinking–feeling–willing, this day has to do with injuries to the will, to the capacity for action. Its healing comes from warm, patient, intimate stroking by one who has heart and life force. Whom can you stroke physically and with your compassion? Who strokes you?

Venus stood here (4° Pisces) at both the Feeding of the Five Thousand and the Walking on Water. We may contemplate where we are feeding our friends, family, and community with the nourishment of love (Pisces), and where we are able to calm the storms in others. Opposite to this would be Venus thwarted, a lover scorned, whereby she becomes jealous and vindictive, nourishing egoism and fanning flames of unrest. "It is I, do not be afraid," are the words from the being of Love who called to the disciples at the Walking on Water. Christ grows in us as we develop the capacity to love one another. Pisces is all about love, and ancient myth tells us that Venus was birthed from this watery region of the heavens. Venus wears the therapeutic gaze and asks, What is missing? And there she serves. May we also find and ask this question today! For what is missing is Christ. First we find him in our own heart, and then we find him in others.

March 21: ASPECT: Sun conjunct Uranus, 5° Pisces. The flight into Egypt by the parents of the

---

[2] Moore, *The Planets Within: The Astrological Psychology of Marsilio Ficino* (Hudson, NY: Lindisfarne Press, 1990).

[3] Paul and Powell, *The Cosmic Dances of the Planets*, p. 21.

Solomon Jesus occurred during a Sun–Uranus conjunction, also in Pisces. Where is our Egypt today? Is it in our heart (Sun)? Herod, the representative of wanton materialism filled with jealousy and rivalry, grew maniacally uneasy regarding the possibility that a Messiah (Uranus bringing the new) had been born. The Messiah threatened Herod's egoistic power. During the night when he resolved to murder the children of Bethlehem, an angel appeared to Joseph, the father of the Solomon Jesus, instructing him to flee with his family into Egypt. The child was one year old at the time. A quiet heart receives guidance from realms of spirit, lending strength and protection to those carrying new mystery streams. Something new is vulnerable and is best protected in the initiation chambers of "Egypt," our hearts. Know when it is prudent to protect. Then, listen!

March 26/27: ASPECT: Venus conjunct Neptune, 4° Aquarius (DT). In its most positive aspect, Neptune can bring high ideals and Venus can lead us each to our karmic group. In this aspect, on December 10, 1997, a young woman with few friends ascended a large redwood tree that she named Luna. Her name was Julia Butterfly Hill, and through this act of asserting her ideals in the heights, she found her karmic group.

Venus conjunct Neptune: Venus was conjunct Neptune at the end of the temptations of Christ in the wilderness and at the Wedding in Cana, site of the first of Christ's miracles:

> Mary reminded Jesus that He was responsible for the second course of wine. Mary's reminder to Jesus reveals something of the guiding quality of Sophia, through Mary addressing the Logos in Jesus. Jesus then gave the command that six vessels of water were to be fetched and, after blessing the water, He performed the miracle of turning the water into wine. The water symbolizes the water of life being transformed into wine through the power of divine love represented by the Logos. Christ brought down the fire of divine love into the water of wisdom, and in this magical act we can see the mystery of the interweaving between the Logos and Sophia. All those who drank of this wine were filled with the power of divine love and were united in the community in which they recognized Christ as the Chosen One.[4]

Christ and Sophia continue their interweaving. They guide us to become the new vessels into which wisdom and love unite. With the First Coming, the independent "I" was developing independence from the group "I." With the Second Coming, the "we" is developing. This happens through the power of humanity's awakened "I" working in union with others. These are Grail mysteries. At the wedding at Cana, Christ brought Divine Love, forming new communities, independent from the ancestral familial "I." It is Sophia who works with us when we stand together in community. Our community task is to form the vessel, out of our independent and free will. These vessels *are* Sophianic communities, and Venus works through such groups. Those communities serve as portals through which spiritual beings may bring healing to humanity in our time of global need. The World Soul (Neptune) is the harmony of the spheres, sounding inspirations from both the depths of the Earth and from the heights of the heavens. The communities of Sophia serve these inspirations. This aspect asks us to create our vessels through the social artistry of Venus: collaboration. This is a day to stand with others.

March 28: ASPECT: Jupiter opposed Saturn, 19° Virgo (DT). The conjunctions and oppositions of Jupiter and Saturn greatly interest astrologers. Here, they are opposed at 19° (Jupiter in Pisces and Saturn in Virgo), which goes by fairly quickly (one-degree orb from March 23 to April 2). This is the last pass of three, beginning on May 23, 2010. The last time they were opposite was in 1991; the next time will be 2029. Jupiter's typical hope, optimism, and light can feel squeezed by Saturn's demands for discipline and emphasis on the hard truths of life. A strong will can link them together into extraordinary power. The Berlin Wall fell under this aspect on November 9, 1989, the grand

---

4 Powell, *The Sophia Teachings,* pp. 48–49.

ramparts of Communist Russia revealed in truth to have little substance. Two examples of people born with this aspect are the Russian composer Sergei Prokofieff (April 23, 1891), whose music shows the grandness of Jupiter in a dance with the melancholy of Saturn, and the Catalan architect Antonio Gaudi (June 25, 1852), whose grand edifices do the same.

ASPECT: Jupiter–Saturn opposition. These oppositions occur approximately ten years after a Jupiter–Saturn conjunction. The *conjunction* tells the opening story; the *opposition* either empowers the good of the conjunction or reveals the forces of hindrance. The last conjunction of Jupiter and Saturn occurred at 28° Aries, May 28, 2000 (see opening commentary for 2011, Jan. 1). Today we stand at the final opposition to this unfolding story.

The opening story: The *conjunction* in Aries foretold new leadership—Aries is the first and leading sign of the zodiac. We are to decide the true nature of the leadership this conjunction revealed. Because it was in Aries, we can attribute the leader with devotion, self-sacrifice, and great spiritual strength. We can think of the crucifixion of Christ, which occurred in Aries. Aries speaks of power *with* another, not power *over* another. A mantra from Revelation 3:11: "Hold fast to what you have, so that no one may seize your crown." We are warned not to give up our inner guidance, no matter the pressures coming from the outer world. It is interesting to note that Venus, at the death of Novalis, was exactly at this conjunction degree (28° Aries). Novalis was the John being. This is the being Rudolf Steiner proclaimed would be assisting us now.

According to Robert Powell, this conjunction marked the birth of a new Christian era coincident with an awakening of a spiritual presence in Mother Nature.[5] Sixteen months after the beginning of this awakening, an anti-force rose from subearthly realms on September 11, 2001. This event can be seen as the entrance of the beast onto the world stage. Through the spread of war, fear, and terror, it changed the world inversely to (and in

---

5 Powell, "The Cosmic Beginning of the New Millennium," *Christian Star Calendar 2000*.

Gaudi's Temple Expiatori de la Sagrada Família
(1882–c. 2026)

direct opposition to) nature's new spiritual awakening, the ripening of goodness, and the potential beginning of Christlike leadership.

Midpoint (time of decision between the opening and the closing chapters of a story): Today's third and last *opposition* can mean that this new leadership and spiritual awakening in nature may be challenged for the third and last time. It is interesting to note that, one month before the *first* opposition between the two planets in May 2010, the BP oil catastrophe began in the Gulf of Mexico and continued through the time of the opposition one month later and beyond. This is certainly an adverse effect for Nature.

Characteristics: Jupiter gives the gift of spiritual sight and the wisdom to behold the true Kingdom: "Your Kingdom Come" (Matt. 6:10). Saturn can be seen as the fire of the cosmic will that lifts thinking to the purity of the virgin intellect, thereby reflecting the One source: "Hallowed be your name" (Matt. 6:9). In opposition *wisdom* and *will* ennoble each other. Inversely, tyrannical kings and kingdoms (negative Jupiter) can bring suffocating conditions in another "one's" name (negative Saturn), thus smothering new initiatives. This current opposition occurs with Jupiter in Pisces and Saturn in Virgo. Pisces bears the gift of psychic perception, and when Jupiter is here and opposed by Saturn this gift can bear astonishing fruits of wisdom through the rigors of Saturnine discipline. Saturn in Virgo suggests cosmic memory standing *with* Sophia. With Wise Jupiter in Pisces and Saturn in the sign of the Virgin, an opposition is created that strengthens love (Pisces) for Sophia (Virgo). Here the theme of an awakening in nature is confirmed. May we attend this!

Historic Parallels: The very long past Jupiter–Saturn *conjunction* in Pisces, in 7 B.C., foretold the rebirth of Zarathustra, an event that sent the Magi on a journey to adore the child of wisdom (the Solomon Jesus) conceived with Jupiter (wisdom) very close to where it is now in this current opposition to Saturn. The Nathan Jesus, the child of Love (Pisces), was conceived with the Sun also very near Jupiter in this current conjunction. The stars spoke of great wisdom and great love uniting. This long past conjunction marked the onset of the First Coming. Now, the stars seem to be aligning to foretell stages of the Second Coming.

Some questions for us: Are the new communities (Jupiter) those gathering around Christ in his Second Coming? Are Novalis's *Hymns to the Night*, his hymns to Sophia, resounding? (At the death of Novalis, Venus was at the conjunction degree.) Was the dawn of the new ministry of the Novalis–John individuality being pointed out at the conjunction more than ten years ago? Are we, through "Michael–Sophia *in nomine Christi*," being shown the way of self-transformation through the initiation trials now facing humanity in the wilderness of materialism? (Saturn is very near where Mars was at the start of the Forty Days.) Will someone stand up to oppose the true leader? Are we the leaders, the ones awaited?

These are questions that history may answer for us if we cannot find the answers now. The greatest challenge during this opposition is discernment between the true and the false. Our greatest deed is to become Christlike and to "hold fast to what we have so that no one may seize our crown."

March 21: Equinox, equal day and equal night, an experience shared the world over, in both hemispheres.

March 31: Sun 15° Pisces. Birth of the Solomon Jesus (March 5, 6 B.C.). The reincarnation of the great teacher, Zarathustra, who was visited by the Three Kings. The kings brought the wisdom gathered by initiates in the three preceding cultural ages: Myrrh from ancient India, Frankincense from ancient Persia, and Gold from ancient Egypt. The influence of this great teacher, the Master Jesus, is always present on Earth. It takes discernment to hear these teachings through the cacophony of distractions, but he is always here. There is always an initiate who is working with him, even if he is not physically with us. This is a good day to open up to what we do not know. Pisces listens to what sounds from behind the veil of the sensory world. Listen!

To starry realms,
To the dwelling places of Gods,
Turns the Spirit gaze of my soul.

From starry realms,
From the dwelling places of Gods,
Streams Spirit power into my soul.

For starry realms,
For the dwelling places of Gods,
Lives my Spirit heart through my soul.
—Rudolf Steiner

APRIL

The Sun begins the month in front of the Fishes (Pisces) moving into Aries on April 15. Saturn is still retrograde, as is Mercury, who stations Direct on April 24. Pluto stations before going Retrograde on the 10th. The new moon is on the 3rd (Sun and Moon in Pisces), and the full moon is on the 18th (Sun in Aries, Moon in Libra).

The Sun continues to cleave to Mars, Uranus, Jupiter, and Mercury. By months end, enough distance will develop between the Sun and the four planets that they will be visible before the early predawn light. Venus continues to be visible as the Morning Star. Saturn will be visible in the evening sky, to the southeast after dusk. The Moon, nearing fullness, will be below Saturn in the Virgin (Virgo) on the 16th. The Lyrids meteor shower reaches its peak on the 21st to 22nd. Look up toward the east and into the constellation of Lyra in the predawn dark.

April 1: Sun 16° Pisces: Conception of the Nathan Jesus (March 6, 2 B.C.). An immaculate conception occurred. This is a day to remember how much our children need love and protection; for the young child bears the innocence of this immaculate being and it is this very innocence that is currently under grave assault.

April 2: Pluto stations 12°36' Sagittarius: The Healing of the Paralyzed Man at the Pool of Bethesda (John 5:2–17). This continues through the 17th of April. The term *station* refers to the points in a planet's retrograde cycle at which it stands still, and hence concentrating its energies heavily on a single zodiacal position. Pluto at station is now concentrating on the third healing miracle of Christ. This miracle healed the paralyzed man who, in his previous incarnation, had an excess of personality that led to egoism. In such a state, motives are based entirely on self-consideration. In his previous life, he had ignored both others and his angel. Now, at the pool of Bethesda, he is ignored by others, as well as by the angel who stirs the waters to call the sick for healing. At the moment of his healing through Christ, who represented both the world of angels and the world of human beings, he was lifted from the horizontal orientation of the negative human past into the vertical of spiritual liberation.

> "I" consciousness of the past, which preserves its activity from the previous incarnation and in which many human beings live and act, is called consciousness of the "dead" in the Gospels, and those who live under the "I" impulse of the past are simply called "the dead." Thus, healing the paralyzed man involved more than merely the present "I"; the "dead," in particular, heard the "voice of the Son" and experienced a conversion in their past consciousness. "For the Father raiseth up the dead, and quickeneth them; even so the Son quickeneth whom he will" (John 5:21)."[1]

If we ignore the voice of conscience that calls our dead to life, we ignore the Christ. Our dead are powerful influences when Pluto is their master. Likewise, our dead are raised when we hear the voice of Christ, our true master. Pluto stationed at the position of this healing is a call to humankind to find the will to be healed. We are living in a time of choosing. We choose either Christ or Antichrist as individuals, as nations, and as a world community. To know our "dead" is to shine light into the darkness. Christ asked the paralyzed man, "Do you want to be healed?" (John 5:6). "Truly, truly, I say to you, an hour is coming, and is now here, when the dead will hear the voice of the Son of God, and those who hear will live" (John 5:25).

April 3: new moon, 18° Pisces (DT): Gratitude for water. In this water sign, it is amazing that the only ceremony in the Oracle of the Solar Cross that is deliberately focused on thanks for water occurs in this degree. This is a day for celebration of water, gratitude for water, penetration of the essence of water.

New moon: Mercury stood at the place of this new moon from the Last Supper through the trial by Caiaphus and into the Passion of Christ. What was witnessed then by the "Messenger of

---
[1] Tomberg, *Christ and Sophia*, p 251.

SIDEREAL GEOCENTRIC LONGITUDES : APRIL 2011 Gregorian at 0 hours UT

DAY	☉	☽	☊	☿	♀	♂	♃	♄	⛢	♆	♇
1 FR	16 ♓ 2	17 ♒ 41	2 ♐ 0R	29 ♓ 23R	10 ♒ 47	4 ♓ 11	20 ♓ 13	19 ♍ 13R	6 ♓ 15	5 ♒ 0	12 ♐ 35
2 SA	17 1	29 33	1 47	29 11	11 59	4 57	20 27	19 8	6 18	5 2	12 36
3 SU	18 0	11 ♓ 24	1 33	28 53	13 11	5 44	20 42	19 3	6 22	5 4	12 36
4 MO	19 0	23 18	1 19	28 29	14 23	6 31	20 56	18 59	6 25	5 6	12 36
5 TU	19 59	5 ♈ 14	1 7	27 59	15 36	7 18	21 11	18 54	6 28	5 8	12 36
6 WE	20 58	17 14	0 57	27 25	16 48	8 4	21 25	18 49	6 32	5 9	12 36
7 TH	21 57	29 20	0 50	26 46	18 0	8 51	21 40	18 45	6 35	5 11	12 36
8 FR	22 56	11 ♉ 35	0 46	26 4	19 13	9 38	21 54	18 40	6 38	5 13	12 36
9 SA	23 55	24 1	0 44	25 20	20 25	10 24	22 9	18 35	6 42	5 14	12 36
10 SU	24 54	6 ♊ 42	0 44D	24 34	21 37	11 11	22 23	18 31	6 45	5 16	12 36R
11 MO	25 53	19 42	0 45	23 48	22 50	11 57	22 38	18 26	6 48	5 18	12 36
12 TU	26 52	3 ♋ 4	0 45R	23 1	24 2	12 44	22 52	18 22	6 51	5 19	12 36
13 WE	27 51	16 51	0 43	22 17	25 14	13 30	23 7	18 17	6 55	5 21	12 36
14 TH	28 49	1 ♌ 5	0 39	21 33	26 27	14 16	23 21	18 12	6 58	5 22	12 36
15 FR	29 48	15 43	0 33	20 53	27 39	15 3	23 36	18 8	7 1	5 24	12 36
16 SA	0 ♈ 47	0 ♍ 42	0 25	20 16	28 52	15 49	23 50	18 3	7 4	5 25	12 36
17 SU	1 46	15 54	0 17	19 42	0 ♓ 4	16 35	24 5	17 59	7 8	5 27	12 35
18 MO	2 44	1 ♎ 7	0 8	19 13	1 17	17 22	24 19	17 55	7 11	5 28	12 35
19 TU	3 43	16 12	0 1	18 49	2 29	18 8	24 33	17 50	7 14	5 30	12 35
20 WE	4 41	0 ♏ 59	29 ♏ 55	18 29	3 42	18 54	24 48	17 46	7 17	5 31	12 35
21 TH	5 40	15 21	29 52	18 14	4 54	19 40	25 2	17 41	7 20	5 32	12 34
22 FR	6 39	29 14	29 51	18 4	6 7	20 26	25 16	17 37	7 23	5 34	12 34
23 SA	7 37	12 ♐ 39	29 52D	18 0	7 20	21 12	25 31	17 33	7 26	5 35	12 33
24 SU	8 36	25 38	29 53	18 0D	8 32	21 58	25 45	17 29	7 29	5 36	12 33
25 MO	9 34	8 ♑ 14	29 53R	18 6	9 45	22 44	25 59	17 25	7 32	5 37	12 33
26 TU	10 32	20 33	29 53	18 16	10 57	23 30	26 14	17 20	7 35	5 39	12 32
27 WE	11 31	2 ♒ 38	29 50	18 31	12 10	24 16	26 28	17 16	7 38	5 40	12 32
28 TH	12 29	14 35	29 46	18 51	13 23	25 2	26 42	17 12	7 41	5 41	12 31
29 FR	13 28	26 27	29 39	19 15	14 35	25 48	26 56	17 8	7 44	5 42	12 30
30 SA	14 26	8 ♓ 18	29 32	19 44	15 48	26 33	27 11	17 5	7 47	5 43	12 30

INGRESSES :

2	☽ → ♓	0:55		☽ → ♏	22:23
4	☽ → ♈	13:30	22	☽ → ♐	1:20
7	☽ → ♉	1:18	24	☽ → ♑	8:14
9	☽ → ♊	11:23	26	☽ → ♒	18:44
11	☽ → ♋	18:34	29	☽ → ♓	7:12
13	☽ → ♌	22:12			
15	☉ → ♈	4:52			
	☽ → ♍	22:52			
16	♀ → ♓	22:35			
17	☽ → ♎	22:13			
19	☊ → ♏	2:25			

ASPECTS & ECLIPSES :

2	☽ N ☊	4:25	9	☽ ☌ ☋	12:47		☽ ☌ ♄	3:16	25	☉ □ ☽	2:46
	☽ ☌ A	8:50		☉ ☌ ☿	19:28		♀ □ ☊	3:38	27	☽ ☌ ♆	6: 4
	☽ ☌ ♂	11:43	10	☽ ☍ ♇	10:59		☽ ☍ ☿	5:48		♀ □ ♇	7: 3
	☽ ☌ ⛢	13:44	11	☉ □ ☽	12: 5		☽ ☌ P	5:55	29	☽ N ☊	6:26
3	☉ ☌ ☽	14:32		♂ □ ♇	20:14		☽ ☍ ♃	13: 5		☽ ☌ A	18: 1
	☽ ☍ ♄	15:21	12	☿ ☌ ♃	3:42	18	☉ ☍ ☽	2:43		☽ ☌ ⛢	22:58
	☽ ☌ ♃	19: 8	14	☽ ☍ ♆	7: 6		♂ ☍ ♄	15:37	30	☽ ☌ ♀	16:54
	♂ ☌ ⛢	20:40	15	☽ ☍ ♀	20:48	19	☿ ☌ ♂	14:41		☽ ☍ ♄	17:39
	☉ ☍ ♄	23:42		☽ S ☊	23:33	22	☽ ☌ ☊	1: 5		♀ ☍ ♄	23:58
4	☽ ☌ ☿	10: 3	16	☽ ☍ ⛢	10: 7		☽ ☌ ♇	23:49			
6	☉ ☌ ♃	14:44	17	☽ ☍ ♂	1: 8	23	♀ ☌ ⛢	2:21			

SIDEREAL HELIOCENTRIC LONGITUDES : APRIL 2011 Gregorian at 0 hours UT

DAY	Sid. Time	☿	♀	⊕	♂	♃	♄	⛢	♆	♇	Vernal Point
1 FR	12:36: 2	20 ♌ 10	18 ♐ 19	16 ♍ 2	25 ♒ 39	21 ♓ 3	18 ♍ 53	5 ♓ 45	3 ♒ 45	10 ♐ 48	5 ♓ 6'11"
2 SA	12:39:58	24 34	19 54	17 1	26 17	21 8	18 55	5 46	3 45	10 48	5 ♓ 6'11"
3 SU	12:43:55	28 50	21 29	18 0	26 55	21 14	18 57	5 47	3 46	10 48	5 ♓ 6'11"
4 MO	12:47:51	2 ♍ 58	23 4	18 59	27 32	21 19	18 59	5 47	3 46	10 49	5 ♓ 6'11"
5 TU	12:51:48	6 58	24 39	19 58	28 10	21 25	19 1	5 48	3 46	10 49	5 ♓ 6'11"
6 WE	12:55:45	10 51	26 14	20 58	28 48	21 30	19 3	5 49	3 47	10 49	5 ♓ 6'11"
7 TH	12:59:41	14 38	27 49	21 57	29 26	21 36	19 4	5 49	3 47	10 50	5 ♓ 6'10"
8 FR	13: 3:38	18 18	29 23	22 56	0 ♓ 4	21 41	19 6	5 50	3 48	10 50	5 ♓ 6'10"
9 SA	13: 7:34	21 52	0 ♑ 58	23 55	0 41	21 47	19 8	5 51	3 48	10 50	5 ♓ 6'10"
10 SU	13:11:31	25 21	2 33	24 54	1 19	21 52	19 10	5 51	3 48	10 51	5 ♓ 6'10"
11 MO	13:15:27	28 46	4 8	25 53	1 57	21 58	19 12	5 52	3 49	10 51	5 ♓ 6'10"
12 TU	13:19:24	2 ♎ 5	5 43	26 51	2 34	22 3	19 14	5 52	3 49	10 51	5 ♓ 6'10"
13 WE	13:23:20	5 20	7 18	27 50	3 12	22 9	19 16	5 53	3 49	10 52	5 ♓ 6'10"
14 TH	13:27:17	8 31	8 53	28 49	3 50	22 14	19 18	5 54	3 50	10 52	5 ♓ 6'10"
15 FR	13:31:13	11 39	10 27	29 48	4 27	22 20	19 20	5 54	3 50	10 52	5 ♓ 6' 9"
16 SA	13:35:10	14 43	12 2	0 ♎ 47	5 5	22 25	19 22	5 55	3 50	10 53	5 ♓ 6' 9"
17 SU	13:39: 7	17 44	13 37	1 45	5 42	22 31	19 24	5 56	3 51	10 53	5 ♓ 6' 9"
18 MO	13:43: 3	20 43	15 12	2 44	6 20	22 36	19 26	5 56	3 51	10 53	5 ♓ 6' 9"
19 TU	13:47: 0	23 39	16 47	3 43	6 57	22 42	19 28	5 57	3 51	10 54	5 ♓ 6' 9"
20 WE	13:50:56	26 33	18 22	4 41	7 35	22 48	19 30	5 58	3 52	10 54	5 ♓ 6' 9"
21 TH	13:54:53	29 25	19 57	5 40	8 12	22 53	19 32	5 58	3 52	10 54	5 ♓ 6' 9"
22 FR	13:58:49	2 ♏ 15	21 32	6 38	8 50	22 59	19 34	5 59	3 53	10 55	5 ♓ 6' 8"
23 SA	14: 2:46	5 4	23 7	7 37	9 27	23 4	19 36	6 0	3 53	10 55	5 ♓ 6' 8"
24 SU	14: 6:42	7 52	24 42	8 35	10 4	23 10	19 38	6 0	3 53	10 55	5 ♓ 6' 8"
25 MO	14:10:39	10 38	26 17	9 34	10 42	23 15	19 40	6 1	3 54	10 56	5 ♓ 6' 8"
26 TU	14:14:36	13 24	27 52	10 32	11 19	23 21	19 42	6 1	3 54	10 56	5 ♓ 6' 8"
27 WE	14:18:32	16 9	29 27	11 31	11 56	23 26	19 44	6 2	3 54	10 56	5 ♓ 6' 8"
28 TH	14:22:29	18 54	1 ♒ 2	12 29	12 33	23 32	19 46	6 3	3 55	10 57	5 ♓ 6' 8"
29 FR	14:26:25	21 39	2 37	13 27	13 10	23 37	19 48	6 3	3 55	10 57	5 ♓ 6' 7"
30 SA	14:30:22	24 23	4 12	14 26	13 47	23 43	19 50	6 4	3 55	10 57	5 ♓ 6' 7"

INGRESSES :

3	☿ → ♍	6:42
7	♂ → ♓	21:42
8	♀ → ♑	9:14
11	☿ → ♎	8:53
15	⊕ → ♎	4:58
21	☿ → ♏	4:55
27	♀ → ♒	8:26

ASPECTS (HELIOCENTRIC +MOON(TYCHONIC)) :

1	☽ ☍ ☿	8: 2	6	⊕ ☍ ♃	14:44		☿ ⚹ ♇	18: 0	22	☿ □ ♆	13:50		☿ △ ♃	17:50
	♀ □ ♄	8:36	8	☿ ☌ ♄	5:25	16	☽ ☍ ♂	7:13		☽ ☌ ♇	20:50		☽ ☌ ⛢	19:29
	☽ ☌ ♂	17: 0		♀ ⚹ ♂	16:52		☽ ☍ ⛢	8:15		♀ ⚹ ♃	23:16		♀ ☌ ♆	19:54
2	☿ ☍ ♂	11:10		☿ ☍ ♃	23:21	17	☽ ☌ ♄	5:32	23	☿ △ ⛢	7:57	30	☽ ☌ ♂	11:43
	☽ ☌ ⛢	12:36	9	☿ ☌ ⊕	19:28		♂ ☌ ⛢	8:41	25	☿ △ ♂	0:36		☽ ☍ ♄	23:22
	♀ □ ♃	19:55	10	☽ ☍ ♇	7:44		☽ ☍ ♃	10:29		♂ □ ♇	9:17			
3	☽ ☍ ♄	15:15	12	♀ ⚹ ⛢	2:26	18	☿ ☌ ☋	23:18	26	⊕ ⚹ ♇	9:54			
	☽ ☌ ♃	19:59		☽ ☍ ♀	5:17	19	♀ ☌ A	0:37		☽ ☌ ♀	16:40			
	⊕ ☌ ♄	23:42		☿ △ ♆	12:45		⊕ △ ♆	3:41	27	☽ ☌ ♆	2:32			
4	☿ ☍ ⛢	16:55	14	☽ ☍ ♆	4:33		☽ ☌ ☿	14:58	28	☿ ⚹ ♄	7:38			
5	☿ □ ♇	23:49		☿ □ ♀	5:26	20	♀ △ ♄	17:36	29	☿ ☌ A	9:31			

the Gods" is remembered during this new moon: love of one's enemies. The Moon marks the watery sphere of the angels; it is the sphere that remembers our karmic debts. This new moon may be a time to ponder inwardly our true nature as children of God. Counter to this is the nature of our double—the caricature of our true self—who tends to judge and react to avoid exposure. The double is the "not us" that can be named but is not to be attended (the knowing glance). We are to attend what we want to grow. That is the spiritual challenge of our time. We can ask our angel for help, for the new moon is the full moon from the perspective of angels. During new moon periods, they are able to pass great wisdom to stir human thought life. With Mercury (the planet of thinking) remembering the most potent events of Earth evolution, we may find this new moon offers imaginations that strengthen us in any personal trials. Christ, in his great time of trial, modeled the way for human beings, who now stand in their great trial. Can we love one another?

ASPECTS: Mars conjunct Uranus (6° Pisces). Heliocentric Mars and Uranus were close together at the Baptism in the Jordan. Here the Living Word became flesh and lived among us. Care with words is a modest practice today, lest we bring to form the negative side of Mars–Uranus: bristling, bruising egoism.

Saturn (18 Virgo) opposite Sun (18 Pisces). Saturn, the guardian to the portal of the Father's Kingdom, opposite Sun, remembers the end of the temptations of Jesus Christ in the wilderness. The Father in the heights shone his brightest light onto his Son, who overcame the onslaughts that rose from the abyss of the Earth against him. Today the trials of Christ, the Baptism, and the end of the Forty Days remind us that the power of Christ is here with us and immeasurably strengthens those who choose to align with him. Christ recognized the tempters. John recognized the true light. Whose words are we following? Whose will moves us? If the beasts of the abyss wear wondrous cloaks and speak like lambs, will we still know them? There is much to contemplate during this new moon.

April 6: ASPECT: Sun conjunct Jupiter, 21° Pisces. With so many planets currently in Pisces (Mercury, Sun, Jupiter, Mars, and Uranus) there is a great cosmic inflowing of love. Today's Sun conjunct Jupiter evokes the Virgin Mary, who was also born during a Sun–Jupiter conjunction. This is she who was the Queen of Sheba, even greater in wisdom than Solomon was. At the holy festival of Pentecost, the Divine Sophia united with the Blessed Virgin Mary. This is the highest example of Sun and Jupiter in conjunction. It is a day to see in all others the spark of spiritual nobility. This is our future.

April 10: Sun 25° Pisces: Feeding of the Four Thousand (Matt. 15:29–39; *Chron.* 284). At the Feeding of the Four Thousand, seven loaves of bread and seven fish were multiplied. After all had eaten their fill, seven baskets full of bread were gathered. Here we see our union with the *temporal* aspect of the Sun Being. Seven signifies our chakras and our sevenfold nature: physical, etheric, astral, "I," spirit self, life spirit, and spirit body.

Human beings develop over the course of *time*. As we purify our bodies, our chakras awaken as organs of perception. Our awakened perceptions draw us ever closer to oneness with Christ. As this occurs, we require less nourishment *from* the elemental world and, instead, become sources of nourishment *for* the elemental world. As we move forward through evolution we will reach ever-higher levels of purity. Sophia's Temple has seven pillars, and we are currently working with the fourth, Earth. This is a good day to ponder the miracles in everyday life and the humility and patience needed for the process of becoming. We can experience the difference between giving and taking. The practice of giving can relieve us of the burden of egoism.

April 14: Sun 29° Pisces: Peter Given the Keys (March 19, 31). Four days after the Feeding of the Four Thousand, Jesus and the disciples had withdrawn to a mountain. At dawn, he goes to them and asks, "Who do you say that I am?" Peter saw the majesty of Jesus, proclaimed His divinity by saying, "You are the Christ, the Son of the living God" (Matthew 16:15–16). Peter was given the keys. The keys to the kingdom of heaven signify the power, drawn from the kingdom of the Father, to be able to hold in check the forces of the underworld arising through the gates of Hell (the moon chakra). The two keys are laid one over the other to form a cross (in eurythmy, the moon gesture forms a cross at the moon chakra). It is precisely the sign of the cross that the Father has empowered to banish the evil forces back into the underworld. The keys once given to Peter are now offered to all humanity. We are to use the keys. This is a day to contemplate our inner power to say "No" to subversive forces.

Noteworthy: The second phase of the volcano in Iceland (April 14, 2010) occurred with Sun at this degree. This second phase spewed an ash cloud disrupting European flights. Are we collectively using the keys to hold the gates of Hell in check?

April 15: Sun enters Aries: Devotion becomes force of sacrifice. Strength of thinking allows the Archangel Michael to pour in forces of will.

April 17/18 (15-17-19): Full moon, 1° to 2° Aries (DT): Make room for the new. We are right at the beginning of Aries, and a fragment form that the Oracle of the Solar Cross gives us: A flash of light from a resplendent cloud. Shock of thunder and words can be heard in the thunder. Again, and yet again: Glory! Glory! With the images of the Oracle of the Solar Cross, it is best to mull over the words and pictures, and then use them in one's own life. The Oracle continues: The tree that could not feed a pregnant mother or her grown child is shocked, crumpled, and killed; the old is swept away to make room for the new.

ASPECT: Mars opposite Saturn (18° Virgo). Mars opposes Saturn during this full moon. Each full moon is a new moon from the perspective of the angels. When full, the Moon is furthest from the Sun and empty of light from the angelic perspective. During this time the angels are active in human dream life. The full moon works most strongly on the base of the spine, affecting the will and instinctual life in the subconscious. This full moon is accompanied by a Mars–Saturn opposition. Heliocentric Mars and Saturn were close to opposition at the birth of Novalis, the great poet who spoke with and through the Saturnine portal into the kingdom of our Divine Mother. In part five of his *Hymns to the Night* he expresses:

> To the marriage Death doth call—
> The virgins standeth back—
> The lamps burn lustrous all—
> Of oil there is no lack—
> If the distance would only fill
> With the sound of you walking alone
> And that the stars would call
> Us all with human tongues and tone.
>
> Unto thee, O Mary
> A thousand hearts aspire.
> In this life of shadows
> Thee only they desire.
> In thee they hope for delivery
> With visionary expectation—
> If only thou, O holy being
> Could clasp them to thy breast.

Novalis exemplifies a spirit united with the Word (Mars) to form (Saturn) Sophianic inspirations (Virgo). The slang of "teen talk" and technological devices is splintering the Word. As all things were created through the Word, we can only ponder the deeper metaphor of tearing the Word apart. This is a day to practice the art of the Word. Novalis recognized the power of the Word and the union of the Word with the Mother. The *Bible* refers to "oil in our lamps," representing recognition and devotion (Sun in Aries) to the Christ and Sophia. This is a day to practice the art of the Word in its poetic wholeness.

April 19: Sun 4° Aries: Woe upon the Pharisees. In this address to the crowds and disciples, Jesus Christ issued a challenge to the Pharisees. Powerful words echo from this "woe" into our own time, and today in particular as Mars (the Word) and Saturn (cosmic memory) continue to stand closely opposed to each other in the heavens. Following is a part of what He then spoke:

They tie up heavy burdens, hard to bear, and lay them on people's shoulders, but they themselves are not willing to move them with their finger. They do all their deeds to be seen by others.... Woe to you, scribes and Pharisees, hypocrites! For you are like whitewashed tombs, which outwardly appear beautiful, but within are full of dead people's bones and all uncleanness. So you also outwardly appear righteous to others, but within you are full of hypocrisy and lawlessness. (Matt. 23:4–5, 27–28 [ESV])

These words thundered from the Lamb of God shortly before his sacrifice (Aries). Who are these hypocrites in today's world? Are we free of hypocrisy? What will we sacrifice to stand with Christ?

April 22/23: ASPECT: Venus conjunct Uranus (DT): We understand Venus as an influence for one to find one's destiny brothers and sisters, and Uranus to work in unexpected and shocking ways. In this aspect, the Healer raised the high initiate Lazarus from the dead, and into a much more intimate association with the students of the Teacher. In this aspect, the last great push of World War II began, D-Day, June 6, 1944.

ASPECT: Venus conjunct Uranus: The Raising of Lazarus (July 26, 32). Through Christ, Lazarus received the seven gifts of the Holy Spirit, as seed impulses in his etheric body. Having passed through death, he had seen another world and experienced the mysteries of the Spirit in the heights of Heaven and in the depths of the underworld. The combination of the tears being shed on Earth and the voice of spiritual thunder speaking, "Lazarus, come forth!" Together they called Lazarus back from the Kingdom of Light to be reborn on Earth with a new mission. Does not this voice call out again from the etheric realms where Christ is now working? Is not each of our names now sounding with spiritual thunder from the Etheric Christ? Is not the Being of Love calling all his children back from the jaws of materialism into the splendor of receiving his name, and the promised future this recognition brings? Christ wept! The gift of tears is our perfect offering as we awaken to the presence of Christ and Sophia in the eternal present. Lazarus journeyed through the underworld. Meeting the underworld, with Christ, is the descent that allows for an ascent. This is a good day to listen attentively to what is rising from the Earth and descending from Heaven. In 1944, during this same aspect, we were in battle against the threat of evil. Valentin Tomberg gives us a different imagination for evil: "For good does not *fight* evil; it does not struggle against it. The good is only present, or it is not. Its victory consists in that it results in being present, its defeat in that it is forced to be absent."[2] What does this mean in the current fight against evil? How do we fill all space with goodness so evil has no breath? Negative Venus goes to war and destroys. Positive Venus goes to peace, guided by new imaginations coming into time (Uranus). May we find the gift of tears rather than the tears of grief. Good simply is!

April 25: Sun 10° Aries: The Visitation (March 30, 2 B.C.). The Nathan Mary, pregnant with Jesus, visited her cousin Elizabeth, who was pregnant with John the Baptist. During that meeting, all four of them were filled with holy awe as the Old Adam, John the Baptist in Elizabeth's womb, was quickened by the presence of the New Adam, Jesus in Mary's womb. The Adam that experienced the Fall (John the Baptist) was reunited with the substance held back at the time of the Fall. When something falls, something else rises. In Paradise the pure substance *rose* from Adam and was guarded in the lodge of the Sun as the Adam being *fell* from Paradise. This chaste and virgin substance of the first Adam was brought into incarnation for the first time through this pure Nathan soul. Through the Mystery of Golgotha the tragedy of this necessary duality was overcome once and for all. The Sun today can remind us that reunion between our fallen self and our higher self is a choice offered in each moment. May we choose wisely.

April 27: Sun 12° Aries: The Last Anointing (April 1, 33). Mary Magdalene enters the room as Jesus

---

2 Anonymous, *Meditations on the Tarot: A Journey into Christian Hermeticism* (New York: Tarcher/Putnam, 1985), p. 114.

Christ is speaking of His approaching death and His betrayal for money. All are indescribably sad. Magdalene casts herself down at Jesus' feet, anointing them with a costly ointment, and she dries His feet with her hair. Judas scolds her and is reprimanded by Jesus. The betrayal is set in motion. Jesus said, "Truly, I say to you, wherever this gospel is proclaimed in the whole world, what she has done will also be told in memory of her" (Matt 26:13). These words were inscribed eternally into the angelic sphere. Judas ran out into the night, all the way to Jerusalem, and presented himself to the high priests and Pharisees. He betrayed Christ for thirty pieces of silver. We can hear an ominous warning in this. Wherein lies the true nature of our devotion (Aries) when money is at stake? Does the muttering of the blind cause us to compromise? Are there souls brave enough to represent the new in spite of the rumbling of those who mutter against them?

April 28–29: Sun 13° Aries: The Last Supper through to the Nailing on the Cross (April 2–3, 33). The Sun today remembers the most wretched moments of the life of Christ up to his final victory on the hill of Golgotha. All that Christ then experienced *from* humanity, allows him to give *to* humanity now. The deeds done to him during the Passion created the karmic field that allows him to touch us spiritually in this time of the Second Coming. Christ gives all his love to humanity, as humanity once gave all their hatred to him. Each step of the way must be contemplated as the greatest mystery of Earth evolution. The Passion of Christ is the path of the initiate. We may pray for the strength to willingly carry the cross of our own burdens. This lightens his Cross. In the words of Judith von Halle:

> There can be no fantasy or even wish on the part of the spiritual pupil of entering upon a path of cognition that would be broad and well trodden, easy and without effort. The path of cognition that one takes is one's own. Hence no one has entered upon it before. At the beginning of the journey, at the time of one's decision to commit, it actually does not exist at all. It is one's task to direct oneself through the morass of one's soul urgings, and to direct one's I through the "soul emptiness of space," through the "destruction of time. [3]

It is sobering indeed to imagine how lonely the path is through space during initiation, and how free human beings must be to find their very own paths. It is the initiates who are restoring time's destruction. We are all to begin this journey toward initiation; it is the path leading us into the future. We have our very own path! What is it?

April 29: Sun 14° Aries: The Death of Jesus on the Cross (April 3, 33). This death marks the birth of Christ into the Earth. This birth was his descent into Hell, a time when the spiritual world held its breath wondering if the Son of God would ever emerge again from the darkness of the Earth. Yet, as the blood spilled from the lance thrust into him at the cross, the entire Earth was surrounded in radiant light. The Sun was at this same degree during the Transfiguration two years earlier (April 4, 31). This is a star language. The path to purification and ascent is through the descent. Christ's descent was not for his being, but for the whole of humanity and the spiritual world. The John–Raphael being's painting of the Transfiguration is an imagination for our future. Raphael sketched the Transfiguration and, before his death, painted the light-filled upper half. His disciples finished the lower (dark) half of the painting based on Raphael's sketches. This lower half shows the picture of the boy possessed. We, as disciples of John, are called to work on this masterpiece by meeting the possessions in our own souls. There comes a time when it is as if our hands and feet are nailed down, as the narrow way of redemption opens before us.

⚘

---

[3] Von Halle, *Der Abstieg in die Erdenschichten* ("The Descent into the Layers of the Earth"; Dornach, Switzerland: Verlag am Goetheanum 2008).

MAY

The Sun is in Aries, entering the Bull (Taurus) on the 15/16th. The Sun will be in front of Aldebaran (the "Eye of the Bull" and a Royal Star of Persia) on the 31st, a good day to sense what might come from this star.

The mornings of May bring an eastern horizon show, beginning about two hours before sunrise on the 1st. Venus and the waning crescent moon rise together followed swiftly by Mercury, then Jupiter and Mars. This continues as the month unfolds, with these planets rearranging their order. By month's end we will see Jupiter rising three hours before the Sun, followed by Mars and Venus. The Moon and Mercury follow them, but may be hidden in the light of the Sun.

The evening sky continues to show us Saturn in Virgo each evening, and is lit by the waxing moon and Saturn together on the 14th.

May 1: Sun 15° Aries: Resurrection of Christ (April 5, 33). According to Judith von Halle, a third and final earthquake occurred as Christ arose from the depths of the Earth in his resurrection body. To behold such magnificent splendor is beyond normal understanding. The words of the Risen Christ to Mary Magdalene sound through time, "Do not cling to me, for I have not yet ascended to the Father; but go to my brothers and say to them, 'I am ascending to my Father and your Father, to my God and your God" (John 20:17). These words contain the powerful *fact* that Christ, from this moment on, is the bridge that restores the unity between above and below, between the Earth and Heaven. From this moment on, he is *in* us. This oneness interconnects the whole of humanity into fellowship. The actual awakening of the disciples to the reality of this oneness comes later at the holy festival of Pentecost. During these forty days, the disciples are in a kind of sleep. Images from their life *with* Christ rise into their consciousness (etheric images), which help them understand the teachings of Christ during the forty days after the Resurrection. This is a wonderful day to remember this oneness and to seek, in all our brothers and sisters, Christ's presence. The forty days until Ascension are potent days to work with etheric echoes. If we hold silence after a conversation, after an event, or at day's end, we may experience an echo. These are etheric responses from angelic realms, inspiring and informing us of hidden dimensions in our daily work.

May 3: new moon, 17° Aries (DT): Expect the unexpected in the deep waters. Fragments for the Oracle of the Solar Cross. If you must have money, go fishing! The fish you catch will have a coin in its mouth, enough to pay the taxes required this day, and those of another, too. And the fish you catch will feed us all. As explanation, when asked to pay the Temple tax, the Teacher instructs Peter to go fishing, predicting that the first fish he catches will have a coin in its mouth. Peter does so and with this he pays the tax for both of them. Expect the unexpected. The whole world is interlinked. All creation is magical and intertwined, but we must learn how to open to it. As a bonus, the magic fish is so large that it feeds everyone.

Sun 17° Aries: Appearance in Emmaus (April 6, 33). May 2 through June 9, we move through the Sun degrees, which remember the forty days of Christ between the Resurrection and the Ascension. These days specifically mark the communion of the disciples and holy women with the resurrection body of Christ. There are several different kinds of communion with Christ, of which four are primary:

Communion with Christ's physical body
    (Resurrection body)—Bread
Communion with Christ's "I"—Wine (Descent
    into Hell)
Communion with Christ's etheric body— the
    Eternal Gospel (Life Tableau of Christ)
Communion with Christ's astral body— the
    Eternal Apocalypse (Book of Revelation is
    a portion of this body)[1]

The day after the Resurrection, Luke and Cleophas were traveling to Emmaus when a third person joined them. That evening, the three went to a guest house, where they were served food. The

---
1 See *Christian Hermetic Astrology*, pp. 236–257.

SIDEREAL GEOCENTRIC LONGITUDES : MAY 2011 Gregorian at 0 hours UT

DAY		☉	☽	☊	☿	♀	♂	♃	♄	♅	♆	♇
1	SU	15 ♈ 24	20 ♓ 10	29 ♏ 23R	20 ♓ 16	17 ♓ 1	27 ♓ 19	27 ♓ 25	17 ♍ 1R	7 ♓ 50	5 ♒ 44	12 ♐ 29R
2	MO	16 22	2 ♈ 7	29 15	20 53	18 13	28 5	27 39	16 57	7 53	5 45	12 28
3	TU	17 21	14 10	29 7	21 33	19 26	28 50	27 53	16 53	7 56	5 46	12 28
4	WE	18 19	26 20	29 2	22 18	20 39	29 36	28 7	16 50	7 59	5 47	12 27
5	TH	19 17	8 ♉ 38	28 58	23 5	21 52	0 ♈ 21	28 21	16 46	8 1	5 48	12 26
6	FR	20 15	21 6	28 56	23 57	23 4	1 7	28 35	16 42	8 4	5 49	12 26
7	SA	21 13	3 ♊ 46	28 55D	24 51	24 17	1 52	28 49	16 39	8 7	5 50	12 25
8	SU	22 11	16 39	28 57	25 48	25 30	2 38	29 3	16 36	8 10	5 51	12 24
9	MO	23 10	29 47	28 58	26 49	26 43	3 23	29 17	16 32	8 12	5 52	12 23
10	TU	24 8	13 ♋ 12	28 59	27 52	27 55	4 8	29 30	16 29	8 15	5 53	12 22
11	WE	25 6	26 57	29 0R	28 58	29 8	4 53	29 44	16 26	8 17	5 53	12 21
12	TH	26 4	11 ♌ 1	28 59	0 ♈ 7	0 ♈ 21	5 39	29 58	16 23	8 20	5 54	12 20
13	FR	27 1	25 24	28 57	1 19	1 34	6 24	0 ♈ 12	16 20	8 23	5 55	12 19
14	SA	27 59	10 ♍ 3	28 53	2 33	2 47	7 9	0 25	16 17	8 25	5 55	12 18
15	SU	28 57	24 52	28 49	3 50	3 59	7 54	0 39	16 14	8 27	5 56	12 17
16	MO	29 55	9 ♎ 44	28 45	5 9	5 12	8 39	0 52	16 12	8 30	5 57	12 16
17	TU	0 ♉ 53	24 32	28 42	6 30	6 25	9 24	1 6	16 9	8 32	5 57	12 15
18	WE	1 51	9 ♏ 6	28 40	7 54	7 38	10 9	1 19	16 6	8 35	5 58	12 14
19	TH	2 48	23 22	28 39	9 21	8 51	10 53	1 33	16 4	8 37	5 58	12 13
20	FR	3 46	7 ♐ 15	28 39D	10 49	10 4	11 38	1 46	16 2	8 39	5 59	12 12
21	SA	4 44	20 42	28 40	12 20	11 16	12 23	1 59	15 59	8 42	5 59	12 11
22	SU	5 42	3 ♑ 45	28 42	13 53	12 29	13 7	2 13	15 57	8 44	6 0	12 10
23	MO	6 39	16 27	28 43	15 29	13 42	13 52	2 26	15 55	8 46	6 0	12 9
24	TU	7 37	28 49	28 44	17 7	14 55	14 37	2 39	15 53	8 48	6 0	12 8
25	WE	8 35	10 ♒ 57	28 44R	18 47	16 8	15 21	2 52	15 51	8 50	6 1	12 6
26	TH	9 32	22 55	28 43	20 29	17 21	16 6	3 5	15 49	8 52	6 1	12 5
27	FR	10 30	4 ♓ 49	28 42	22 13	18 34	16 50	3 18	15 47	8 54	6 1	12 4
28	SA	11 28	16 41	28 39	24 0	19 47	17 34	3 31	15 46	8 56	6 1	12 3
29	SU	12 25	28 36	28 37	25 49	21 0	18 19	3 44	15 44	8 58	6 2	12 1
30	MO	13 23	10 ♈ 37	28 35	27 40	22 13	19 3	3 57	15 43	9 0	6 2	12 0
31	TU	14 20	22 47	28 33	29 34	23 26	19 47	4 9	15 41	9 2	6 2	11 59

INGRESSES :

1	☽ → ♈	19:45	16	☉ → ♉	2: 2
4	☽ → ♉	7:11	17	☽ → ♏	8:57
	♂ → ♈	12:44	19	☽ → ♐	11:22
6	☽ → ♊	16:54	21	☽ → ♑	17: 1
9	☽ → ♋	0:23	24	☽ → ♒	2:19
11	☽ → ♌	5:14	26	☽ → ♓	14:16
	♀ → ♈	17: 4	29	☽ → ♈	2:48
	☿ → ♈	21:28	31	☿ → ♉	5:28
12	♃ → ♈	3:36		☽ → ♉	14: 3
13	☽ → ♍	7:33			
15	☽ → ♎	8:16			

ASPECTS & ECLIPSES :

1	☽ ☌ ☿	0:12		☿ ☌ ♃	19:58	19	☽ ☌ ☊	9: 2	29	☽ ☌ ♃	10:27
	♂ ☌ ♃	4:18	13	☽ □S ☊	5:48	20	☽ ☌ ♇	8:44	30	☽ ☌ ♂	17:43
	☽ ☌ ♃	14:51		☽ ☍ ♅	21:19	21	☿ ☌ ♂	1:19	31	☽ ☌ ♀	1:23
	☽ ☌ ♂	15:20	14	☽ ☌ ♄	10: 5	22	☉ □ ♆	7:31		☽ ☌ ☿	15:38
3	☉ ☌ ☽	6:50	15	☽ ☍ ♃	9:28	23	♀ ☌ ♂	8:22			
6	☽ ☌ ☋	14:51		☽ ☌ P	11:23	24	☽ ☌ ♆	14:10			
7	☽ ☍ ♇	16: 8		☽ ☍ ☿	15:51		☉ □ ☽	18:52			
9	☿ ☌ ♀	14:54		☽ ☍ ♀	16: 1	26	☽ N□ ☊	11:40			
10	☉ □ ☽	20:32		☽ ☍ ♂	22: 8	27	☽ ☌ ♅	8:18			
11	♀ ☌ ♃	14:37	16	☿ ☌ ♀	9:53		☽ ☌ A	9:43			
	☽ ☍ ♆	15:19	17	☉ ☍ ☽	11: 8		☽ ☍ ♄	22: 9			

SIDEREAL HELIOCENTRIC LONGITUDES : MAY 2011 Gregorian at 0 hours UT

DAY		Sid. Time	☿	♀	⊕	♂	♃	♄	♅	♆	♇	Vernal Point
1	SU	14:34:18	27 ♏ 8	5 ♒ 47	15 ♎ 24	14 ♓ 24	23 ♓ 48	19 ♍ 52	6 ♓ 5	3 ♒ 56	10 ♐ 58	5♓ 6' 7"
2	MO	14:38:15	29 54	7 22	16 22	15 1	23 54	19 54	6 5	3 56	10 58	5♓ 6' 7"
3	TU	14:42:11	2 ♐ 40	8 57	17 20	15 38	23 59	19 56	6 6	3 57	10 58	5♓ 6' 7"
4	WE	14:46: 8	5 27	10 32	18 19	16 15	24 5	19 58	6 7	3 57	10 59	5♓ 6' 7"
5	TH	14:50: 5	8 15	12 7	19 17	16 52	24 10	20 0	6 7	3 57	10 59	5♓ 6' 7"
6	FR	14:54: 1	11 4	13 42	20 15	17 29	24 16	20 2	6 8	3 58	11 0	5♓ 6' 6"
7	SA	14:57:58	13 54	15 17	21 13	18 6	24 21	20 4	6 9	3 58	11 0	5♓ 6' 6"
8	SU	15: 1:54	16 47	16 52	22 11	18 43	24 27	20 6	6 9	3 58	11 0	5♓ 6' 6"
9	MO	15: 5:51	19 41	18 28	23 9	19 20	24 32	20 8	6 10	3 59	11 1	5♓ 6' 6"
10	TU	15: 9:47	22 38	20 3	24 7	19 56	24 38	20 10	6 10	3 59	11 1	5♓ 6' 6"
11	WE	15:13:44	25 37	21 38	25 5	20 33	24 43	20 11	6 11	3 59	11 1	5♓ 6' 6"
12	TH	15:17:40	28 38	23 13	26 3	21 9	24 49	20 13	6 12	4 0	11 2	5♓ 6' 6"
13	FR	15:21:37	1 ♑ 43	24 49	27 1	21 46	24 54	20 15	6 12	4 0	11 2	5♓ 6' 6"
14	SA	15:25:34	4 50	26 24	27 59	22 23	25 0	20 17	6 13	4 1	11 2	5♓ 6' 5"
15	SU	15:29:30	8 2	27 59	28 57	22 59	25 5	20 19	6 14	4 1	11 3	5♓ 6' 5"
16	MO	15:33:27	11 17	29 35	29 55	23 36	25 11	20 21	6 14	4 1	11 3	5♓ 6' 5"
17	TU	15:37:23	14 36	1 ♓ 10	0 ♏ 53	24 12	25 16	20 23	6 15	4 2	11 3	5♓ 6' 5"
18	WE	15:41:20	17 59	2 45	1 50	24 48	25 22	20 25	6 16	4 2	11 4	5♓ 6' 5"
19	TH	15:45:16	21 27	4 21	2 48	25 25	25 27	20 27	6 16	4 2	11 4	5♓ 6' 5"
20	FR	15:49:13	25 0	5 56	3 46	26 1	25 33	20 29	6 17	4 3	11 4	5♓ 6' 5"
21	SA	15:53: 9	28 39	7 32	4 44	26 37	25 38	20 31	6 18	4 3	11 5	5♓ 6' 4"
22	SU	15:57: 6	2 ♒ 23	9 7	5 41	27 13	25 44	20 33	6 18	4 3	11 5	5♓ 6' 4"
23	MO	16: 1: 3	6 14	10 43	6 39	27 49	25 49	20 35	6 19	4 4	11 5	5♓ 6' 4"
24	TU	16: 4:59	10 11	12 18	7 37	28 25	25 55	20 37	6 19	4 4	11 6	5♓ 6' 4"
25	WE	16: 8:56	14 15	13 54	8 34	29 1	26 0	20 39	6 20	4 4	11 6	5♓ 6' 4"
26	TH	16:12:52	18 26	15 29	9 32	29 37	26 6	20 41	6 21	4 5	11 6	5♓ 6' 4"
27	FR	16:16:49	22 45	17 5	10 30	0 ♈ 13	26 11	20 43	6 21	4 5	11 7	5♓ 6' 4"
28	SA	16:20:45	27 11	18 40	11 27	0 49	26 17	20 45	6 22	4 6	11 7	5♓ 6' 3"
29	SU	16:24:42	1 ♓ 47	20 16	12 25	1 25	26 22	20 47	6 23	4 6	11 7	5♓ 6' 3"
30	MO	16:28:38	6 30	21 52	13 22	2 1	26 28	20 49	6 23	4 6	11 8	5♓ 6' 3"
31	TU	16:32:35	11 23	23 27	14 20	2 36	26 33	20 51	6 24	4 7	11 8	5♓ 6' 3"

INGRESSES :

2	☿ → ♐	0:54
12	☿ → ♑	10:41
16	⊕ → ♏	2: 9
	♀ → ♓	6:24
21	☿ → ♒	8:44
26	♂ → ♈	15:10
28	☿ → ♓	14:47

ASPECTS (HELIOCENTRIC +MOON(TYCHONIC)) :

1	☽ ☌ ♃	7:21		☿ □ ♃	16:38	18	☿ △ ♄	17: 4		♀ □ ♇	5:43	30	☿ □ ♇	22:48
3	☿ ⚹ ♆	11: 5		☿ ⚹ ⊕	17:50	19	♂ ☌ ♃	2: 1	24	☿ ⚹ ♇	5:26	31	☿ △ ⊕	17:32
4	☿ □ ♅	5:45	11	♀ □S ☊	3:45		☿ □S ☊	14:20		☽ ☌ ♆	10:20			
	♀ ⚹ ♇	6:49		☽ ☍ ♆	12: 4	20	☿ ⚹ ♃	3:40	25	☽ ☌ ☿	10: 3			
5	☿ ☌ ♇	23:24	12	☽ ☍ ♀	22:53		♀ ☌ ♅	5:16	27	☽ ☌ ♅	3: 8			
7	☽ ☍ ♇	13:32	13	☽ ☍ ♅	17:44		☽ ☌ ♇	6:45	28	☽ ☌ ♀	4:38			
8	☽ ☍ ☿	0:19	14	☿ ⚹ ♅	10:27		⊕ □ ♆	6:59		☽ ☍ ♄	8:14			
	☿ ⚹ ♀	1:43		☽ ☌ ♄	16:38		☿ ⚹ ♂	8: 1		☽ ☌ ♃	19:29			
	☿ □ ♂	20:14		☽ ☍ ♂	20:49	22	☿ ☌ ♆	10:30	29	☽ ☌ ♂	5:56			
9	☿ □ ♄	3:39	15	☽ ☍ ♃	0:21		⊕ △ ♅	15:29		♀ ☍ ♄	7:55			
10	♂ ☍ ♄	9:12	16	♀ △ ⊕	12:57	23	☿ □ ⊕	3:25		☿ ☌ ♅	23:25			

third person took the bread, blessed it, and broke it into small pieces. Through this act, the disciples recognized Christ. This was communion with the resurrection body of Christ, accompanied by his words, "I am the bread of life." This bread of life is the substance of the Word of God living in all pure nourishment, as the antidote to destructive manipulation of the Mother's archetypes in seeds. Christ, throughout the forty days, was ministering the bread of life to his disciples. Through his wounds and from his mouth flowed pure light, giving them the power to forgive sins, to baptize, to heal, and to lay on hands. As communion with the resurrection body was the forty days between the Resurrection and the Ascension, so is communion with the "I" of Christ (wine). His descent into Hell and into the heart of the Mother.

The Grail Knights were schooled in developing the courage to descend into Hell, confront evil, and overcome it. Parsifal took up this battle with evil for the sake of human beings and the Mother Earth. He is the human being of the future, the Jupiter human being. In the twelve-year rhythm of Jupiter, we follow Christ as he penetrates the subearthly realms on behalf of the Mother, which began in 1945. We are currently in the seventh interior sphere, the *Earth Mirror* (July 24, 2004 to June 5, 2016), connected with the manas cognition of the spirit self.[2] The Beatitude that counteracts the evil of this sphere is "Blessed are the peacemakers for they shall be called the children of God." Valentin Tomberg speaks of the peacemakers:

> If the consciousness soul is filled with consciousness of the guilt and need of earthly life, it lifts it like a cup, interceding for the need of Earth. It can then encounter a current descending from above, one that absorbs the darkness of guilt and need into its own clear light, carried upward by the consciousness soul. It may happen then that the ascending darkness and the descending light unite, which leads to a "rainbow" of reconciliation between the two worlds. For example, Goethe, in his soul, carried knowledge of this process of reconciliation and peace between the two

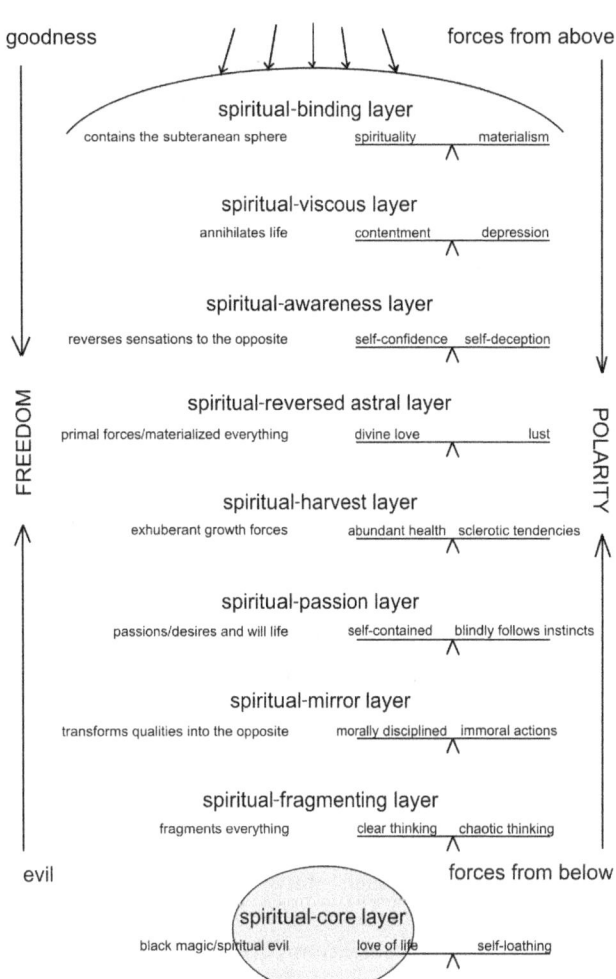

worlds. Such knowledge became not only the basis of his theory of color, but also of his fairytale *The Green Snake and the Beautiful Lily*.[3]

The fruition of Earth's evolution is the ripening of the consciousness soul to receive the angelic sphere into itself. We reach this fruition by partaking in communion with Christ and Sophia. If Christ, or an ambassador of Christ, were among us—would we know this, or would we persecute him in this Second Coming as we did in the first? Such is food for thought on this new moon as we contemplate these forty days. Are we aware of unseen beings moving among us? Can we sacrifice (Aries) our self-interest, to find higher beings whose interest is in us? We are not alone!

---

2 See Powell, *The Inner Life of the Earth*, p. 121.

3 Tomberg, *Christ and Sophia*, p. 220.

May 4: Sun 19° Aries: Conversation with the Pharisee Nicodemus (April 9, 30). A great mystery lives in this conversation, which occurred in the *night* (John 3:1–21).

May 9: ASPECT: Mercury conjunct Venus, 27° Pisces. Square to this conjunction today was the Mercury–Venus conjunction at the second raising of Salome, the daughter of Jairus, who was the head of the synagogue at Capernaum. Salome fell ill for a second time, owing to her parents' dismissive attitude toward Jesus after the first healing.

> In this example of Jairus's daughter is contained a teaching concerning the Second Coming of the Lord. Many are those who received the grace of Jesus Christ through his First Coming, but in later incarnations have forgotten it. Like Jairus and his wife, they have lived frivolous lives based on worldly concerns, even mocking the memory of the Holy One of Israel, the Saviour of humankind. But misfortune is bound to strike whosoever turns away from the Source of all Goodness. And this is the situation in which many find themselves in their incarnations in the Age of the Second Coming. Salvation can be found only by turning to Jesus Christ, and as in the case of Jairus, a second opportunity will be given to all who sincerely seek Him. And in the case of those who have missed the grace of Jesus Christ in their incarnations up until now, there is now another opportunity—as in the case of the pagan woman Enue[4]—to seek out Jesus Christ and make contact with him. However great the throng, He notices each one, and His healing power of love and compassion goes forth to each who seeks it and needs it.[5]

Mercury, our personal seat of action and intelligence, in union with Venus, our karmic group, tells the story of rising from the dead of forgetfulness to remember what once touched us. The pagans, the Jews, the Christians and all petals of the Rose of the World can touch him now. Christ, the being of love, is the center of all karmic groups until the end of time. Where Christ has been usurped, the soul of the person, the circle, organization, or society is dying, just as Salome died when her father dismissed the presence of Christ. We are given a second chance. Do we seek power *over* others or power *with* others? This is a question Mercury conjunct Venus asks. Collaboration is the "way of the Grail."

May 11: Sun 25° Aries: The appearance of the Risen One to the seven disciples at the northeast end of the Sea of Galilee (John 21:1–23). Here Christ bids Peter, "Feed my lambs.... Tend my sheep.... Feed my sheep" (John 21:15–17). He is called to be the spiritual leader of the Church, to ensure that the sacraments, above all Holy Communion, continue to be celebrated for all time. Peter asks what will become of John, and the Risen One answers: "If it is my will that he remain until I come, what is that to you?" Implicit here is the task of the Church of John to wait until the Second Coming of Christ in the etheric realm. The Church of Peter has the task to lead human beings to the threshold of the spiritual world, and the Church of John must lead them across the threshold. John and Peter work together, united in their service to Christ and Sophia. The Church of John is centered in the heart, and those who choose to join this Church are summoned by the call of the Grail. Mass in the exoteric church is comparable to the Grail Mystery in the esoteric church.

Grail communion is communion with the beings of the stars, requiring one to cross the threshold. Crossing the threshold requires a meeting with the soul's fallen nature in the depths of the underworld. This is why it is the John being that Rudolf Steiner claims will be with us at the end of the century. John is the one who accompanied Lazarus through the underworld after his death, and before he was raised by Christ. We live in the time of the Second Coming, when the Church of John is opening, and this is a time when humanity is both collectively and individually crossing the threshold.

Finally, we live in a time when star wisdom is being reborn as communion with the beings of

---

4 Enue was the woman healed of the "issue of blood." Her destiny was intricately intertwined with that of Salome (see lecture referred to above).

5 Powell, *Christian Hermetic Astrology*, p. 122.

the stars. Aries is the constellation of self-sacrifice, spiritual strength, and leadership. On this day we may ask: Are we are even awake to the vastness of the mysteries surrounding us in our everyday life? Alternatively we may find we are excessively caught up in the small story of our "little" biography. As our interest in others and in the vastness of other worlds that interact with us increases, we open to new possibilities. We may ask ourselves: "What about John?" Where do I stand before the hermetic mysteries of the stars?

ASPECT: Venus conjunct Jupiter, 29° Pisces. Venus and Jupiter were in hermetic (viewed from the Sun) conjunction in Pisces at the start of the temptations in the wilderness. Through his victory over the tempters, Christ was able to form a new karmic community. From a certain perspective, Venus represents the archai, who were at their human stage of evolution during ancient Saturn (a much earlier incarnation of the Earth). The archai who remained behind we know as the *Asuras*, who tempt human beings into destructive acts through abject egoism. The Asuras wield the strongest will to evil, and because of this our present-day self-development is under constant threat. There are communities whose members love one another (Venus) and there are those that seek to rule over others (negative Jupiter). Both the highest and the lowest manifest on Earth. It takes courage to see through the times to underlying agendas.

Pisces—the sign under which this conjunction occurs—invites us to discern communities of love from agendas of tyranny. Peace, harmony, and protection for all beings, including the beings of nature, represent the fruits of Venus and Jupiter conjoined in Pisces.

ASPECT: Venus conjunct Jupiter, 29° Pisces (DT): We see Venus as the beacon of one's destiny brothers and sisters, and Jupiter as something that could be large, dignified, and full of light (see the relevant article in the *Journal* for 2010). In this aspect, Paul Revere made his famous ride on April 18, 1775, through the dark and stormy night, setting up a lamp in the steeple of a church, an act that connected him with his destiny brothers and separated him from his (English) forebears.

May 16: Sun enters Taurus: Inner Balance becomes Progress. The work of the transformation of the will: "May the world thought think in me."

May 17 (14-17-20): Full moon, 2° Taurus (DT). The Taurus full moon has been called the *Wesak* (Pentecost) *full moon*, when the Buddha and the Christ become active in the world, renewing a blessing. This year, the festival of Pentecost occurs in the Great Circle of Algol, the Eye of Medusa, with very difficult themes (uncharacteristic of Taurus in general). The themes of this location concern death, turning to stone, mastering the art of poetry. How appropriate that John Donne died when the Sun was at this degree. His *Ode* summarizes the power available in this full moon. Read it aloud:

> When in mid-air the golden trump shall
>   sound,
> To raise the nations under ground;
> When, in the Valley of Jehoshaphat,
> The judging God shall close the
>   book of Fate,
> And there the last assizes keep
> For those who wake and those who sleep;
> When rattling bones together fly
> From the four corners of the sky;
> When sinews o'er the skeletons are spread,
> Those clothed with flesh, and life
>   inspires the dead;
> The sacred poets first shall hear
>   the sound,
> And foremost from the tomb shall bound,
> For they are cover'd with the lightest
>   ground;
> And straight, with inborn vigour, on
>   the wing,
> Like mounting larks, to the new
>   morning sing.
> There thou, sweet Saint, before the quire
>   shall go,
> As harbinger of Heaven, the way to show,
> The way which thou so well hast
>   learn'd below.

Sun 2° Taurus. The Virgin Mary receives her first communion (April 23, 33). Shortly after midnight the Blessed Virgin Mary receives the holy sacrament from Peter (three weeks after the Last Supper). During this communion, Jesus appears to her. Later she retires to her room to pray, and toward dawn the Lord appears to her again and gives her power over the church, a protective force, such that light flows from him into her. In this we see the preparation for the event of Pentecost coming in the weeks that follow. Under this full moon, we may ask where we are able to reverently hold the place of center for a family or group—in anticipation of leading inspirations. Taurus shapes our larynx and Eustachian tubes, mirrored by the stethoscope. Through the organ of the larynx we can listen to the heart of God. This full moon is a beautiful Moon for spiritual listening. This is an antidote to hardening forces that atrophy our subtle higher senses.

May 21: Mercury conjunct Mars, 12° Aries: The Sun was at this degree when Mary Magdalene last anointed Jesus Christ (April 1, 33). In the event of this anointing we see the devotion (Aries) in Magdalene's soul opposite the restlessness in Judas's soul. The healing forces of Mercury conjunct the restless astral forces (negative Mars) of Judas. One either tames these passions into devotion (Magdalene), or one betrays oneself and others as though driven by demons (Judas). We may ask: Where can we bring healing words to ennoble passions as we humble ourselves to serve? When we are restless, Nature is a calming influence.

May 23: ASPECT: Venus conjunct Mars (DT): We are watching Venus in her conjunctions with other planets, preparing for the Venus conjunction with the Sun in 2012. We understand Venus as the matron of our karmic group, connecting us with our destiny kin; Mars in its highest aspect can bring us true speaking, the power of the voice. Together they can work very strongly, as in this aspect the North Atlantic Treaty Organization (NATO) was established. The karmic group of the Jesus children is strong here, too. In this aspect, we have the birth of Nathan Jesus (whom we identify as the Teacher), the death of Solomon Jesus (who transferred the power of Zarathustra to the Nathan Jesus), and the birth of the Nathan Mary (the biological mother of the Teacher).

A star is above my head.
  Christ speaks from the star:
"Let your soul be borne
  Through my strong force.
  I am with you.
  I am in you.
  I am for you.
  I am your I."
—RUDOLF STEINER

When the Christ impulse entered the evolution of humanity in the way known to us, one result was that the chaotic forces of the sibyls were thrust back for a time, as when a stream disappears below ground and reappears later on. These forces were indeed to reappear in another form, a form purified by the Christ impulse.... Yes, a time is coming when the old astrology will live again in a new form, a Christ-filled form, and then, if one can practice it properly so that it will be permeated with the Christ impulse, one may venture to look up to the stars and question them about their spiritual script.
—RUDOLF STEINER (*Christ and the Spiritual World and the Search for the Holy Grail*, pp. 94, 122)

JUNE

The Sun is in Taurus to begin the month, moving into Gemini (the Twins) on the 16th. Neptune stations before going retrograde on the 4th, returning to Direct motion on November 10th. Saturn stations Direct on the 14th. The new moon (Sun and Moon in Taurus) and partial solar eclipse is on the 1st, in front of Aldebaran (the eye of the Bull and a Royal Star of Persia). The full moon (Sun in Taurus, Moon in Scorpio) and total lunar eclipse is on the 15th.

The evening sky continues to be somewhat starless through the month with only Saturn in Virgo (the Virgin) in the southeastern sky after sunset. Saturn partners with the Moon on the 10th and Mercury emerges as the evening star toward the end of the month.

Rising before the Sun, Jupiter and Mars are visible for the entire month. Venus continues to be visible as a morning star until around the 22nd. The waning Moon will join Jupiter in Aries before sunrise on the 26th, Mars on the 28th, and Venus on the 30th—though they may be too close to the Sun to be seen.

June 1: New moon and partial solar eclipse, 16° Taurus (DT): Paradise. This degree brings us one of the sweetest images from the Oracle of the Solar Cross; here a fragment:

> There is a profusion of wildflowers of every color and variety in every direction. Bees enter every flower cup, finding perfume, sweetness, and pollen. Traveling from flower to flower, the bees bring the male pollen to the waiting female ovaries. Lulled by the murmur of the buzzing, people stretch out on the green grass to hear pearls of wisdom spoken by a wise visitor. Paradise. In this new moon, one can access a sense of the beauteous forms of Natura in her full beauty.

Heliocentric Venus stood at this degree at the end of the Temptations of Jesus Christ. During the Forty Days, Jesus was daily submitted to temptation. The three temptations described in the Gospels took place on the last three days of the forty-day period (November 27–29). On the next day, the 30th, having overcome the last temptation, twelve angels served him heavenly food. Venus, the planet of love who loves the Earth, sent forth the angels that ministered to Christ, the coming spirit of the Earth. Today is a day both to remember and to celebrate each and every victory over doubt, cynicism, and hatred, forces that eclipse the Sun of our conscience and separate us from the Mother. What is the connection between the Forty Days that began the ministry and the forty days following the Resurrection and form the culmination of Jesus Christ's ministry? Moon and Sun stand together as representatives of the two eyes of God. We may ask: Who is looking through my eyes?

June 3: ASPECT: Moon opposite Pluto 11°55' Sagittarius. This same aspect, at this same degree, occurred at the second conversion of Mary Magdalene (December 26, 30). Through the power of Jesus' words, three times Mary Magdalene fell unconscious to the ground. After the third fall, she wept bitterly and asked her sister Martha to bring her to join the holy women (*Chron.* p. 267). Here are the words he spoke:

> When the unclean spirit has gone out of a person, it passes through waterless places seeking rest, but finds none. Then it says, "I will return to my house from which I came." And when it comes, it finds the house empty, swept, and put in order. Then it goes and brings with it seven other spirits more evil than itself, and they enter and dwell there, and the last state of that person is worse than the first. So also will it be with this evil generation. (Matt. 12:43–45 [ESV])

Until the Mystery of Golgotha, Christ could heal only by working on people from without. In those times, the human astral body had contracted, through the gradual process of the Fall, to such an extent that it had completely separated from the seven planetary spirits. This resulted in what could be seen as seven hollow spheres within the human astral body that had previously been filled with the seven planetary spirits. These empty spheres were perfect dwelling places for adversarial forces.[1] When Christ cast out possessions,

---
1 See von Halle, *Illness and Healing*, pp. 60–61.

SIDEREAL GEOCENTRIC LONGITUDES : JUNE 2011 Gregorian at 0 hours UT											
DAY	☉	☽	☊	☿	♀	♂	♃	♄	⛢	♆	♇
1 WE	15 ♉ 18	5 ♉ 8	28 ♏ 31R	1 ♉ 29	24 ♈ 39	20 ♈ 31	4 ♈ 22	15 ♍ 40R	9 ♓ 4	6 ♒ 2	11 ♐ 58R
2 TH	16 15	17 42	28 30	3 27	25 52	21 15	4 34	15 39	9 6	6 2	11 56
3 FR	17 13	0 ♊ 28	28 30D	5 27	27 5	21 59	4 47	15 38	9 7	6 2	11 55
4 SA	18 10	13 28	28 30	7 29	28 18	22 43	4 59	15 37	9 9	6 2R	11 53
5 SU	19 8	26 42	28 31	9 32	29 31	23 27	5 12	15 36	9 11	6 2	11 52
6 MO	20 5	10 ♋ 9	28 32	11 38	0 ♉ 44	24 11	5 24	15 35	9 12	6 2	11 51
7 TU	21 3	23 49	28 33	13 45	1 57	24 55	5 36	15 35	9 14	6 2	11 49
8 WE	22 0	7 ♌ 42	28 33	15 53	3 10	25 38	5 48	15 34	9 15	6 2	11 48
9 TH	22 58	21 46	28 33R	18 3	4 23	26 22	6 0	15 34	9 17	6 1	11 46
10 FR	23 55	6 ♍ 0	28 33	20 13	5 36	27 6	6 12	15 33	9 18	6 1	11 45
11 SA	24 52	20 21	28 33	22 25	6 49	27 49	6 24	15 33	9 20	6 1	11 44
12 SU	25 50	4 ♎ 47	28 32	24 36	8 2	28 33	6 36	15 33	9 21	6 1	11 42
13 MO	26 47	19 12	28 32	26 48	9 15	29 16	6 47	15 33	9 22	6 0	11 41
14 TU	27 44	3 ♏ 32	28 32	29 0	10 28	0 ♉ 0	6 59	15 33D	9 24	6 0	11 39
15 WE	28 42	17 43	28 32D	1 ♊ 12	11 41	0 43	7 11	15 33	9 25	6 0	11 38
16 TH	29 39	1 ♐ 41	28 32	3 23	12 55	1 26	7 22	15 33	9 26	5 59	11 36
17 FR	0 ♊ 36	15 20	28 32R	5 33	14 8	2 9	7 33	15 33	9 27	5 59	11 35
18 SA	1 33	28 41	28 32	7 42	15 21	2 52	7 45	15 34	9 28	5 58	11 33
19 SU	2 31	11 ♑ 41	28 31	9 50	16 34	3 36	7 56	15 34	9 29	5 58	11 32
20 MO	3 28	24 22	28 31	11 57	17 47	4 19	8 7	15 35	9 30	5 57	11 30
21 TU	4 25	6 ♒ 46	28 30	14 1	19 0	5 2	8 18	15 36	9 31	5 57	11 29
22 WE	5 22	18 56	28 30	16 4	20 14	5 44	8 29	15 37	9 32	5 56	11 27
23 TH	6 20	0 ♓ 56	28 29	18 5	21 27	6 27	8 39	15 38	9 33	5 56	11 26
24 FR	7 17	12 50	28 29D	20 5	22 40	7 10	8 50	15 39	9 34	5 55	11 24
25 SA	8 14	24 43	28 30	22 2	23 53	7 53	9 1	15 40	9 34	5 54	11 23
26 SU	9 11	6 ♈ 40	28 30	23 57	25 7	8 35	9 11	15 41	9 35	5 54	11 21
27 MO	10 9	18 44	28 31	25 50	26 20	9 18	9 21	15 42	9 36	5 53	11 20
28 TU	11 6	1 ♉ 0	28 32	27 41	27 33	10 1	9 32	15 44	9 36	5 52	11 18
29 WE	12 3	13 31	28 33	29 30	28 47	10 43	9 42	15 45	9 37	5 51	11 17
30 TH	13 0	26 18	28 34	1 ♋ 16	0 ♊ 0	11 26	9 52	15 47	9 37	5 51	11 15

INGRESSES :

2 ☽ → ♊ 23: 7	18 ☽ → ♑ 2:24
5 ☽ → ♋ 5:55	20 ☽ → ♒ 10:49
♀ → ♉ 9:36	22 ☽ → ♓ 22: 7
7 ☽ → ♌ 10:44	25 ☽ → ♈ 10:37
9 ☽ → ♍ 13:55	27 ☽ → ♉ 22: 3
11 ☽ → ♎ 16: 3	29 ☿ → ♋ 6:46
13 ☽ → ♏ 18: 3	♀ → ♊ 23:59
14 ♂ → ♉ 0:14	30 ☽ → ♊ 6:50
☿ → ♊ 10:50	
15 ☽ → ♐ 21: 5	
16 ☉ → ♊ 8:51	

ASPECTS & ECLIPSES :

1 ☉ ☌ ☽ 21: 2	12 ☽ ☌ P 1:32	☽ ☌ ♇ 17:21	26 ☽ ☌ ♃ 5: 6
☉ ● P 21:14	☽ ☍ ♃ 3: 4	18 ☿ □ ⛢ 20: 0	☉ □ ⛢ 10: 3
2 ☽ ☌ ☋ 20:19	☉ ˢ☋ ☿ 23:30	19 ☿ ☍ ♇ 19: 1	27 ☉ □ Π 2:22
3 ☿ □ ♆ 6:57	13 ☽ ☍ ♂ 17:43	20 ☽ ☌ ♆ 22:23	28 ☉ ☍ ♇ 4:59
☽ ☍ ♇ 21: 6	☿ ☍ ☊ 18:48	21 ☿ □ ♄ 18:31	☽ ☌ ♂ 18:22
7 ☽ ☍ ♆ 21: 7	14 ☽ ☍ ♀ 12:47	22 ♂ □ ♆ 6:32	♀ ☍ ☊ 19:31
9 ☉ □ ☽ 2:10	☉ ☍ ☊ 19:58	☽ ᴺ⊓ ☊ 19: 5	30 ☽ ☌ ☋ 4:11
☽ ⚼ ☊ 11:28	15 ☽ ☌ ☊ 18:33	23 ☉ □ ☽ 11:48	☽ ☌ ♀ 7:33
10 ☽ ☍ ⛢ 5:33	☽ ●☍ T 20: 9	☽ ☌ ⛢ 17:22	
♀ □ ♆ 8:15	☉ ☍ ☽ 20:13	24 ☽ ☌ A 4: 6	
☽ ☌ ♄ 15:59	16 ☽ ☍ ☿ 3:31	☽ ☍ ♄ 5:40	

SIDEREAL HELIOCENTRIC LONGITUDES : JUNE 2011 Gregorian at 0 hours UT											
DAY	Sid. Time	☿	♀	⊕	♂	♃	♄	⛢	♆	♇	Vernal Point
1 WE	16:36:32	16 ♓ 24	25 ♓ 3	15 ♏ 18	3 ♈ 12	26 ♓ 39	20 ♍ 53	6 ♓ 25	4 ♒ 7	11 ♐ 8	5 ♓ 6' 3"
2 TH	16:40:28	21 35	26 39	16 15	3 48	26 44	20 55	6 25	4 7	11 9	5 ♓ 6' 3"
3 FR	16:44:25	26 54	28 15	17 13	4 23	26 50	20 57	6 26	4 8	11 9	5 ♓ 6' 3"
4 SA	16:48:21	2 ♈ 23	29 50	18 10	4 59	26 55	20 59	6 27	4 8	11 9	5 ♓ 6' 2"
5 SU	16:52:18	8 1	1 ♈ 26	19 8	5 34	27 1	21 1	6 27	4 8	11 10	5 ♓ 6' 2"
6 MO	16:56:14	13 46	3 2	20 5	6 10	27 6	21 3	6 28	4 9	11 10	5 ♓ 6' 2"
7 TU	17: 0:11	19 40	4 38	21 2	6 45	27 12	21 5	6 28	4 9	11 10	5 ♓ 6' 2"
8 WE	17: 4: 7	25 41	6 14	22 0	7 20	27 17	21 7	6 29	4 10	11 11	5 ♓ 6' 2"
9 TH	17: 8: 4	1 ♉ 48	7 50	22 57	7 55	27 23	21 9	6 30	4 10	11 11	5 ♓ 6' 2"
10 FR	17:12: 1	8 0	9 26	23 55	8 31	27 28	21 11	6 30	4 10	11 11	5 ♓ 6' 2"
11 SA	17:15:57	14 16	11 2	24 52	9 6	27 34	21 12	6 31	4 11	11 12	5 ♓ 6' 2"
12 SU	17:19:54	20 34	12 38	25 49	9 41	27 39	21 14	6 32	4 11	11 12	5 ♓ 6' 1"
13 MO	17:23:50	26 53	14 14	26 47	10 16	27 45	21 16	6 32	4 11	11 12	5 ♓ 6' 1"
14 TU	17:27:47	3 ♊ 12	15 50	27 44	10 51	27 50	21 18	6 33	4 12	11 13	5 ♓ 6' 1"
15 WE	17:31:43	9 29	17 26	28 41	11 26	27 56	21 20	6 34	4 12	11 13	5 ♓ 6' 1"
16 TH	17:35:40	15 42	19 2	29 39	12 1	28 1	21 22	6 34	4 12	11 13	5 ♓ 6' 1"
17 FR	17:39:36	21 51	20 38	0 ♐ 36	12 35	28 7	21 24	6 35	4 13	11 14	5 ♓ 6' 1"
18 SA	17:43:33	27 53	22 14	1 33	13 10	28 12	21 26	6 36	4 13	11 14	5 ♓ 6' 1"
19 SU	17:47:30	3 ♋ 48	23 50	2 30	13 45	28 18	21 28	6 36	4 13	11 14	5 ♓ 6' 0"
20 MO	17:51:26	9 35	25 26	3 28	14 19	28 23	21 30	6 37	4 14	11 15	5 ♓ 6' 0"
21 TU	17:55:23	15 14	27 3	4 25	14 54	28 29	21 32	6 38	4 14	11 15	5 ♓ 6' 0"
22 WE	17:59:19	20 43	28 39	5 22	15 29	28 34	21 34	6 38	4 15	11 15	5 ♓ 6' 0"
23 TH	18: 3:16	26 3	0 ♉ 15	6 19	16 3	28 40	21 36	6 39	4 15	11 16	5 ♓ 6' 0"
24 FR	18: 7:12	1 ♌ 13	1 52	7 17	16 37	28 45	21 38	6 39	4 15	11 16	5 ♓ 6' 0"
25 SA	18:11: 9	6 13	3 28	8 14	17 12	28 51	21 40	6 40	4 16	11 16	5 ♓ 6' 0"
26 SU	18:15: 5	11 4	5 4	9 11	17 46	28 56	21 42	6 41	4 16	11 17	5 ♓ 5'59"
27 MO	18:19: 2	15 46	6 41	10 8	18 20	29 2	21 44	6 41	4 16	11 17	5 ♓ 5'59"
28 TU	18:22:59	20 18	8 17	11 6	18 55	29 7	21 46	6 42	4 17	11 17	5 ♓ 5'59"
29 WE	18:26:55	24 42	9 54	12 3	19 29	29 13	21 48	6 43	4 17	11 18	5 ♓ 5'59"
30 TH	18:30:52	28 58	11 30	13 0	20 3	29 18	21 50	6 43	4 17	11 18	5 ♓ 5'59"

INGRESSES :

3 ☿ → ♈ 13:37
4 ♀ → ♈ 2:25
8 ☿ → ♉ 16:59
13 ☿ → ♊ 11:49
16 ⊕ → ♐ 8:58
18 ☿ → ♋ 8:31
22 ♀ → ♉ 20:11
23 ☿ → ♌ 18:16
30 ☿ → ♍ 5:58

ASPECTS (HELIOCENTRIC +MOON(TYCHONIC)) :

1 ☿ ☍ ♄ 20:56	☿ ☌ ☊ 15:36	☽ ☍ ♂ 8:29	☿ ⚹ ♀ 17:32	☽ ☌ ⛢ 11:30	☿ △ ♂ 15:26
2 ♀ ☌ ♃ 1:26	☽ ☍ ♆ 17:54	☽ ☍ ♀ 14:40	☿ □ ♄ 22:15	☿ △ ♃ 12:15	28 ⊕ ☌ ♇ 4:59
♂ ⚹ ♆ 13:27	9 ♀ ☌ ♂ 2:16	☿ ☍ ⊕ 23:30	17 ☽ ☍ ☿ 21:20	24 ☿ □ ♀ 4:26	☽ ☌ ♀ 16: 6
☿ ☌ ♃ 23:38	☿ □ ♆ 9:12	13 ☿ ⚹ ♃ 3:18	18 ☿ □ ♃ 1:18	☿ ☍ ♆ 14:29	
3 ☿ ☌ ♀ 8:21	☿ ⚹ ⛢ 18:14	14 ⊕ △ ♃ 2:52	19 ☿ △ ⛢ 11:34	☽ ☍ ♄ 17:48	
☽ ☍ ♇ 19:44	10 ☽ ☍ ⛢ 0:51	☿ △ ♆ 3:47	20 ☽ ☌ ♆ 19: 3	25 ☽ ☌ ♃ 8:21	
4 ☿ ⚹ ♆ 7:32	11 ☽ ☌ ♄ 1:25	☿ □ ⛢ 12:47	⊕ ⚹ ♆ 19:30	♀ □ ♆ 11:55	
☿ ☌ ♂ 12:26	♀ △ ♇ 2:32	♂ △ ♇ 15:10	☿ □ ♂ 22:24	☿ △ ⊕ 12:14	
5 ☿ △ ♇ 13:11	☽ ☍ ♃ 12: 4	15 ☿ ☍ ♇ 6:40	22 ☿ ⚹ ♄ 3:48	26 ☿ △ ♇ 1: 1	
6 ♀ ⚹ ♆ 16:47	12 ☿ △ ♄ 2:34	☿ ⚹ ♂ 8:15	☿ ᴺ⊓ ☊ 12:44	☽ ☌ ♂ 23:10	
7 ⊕ ⚹ ♄ 0:55	☿ ☌ P 8:14	16 ☽ ☌ ♇ 16:43	23 ⊕ □ ⛢ 8:14	27 ♀ ⚹ ⛢ 0: 9	

and the recipients returned to the same behaviors, the situation became even worse for them. Why? Perhaps because as we are purified we become aware of what had bound us. Not only do we *see* more clearly, but we are also *seen* more clearly by the adversaries. The greater the light, the greater the shadow. In healing, we rise. To be freed and then to fall again invites greater demons, for we fall further. It is necessary, after releasing negative entities, to fill our seven chakras consciously with spiritual practices; this realigns our astral bodies with the seven planetary spirits. The Moon is the portal both to the abyss and to the sphere of the angels. Pluto is either the destroying adversary or the Divine Love of Phanes; both possibilities exist. In this healing, it was Phanes who worked through Christ, healing Magdalene from her lower passions (Moon). Her protection in this final conversion was the circle of holy women. Strong memories live in today's alignment. We may ask: What is our equivalent to the circle of holy women?

June 9: Sun 23° Taurus: The Ascension of Christ. Early in the morning of this day Jesus presented the Blessed Virgin Mary to the apostles and disciples as their advocate and as the center of their community. Here we see another stage in preparation for the coming event of Pentecost. (A preceding stage was when Mary received communion.) As the Sun climbed higher in the sky, Christ continued to the Mount of Olives and ascended to the top, all the while becoming increasingly radiant with light until he became more radiant than the midday Sun. Then he disappeared into this radiance. Two angels then appeared saying:

> Men of Galilee, why do you stand looking into heaven? This Jesus, who was taken up from you into heaven, will come in the same way as you saw him go into heaven. (Acts 1:11 [ESV])

The Angelic voice sounds again in our time as Christ's appearance in the etheric realm becomes increasingly self-evident. The Resurrection of Christ portrayed by Matthias Grünewald, in his painting of the Isenheim Altarpiece, clearly shows the wounds of Christ. These wounds are the new organs of the will streaming from the ascended Christ. Under the auspices of Taurus, an Earth sign ruled by Venus, we see how our love of humanity and of the elemental beings of the Earth can bring us into ever-closer connection with these organs of the Christ will that are streaming around the Earth.

June 12: Sun 26° Taurus: Blessing of the Children (May 17, 32). Jesus blesses a thousand children. This is a very important component in this land of milk and honey, streaming with the soul of Sophia. Sophia breathes familial love creating deep bonds between mothers and children. Later that evening, Jesus dines with ten of the holy women, as He continues to teach. The women and the children! Are we blessing the feminine aspect of our nature and working to protect the innocence of our children?

June 15 (12-15-18): Full moon, 29° Taurus (DT). The main theme here from this fragment of the Oracle of the Solar Cross is renunciation of the materialistic world: A fine estate, a large house, a pleasant farm, and easy living. Material wealth. The family leaves it all behind to dwell in a tent in the desert because it rests upon holy ground. Rather than hoist yourself up and away from Nature, feel the holy Earth with your bare feet.

June 16: Sun enters Gemini: Perseverance becomes Faithfulness. Control of one's feeling nature is the key.

June 19: Sun 2° Gemini: Cosmic Pentecost. The Holy Festival of Pentecost, the descent of the Holy Spirit (May 24, 33). The zodiacal position of 2° Gemini is directly opposite the Galactic Center (2° Sagittarius). The Galactic Center, also known as the Central Sun, is the Divine Heart of the galaxy and the source of the Holy Spirit. The Blessed Virgin Mary, presented by Jesus Christ before the Ascension as the center of the community, here served as this center and as the bearer of Divine Sophia. The sparks of fire that issued from her blessed soul were the manifestation of Christ's Cosmic I Am. The "I" of the world was born through the immaculate heart of the divine Mary–Sophia. Since that first Pentecost, the Christ spirit has lived within human souls on Earth. Pentecost was the awakening of Christ's apostles from a dreamlike state, when they united with the principle of Christ's love as an experience *within* their own beings. Emanations from the heart of the galaxy are increasing in our time, leading up to a Pentecost on a world scale (see Robert Powell's article: "World Pentecost," *Journal for Star Wisdom 2010*). In remembrance of this profound moment, which today strongly quickens, we are encouraged to wrest ourselves from the distractions of materialism. Walk in nature, star gaze in the evening, assemble with friends. Remember the grace and love of Sophia.

ASPECT: Mercury opposite Pluto 11° Sagittarius. At the first Pentecost, Mercury and Pluto were close to an opposition in Sagittarius. A mind (Mercury) that contemplates the stars is attending the future.

June 28: ASPECT: Sun opposite Pluto, 11°18' Sagittarius. The Sun was opposite Pluto at both the birth of the Solomon Jesus and at the conception of the Nathan Jesus. Jesus Christ opposed evil throughout His biography, thus paving the way for humanity's confrontation with the tempters. The confrontation of Pluto, the god of the underworld, with the Sun, the Christ-filled heart, continues. We remember two years ago when Pluto stood at the place of the Baptism (6° Sagittarius) during the 2009 solar eclipse (the longest solar eclipse of the twenty-first century). Something may have begun then that every Pluto–Sun opposition challenges. Today we may contemplate our willingness to face the forces moving behind the scenes of ordinary reality. To name the workings of the adversarial forces decreases their power. Their power is based on fear, terror, war, and hatred; naming diminishes their effectiveness. The god of the underworld divested of the concealment of his dark garments is powerless. This is a good day to hear the words of the Delphic Oracle: "Know thyself."

June 30: ASPECT: Venus conjunct Moon, 29° Taurus. Venus stood at this degree during the union in the temple of the two Jesus children (April 3, 12). The elder Jesus, the Solomon Jesus, is from the kingly lineage of Solomon, and the younger Jesus, the Nathan Jesus, is from the priestly lineage of Nathan. John the Baptist filled the third post, that of prophet, completing the three sacred posts of Holy Israel. The Solomon Jesus (the reincarnated Zarathustra) was four years and nine months older than the younger Jesus (the paradisiacal immaculate soul). With this union in the temple at the time of the Feast of the Passover, the soul of the elder Jesus' separated from his body and united with the immaculate soul to indwell the latter's body. Thus was the union of the kingly and priestly lines joined. Later, at the Baptism, John the Baptist would fulfill the third post.

The next day, the transformed twelve-year old Jesus went to one of the rabbinic schools in Jerusalem and astounded the doctors and scribes with His knowledge. Venus remembers this union, and the Moon cradles this memory. The Moon holds the key to our karmic burdens. As our love (Venus) of Christ and Sophia increases, we meet these burdens of karma (Moon), making way for a similar unity in our own heart between love and wisdom. Two becoming one is a sign of the potential for all humanity. This is a good day to focus on any impediment to love that we meet in our own being, most productively revealed through our community relationships. Wherever we find impediments in our ability to love one another, we stand before our karmic limitations. Are we able to stand with John as those who love one another?

JULY

The Sun begins July in Gemini (the Twins), moving into Cancer (the Crab) on the 17th. Uranus stations before going Retrograde on the 10th (remaining so for the rest of 2011). The new moon and partial solar eclipse is on the 1st (Sun and Moon in Gemini). The full moon is on the 15th (Sun in Gemini, Moon in Sagittarius), and the 2nd new moon of the month is July 30 (Sun and Moon in the Crab). The night sky brings the Moon, in her different phases, and Saturn in the south-southwest each evening, with the waxing half moon just below Saturn in Virgo on the 7th.

Jupiter and Mars are visible in the southeast before sunrise through the month. The waning crescent moon joins Jupiter on the 23rd in Aries, with the waning crescent above Jupiter. The Moon then joins Mars on the 27th, but may be best viewed the day before and after, as the Moon is right on top of Mars.

July 1: New moon and partial solar eclipse, 14° Gemini (DT): Forgiveness. The Oracle of the Solar Cross speaks of a righteous man who has severely criticized and persecuted those whose beliefs deviate from his own, which is the party line. For weeks his upper body has become contorted by convulsions and vomiting. He asks for forgiveness for his severity, and the symptoms disappear.

The Sun was 14° Gemini at the death of the Solomon Jesus (June 5, 12). It is the death of wisdom that is most remarkable in world headlines. This new moon accompanies a Moon opposition to Pluto. Now is a time to ponder the relationship between our faithfulness to peace, harmony, and unity in the face of persevering fear mongering, war, tragedy, and fragmentation. The Moon gesture in eurythmy closes the gates to the underworld. The voice within us that does not like us is *not* our voice. Close the gates!

July 6: Sun 19° Gemini. This position is aligned exactly with the most radiant star in our heavens, Sirius, known as the star of the Master Jesus and revered by the Egyptians as the star of Isis (a pre-Christian manifestation of Sophia). A triangular relationship is formed between Sirius, our Sun and Shambhala, the golden realm at the heart of the Earth, the Earth's heart chakra. Today's Sun suggests mighty influences sounding through the meridian connections of the Daughter in the Heights, the Mother in the Depths, and Christ in the encircling round. Today, Pluto is in exactly its location at the conversation with Nicodemus. Anne Catherine Emmerich saw a meeting among Jesus, Nicodemus, and Joseph of Arimathea:

> I saw Jesus during the night reclining with [Nicodemus] on the ground and instructing him. Before daybreak both started for Jerusalem, where they went to Lazarus on Sion. Here came Joseph of Arimathea also to see Jesus.[1]

On this day of Sun conjunct Sirius we can ponder the mystery of the conversation between Nicodemus and Jesus in the night. According to Judith von Halle:

> The Grail story can be traced back to Joseph of Arimathea and Nicodemus, who asked Pilate for permission to take the body of Christ down from the Cross and to lay it in the grave, which was granted them.[2]

The chalice that caught the blood of Christ went with these two and spread across Europe as the Grail Legend. According to Robert Powell:

> A new star wisdom embodied in the new science of the Grail is concerned with, among other things, the mystery of communion, that is, the cosmic communion between humanity and the world of stars. Star wisdom, in the light of the Holy Grail, has the task of discerning when the cosmic configurations arise that are propitious for the inner communion of the human being with the Risen Christ.[3]

Putting together the Sirius position of the Sun, the Pluto memory of the conversation with the

---

1 Emmerich, *LJC*, vol.2, p. 122.
2 Von Halle, *And if He Had Not Been Raised...: The Stations of Christ's Path to Spirit Man* (London: Temple Lodge, 2007), p. 33.
3 Powell, *The Christ Mystery*, p. 17.

SIDEREAL GEOCENTRIC LONGITUDES : JULY 2011 Gregorian at 0 hours UT											
DAY	☉	☽	☊	☿	♀	♂	♃	♄	♅	♆	♇
1 FR	13 ♊ 58	9 ♊ 23	28 ♏ 34R	3 ♋ 1	1 ♊ 13	12 ♉ 8	10 ♈ 2	15 ♍ 49	9 ♓ 38	5 ♒ 50R	11 ♐ 13R
2 SA	14 55	22 46	28 33	4 43	2 27	12 50	10 12	15 50	9 38	5 49	11 12
3 SU	15 52	6 ♋ 25	28 31	6 23	3 40	13 32	10 21	15 52	9 39	5 48	11 10
4 MO	16 49	20 18	28 29	8 1	4 54	14 15	10 31	15 54	9 39	5 47	11 9
5 TU	17 46	4 ♌ 22	28 26	9 37	6 7	14 57	10 40	15 56	9 39	5 46	11 7
6 WE	18 44	18 33	28 24	11 10	7 20	15 39	10 50	15 59	9 39	5 45	11 6
7 TH	19 41	2 ♍ 48	28 23	12 42	8 34	16 21	10 59	16 1	9 40	5 44	11 4
8 FR	20 38	17 3	28 22	14 11	9 47	17 3	11 8	16 3	9 40	5 43	11 3
9 SA	21 35	1 ♎ 16	28 22D	15 38	11 1	17 45	11 17	16 6	9 40	5 42	11 1
10 SU	22 32	15 24	28 23	17 2	12 14	18 26	11 26	16 8	9 40R	5 41	11 0
11 MO	23 30	29 26	28 24	18 24	13 28	19 8	11 34	16 11	9 40	5 40	10 58
12 TU	24 27	13 ♏ 19	28 26	19 44	14 41	19 50	11 43	16 14	9 40	5 39	10 57
13 WE	25 24	27 3	28 26	21 2	15 55	20 31	11 51	16 17	9 40	5 38	10 55
14 TH	26 21	10 ♐ 36	28 26R	22 17	17 9	21 13	12 0	16 20	9 39	5 37	10 54
15 FR	27 18	23 55	28 24	23 30	18 22	21 54	12 8	16 23	9 39	5 35	10 52
16 SA	28 16	7 ♑ 0	28 20	24 40	19 36	22 36	12 16	16 26	9 39	5 34	10 51
17 SU	29 13	19 50	28 16	25 47	20 49	23 17	12 24	16 29	9 39	5 33	10 50
18 MO	0 ♋ 10	2 ♒ 24	28 11	26 52	22 3	23 59	12 31	16 32	9 38	5 32	10 48
19 TU	1 7	14 45	28 5	27 54	23 17	24 40	12 39	16 36	9 38	5 30	10 47
20 WE	2 5	26 53	28 1	28 53	24 30	25 21	12 46	16 39	9 37	5 29	10 45
21 TH	3 2	8 ♓ 53	27 57	29 49	25 44	26 2	12 54	16 43	9 37	5 28	10 44
22 FR	3 59	20 46	27 54	0 ♌ 42	26 58	26 43	13 1	16 46	9 36	5 26	10 43
23 SA	4 56	2 ♈ 39	27 53	1 31	28 12	27 24	13 8	16 50	9 36	5 25	10 41
24 SU	5 54	14 35	27 53D	2 18	29 25	28 5	13 15	16 54	9 35	5 24	10 40
25 MO	6 51	26 39	27 54	3 0	0 ♋ 39	28 46	13 22	16 58	9 34	5 22	10 39
26 TU	7 48	8 ♉ 56	27 56	3 39	1 53	29 27	13 28	17 2	9 34	5 21	10 37
27 WE	8 46	21 31	27 57	4 14	3 7	0 ♊ 7	13 34	17 6	9 33	5 20	10 36
28 TH	9 43	4 ♊ 27	27 57R	4 45	4 21	0 48	13 41	17 10	9 32	5 18	10 35
29 FR	10 40	17 46	27 55	5 12	5 34	1 29	13 47	17 14	9 31	5 17	10 33
30 SA	11 38	1 ♋ 28	27 52	5 35	6 48	2 9	13 53	17 18	9 30	5 15	10 32
31 SU	12 35	15 32	27 47	5 53	8 2	2 50	13 58	17 23	9 29	5 14	10 31

INGRESSES :

2 ☽ → ♋ 12:46
4 ☽ → ♌ 16:34
6 ☽ → ♍ 19:17
8 ☽ → ♎ 21:52
11 ☽ → ♏ 0:58
13 ☽ → ♐ 5:11
15 ☽ → ♑ 11: 6
17 ☽ → ♒ 19:22
☉ → ♋ 19:47
20 ☽ → ♓ 6:11
21 ☿ → ♌ 4:57
22 ☽ → ♈ 18:39
24 ♀ → ♋ 11:16
25 ☽ → ♉ 6:35
26 ♂ → ♊ 19:37
27 ☽ → ♊ 15:48
29 ☽ → ♋ 21:27

ASPECTS & ECLIPSES :

1 ☽ ☍ ♇ 3:19
☉ ● P 8:37
☉ ☌ ☽ 8:53
2 ☽ ☌ ☿ 23:55
3 ☉ □ ♄ 0:10
5 ☽ ☍ ♆ 2:22
☿ □ ♃ 18: 2
6 ☽ S ☊ 16:34
7 ☽ ☍ ♅ 11:33
☽ ☌ P 13:41
♀ □ ♅ 21:27
☽ ☌ ♄ 22:19
8 ☉ □ ☽ 6:29
9 ♀ ☍ ♇ 0: 7
☽ ☍ ♃ 17:10
12 ☉ □ Π 2:59
☽ ☍ ♂ 11:56
13 ☽ ☌ ☊ 2:25
♀ □ ♄ 7:23
14 ☽ ☌ ♇ 0:32
☽ ☍ ♀ 12:55
15 ☉ ☍ ☽ 6:39
16 ☉ □ Π 16:30
17 ☽ ☍ ☿ 12:22
18 ☽ ☌ ♆ 6: 0
20 ☽ N ☊ 2:12
21 ☽ ☌ ♅ 1:28
☽ ☍ ♄ 15:52
☽ ☌ A 22:36
23 ☉ □ ☽ 5: 1
♂ ☍ ☊ 16:57
☽ ☌ ♃ 21:18
27 ☽ ☌ ☋ 12: 0
☽ ☌ ♂ 16:55
28 ☽ ☍ ♇ 11: 6
29 ☿ ☍ ♆ 3:58
30 ☽ ☌ ♀ 10: 3
☉ ☌ ☽ 18:39

SIDEREAL HELIOCENTRIC LONGITUDES : JULY 2011 Gregorian at 0 hours UT											
DAY	Sid. Time	☿	♀	⊕	♂	♃	♄	♅	♆	♇	Vernal Point
1 FR	18:34:48	3 ♍ 5	13 ♉ 7	13 ♐ 57	20 ♈ 37	29 ♓ 24	21 ♍ 52	6 ♓ 44	4 ♒ 18	11 ♐ 18	5 ♓ 5'59"
2 SA	18:38:45	7 5	14 43	14 54	21 11	29 29	21 54	6 45	4 18	11 19	5 ♓ 5'59"
3 SU	18:42:41	10 58	16 20	15 52	21 45	29 35	21 56	6 45	4 19	11 19	5 ♓ 5'58"
4 MO	18:46:38	14 44	17 56	16 49	22 18	29 40	21 58	6 46	4 19	11 19	5 ♓ 5'58"
5 TU	18:50:34	18 25	19 33	17 46	22 52	29 46	22 0	6 47	4 19	11 20	5 ♓ 5'58"
6 WE	18:54:31	21 59	21 10	18 43	23 26	29 51	22 2	6 47	4 20	11 20	5 ♓ 5'58"
7 TH	18:58:28	25 28	22 46	19 41	24 0	29 57	22 4	6 48	4 20	11 20	5 ♓ 5'58"
8 FR	19: 2:24	28 52	24 23	20 38	24 33	0 ♈ 2	22 5	6 48	4 20	11 21	5 ♓ 5'58"
9 SA	19: 6:21	2 ♎ 11	26 0	21 35	25 7	0 8	22 7	6 49	4 21	11 21	5 ♓ 5'58"
10 SU	19:10:17	5 26	27 37	22 32	25 40	0 13	22 9	6 50	4 21	11 21	5 ♓ 5'58"
11 MO	19:14:14	8 37	29 14	23 29	26 14	0 19	22 11	6 50	4 21	11 22	5 ♓ 5'57"
12 TU	19:18:10	11 45	0 ♊ 50	24 27	26 47	0 24	22 13	6 51	4 22	11 22	5 ♓ 5'57"
13 WE	19:22: 7	14 49	2 27	25 24	27 20	0 30	22 15	6 52	4 22	11 22	5 ♓ 5'57"
14 TH	19:26: 3	17 50	4 4	26 21	27 54	0 35	22 17	6 52	4 23	11 23	5 ♓ 5'57"
15 FR	19:30: 0	20 48	5 41	27 18	28 27	0 41	22 19	6 53	4 23	11 23	5 ♓ 5'57"
16 SA	19:33:57	23 44	7 18	28 15	29 0	0 46	22 21	6 54	4 23	11 23	5 ♓ 5'57"
17 SU	19:37:53	26 38	8 55	29 13	29 33	0 52	22 23	6 54	4 24	11 24	5 ♓ 5'57"
18 MO	19:41:50	29 30	10 32	0 ♑ 10	0 ♉ 6	0 57	22 25	6 55	4 24	11 24	5 ♓ 5'56"
19 TU	19:45:46	2 ♏ 20	12 9	1 7	0 39	1 3	22 27	6 56	4 24	11 24	5 ♓ 5'56"
20 WE	19:49:43	5 9	13 46	2 4	1 12	1 8	22 29	6 56	4 25	11 25	5 ♓ 5'56"
21 TH	19:53:39	7 57	15 24	3 1	1 45	1 14	22 31	6 57	4 25	11 25	5 ♓ 5'56"
22 FR	19:57:36	10 43	17 1	3 59	2 18	1 19	22 33	6 57	4 25	11 25	5 ♓ 5'56"
23 SA	20: 1:32	13 29	18 38	4 56	2 51	1 25	22 35	6 58	4 26	11 26	5 ♓ 5'56"
24 SU	20: 5:29	16 14	20 15	5 53	3 23	1 30	22 37	6 59	4 26	11 26	5 ♓ 5'56"
25 MO	20: 9:26	18 59	21 52	6 51	3 56	1 36	22 39	6 59	4 26	11 26	5 ♓ 5'55"
26 TU	20:13:22	21 44	23 29	7 48	4 29	1 41	22 41	7 0	4 27	11 27	5 ♓ 5'55"
27 WE	20:17:19	24 28	25 7	8 45	5 1	1 47	22 43	7 1	4 27	11 27	5 ♓ 5'55"
28 TH	20:21:15	27 13	26 44	9 43	5 34	1 52	22 45	7 1	4 28	11 27	5 ♓ 5'55"
29 FR	20:25:12	29 59	28 21	10 40	6 6	1 58	22 47	7 2	4 28	11 28	5 ♓ 5'55"
30 SA	20:29: 8	2 ♐ 45	29 59	11 37	6 38	2 3	22 49	7 3	4 28	11 28	5 ♓ 5'55"
31 SU	20:33: 5	5 32	1 ♋ 36	12 35	7 11	2 9	22 51	7 3	4 29	11 28	5 ♓ 5'55"

INGRESSES :

7 ♃ → ♈ 14:28
8 ☿ → ♎ 8: 9
11 ♀ → ♊ 11:29
17 ♂ → ♉ 19:27
⊕ → ♑ 19:54
18 ☿ → ♏ 4:10
29 ☿ → ♐ 0:10
30 ♀ → ♋ 0:19

ASPECTS (HELIOCENTRIC +MOON(TYCHONIC)) :

1 ☽ ☍ ♇ 3:28
☿ ☍ ♅ 21:54
3 ☿ □ ♇ 2:11
4 ☿ □ ⊕ 18:14
☽ ☍ ♆ 23:55
5 ⊕ ☌ A 11:43
☿ △ ♀ 13:50
6 ☿ ☌ ♄ 0:18
♀ ☌ ☊ 10:43
♀ △ ♄ 13: 7
7 ☽ ☍ ♅ 6:44
8 ♂ ☌ ☊ 8:15
☽ ☌ ♄ 8:31
☿ ☍ ♃ 8:39
☽ ☍ ♃ 22: 4
9 ☽ ☌ ☿ 2: 2
⊕ □ ♄ 14: 7
☿ △ ♆ 15:55
10 ☽ ☍ ♂ 18:16
11 ♀ ⚹ ♃ 17: 5
☿ ⚹ ♇ 21: 5
13 ☽ ☍ ♀ 10:48
14 ☽ ☌ ♇ 1:23
♀ △ ♆ 4:31
15 ♀ □ ♅ 17:51
☿ ☌ ☋ 22:34
17 ⊕ △ ♂ 20:32
18 ☽ ☌ ♆ 3:50
☿ ☍ ♂ 6:16
☿ ⚹ ⊕ 8:21
♀ ☍ ♇ 12:51
⊕ □ ♃ 21:59
19 ☿ □ ♆ 17:37
20 ☿ △ ♅ 15:21
☽ ☌ ♅ 20: 6
22 ☽ ☍ ♄ 3:36
☽ ☌ ♃ 21:29
25 ⊕ ⚹ ♅ 3:43
♀ □ ♄ 11:44
☽ ☌ ♂ 14:56
♂ □ ♆ 22:42
26 ☿ ⚹ ♄ 8:24
☿ ☌ A 8:47
27 ☽ ☍ ☿ 7: 2
28 ☽ ☍ ♇ 12:42
29 ☿ △ ♃ 17:46
☽ ☌ ♀ 21: 4
30 ☿ ⚹ ♆ 14:55
♂ ⚹ ♅ 18:20
31 ♀ □ ♃ 8:30
☿ □ ♅ 13: 8

Grail founders, and the presence of the etheric Christ, we have the golden triangle: Sirius (Sophia), our Sun (Christ), and the heart of the Earth (on the altar of which stands the Grail chalice). We are all making our way through the dark forests of materialism, as were the Grail Knights before us. We are seeking the Grail Castle, where spiritual nourishment again finds willing disciples in human beings. This is a good day to ponder the subtle and to find the connection between the heights, the depths, and the encircling round.

July 14 (11-14-17): Full moon, 27° Gemini (DT): The Teacher visits the families of the shepherds, who recall the night of living stars at the birth of Jesus. The marriage of a son and daughter of the shepherds takes place this day, and the Teacher is there to bless them. What goes around comes around.

Saturn 26° Gemini: The Raising of the Youth of Nain (November 13, 30). This full moon remembers the Youth of Nain (Luke 7:11–17), the Son of the Widow, who is a significant figure for the entire history of humanity. We can follow the incarnations: Youth of Nain–Mani–Parsifal. Rudolf Steiner called Mani one of the greatest beings to incarnate on this planet. Further, he indicates that he will most likely incarnate again in the twenty-first century if conditions are right. Parsifal was also a Son of a Widow. What does the "Son of the Widow" indicate? In this regard, Rudolf Steiner noted:

> During the fifth Root Race [present post-Atlantean great epoch], the father withdraws. The soul is widowed. Humanity is thrown back onto itself. It must find the light of truth within its own soul in order to act as its own guide. Everything of a soul nature has always been expressed in terms of the feminine. Therefore the feminine element—which exists only in a germinal state today and will later be fully developed—this self-directing feminine principle, which is no longer confronted by the divine fructifier, is called by Mani the "Widow." And therefore he calls himself "Son of the Widow."... [Mani said]:

> "You must lay aside everything that you have acquired as outer revelation by means of the senses. You must lay aside all things that come to you via outer authority; then you must become ripe to gaze into your own soul." [4]

Clearly the teachings of Mani direct widowed souls (sons and daughters of Sophia) to become spiritual investigators in their own right through inner ripening. Mani teaches the healing of evil. The first step in this direction is to confront one's shadow. The planet of memory, Saturn, recalls the Youth of Nain. On this occasion of a full moon we may ask: What ails you and me? Where am I widowed from my spiritual aims? Where does my faithfulness to my spiritual resolves (Saturn) need resurrection? A full moon calls for action. What deed is called for so that I may be called back to my mission in life?

July 17: Sun enters Cancer: Selflessness becomes Catharsis. The instinct to purify oneself is invoked. (The Cathars were the "pure ones.")

July 18: Sun 1 degree Cancer, aligned with Procyon (redeemed or redeeming) in the Lesser Dog. This is where the Sun was when Jesus taught concerning the Baptism by Fire (Luke 12:49; *Chron.* 305). In this discourse He chastises the people for not being able to interpret the signs of the times. These are applicable words for all of us:

> "I came to cast fire on the earth, and would that it were already kindled! I have a baptism to be baptized with, and how great is my distress until it is accomplished! Do you think that I have come to give peace on Earth? No, I tell you, but rather division. For from now on in one house there will be five divided, three against two and two against three. They will be divided, father against son and son against father, mother against daughter and daughter against mother, mother-in-law against her daughter-in-law and daughter-in-law against mother-in-law." (Luke 12:49–53 [ESV])

---

4 Steiner, *The Temple Legend*, p. 62.

Fire has many meanings. The Sun today remembers these words of Christ. With the Sun conjunct the redeeming Procyon, we can assume Jesus is speaking of redeeming fire. Is this the fire of the Holy Spirit that he wishes were burning already—the Pentecostal revelation? Is this the fire of "I" consciousness, born to humanity through the Mystery of Golgotha and Pentecost? Is the separating factor between families and nations the "I" that burns with egoism rather than love? Are the new disciples of Christ and Sophia being divided from Pharisaic influences? This is a powerful day to contemplate fire and its origin and effect. One fire warms while the other burns. It is a good day to search for clarity about which fire burns in us. The division mentioned here may indicate that, whereas some will choose to read the signs of the times, others will not.

July 20: Sun 3° Cancer (June 25, 31). Jesus teaches the significance of the word *Amen*. This is also where the Sun was at the July 2009 eclipse, when Pluto stood exactly where it was at the Baptism of Christ. The Sun at this degree remembers the teachings of the Amen, as well as the solar eclipse of 2009. Valentin Tomberg addresses the Amen:

> A: the risen head; M: the risen hands; E: the inner life of the resurrection body; N: the force of [the resurrection body's] denial of evil.[5]

And: "The words of the Amen, the faithful and true witness, the beginning of God's creation" (Revelation 3:14). Meditation on this verse brings us into contact with the mystery of the resurrection body. *Putting on the resurrection body*[6] is the goal of all humanity.

The *head of the Amen* is the Kingdom of stars in the heavens; the *heart of the Amen* is the Power of the radiant cross of Sun's light; and the *limbs of the Amen* are the rainbow of Glory when matter is permeated by spirit. The Kingdom, the Power, and the Glory of the Amen stand as the antidote to the adversarial forces confronting humanity today.

---

5   Tomberg, *Christ and Sophia*, p. 300.
6   This is a term used by St. Paul, who recognized immortality as "putting on the resurrection body."

The Amen is Christ in his cosmic robes. This is a day to experience the presence of the Amen and the strength of the N as "No" to forces rising from the abyss. What is the experience of contemplating the vastness of the Amen?

July 23: ASPECT: Moon conjunct Jupiter, 13° Aries. Moon was conjunct Jupiter at the conception of the Virgin Mary. The Blessed Virgin was a vessel for wisdom (Jupiter) down into the depths of her will (Moon). Thoughts filled with Divine Wisdom (Jupiter) are streaming in from the periphery in ever-increasing radiance. As these wisdom-filled thoughts are received, the experience of *holy awe* can rise from the lunar depths of our subconscious, filling us with peace.

What might be the experience of witnessing this conjunction in the evening sky? Jupiter at 13° Aries remembers the Passion of Christ. When the lunar gates are held in check, one sacrifices self for others. When the lunar gate has been trespassed from below, one sacrifices others for the self. This is a day to ponder the wisdom we command over our personal subearthly forces and to take stock of the world's command over such forces. Do we see holy awe and self-sacrifice (Moon in Aries), or tyranny (negative Jupiter)?

July 27: ASPECT: Moon conjunct Mars, 0° Gemini. This aspect occurred at several special events: at both the death and birth of the Nathan Mary, at the birth of John the Baptist, and as Christ delivered his "Woe upon the Pharisees." The beings of Gemini represent the union of intelligence and spontaneous wisdom; this is intuition. Nathan Mary, John the Baptist, and Jesus Christ are supreme examples of the marriage of intelligence and wisdom becoming intuition.

The Nathan Mary experienced an intuitive union with the Solomon Mary at the conversation before the Baptism; John the Baptist experienced an intuitive union with Lazarus at the latter's death; and Christ was in continual union with the Father and all the Beings of the stars. The Living Word (Mars), when brought into the depths of our individual will (Moon), prepares us for the experience of intuition. Those who fail to hold lower forces in check are addressed in the "Woe to the Pharisees."

This is a fine day to meditate on our ability, as masters over lower influences, to direct our words. Such self-mastery sets us on a path toward the union of intelligence and spontaneous wisdom. We may ask: What type of union is encouraged by our words? There is union with beings of truth, for example, and there is union with beings of slander. Some unions are harmless; others tend to overwhelm us.

July 29: ASPECT: Mercury (5° Leo) opposite Neptune (5° Aquarius). Heliocentric Mercury and Neptune were in opposition at the Ascension of Christ. Neptune, in its highest aspect, is the *Harmony of the Spheres,* and Mercury is the messenger of the gods. At the Ascension, Christ was taken into the Harmony of the Spheres, and the sound of his being will continue as the healing message of the gods until the end of time. We may ask if we can hear this sound in our quiet heart. Leo represents the heart and wellspring of compassion and mercy. When our heart sounds with mercy we meet the sound of the Divine Heart.

This is a good day to devote even a single moment to remembering the harmonic sounds of creation and the One who bore this sound into Earth's evolution. We hear this harmony in places where nature is filled with good elemental spirits. We need to nourish ourselves in such places, for they are the antidotes to distraction (negative Mercury). Can we wrest ourselves from distraction and find replenishment in nature?

July 30: Second new moon of this month, 12° Cancer (DT): Three waters to drink. Fragment from the Oracle of the Solar Cross:

> A little voice—is it inside or outside?—calls you, and you follow to a grassy field of peace. Three beautiful wells are there, as well as arbors of fruit trees heavily laden. The Good Shepherd greets you, washes off the dust of your journey, and gives you

The Beehive Cluster
(2MASS/UMass/IPAC-Caltech/NASA/NSF)

three waters to drink. You know his voice. He offers you fruit, honey, and bread. This combines easily imagined pictures with ones that require effort to imagine. Three waters; from where do they come?

Sun 12½° Cancer, Praesepe ("manger"), the beehive. The beehive is at the center of the spiraling arms of Cancer, the heart of the Crab. It was through this gateway that the Greeks believed human souls entered earthly incarnation in order to gather the golden nectar of earthly experience to take back to Sophia, the Queen of the cosmic realm. Cancer marks a point of decision: *Development* or *envelopment?* The spiraling arms of Cancer invite us to breathe in the Light and to move forward with the evolution of life and consciousness. The opposite is *envelopment*, whereby we are arrested in our progress and are thus relegated to the dark corridors of rigidified convention. The healing waters of this new moon ask us to develop our light. Where may we be stuck? What might we change if we were to re-think old assumptions?

AUGUST

The month begins with the Sun in the Crab (Cancer), moving into the Lion (Leo) on the 18th. Uranus, Neptune, and Pluto continue to be Retrograde, while Mercury stations before going Retrograde on the 4th in Leo, moving back into Cancer and stationing Direct on the 27th. Jupiter, in Aries, stations before going Retrograde on the 31st (until stationing Direct December 26).

The new crescent moon may be visible on the 1st, low in the west along with Mercury as the Sun sets. As the crescent grows, the Moon joins Saturn on the 4th, in Virgo, and again on the 31st, but by now the Sun has traveled far enough in its yearly journey around the zodiac that it brings this Moon–Saturn cycle too near the western horizon to be seen.

The full moon is on the 13th this month (Sun in Cancer, Moon in Capricorn) and may obscure the Perseid meteor shower peak, August 13 to 14. These meteor showers, however, date from July 23 through August 22, so make time to scan the northeast after midnight.

The Sun joins with Venus and Mercury on the 16th to 17th in Leo, marking Venus's disappearance into the Sun to reemerge as Evening Star in October. The waning half moon shines above Jupiter on the 20th, and can be seen to the east around midnight in Aries. Then the Moon meets with Mars, to be seen in the east-southeast just before sunrise in Gemini. The Moon joins the Sun and Venus for the new moon on the 29th.

August 8: ASPECT: Mercury opposite Neptune, 5° Aquarius. Neptune and Mercury were conjunct at the birth of the Nathan Jesus, who became one with Christ and later bore the five wounds that brought healing to the world. If the self-will (Mercury) rules over one's higher will, one is vulnerable to becoming caught up in the illusions (Neptune) of the egoistic person. This is a good day to ponder the difference between *ruler* and *servant*. Inspirations bearing cosmic thoughts surround us. May we invite these healing messages!

August 10: Sun 22° Cancer: Death of Lazarus (July 15, 32). Today through August 21 the Sun traces the journey of Lazarus, through the spiritual worlds after his death, to his raising July 26, 32. During the days between his death and rebirth, Lazarus united with John the Baptist and is referred to after this as Lazarus–John. It is this individuality who wrote the Gospel of St. John and Revelation.

What happened in these days of spirit journeying? The Temple Legend holds many secrets based on King Solomon and his master builder, Hiram, who, coming from the stream of Cain, could use technology to transform the Earth. Solomon, from the stream of Abel could envision what the gods wanted built on Earth but could not build it. Both as Hiram and in his later incarnation as Lazarus, he was initiated into the mystery of fire (human passions, desires and instincts) through journeying into the interior of the Earth. Hiram learned how to transform the Earth into a work of art (transformation connected to divine intention). Lazarus saw into the heights through his union with the John being.

In these next few days we can contemplate the nature of our desires and passions and ask if they are in accord with our higher wishes and intentions. When in accord, our will transforms the Earth into a work of art. We live in a world that is not transforming the Earth to be a work of art, but instead is transforming her into an ecological disaster. Cain reflects more our masculine nature, and Abel more our feminine nature. In mysterious ways these streams were united under the cross. Are we truly open to the Abel nature in ourselves and in others? The ideal is the meeting between the two. Through this union Cain serves the intuitive feminine and can reach into the material world with artistry. What once we could experience only after death is increasingly available in life, but this requires the cooperation between our Cain and Abel natures. This is the recognition of karma (karmic clairvoyance). The constellation of Cancer keeps asking: Development or envelopment? Development is contingent upon meeting and redeeming our karma: Catharsis.

August 11: ASPECT: Mars opposite Pluto, 10°19' Sagittarius. Mars events occurring close to this degree (9° to 10° Gemini) give us a picture of the gravity of the situation: betrayal by Judas, Gethsemane, Crucifixion, the Passion, and the Descent into Hell. This degree marks Christ's entrance into the last stages of His mission. Just three days before these events, Christ teaches of the Second Coming (March 30, 33):

> [Christ] used the analogy of fire and water, which are inimical. When water does not overpower fire, the flames become greater and more powerful. He spoke of persecution and martyrdom. By the flames of fire, he was referring to those disciples who would remain true to him, and by water he meant those who would leave him and seek the abyss. (*Chron.* p. 248)

These teachings preceded the greatest trials of Christ. Today, Mars remembers these events. Now humanity faces its great trials. It takes fire to stand in our spirit with Christ. "Political correctness" is often the excuse of those afraid of the truth. Today we may ask: Are we water or are we fire...believers or nonbelievers?

Pluto at this degree is where it was at the raising of the Youth of Nain (November 13, 30).

August 13 (10-13-16): Full moon, 25° Cancer (DT): My greatest deed. When John the Water Initiator arrives this day at the third place where he performed the water initiation, he knows that his greatest deed will be done here, the Water Initiation of the Teacher, through which divine energy will enter a human being in a new way. One can affirm: "I come to the place of my greatest deed."

Sun 25° Cancer: The birth of the Nathan Mary—she who bore the vessel for the Logos. Purity and gentleness bring forth our greatest and most enduring deeds.

August 16: ASPECT: Superior conjunction of Venus and the Sun, 28° Cancer (DT). Superior means Venus is farther away. This conjunction at 28° of Cancer sets us up for the inferior conjunction directly in front of the face of the Sun on June 5, 2012 (at 20°50' Taurus), a very rare event (about which more will follow in the *Journal* for 2012). Many events have occurred with this aspect, suggesting that it is particularly fruitful in the world arena. In the time of the Teacher, this marks the day that the Teacher summoned Thomas to be a student, as well as the call to Judas to join the group of students, and also as the call to Zaccheus hiding behind the foliage of a ficus tree. It is a day when a call comes to join one's karmic group, those with whom one has important destiny. The Magna Carta was signed in this aspect on June 15, 1215. Martin Luther King gave his "I Have a Dream" speech in this aspect on August 28, 1963. The cathedral of Chartres was reopened after reconstruction following a fire on this day on March 27, 1220.

August 18: Sun enters Leo: Compassion becomes Freedom. This is the foundation of the true king, the spiritualized "I."

August 21: Sun 2° Leo: Conversation at Jacob's Well with the Samaritan woman (July 26, 30). The zodiacal sign Leo corresponds to the human heart. At this conversation the Samaritan woman's heart opened to Christ and to the living waters—the spring of water welling up to eternal life. This is a good day to pay attention to our own hearts. Do we find merciful waters?

ASPECT: Venus opposite Neptune (4°41' Aquarius). Venus was opposite Neptune at the attempted murder of Jesus (Luke 4:29–30).

> At the close of the Sabbath, when Jesus came out of the synagogue, he was immediately surrounded by about twenty Pharisees. They began to lead him out of the town toward a nearby hill, for they intended to cast him down from the brow of the hill. Suddenly, however, Jesus stopped, stood still, and with the help of angelic beings passed—as if invisible—through the midst of the crowd to his escape. (*Chron.* 241)

The sphere of Venus holds the beings of the archai—the Time Spirits, who stand guard over great evolutionary cycles. Neptune is the sphere of inspiration or illusion. In this event, the Time Spirits (Venus) guard the being who would bring about

SIDEREAL GEOCENTRIC LONGITUDES : AUGUST 2011 Gregorian at 0 hours UT

DAY	☉	☽	☊	☿	♀	♂	♃	♄	♅	♆	♇
1 MO	13 ♋ 32	29 ♋ 52	27 ♏ 40R	6 ♌ 6	9 ♋ 16	3 ♊ 30	14 ♈ 4	17 ♍ 27	9 ♓ 28R	5 ♒ 12R	10 ♐ 30R
2 TU	14 30	14 ♌ 23	27 33	6 15	10 30	4 10	14 9	17 32	9 27	5 11	10 28
3 WE	15 27	28 59	27 27	6 18	11 44	4 51	14 15	17 36	9 26	5 9	10 27
4 TH	16 25	13 ♍ 33	27 21	6 16R	12 58	5 31	14 20	17 41	9 25	5 8	10 26
5 FR	17 22	27 59	27 18	6 9	14 12	6 11	14 25	17 46	9 24	5 6	10 25
6 SA	18 20	12 ♎ 14	27 16	5 57	15 26	6 51	14 29	17 50	9 22	5 5	10 24
7 SU	19 17	26 16	27 16D	5 39	16 40	7 31	14 34	17 55	9 21	5 3	10 23
8 MO	20 15	10 ♏ 3	27 17	5 16	17 54	8 11	14 38	18 0	9 20	5 1	10 22
9 TU	21 12	23 37	27 18	4 49	19 8	8 51	14 42	18 5	9 19	5 0	10 21
10 WE	22 10	6 ♐ 58	27 18R	4 16	20 22	9 31	14 46	18 10	9 17	4 58	10 19
11 TH	23 7	20 7	27 15	3 39	21 36	10 10	14 50	18 16	9 16	4 57	10 18
12 FR	24 5	3 ♑ 5	27 11	2 58	22 50	10 50	14 54	18 21	9 14	4 55	10 17
13 SA	25 2	15 51	27 3	2 14	24 5	11 30	14 57	18 26	9 13	4 54	10 16
14 SU	26 0	28 25	26 54	1 27	25 19	12 9	15 1	18 31	9 11	4 52	10 16
15 MO	26 57	10 ♒ 49	26 43	0 37	26 33	12 49	15 4	18 37	9 10	4 50	10 15
16 TU	27 55	23 2	26 32	29 ♋ 47	27 47	13 28	15 7	18 42	9 8	4 49	10 14
17 WE	28 53	5 ♓ 6	26 21	28 57	29 1	14 7	15 9	18 48	9 6	4 47	10 13
18 TH	29 50	17 2	26 12	28 7	0 ♌ 15	14 47	15 12	18 53	9 5	4 45	10 12
19 FR	0 ♌ 48	28 53	26 5	27 19	1 30	15 26	15 14	18 59	9 3	4 44	10 11
20 SA	1 46	10 ♈ 44	26 1	26 34	2 44	16 5	15 16	19 5	9 1	4 42	10 10
21 SU	2 43	22 38	25 59	25 53	3 58	16 44	15 18	19 10	9 0	4 40	10 9
22 MO	3 41	4 ♉ 40	25 58	25 16	5 12	17 23	15 20	19 16	8 58	4 39	10 9
23 TU	4 39	16 55	25 58D	24 45	6 27	18 2	15 22	19 22	8 56	4 37	10 8
24 WE	5 37	29 29	25 58R	24 20	7 41	18 41	15 23	19 28	8 54	4 36	10 7
25 TH	6 35	12 ♊ 26	25 57	24 2	8 55	19 19	15 24	19 34	8 52	4 34	10 7
26 FR	7 32	25 50	25 54	23 51	10 10	19 58	15 25	19 40	8 50	4 32	10 6
27 SA	8 30	9 ♋ 42	25 48	23 48D	11 24	20 37	15 26	19 46	8 48	4 31	10 5
28 SU	9 28	24 0	25 40	23 52	12 38	21 15	15 27	19 52	8 46	4 29	10 5
29 MO	10 26	8 ♌ 40	25 30	24 5	13 53	21 54	15 27	19 58	8 44	4 27	10 4
30 TU	11 24	23 35	25 20	24 26	15 7	22 32	15 27	20 5	8 42	4 26	10 4
31 WE	12 22	8 ♍ 36	25 9	24 55	16 21	23 10	15 27R	20 11	8 40	4 24	10 3

INGRESSES :

1	☽ → ♌	0:13	19	☽ → ♈	2:15
3	☽ → ♍	1:40	21	☽ → ♉	14:45
5	☽ → ♎	3:22	24	☽ → ♊	0:58
7	☽ → ♏	6:28	26	☽ → ♋	7:18
9	☽ → ♐	11:25	28	☽ → ♌	9:53
11	☽ → ♑	18:16	30	☽ → ♍	10:15
14	☽ → ♒	3: 2			
15	☿ → ♋	17:54			
16	☽ → ♓	13:49			
17	♀ → ♌	19: 2			
18	☉ → ♌	4: 4			

ASPECTS & ECLIPSES :

1	☽ ☍ ♆	8:50	9	☽ ☌ ☊	6:34		☿ ☌ ♀	23: 9	25	♂ □ ♄	10:42
	☽ ☌ ☿	10:27		♂ □ ♅	16: 7	17	☉ i☌ ☿	0:56		☽ ☌ ♂	13: 4
	☉ □ ♃	14:35	10	☽ ☍ ♂	4:51		☽ ☌ ♅	8: 1	27	☽ ☌ ☿	23:47
2	☽ ☌ P	21: 6		☽ ☌ ♇	6: 4	18	☽ ☍ ♄	3:46	28	☽ ☍ ♆	17:10
	☽ ⊓S ☊	21:28	11	♂ ☍ ♇	4:44		☽ ☌ A	16:12	29	☉ ☌ ☽	3: 3
3	☽ ☍ ♅	17:10	13	☽ ☍ ♀	17:22	20	☽ ☌ ♃	9:12		☽ ☌ ♀	9:10
4	☽ ☌ ♄	6:52		☉ ☍ ☽	18:57	21	♀ ☍ ♆	13:25	30	☽ ⊓S ☊	2:45
5	♀ □ ♃	4:20	14	☽ ☍ ☿	5:27		☉ □ ☽	21:54		☽ ☌ P	17:25
6	☽ ☍ ♃	3:51		☽ ☌ ♆	12:24	22	☉ ☍ ♆	23:18	31	☽ ☍ ♅	0: 6
	☉ □ ☽	11: 8	16	☽ N⊔ ☊	6:50	23	☽ ☌ ☋	17:21		☽ ☌ ♄	18:43
8	☿ ☍ ♆	14:17		☉ s☌ ♀	11:31	24	☽ ☍ ♇	19:45			

SIDEREAL HELIOCENTRIC LONGITUDES : AUGUST 2011 Gregorian at 0 hours UT

DAY	Sid. Time	☿	♀	⊕	♂	♃	♄	♅	♆	♇	Vernal Point
1 MO	20:37: 1	8 ♐ 20	3 ♋ 13	13 ♑ 32	7 ♉ 43	2 ♈ 14	22 ♍ 53	7 ♓ 4	4 ♒ 29	11 ♐ 29	5 ♓ 5'55"
2 TU	20:40:58	11 9	4 51	14 29	8 15	2 20	22 55	7 5	4 29	11 29	5 ♓ 5'54"
3 WE	20:44:55	14 0	6 28	15 27	8 47	2 25	22 56	7 5	4 30	11 29	5 ♓ 5'54"
4 TH	20:48:51	16 52	8 6	16 24	9 19	2 31	22 58	7 6	4 30	11 30	5 ♓ 5'54"
5 FR	20:52:48	19 47	9 43	17 22	9 51	2 36	23 0	7 6	4 30	11 30	5 ♓ 5'54"
6 SA	20:56:44	22 43	11 20	18 19	10 23	2 42	23 2	7 7	4 31	11 30	5 ♓ 5'54"
7 SU	21: 0:41	25 42	12 58	19 17	10 55	2 47	23 4	7 8	4 31	11 31	5 ♓ 5'54"
8 MO	21: 4:37	28 44	14 35	20 14	11 27	2 53	23 6	7 8	4 32	11 31	5 ♓ 5'54"
9 TU	21: 8:34	1 ♑ 48	16 13	21 12	11 59	2 58	23 8	7 9	4 32	11 31	5 ♓ 5'53"
10 WE	21:12:30	4 56	17 50	22 9	12 31	3 4	23 10	7 10	4 32	11 32	5 ♓ 5'53"
11 TH	21:16:27	8 8	19 28	23 7	13 2	3 9	23 12	7 10	4 33	11 32	5 ♓ 5'53"
12 FR	21:20:24	11 23	21 5	24 4	13 34	3 15	23 14	7 11	4 33	11 33	5 ♓ 5'53"
13 SA	21:24:20	14 42	22 43	25 2	14 6	3 20	23 16	7 12	4 33	11 33	5 ♓ 5'53"
14 SU	21:28:17	18 5	24 20	25 59	14 37	3 25	23 18	7 12	4 34	11 33	5 ♓ 5'53"
15 MO	21:32:13	21 34	25 58	26 57	15 9	3 31	23 20	7 13	4 34	11 34	5 ♓ 5'53"
16 TU	21:36:10	25 7	27 35	27 55	15 40	3 36	23 22	7 14	4 34	11 34	5 ♓ 5'52"
17 WE	21:40: 6	28 46	29 13	28 52	16 11	3 42	23 24	7 14	4 35	11 34	5 ♓ 5'52"
18 TH	21:44: 3	2 ♒ 30	0 ♌ 50	29 50	16 43	3 47	23 26	7 15	4 35	11 35	5 ♓ 5'52"
19 FR	21:47:59	6 21	2 28	0 ♒ 48	17 14	3 53	23 28	7 15	4 35	11 35	5 ♓ 5'52"
20 SA	21:51:56	10 18	4 6	1 45	17 45	3 58	23 30	7 16	4 36	11 35	5 ♓ 5'52"
21 SU	21:55:53	14 22	5 43	2 43	18 16	4 4	23 32	7 17	4 36	11 36	5 ♓ 5'52"
22 MO	21:59:49	18 34	7 21	3 41	18 48	4 9	23 34	7 17	4 37	11 36	5 ♓ 5'52"
23 TU	22: 3:46	22 53	8 58	4 39	19 19	4 15	23 36	7 18	4 37	11 36	5 ♓ 5'51"
24 WE	22: 7:42	27 20	10 36	5 36	19 50	4 20	23 38	7 19	4 37	11 37	5 ♓ 5'51"
25 TH	22:11:39	1 ♓ 55	12 13	6 34	20 21	4 26	23 40	7 19	4 38	11 37	5 ♓ 5'51"
26 FR	22:15:35	6 39	13 50	7 32	20 51	4 31	23 41	7 20	4 38	11 37	5 ♓ 5'51"
27 SA	22:19:32	11 32	15 28	8 30	21 22	4 37	23 43	7 21	4 38	11 38	5 ♓ 5'51"
28 SU	22:23:28	16 33	17 5	9 28	21 53	4 42	23 45	7 21	4 39	11 38	5 ♓ 5'51"
29 MO	22:27:25	21 44	18 43	10 26	22 24	4 48	23 47	7 22	4 39	11 38	5 ♓ 5'51"
30 TU	22:31:22	27 4	20 20	11 24	22 55	4 53	23 49	7 23	4 39	11 39	5 ♓ 5'51"
31 WE	22:35:18	2 ♈ 33	21 58	12 22	23 25	4 59	23 51	7 23	4 40	11 39	5 ♓ 5'50"

INGRESSES :

8	☿ → ♑	9:57
17	☿ → ♒	7:59
	♀ → ♌	11:34
18	⊕ → ♒	4:12
24	☿ → ♓	14: 3
30	☿ → ♈	12:53

ASPECTS (HELIOCENTRIC +MOON(TYCHONIC)) :

1	☽ ☍ ♆	7:39	10	☽ ☌ ♇	8:17	17	☿ ☌ ⊕	0:56		⊕ ✶ ♃	13: 7		☽ ☌ ♀	18: 9
2	☿ ☌ ♇	2:51		☿ ✶ ♅	16:50		☽ ☌ ♅	4:17		⊕ ☌ ♆	23:18	30	⊕ ✶ ♇	6: 4
3	♀ △ ♅	9:10	11	⊕ △ ♄	2:20		☿ ☍ ♀	5:13	23	☽ ☌ ♂	4:49		☽ ☍ ♅	22: 3
	☽ ☍ ♅	13:20	12	☿ △ ♂	18:52	18	☿ ✶ ♃	8:17	24	♀ △ ♇	15: 4		♀ N⊔ ☊	22:51
4	☽ ☌ ♄	15:40		☽ ☌ ☿	21: 3		☽ ☍ ♄	12:58		☽ ☍ ♇	22:30	31	☿ ✶ ♆	9: 4
5	♀ ✶ ♂	3: 4	13	♀ ✶ ♄	8:19		☿ ☌ ♆	13: 4	26	☿ ☌ ♅	3:24		☿ ☌ ♃	10:35
	☽ ☍ ♃	7:47		☽ ☍ ♀	15: 0	19	☽ ☌ ♃	10:12	27	☿ □ ♇	0:28		♂ △ ♄	21:52
6	☿ □ ♄	2:37	14	☽ ☌ ♆	11:51		♀ △ ♃	22: 8		♃ ✶ ♆	7: 7			
8	☽ ☍ ♂	2:33	15	☿ △ ♄	12: 8	20	♀ ☍ ♆	7:29	28	☽ ☍ ♆	17:28			
9	♀ ☌ P	9: 0		☿ ⊓S ☊	13:36		☿ ✶ ♇	7:38	29	☿ ✶ ♂	3:19			
	☿ □ ♃	9:12	16	♀ ☍ ⊕	11:31	22	☿ □ ♂	1:28		☿ ☍ ♄	9:21			

the "turning point of time." Perhaps this aspect and event are describing the art (Venus) of illusion (Neptune) as protection against malignant forces. The use of this art would require that no attention leak into the horizontal. This is the way of invisibility that trackers and scouts of the Native American tradition know. It is the art of Neptune's illusion serving the good. The practice of invisibility is the practice of concentration without effort. This is a good day to ponder the help, always at hand, that guards us through our most dangerous trials. We may ask: Do we remember to open to the guiding hand of other-world helpers?

August 22: Sun 3° Leo: The Raising of Lazarus (July 26, 32). Before the tomb of Lazarus, Jesus wept!

> Tears have a spiritual, magical power and significance. Goethe indicates this by letting Faust say: "My tears are flowing, the earth takes me back again!"
>
> There exists indeed a whole rainbow of tears—tears of gratitude, of admiration, of compassion, of suffering, of joy, and of sorrow...but always their characteristic is (whether they express an over-measure of deprivation or an over-measure of grace) that they are the bearers of a humility capable of mirroring the light. The eye of pride is always dry. He who weeps also kneels. And he who kneels weeps inwardly. And to kneel signifies an inner approach to the earth, a partaking in the Earth's humility, in the presence of heaven's sublimity. "My tears are flowing, the Earth takes me back again!"...The miracle of the raising of Lazarus works irrespective of time and place, where what is forgotten is remembered, where what sleeps is awakened, and where what is dead is brought to life.[1]

This is a day to listen for the world call to awaken from our sleep in the increasingly ominous illusions of materialism. The "Gift of Tears" has been revered through the ages. It is our perfect offering. Are we willing to be called from the grave of our entombment?

ASPECT: Sun opposite Neptune 4° Aquarius. There was an opposition between Sun and Neptune at the Raising of Lazarus, the death of Master Jesus (Solomon Jesus) and at the death of the Virgin Mary in Ephesus (*Chron.* 136, 157). All three of these beings were raised, one way or another, into the harmony of the spheres at death. Death reveals whom we truly served—the good spirits or the impostors. In life it takes a community to help us know the difference. Our spiritual brothers and sisters reflect back to us our effect. This reflection helps us stay true. Can we receive these reflections?

August 23: Sun 5° Leo, Regulus, the Lion's Heart.

August 28: New moon, 10° Leo (DT): Possession. The events from the life of Jesus Christ are very challenging this day, involving demonic possession and being struck mute—what one would call extreme acting out and psychotic behavior. It is interesting that Mother Teresa, who was born with the Sun in this degree, once went through a similar experience in a hospital, pulling out all the tubes from her body, until a healer arrived, who prayed, and she calmed. She was never able to speak about it. Be strong in the new moon.

Sun 10° Leo: Healing of the Nobleman's Son. The nature of this child's illness was caused by the failure of the father to maintain his spiritual uprightness. Instead he became, as it were, a satellite circling around his earthly master. The greater our neglect of spirit, the more susceptible we become to leaning into false masters. We compromise our cross. Our cross is our balance between the horizontal realm of earthly life and the vertical world of spiritual life. The crossing point between the two creates the sovereign middle space wherein the human being is free. Hindering forces strive against this balance, luring us one way or another. The more we succumb to these forces the less certain our moral character. The less certain our moral character the greater our vulnerability to negative forces. Who is our master? This is truly a question for us all to reflect upon during this new moon.

---

1 Tomberg, *Lazarus, Come Forth!*, p. 87, 89.

August 31: ASPECT (DT): Jupiter rests at 15° Aries, before turning retrograde. This resting ("going stationary") emphasizes that particular degree of the heavens, the zone where the Sun was situated at the resurrection of the Healer—a complete mystery to most! Contemplation of the event during these few days may help one penetrate into the mystery.

Sun 12° Leo: Death of the Nathan Mary (August 5, 12). This is the gentle and pure being who united with the Virgin Mary just before the Baptism in the Jordan. The Virgin Mary was the first to encounter Christ in his resurrection body. Jupiter (wisdom) rests at the Resurrection. The Virgin Mary, in union with the purity of humanity's pre-Fall substance (Nathan Mary), *rests* in future Jupiter, the next planetary incarnation of Earth. She was so pure that she was assumed into Heaven. This is a good day to contemplate the movement of evolution and the necessity of change as we progress toward our future. Evolution is constantly in the process of becoming. One of Rudolf Steiner's definitions of evil is of "good in the wrong time." The question arises: Where am I resting in wisdom, where resisting?

O Spirit of God...
Fill the hearts that seek Thee,
Seek Thee in deep longing,
Deep longing for health
For health and strong courage,
Strong courage that flows
    within our limbs,
Flows as a precious divine gift,
Divine gift from Thee,
O Spirit of God.

My heart radiates.
Above my head radiates a star.
Heart and star radiate together.
I feel soul warmth
In radiance of the stars
    In warmth of heart.
—RUDOLF STEINER

SEPTEMBER

Sun begins in Leo and enters Virgo on the 18th. Pluto stations Direct on the 17th, Retrograde since April.

The full moon is on the 12th (Sun in Leo, Moon in Aquarius). The waning Moon is above Jupiter on the 16th, both rising about 2 hours after sunset, allowing for a beautiful east-southeastern view in twilight. The last waning crescent Moon hangs beneath Mars in Cancer on the 23rd, in the east-southeast, disappearing into the Sun's light as day breaks. The new moon is in Virgo on the 27th, and includes Mercury conjunct the Sun and Moon. On the 28th, the Moon joins Venus and Saturn, invisible in the Sun's light, with Venus and Saturn exactly conjunct on the 29th.

September 8: Sun 20° Leo. Uranus was at 20° Leo at the conversion of Lucifer. Christ on the cross signified the Tree of Life, raised up for the first time on Earth since the expulsion of human beings from Paradise. God had set up his cross in the wilderness of the world, as the seed of redemption—a sign for all posterity. And it was this situation to which the planet Uranus (20° Leo) bore witness as it rose about two o'clock that afternoon. Lucifer, beholding the innocent Son of Man on the cross, was taken over by his guilt and underwent a profound conversion. This conversion can be conceived of as the redemption of the Cosmic Lucifer (see *Christian Hermetic Astrology*, "The Mystery of Golgotha"). Uranus brings lightning bolts to either illumine or destroy the works of human beings, depending upon their moral character.

> In order to arrive at Illumination, a subtle temptation must be met. Instead of thinking becoming a vehicle for divine truth, it can become "brilliant" and then "electrified." And there is a world of difference between an illumined person and a brilliant thinker. The brilliant thinker is able to combine thoughts to his own pleasing, to make everything conform to the way in which he wants to see things, whilst an illumined person is interested solely in divine truth, for which he sacrifices his personal viewpoints.[1]

The world is intricately woven with distortions of truth. Within public media is a vehicle for brilliant thinkers to fashion mass opinion. When the truth is altered, by even one degree, the arc of projection will cause it ultimately to miss its mark. This is a very good day to meditate on the uncompromising power of truth. How do we live it and how do we protect our children from becoming pawns of the virtual world's brilliance? The heart is the great thinker and Uranus in Leo points us to this future potential. Negative Uranus works against this potential, luring human souls into virtual brilliance. Can we practice the art of stillness beyond attachment to our personal viewpoints? In stillness the mind becomes a sea of glass into which cosmic thoughts can be reflected.

September 10: Sun 22° Leo: Death of the Virgin Mary (August 15, 44). Anne Catherine's visions indicate that, after the Ascension of Jesus Christ, Mary lived for three years alternately in Jerusalem in a house on Mount Zion and at the home of Lazarus in Bethany. After this, she traveled with the Apostle John to Ephesus. Under the cross, Christ spoke to John: "Behold, your mother!" And from that hour the disciple took her to his own home" (John 19:27). Adhering to this command John stayed with the Blessed Virgin in Ephesus. Anne Catherine gives the following account:

> A short time before the Blessed Virgin's death, as she felt the approach of her reunion with her God, her Son, and her Redeemer, she prayed that there might be fulfilled what Jesus had promised to her in the house of Lazarus at Bethany on the day before His Ascension. It was shown to me in the spirit how at that time, when she begged him that she might not live for long in this vale of tears after He had ascended, Jesus told her in general what spiritual works she was to accomplish before her end on Earth. He told her, too, that in answer to her prayers the apostles and several disciples would be present at

---
1 Powell, *Hermetic Astrology*, Volume 2, p. 312.

SIDEREAL GEOCENTRIC LONGITUDES : SEPTEMBER 2011 Gregorian at 0 hours UT

DAY	☉	☽	☊	☿	♀	♂	♃	♄	♅	♆	♇
1 TH	13 ♌ 20	23 ♍ 32	25 ♏ 1R	25 ♋ 32	17 ♌ 36	23 ♊ 49	15 ♈ 27R	20 ♍ 17	8 ♓ 38R	4 ♒ 22R	10 ♐ 3R
2 FR	14 18	8 ♎ 17	24 54	26 17	18 50	24 27	15 26	20 24	8 36	4 21	10 2
3 SA	15 16	22 43	24 51	27 10	20 5	25 5	15 26	20 30	8 34	4 19	10 2
4 SU	16 15	6 ♏ 49	24 49	28 10	21 19	25 43	15 25	20 36	8 32	4 18	10 1
5 MO	17 13	20 33	24 49	29 17	22 34	26 21	15 24	20 43	8 29	4 16	10 1
6 TU	18 11	3 ♐ 58	24 49	0 ♌ 30	23 48	26 59	15 23	20 49	8 27	4 14	10 1
7 WE	19 9	17 5	24 48	1 49	25 2	27 36	15 21	20 56	8 25	4 13	10 0
8 TH	20 7	29 58	24 45	3 14	26 17	28 14	15 20	21 3	8 23	4 11	10 0
9 FR	21 5	12 ♑ 37	24 38	4 43	27 31	28 52	15 18	21 9	8 20	4 10	10 0
10 SA	22 4	25 6	24 29	6 18	28 46	29 29	15 16	21 16	8 18	4 8	10 0
11 SU	23 2	7 ♒ 26	24 17	7 55	0 ♍ 0	0 ♋ 7	15 14	21 23	8 16	4 7	9 59
12 MO	24 0	19 38	24 3	9 37	1 15	0 44	15 11	21 29	8 14	4 5	9 59
13 TU	24 59	1 ♓ 42	23 49	11 21	2 29	1 21	15 9	21 36	8 11	4 4	9 59
14 WE	25 57	13 39	23 35	13 7	3 44	1 59	15 6	21 43	8 9	4 2	9 59
15 TH	26 55	25 32	23 24	14 56	4 58	2 36	15 3	21 50	8 6	4 1	9 59
16 FR	27 54	7 ♈ 22	23 14	16 45	6 13	3 13	15 0	21 57	8 4	3 59	9 59
17 SA	28 52	19 11	23 8	18 36	7 27	3 50	14 56	22 4	8 2	3 58	9 59D
18 SU	29 51	1 ♉ 4	23 4	20 28	8 42	4 27	14 53	22 11	7 59	3 56	9 59
19 MO	0 ♍ 49	13 4	23 2	22 20	9 56	5 3	14 49	22 18	7 57	3 55	9 59
20 TU	1 48	25 17	23 2	24 12	11 11	5 40	14 45	22 25	7 55	3 53	9 59
21 WE	2 47	7 ♊ 48	23 2	26 4	12 26	6 17	14 41	22 32	7 52	3 52	9 59
22 TH	3 45	20 41	23 1	27 56	13 40	6 53	14 36	22 39	7 50	3 51	9 59
23 FR	4 44	4 ♋ 1	22 58	29 48	14 55	7 30	14 32	22 46	7 47	3 49	10 0
24 SA	5 43	17 51	22 53	1 ♍ 39	16 9	8 6	14 27	22 53	7 45	3 48	10 0
25 SU	6 41	2 ♌ 10	22 45	3 30	17 24	8 42	14 22	23 0	7 43	3 47	10 0
26 MO	7 40	16 56	22 35	5 20	18 38	9 19	14 17	23 7	7 40	3 45	10 0
27 TU	8 39	2 ♍ 2	22 25	7 9	19 53	9 55	14 12	23 14	7 38	3 44	10 1
28 WE	9 38	17 18	22 14	8 57	21 8	10 31	14 7	23 22	7 35	3 43	10 1
29 TH	10 37	2 ♎ 32	22 6	10 45	22 22	11 7	14 1	23 29	7 33	3 42	10 1
30 FR	11 36	17 34	21 59	12 32	23 37	11 42	13 56	23 36	7 30	3 40	10 2

INGRESSES :

1 ☽ → ♎ 10:28	18 ☉ → ♍ 3:44
3 ☽ → ♏ 12:19	20 ☽ → ♊ 9: 7
5 ☿ → ♌ 14:27	22 ☽ → ♋ 16:51
☽ → ♐ 16:50	23 ☿ → ♍ 2:33
8 ☽ → ♑ 0: 4	24 ☽ → ♌ 20:24
10 ☽ → ♒ 9:29	26 ☽ → ♍ 20:47
♂ → ♋ 19:42	28 ☽ → ♎ 20: 0
♀ → ♍ 23:54	30 ☽ → ♏ 20:14
12 ☽ → ♓ 20:37	
15 ☽ → ♈ 9: 3	
17 ☽ → ♉ 21:51	

ASPECTS & ECLIPSES :

2 ☽ ☍ ♃ 11:49	☉ ☍ ☽ 9:26	21 ☽ ☍ ♇ 4: 8	☉ □ ♇ 9:25
4 ☉ □ ☽ 17:39	13 ☽ ☍ ♀ 1:46	23 ☽ ☌ ♂ 6:24	☽ ☌ ♄ 9:36
5 ☽ ☌ ☊ 7:33	☽ ☌ ♅ 12:57	25 ☽ ☍ ♆ 2:38	☿ □ ♇ 14:12
6 ☽ ☌ ♇ 10:59	14 ☽ ☍ ♄ 16:26	☉ ☍ ♅ 23:57	☉ ☋ ☿ 19:59
♀ □ ☊ 19:27	15 ☽ ☌ A 6:16	26 ☽ S ☊ 8:55	29 ☽ ☍ ♃ 18:11
7 ☽ ☍ ♂ 20:35	16 ☽ ☌ ♃ 15:25	27 ☿ ☍ ♅ 6:13	♀ ☌ ♄ 23:40
8 ☿ ☍ ♆ 15:16	17 ♀ ☍ ♅ 10:44	☽ ☍ ♅ 8:47	
10 ☽ ☌ ♆ 17:30	19 ♀ □ ♇ 0:49	☽ ☌ ☿ 9: 8	
11 ☽ ☍ ☿ 1: 6	☿ □ ☊ 8:59	☉ ☌ ☽ 11: 8	
12 ☉ □ ☊ 0:58	☽ ☌ ☋ 19:36	28 ☽ ☌ P 0:49	
☽ N ☊ 8:36	20 ☉ □ ☽ 13:38	☽ ☌ ♀ 6:33	

SIDEREAL HELIOCENTRIC LONGITUDES : SEPTEMBER 2011 Gregorian at 0 hours UT

DAY	Sid. Time	☿	♀	⊕	♂	♃	♄	♅	♆	♇	Vernal Point
1 TH	22:39:15	8 ♈ 11	23 ♌ 35	13 ♒ 20	23 ♉ 56	5 ♈ 4	23 ♍ 53	7 ♓ 24	4 ♒ 40	11 ♐ 39	5 ♓ 5'50"
2 FR	22:43:11	13 57	25 12	14 18	24 26	5 10	23 55	7 24	4 41	11 40	5 ♓ 5'50"
3 SA	22:47: 8	19 51	26 50	15 16	24 57	5 15	23 57	7 25	4 41	11 40	5 ♓ 5'50"
4 SU	22:51: 4	25 52	28 27	16 14	25 27	5 21	23 59	7 26	4 41	11 40	5 ♓ 5'50"
5 MO	22:55: 1	1 ♉ 59	0 ♍ 4	17 12	25 58	5 26	24 1	7 26	4 42	11 41	5 ♓ 5'50"
6 TU	22:58:57	8 11	1 41	18 11	26 28	5 32	24 3	7 27	4 42	11 41	5 ♓ 5'50"
7 WE	23: 2:54	14 27	3 19	19 9	26 58	5 37	24 5	7 28	4 42	11 41	5 ♓ 5'49"
8 TH	23: 6:51	20 46	4 56	20 7	27 29	5 43	24 7	7 28	4 43	11 42	5 ♓ 5'49"
9 FR	23:10:47	27 5	6 33	21 5	27 59	5 48	24 9	7 29	4 43	11 42	5 ♓ 5'49"
10 SA	23:14:44	3 ♊ 24	8 10	22 3	28 29	5 54	24 11	7 30	4 43	11 42	5 ♓ 5'49"
11 SU	23:18:40	9 40	9 47	23 2	28 59	5 59	24 13	7 30	4 44	11 43	5 ♓ 5'49"
12 MO	23:22:37	15 53	11 24	24 0	29 29	6 5	24 15	7 31	4 44	11 43	5 ♓ 5'49"
13 TU	23:26:33	22 2	13 1	24 58	29 59	6 10	24 17	7 32	4 45	11 43	5 ♓ 5'49"
14 WE	23:30:30	28 4	14 38	25 57	0 ♊ 29	6 16	24 19	7 32	4 45	11 44	5 ♓ 5'48"
15 TH	23:34:26	3 ♋ 59	16 15	26 55	0 59	6 21	24 21	7 33	4 45	11 44	5 ♓ 5'48"
16 FR	23:38:23	9 46	17 52	27 54	1 29	6 27	24 23	7 33	4 46	11 44	5 ♓ 5'48"
17 SA	23:42:20	15 24	19 29	28 52	1 59	6 32	24 25	7 34	4 46	11 45	5 ♓ 5'48"
18 SU	23:46:16	20 53	21 5	29 51	2 28	6 38	24 26	7 35	4 46	11 45	5 ♓ 5'48"
19 MO	23:50:13	26 12	22 42	0 ♓ 49	2 58	6 43	24 28	7 35	4 47	11 45	5 ♓ 5'48"
20 TU	23:54: 9	1 ♌ 22	24 19	1 48	3 28	6 49	24 30	7 36	4 47	11 46	5 ♓ 5'48"
21 WE	23:58: 6	6 22	25 56	2 46	3 57	6 54	24 32	7 37	4 47	11 46	5 ♓ 5'47"
22 TH	0: 2: 2	11 13	27 32	3 45	4 27	6 59	24 34	7 37	4 48	11 46	5 ♓ 5'47"
23 FR	0: 5:59	15 54	29 9	4 44	4 56	7 5	24 36	7 38	4 48	11 47	5 ♓ 5'47"
24 SA	0: 9:55	20 27	0 ♎ 45	5 42	5 26	7 10	24 38	7 39	4 48	11 47	5 ♓ 5'47"
25 SU	0:13:52	24 50	2 22	6 41	5 55	7 16	24 40	7 39	4 49	11 47	5 ♓ 5'47"
26 MO	0:17:49	29 5	3 58	7 40	6 25	7 21	24 42	7 40	4 49	11 48	5 ♓ 5'47"
27 TU	0:21:45	3 ♍ 13	5 35	8 39	6 54	7 27	24 44	7 41	4 50	11 48	5 ♓ 5'47"
28 WE	0:25:42	7 12	7 11	9 38	7 24	7 32	24 46	7 41	4 50	11 48	5 ♓ 5'47"
29 TH	0:29:38	11 5	8 48	10 37	7 53	7 38	24 48	7 42	4 50	11 49	5 ♓ 5'46"
30 FR	0:33:35	14 51	10 24	11 36	8 22	7 43	24 50	7 42	4 51	11 49	5 ♓ 5'46"

INGRESSES :

4 ☿ → ♉ 16:15
♀ → ♍ 22:59
9 ☿ → ♊ 11: 5
13 ♂ → ♊ 0:47
14 ☿ → ♋ 7:47
18 ⊕ → ♓ 3:51
19 ☿ → ♌ 17:32
23 ♀ → ♎ 12:42
26 ☿ → ♍ 5:14

ASPECTS (HELIOCENTRIC +MOON(TYCHONIC)) :

1 ☽ ☌ ♄ 0:33	6 ☽ ☌ ♇ 14: 3	☿ ☍ ♇ 7:50	☿ N ☊ 12: 0	25 ☽ ☍ ♆ 4:20	♂ □ ♅ 14:47
♀ □ ♂ 7:29	7 ☿ □ ⊕ 21: 6	12 ♀ □ ♇ 4:41	☿ ✶ ♄ 16: 3	⊕ ☌ ♅ 23:57	☿ ☍ ⊕ 19:59
☿ △ ♇ 14:30	8 ☿ ☌ P 7:30	13 ☿ □ ♄ 8:56	20 ♀ ☌ ♄ 2:53	26 ♀ △ ♆ 12:41	29 ☿ □ ♇ 4:33
☽ ☍ ♃ 18:51	☿ △ ♄ 12:48	☽ ☌ ♅ 11:41	☿ ✶ ♂ 11: 1	27 ☽ ☌ ☿ 2:31	☽ ☍ ♃ 8: 8
2 ☿ ✶ ⊕ 1:42	9 ☿ ☌ ♂ 3:42	☿ △ ⊕ 13:53	☿ ☍ ♆ 16:18	☽ ☍ ♅ 8:53	☽ ☌ ♀ 11: 7
☽ ☍ ☿ 15:47	♀ ☍ ♅ 13:57	14 ☽ ☍ ♀ 2:16	☽ ☌ ♂ 16:24	28 ☿ □ ♂ 1:17	30 ⊕ □ ♇ 5:30
3 ☿ ☌ ☊ 14:52	10 ☿ △ ♆ 5: 4	☽ ☍ ♄ 21:34	21 ☿ △ ♃ 2:36	☿ ☍ ♅ 2:55	♀ ✶ ♇ 21:18
4 ☿ △ ♀ 13:49	☿ ✶ ♃ 9:40	15 ☿ □ ♃ 9:55	☽ ☍ ♇ 7:28	♀ △ ♂ 4:23	
5 ☽ ☍ ♂ 9:58	☿ □ ♅ 15:40	☿ △ ♅ 14:45	22 ☿ △ ♇ 2:47	♀ ☍ ♃ 5:35	
☿ □ ♆ 10:31	☽ ☌ ♆ 18:42	☽ ☌ ♃ 22: 7	♂ △ ♆ 17: 7	♂ ✶ ♃ 8:56	
☿ ✶ ♅ 21: 9	11 ☿ □ ♀ 0:34	18 ☿ ✶ ♀ 1:19	23 ⊕ □ ♂ 10:31	☽ ☌ ♄ 11:46	

her death, and what she was to say to them and how she was to bless them.... After the Blessed Virgin had prayed that the apostles should come to her, I saw the call going forth to them in many different parts of the world.... I saw all, the farthest as well as the nearest, being summoned by visions to come to the Blessed Virgin.[2]

This is the great being who goes before us into future Jupiter evolution. She who was Eve, the mother of all, prepares the way. The Blessed Virgin helps all her children find their way home. We are encouraged to keep the light of goodness shining for all children.

September 11: Pluto stations at 9°59' Sagittarius for approximately the next eleven days: The Wedding in Cana (December 28, 29). The term *station* refers to the points in a planet's retrograde cycle where it is standing still and, hence, concentrating its energies heavily on a single zodiacal position. With Pluto stationed at this location, a concentration of forces is focused on the first miracle of Christ following his Baptism in the Jordan: the Wedding in Cana in Galilee. This concentration continues until September 22. At the Wedding in Cana, Christ turned water into wine, signifying the formation of communities based on spiritual kinship rather than on blood kinship. In spiritual kinship, we are united through the new wine of Christ working in us. We witness the words of the Resurrected Christ who speaks:

> And he said to them, "Go into all the world and proclaim the gospel to the whole creation. Whoever believes and is baptized will be saved, but whoever does not believe will be condemned. And these signs will accompany those who believe: in my name they will cast out demons; they will speak in new tongues; they will pick up serpents with their hands; and if they drink any deadly poison, it will not hurt them; they will lay their hands on the sick, and they will recover." (Mark 16:15–18 [ESV])

---

2 Emmerich, *The Life of the Blessed Virgin Mary: From the Visions of Ven. Anne Catherine Emmerich*, (Rockford, IL: Tan Books, 1970), pp. 363–364.

When our blood is lifted from its horizontal position connected with heredity, into the vertical position connected with spiritual destinies, we are lifting the serpent nature of the blood into the Christ-ennobled blood. This was ordained as the future state of human communities by the *sign* of this first miracle. The result mentioned in the Gospels is that Jesus Christ "manifested his glory," and "his disciples believed in him" (John 2:11). This miracle foretold the blood becoming a bearer of the Christ impulse.

Now, in this time of the Second Coming, Pluto stations at the event of this miracle asking whether humanity will become a bearer of Christ or a pawn of the serpent. This transformation of the blood is needed to become a witness to the true light of the Second Coming. We are invited to the wedding, where the faith of the disciples then becomes the experience of all disciples now; we witness the "glory" and experience him.

Ten years after 9/11 to the day, we face the question this miracle poses, and the force opposing this miracle—the dragon forces of the blood (Pluto–Hades). Will humanity choose the marriage to Christ as the new wine of the ennobled human heart, or will humanity slither with the fear and hatred of the serpent who announced another level of his arrival at the event of September 11, 2001?

September 12 (9-12-15): Full moon, Sun at 24° Leo (DT): Senior students discovered that mother Mary's tomb was empty. A fragment from the Oracle of the Solar Cross:

> Prayers of mourning turn to awe. Glory! Consummation! Heaven trembles and opens. Glory! Angels increase in number, depth, sound—circles of angels, the closest with the faces of infants. They receive every particle of the physical body turned to light. Glory!

The exclamation "Glory!" occurs in only two places in the Oracle of the Solar Cross (the other being April 17), and both are stimulated by full moons this year.

Full moon 24° Aquarius. The Sun was here at the healing of the Syrophoenician woman and her daughter. Jesus healed the daughter of possession. In healing possession, he would stand back from the person and speak in a great thundering voice filled with the Living Word. Jesus would stand back so that he could drive the demon out of the person into open space. If he had stood close to the person, the demon would react within the body it possessed, bringing physical harm.[3] Jesus laid one hand upon her head, the other on her side, and said: "Straighten up! May it be done to you as you also will it to be done! The devil has gone out of your daughter."[4] Clearly this woman was given the free will to accept or reject healing. It depended on her willingness to feel worthy. Do we feel worthy? If not, we may ask this full moon about the nature of our perceived unworthiness.

September 18: Sun enters Virgo: Courtesy becomes Tactfulness of Heart. The inner work of descent (Persephone) brings awareness of self-knowledge.

Sun 0°19' Virgo: The Moon (portal to both angels and demons) stood here at the beginning of the Forty Days in the Wilderness. During those forty days of continual temptation, Anne Catherine describes how the Christ never once looked at his tempters. Instead he addressed himself directly to his Father in Heaven. This is a powerful example for humanity, which is now facing the combined activity of the tempters on a global scale. May we remember to keep our attention on the in-streaming spiritual Light and Love! This is what guides us through the changes so necessary in our time. What we attend will grow, and as the Sun enters Virgo, the sign of the Divine Sophia, we are to tend our garden gate. This means having the appropriate boundaries. Our boundaries protect us and allow us to choose what shall enter and what shall leave. In eurythmy, the gesture for "B" forms our essential cloak of protection. May we thus practice wrapping ourselves in the starry mantle of Sophia!

September 25/26: ASPECT: Sun opposite Uranus. Under this aspect Jesus taught the Bread of Life (John 6:52–59). Jesus spoke of his body and blood as humanity's true nourishment. The Holy Sacrament is to exist until the end of time, and it continues to feed and give us sustenance, leading us ever nearer to union with Christ. The heart (Sun) receives the true Light (Uranus) when it hungers and thirsts for righteousness. The inverse to this could be the hunger and thirst to build empires (negative Uranus).

September 27: New moon, 9° Virgo (DT): The mouth. A small fragment from the Oracle of the Solar Cross: Enemies open their mouths; out come hisses and gnashing of teeth; they clamor to devour the daughter, who is Peace.

Watch for what comes out of your mouth, what effect that your words have. Pay particular attention to gossip. The Oracle goes on: Divinity speaks: "I bring comfort to you. I put my words in your mouth." We can take words in through the mouth, and perhaps learn from these, thus softening the words that come out of our mouths.

Sun 9° Virgo: Raising of Nazor (September 1, 32). Jesus goes to the field in which Nazor had died and prays. Returning to the house they find Nazor sitting upright in his coffin. Nazor was raised from a distance. Christ went to where his soul and spirit lingered over the field of his death. This is similar to the way thoughts and words linger over the places in which they were expressed. We live in times when it is prudent to surround ourselves with a protective sheath born of conscious attention. This can be likened to wrapping oneself in Sophia's (Virgo) protection. As we become more skilled at this ownership of our personal "field," we are protected from corrupt thoughts, feelings, and actions in our environment. The voice of spiritual guidance is more easily heard in such a conscientiously tended space. We are guided to know when certain spaces and beings need to be cleared of ill will. By cleansing our environments, we help raise the fallen from the dead. This can be done while in the location or even from a distance. These capacities are awaking as gifts from Sophia. Nazor was instructed, after being raised from the dead, to be kinder to his servants. We can remember to be kinder in our words, thoughts, and deeds to

---

3 Von Halle, *Illness and Healing*, pp. 78–79.
4 Emmerich, *LJC*, vol. 3, p. 235.

preserve the environments of this kingdom: the kingdom of our Mother. Elemental beings long to serve the good. Today, we can be particularly attentive to elemental beings. The constellation of Virgo asks this of us and gives us "courtesy" as her virtue.

September 29: ASPECT: Venus conjunct Saturn, 23° Virgo: Venus and Saturn were in opposition at the start of the forty days. The Being of Love in the wilderness of Earth faced his Father in the heights of Heaven. Today, these two planets stand together. This can be experienced as oppressive or as a catalyst for receiving intuitions. This depends on our willingness to defer to our higher resolve.

Saturn at 23° Virgo. Saturn, the planet of cosmic memory, remembers Mars at the beginning of the Forty Days (22° Virgo). Mars is the planet of the Word. It is also a signature of the condition of our astral body. One receives spiritual counsel to the degree the astral body is pure (Virgin Sophia). One who can *receive* spiritual counsel is fit to spiritually counsel others. In spiritual counsel it is as if the angel of the other speaks with and through the one counseling. If the astral body is fallen it is very difficult to distinguish between good and evil, making spiritual counseling dangerous.

Hearing what life stands behind a person's words affords us the discrimination to know who is speaking. Today, Saturn remembers Mars in Virgo and the beginning of the Forty Days. Our conscience (Saturn) bears discernment of good from evil. "Speak that I may know you," were words of Christ, illumining the revealing nature of our speech.

Today Saturn remembers the tempters, who were speaking against Christ in the wilderness. Saturn, as portal to the kingdom of the Father, is inversely the portal to the kingdom of the Asuras who seek to destroy the glory of physical creation. We are advised to mind our words and listen carefully, discerning who actually stands behind the words of others. As Venus stands now in conjunction with Saturn, the possibility of attentive listening is greatly enhanced.

KNIGHTHOOD OF THE TWENTY-FIRST CENTURY

There is a knighthood of the twenty-first century
Whose riders do not ride through the darkness
    of physical forests,
As of old, but through the forest
    of darkened minds.

They are armed with a spiritual armor,
And an inner sun makes them radiant.

Out of them shines healing,
Healing that flows from the knowledge
    of the human being
As a spiritual being.

They must create inner order, inner justice,
Peace, and conviction in the darkness of our time.

They must learn to work side by side
    with angels.

(additional last line from William Bento;
revised by Leslie Loy)

OCTOBER

The Sun begins in Virgo, moving into Libra (the Scales) on the 18th. This month brings Saturn into conjunction with Mercury (on the 6th), the Sun (13th), and Moon (26th), but all are hidden in the light of the Sun's radiance. This invites more daytime stargazing, developing capacities of the heart complementary to the physical eyes! The full moon (Sun in Virgo, Moon in Pisces) is on the 12th and includes Saturn (in opposition to the Moon). The new moon on the 26th (Sun and Moon in Virgo) includes Saturn as well. Mid-month Venus becomes visible as evening star, visible as a shining diamond in the west as twilight deepens into night.

On the 13th, the full moon (actually just past full) shines below Jupiter near the star Regulus (the Heart of the Lion and a Royal Star of Persia, 5° Leo). They can be seen in the east-southeast before dawn. October also brings the Orionid meteor shower, with its peak the 20th to 22nd. Look in the direction of the Orion constellation. On the 28th, the Moon joins Mercury and Venus, again hidden within the light of the Sun.

October 4: Sun 16° Virgo: Birth of the Solomon Mary (September 7, 21). The Solomon Mary is the one whom we refer to as the Virgin Mary. At her *conception* the Sun stood at 17° Sagittarius, which is almost exactly the birth Sun of the Nathan Jesus (16° Sagittarius). This is a star language speaking a profound affinity between the Virgin Mary and the Nathan Jesus.

Robert Powell speaks of the cross the Holy births create in the heavens: Birth of Nathan Jesus (Luke Jesus), Sun 16° Sagittarius; Birth of Solomon Jesus (Matthew Jesus), Sun 15½° Pisces; Birth of John the Baptist, Sun 12° Gemini; Birth of Virgin Mary, Sun 16° Virgo.[1] Today we touch into this cosmic cross that marked the births of the high initiates participating in turning the point of time from its descending stream of involution to its ascending stream of evolution.

Noteworthy: We have a cross in the sky for most of this year. Pluto in Sagittarius (Sun of Nathan Jesus), Uranus in Pisces (Sun of Solomon Jesus), Saturn in Virgo (Sun of Virgin Mary), and the place of John is open. This open place in Gemini holds the mystery of the Baptism. Are we being asked to stand here to conceive our higher natures, lest our lower natures stand in for us? This cross was marked by the giant comets Hayakutake and Hale Bopp of 1996 and 1997, and here again it is marked by the outer planets. Reading the signs in the heavens brings wonder to the open human mind. In contemplating the cross of the great initiates today we can ask: What part do we play in this mystery? Are we willing to take up the place of the Baptist who came as a witness to the true light?

October 5: Sun 17° Virgo: Conception of John the Baptist (September 9, 3 B.C.). The *conception* of this great being, when the Sun was in Virgo prefigures his mission after his death. Virgo is the sign of Wisdom Sophia, the World Soul. John, after his death, became guardian over the souls of the disciples, just as Sophia is guardian over all the souls of humanity. "John's mighty spirit lived on after the beheading, powerfully inspiring the apostles and disciples, becoming a kind of protecting spirit over the Twelve."[2]

This day remembers the protecting forces (Virgo) surrounding each human being. Today, as at the turning point of time, it is the John being, along with many other high initiates, who watch over all those who turn to Christ and Sophia. We are to remember that our angels and guides cannot approach us uninvited. They cannot interfere with humanity's free will. May we make our invitations and invocations a daily habit!

October 11 (8-11-14): Full moon, 23° Virgo (DT): This is the degree of the story of the globe of light, used to illustrate Jupiter, which was prominent at that event.[3] Here we contemplate light and the power of light, and what lives in the light.

Mars was very close to this degree (22° Virgo) at the start of the Forty Days, where the fallen light

---

1 Powell, *Christian Hermetic Astrology,* "The Adoration of the Shepherds."

2 Powell, *Christian Hermetic Astrology,* "The Ministry up to the Beheading of John the Baptist."

3 See the *Journal for Star Wisdom 2010* (also available in the newsletter at www.starwisdom.org).

SIDEREAL GEOCENTRIC LONGITUDES : OCTOBER 2011 Gregorian at 0 hours UT

DAY	☉	☽	☊	☿	♀	♂	♃	♄	⛢	♆	♇
1 SA	12 ♍ 35	2 ♏ 17	21 ♏ 55R	14 ♍ 18	24 ♍ 52	12 ♋ 18	13 ♈ 50R	23 ♍ 43	7 ♓ 28R	3 ♒ 39R	10 ♐ 2
2 SU	13 34	16 34	21 53	16 3	26 6	12 54	13 44	23 50	7 26	3 38	10 3
3 MO	14 33	0 ♐ 26	21 53D	17 47	27 21	13 29	13 38	23 58	7 23	3 37	10 3
4 TU	15 32	13 52	21 54	19 30	28 35	14 4	13 32	24 5	7 21	3 36	10 4
5 WE	16 31	26 57	21 54R	21 13	29 50	14 40	13 25	24 12	7 19	3 35	10 4
6 TH	17 30	9 ♑ 42	21 51	22 54	1 ♎ 5	15 15	13 19	24 20	7 16	3 34	10 5
7 FR	18 29	22 11	21 47	24 35	2 19	15 50	13 12	24 27	7 14	3 33	10 5
8 SA	19 28	4 ♒ 29	21 40	26 15	3 34	16 25	13 5	24 34	7 11	3 31	10 6
9 SU	20 28	16 37	21 30	27 54	4 48	17 0	12 58	24 41	7 9	3 30	10 7
10 MO	21 27	28 39	21 19	29 33	6 3	17 35	12 51	24 49	7 7	3 30	10 7
11 TU	22 26	10 ♓ 35	21 7	1 ♎ 10	7 18	18 9	12 44	24 56	7 5	3 29	10 8
12 WE	23 25	22 28	20 56	2 47	8 32	18 44	12 37	25 3	7 2	3 28	10 9
13 TH	24 25	4 ♈ 19	20 46	4 23	9 47	19 18	12 30	25 11	7 0	3 27	10 10
14 FR	25 24	16 10	20 38	5 59	11 1	19 53	12 22	25 18	6 58	3 26	10 11
15 SA	26 23	28 2	20 33	7 34	12 16	20 27	12 15	25 25	6 55	3 25	10 11
16 SU	27 23	9 ♉ 58	20 30	9 8	13 31	21 1	12 7	25 33	6 53	3 24	10 12
17 MO	28 22	22 1	20 30D	10 41	14 45	21 35	11 59	25 40	6 51	3 23	10 13
18 TU	29 22	4 ♊ 16	20 30	12 14	16 0	22 9	11 52	25 47	6 49	3 23	10 14
19 WE	0 ♎ 21	16 46	20 32	13 46	17 14	22 43	11 44	25 55	6 47	3 22	10 15
20 TH	1 21	29 35	20 32	15 18	18 29	23 16	11 36	26 2	6 45	3 21	10 16
21 FR	2 21	12 ♋ 49	20 32R	16 48	19 44	23 50	11 28	26 9	6 42	3 21	10 17
22 SA	3 20	26 30	20 29	18 19	20 58	24 23	11 20	26 17	6 40	3 20	10 18
23 SU	4 20	10 ♌ 40	20 25	19 48	22 13	24 56	11 12	26 24	6 38	3 19	10 19
24 MO	5 20	25 16	20 19	21 17	23 27	25 29	11 4	26 31	6 36	3 19	10 20
25 TU	6 20	10 ♍ 15	20 13	22 46	24 42	26 2	10 56	26 38	6 34	3 18	10 22
26 WE	7 19	25 28	20 6	24 14	25 57	26 35	10 48	26 46	6 32	3 18	10 23
27 TH	8 19	10 ♎ 45	20 0	25 41	27 11	27 8	10 40	26 53	6 30	3 17	10 24
28 FR	9 19	25 55	19 56	27 7	28 26	27 41	10 31	27 0	6 28	3 17	10 25
29 SA	10 19	10 ♏ 48	19 54	28 33	29 40	28 13	10 23	27 7	6 27	3 17	10 26
30 SU	11 19	25 18	19 54D	29 58	0 ♏ 55	28 45	10 15	27 15	6 25	3 16	10 28
31 MO	12 19	9 ♐ 22	19 55	1 ♏ 22	2 10	29 17	10 7	27 22	6 23	3 16	10 29

INGRESSES :

2 ☽ → ♐ 23:14	22 ☽ → ♌ 6: 0
5 ♀ → ♎ 3:13	24 ☽ → ♍ 7:38
☽ → ♑ 5:42	26 ☽ → ♎ 7: 7
7 ☽ → ♒ 15:12	28 ☽ → ♏ 6:32
10 ☽ → ♓ 2:42	29 ♀ → ♏ 6:16
☿ → ♎ 6:43	30 ☿ → ♏ 0:31
12 ☽ → ♈ 15:14	☽ → ♐ 7:55
15 ☽ → ♉ 3:58	
17 ☽ → ♊ 15:41	
18 ☉ → ♎ 15:21	
20 ☽ → ♋ 0:45	

ASPECTS & ECLIPSES :

2 ☽ ☌ ☊ 9: 7	☽ ☌ A 11:30	22 ☽ ☍ ♆ 11:40	29 ☉ ☍ ♃ 1:30
3 ♂ □ ♃ 5: 2	13 ☽ ☍ ☿ 0: 9	23 ☽ [S] ☊ 16: 0	☽ ☌ ☊ 14:58
☽ ☌ ♇ 17: 6	☽ ☍ ♀ 12:21	24 ☽ ☍ ⛢ 18:10	31 ☽ ☌ ♇ 1:57
4 ☉ □ ☽ 3:14	☽ ☌ ♃ 16:23	26 ☽ ☌ ♄ 2: 3	♀ □ ♆ 21:10
6 ☽ ☍ ♂ 11: 8	☉ ☌ ♄ 21:15	☽ ☌ P 12:15	
☿ ☌ ♄ 21:54	14 ♀ ☍ ♃ 23:37	☉ ☌ ☽ 19:55	
7 ☽ ☌ ♆ 22: 7	16 ☽ ☌ ☋ 20:58	♀ □ ♂ 22: 9	
9 ☽ [N] ☊ 9:33	17 ☿ ☍ ♃ 18:41	☽ ☍ ♃ 23:52	
10 ☽ ☌ ⛢ 16:56	18 ☽ ☍ ♇ 11:33	28 ☽ ☌ ☿ 2: 8	
12 ☉ ☍ ☽ 2: 5	20 ☉ □ ☽ 3:30	☽ ☌ ♀ 4:23	
☽ ☍ ♄ 5:16	21 ☽ ☌ ♂ 20:11	☿ □ ♂ 14:57	

SIDEREAL HELIOCENTRIC LONGITUDES : OCTOBER 2011 Gregorian at 0 hours UT

DAY	Sid. Time	☿	♀	⊕	♂	♃	♄	⛢	♆	♇	Vernal Point
1 SA	0:37:31	18 ♍ 31	12 ♎ 0	12 ♓ 34	8 ♊ 51	7 ♈ 49	24 ♍ 52	7 ♓ 43	4 ♒ 51	11 ♐ 49	5 ♓ 5'46"
2 SU	0:41:28	22 5	13 36	13 33	9 20	7 54	24 54	7 44	4 51	11 50	5 ♓ 5'46"
3 MO	0:45:24	25 34	15 12	14 33	9 49	8 0	24 56	7 44	4 52	11 50	5 ♓ 5'46"
4 TU	0:49:21	28 58	16 49	15 32	10 19	8 5	24 58	7 45	4 52	11 50	5 ♓ 5'46"
5 WE	0:53:18	2 ♎ 17	18 25	16 31	10 48	8 11	25 0	7 46	4 52	11 51	5 ♓ 5'46"
6 TH	0:57:14	5 32	20 1	17 30	11 17	8 16	25 2	7 46	4 53	11 51	5 ♓ 5'45"
7 FR	1: 1:11	8 43	21 37	18 29	11 45	8 22	25 4	7 47	4 53	11 51	5 ♓ 5'45"
8 SA	1: 5: 7	11 50	23 12	19 28	12 14	8 27	25 6	7 48	4 54	11 52	5 ♓ 5'45"
9 SU	1: 9: 4	14 54	24 48	20 27	12 43	8 33	25 7	7 48	4 54	11 52	5 ♓ 5'45"
10 MO	1:13: 0	17 55	26 24	21 27	13 12	8 38	25 9	7 49	4 54	11 52	5 ♓ 5'45"
11 TU	1:16:57	20 54	28 0	22 26	13 41	8 44	25 11	7 50	4 55	11 53	5 ♓ 5'45"
12 WE	1:20:53	23 50	29 36	23 25	14 10	8 49	25 13	7 50	4 55	11 53	5 ♓ 5'45"
13 TH	1:24:50	26 44	1 ♏ 11	24 24	14 38	8 55	25 15	7 51	4 55	11 53	5 ♓ 5'44"
14 FR	1:28:47	29 35	2 47	25 24	15 7	9 0	25 17	7 51	4 56	11 54	5 ♓ 5'44"
15 SA	1:32:43	2 ♏ 26	4 23	26 23	15 36	9 6	25 19	7 52	4 56	11 54	5 ♓ 5'44"
16 SU	1:36:40	5 14	5 58	27 23	16 4	9 11	25 21	7 53	4 56	11 54	5 ♓ 5'44"
17 MO	1:40:36	8 2	7 34	28 22	16 33	9 16	25 23	7 53	4 57	11 55	5 ♓ 5'44"
18 TU	1:44:33	10 48	9 9	29 22	17 1	9 22	25 25	7 54	4 57	11 55	5 ♓ 5'44"
19 WE	1:48:29	13 34	10 45	0 ♈ 21	17 30	9 27	25 27	7 55	4 57	11 55	5 ♓ 5'44"
20 TH	1:52:26	16 19	12 20	1 21	17 58	9 33	25 29	7 55	4 58	11 56	5 ♓ 5'44"
21 FR	1:56:22	19 4	13 56	2 20	18 26	9 38	25 31	7 56	4 58	11 56	5 ♓ 5'43"
22 SA	2: 0:19	21 49	15 31	3 20	18 55	9 44	25 33	7 57	4 59	11 56	5 ♓ 5'43"
23 SU	2: 4:16	24 34	17 6	4 20	19 23	9 49	25 35	7 57	4 59	11 57	5 ♓ 5'43"
24 MO	2: 8:12	27 18	18 42	5 20	19 51	9 55	25 37	7 58	4 59	11 57	5 ♓ 5'43"
25 TU	2:12: 9	0 ♐ 4	20 17	6 19	20 20	10 0	25 39	7 59	5 0	11 57	5 ♓ 5'43"
26 WE	2:16: 5	2 50	21 52	7 19	20 48	10 6	25 41	7 59	5 0	11 58	5 ♓ 5'43"
27 TH	2:20: 2	5 37	23 27	8 19	21 16	10 11	25 43	8 0	5 0	11 58	5 ♓ 5'43"
28 FR	2:23:58	8 25	25 3	9 19	21 44	10 17	25 45	8 0	5 1	11 58	5 ♓ 5'42"
29 SA	2:27:55	11 14	26 38	10 19	22 12	10 22	25 46	8 1	5 1	11 59	5 ♓ 5'42"
30 SU	2:31:51	14 5	28 13	11 19	22 40	10 28	25 48	8 2	5 1	11 59	5 ♓ 5'42"
31 MO	2:35:48	16 57	29 48	12 19	23 8	10 33	25 50	8 2	5 2	11 59	5 ♓ 5'42"

INGRESSES :

4 ☿ → ♎ 7:25
12 ♀ → ♏ 6: 5
14 ☿ → ♏ 3:26
18 ⊕ → ♈ 15:28
24 ☿ → ♐ 23:26
31 ♀ → ♐ 3: 1

ASPECTS (HELIOCENTRIC +MOON(TYCHONIC)) :

2 ☿ ☌ ♄ 19:30	12 ☽ ☍ ♄ 5:34	19 ☽ ☌ ♂ 1:26	28 ♀ ✶ ♄ 10:47
3 ☽ ☍ ♂ 17:19	13 ☽ ☌ ♃ 9:22	22 ☿ ☌ A 8: 3	☿ △ ⊕ 11:53
☽ ☌ ♇ 20:19	⊕ ☍ ♄ 21:15	☽ ☍ ♆ 14:27	☿ △ ♃ 16:24
5 ☿ △ ♆ 19: 7	15 ♀ □ ♆ 8:23	23 ☿ ✶ ♄ 9: 1	29 ⊕ ☌ ♃ 1:30
6 ☿ ☍ ♃ 21:13	☽ ☍ ☿ 11:36	⊕ ✶ ♆ 15:49	☿ ☌ ♇ 6:17
7 ♂ ☍ ♇ 4:54	☽ ☍ ♀ 14:45	24 ☽ ☍ ⛢ 20:23	30 ☽ ☌ ♀ 5:31
8 ☿ ✶ ♇ 0:10	☿ □ ♆ 21:25	26 ♀ ☌ ☋ 0:10	⊕ △ ♀ 16:13
☽ ☌ ♆ 0:48	16 ☿ ☌ ♀ 14:36	☽ ☌ ♄ 0:20	31 ☽ ☌ ♇ 4:34
☿ △ ♂ 3:41	☿ △ ⛢ 22:46	☿ ✶ ♆ 18:45	☽ ☌ ☿ 16:56
10 ☽ ☌ ⛢ 18:25	17 ♀ △ ⛢ 4:56	☽ ☍ ♃ 23: 7	
11 ☿ ☌ ☋ 21:49	18 ☽ ☍ ♇ 14:46	27 ☿ □ ⛢ 20:30	

of dark forces stood before the Light of the World. Contemplating our actions today, along with our inner condition of loneliness or togetherness, will show us where we are in relationship to the Light. Loneliness is the state of the soul when encapsulated in itself. Togetherness is the state of the soul when in communion with the light of the world. The true light unites; the false light divides. A full moon is an opportunity, under which we may contemplate the light. This is the light within, in others, in nature and in the stars.

October 17: Sun 29° Virgo: Conjunct Spica. The ancient clairvoyants saw Virgo as a young woman holding an ear of corn or shaft of wheat. The tip of the shaft of wheat marks the star Spica. This heavenly virgin holds the mysteries of feminine wisdom and the star Spica blesses us with the grace and love of this wisdom. Beneath the feet of this woman, we find the body of Hydra, "the Serpent," stretching its undulating life force throughout the entire region beneath Virgo. To find the blessing of the wheat, the daily bread, we must overcome the temptation of the serpent. This is a day to rejoice in the awakening of the Divine Feminine within and without, in nature, in the depths of the Earth and in the heights of Heaven.

Sun conjunct Spica: Conversation before the Baptism (September 22, 29). The evening before the Baptism, Jesus had a deep and spiritually profound conversation with his mother.

At this moment in time, Jesus was in a condition of emptiness, having seen everywhere on his travels the dire need of human beings, especially the poor and the sick; and having witnessed the utter decadence of humankind's spiritual life. The wisdom-filled soul of "Radiant Star" saw that only a miracle could save humanity, one that would involve sacrifice. During the course of the conversation with Mary, it came to Jesus as a flash of lightning that he should sacrifice himself and make way for the Sun Spirit, *Christ,* whom he (Zarathustra) had known earlier as Ahura Mazda, the Sun's "Aura of Light."[4]

This conversation marked the second death of "Radiant Star" (the first was at the age of seventeen, when he united with the Nathan Jesus in the temple). During this conversation with Mary, the very soul and spirit of the Zarathustra being poured into the heart of the Blessed Virgin Mary. The profundity of this conversation, under the star Spica, has great meaning for the mystery of Mary's continuous connection with Jesus throughout his coming life and trials. It was here that words resounded spiritually "Go to the place of baptism in the Jordan!"[5] The presence of Christ made itself known from this moment onward. The condition of humanity then witnessed by Jesus sounds eerily familiar today.

Sun conjunct Spica: Jesus visits Mensor and Theokeno in their tent city (September 21, 32): These were the two still living of the Three Kings. It is interesting to note that this visit occurred with the Sun conjunct this significant star—Spica. Recalling that it was the vision of the Virgin (see Jan. 21) that initially led the Three Kings to visit the Solomon Jesus (Zarathustra) in 6 B.C., it seems prophetic that now Jesus goes to meet the remaining kings when the Sun is conjunct the great star Spica in the constellation of the Virgin. This meeting occurs three years *after* the Baptism and approximately thirty-seven years after the kings visit the baby Jesus. Mensor, the eldest of the kings was alive and well; Theokeno, the second born, was weakened by old age. The kings told Jesus how they knew something of Melchizedek and his sacrifice of bread and wine.[6]

The virgin, in the constellation of Virgo, holds the bread (shaft of wheat), and on her left side is a vine (wine). In the vision of the Three Kings thirty-seven years earlier, the kings had witnessed the full moon in Virgo and saw the Virgin standing on the Moon, holding a sheaf of wheat in her right hand and on her left side a vine (Spica). Now, thirty-seven years later, this prophecy of the consecration of the bread and wine is fulfilled.

Bringing together the star Spica, the conversation before the Baptism, and the visit to the Three

---

4 See Powell, *Christian Hermetic Astrology,* "The Start of Christ's Ministry."

5 Ibid., p. 60.

6 See Emmerich, *LJC,* vol. 3, pp. 539–549.

Kings, an image arises of Sophia's subtle participation in key events on Earth. The Spica question: Can we empty, so that something greater may enter?

October 18: Sun enters Libra: Contentment becomes Equanimity. Blessed are the contented, for they shall have equanimity.

October 19: Sun 1° Libra: Baptism in the Jordan (September 23, 29). Jesus, having become an empty vessel, makes his way to the Jordan, accompanied by Lazarus. At the moment of the Baptism, a thunderous voice resounds from the heavens: "This is my beloved Son; today I have begotten thee!"[7] Christ, the Great Spirit of the Sun, entered the vessel vacated by "Radiant Star." The Son of God became a human being. Anne Catherine speaks of how perfectly transparent, entirely penetrated by light, the Jesus being became. She also sees:

> But off at some distance on the waters of the Jordan, I saw Satan, a dark, black figure, as if in a cloud, and myriads of horrible black reptiles and vermin swarming around him. It was as if all the wickedness, all the sins, all the poison of the whole region took a visible form at the outpouring of the Holy Ghost, and fled into that dark figure as into their original source.[8]

This is a profound day to meditate on the Divine Light that came into the world at this Baptism and how the equal opposite to the light witnessed the event from the other shore of the Jordan. As the dark being Anne Catherine saw spreads his poisons so blatantly in our time, right before our very eyes, it is clear who is the antidote. It has always been clear. This is a day to meditate on the presence of Christ. At the threshold into Libra stands the Michaelic figure of Arcturus, whose name means "the Watcher" (or Guardian). Christ, the Greater Guardian of the threshold, was born this day. Emblazoned in the stars is the story of *Michael* (Arcturus), *Sophia* (Spica), *in nomine Christi*.

October 24: Sun 6° Libra: Healing of Theokeno (September 28, 32). At this healing, we find the Sun exactly square to where it was when the kings came to adore Jesus thirty-seven years earlier (6° Capricorn). Jesus takes Mensor and visits Theokeno, who is confined to his bed. Jesus takes him by the hand and lifts him. After this Theokeno is no longer bedridden. Then the three go to the temple where Jesus taught.

> He explained that when the good angels withdraw, Satan takes possession of a temple service. He said that they should remove the various animal idols and teach love and compassion and give thanks to the Father in Heaven. Jesus now took bread and wine, which had been prepared beforehand. Having consecrated the bread and wine, He placed them upon a small altar. He prayed and blessed everyone. Mensor, Theokeno, and the four priests knelt before Him with their hands folded across their chests.[9]

Satan not only takes possession of a temple service, but also takes hold of human beings when they allow animal instinct to rule in the temple of the human body. From the time of Christ forward, the "I" is to govern the animal forces in the astral body. Those who have animals on their altars will not attract good angels. It is no longer animals we offer for sacrifice, but rather our lower human passions. Christ now works in the "I," which governs the animal nature and shows compassion to the animal kingdoms. One whose "I" is entangled in human animal nature will be deaf to the sufferings of animals. Our hearts are the altars in our human temple, and upon this altar we offer gratitude and partake in communion with the spiritual world. The human kingdom is now to rise from their beds of contentment and work for the salvation of the Earth and all humanity. This attracts the good angels.

Today Jupiter stands where Mars was at this healing (11° Aries). Wise Jupiter (whose sphere holds the majesty of great cosmic thoughts) remembers the words (Mars) Jesus spoke regarding the purity of temple services. Jupiter inspires

---

7 Emmerich, *LJC,* vol. 1, p. *441.*

8 Ibid., pp. 441–142.

9 Powell, *Chron.* pp. 328–329.

priests, male and female, to tend the good angels in their services for all time. Christ, through his words and through the consecration of bread and wine, infused the altars of the next three cultural epochs with his presence: the European age of Pisces, the Slavic age of Aquarius, and the American age of Capricorn were destined then and there to celebrate the Christianizing of ancient mystery streams. Through this blessing, the relationship (Libra) was inaugurated between the past wisdom streams of ancient Egypt, Persia, and India and the future resurrection of these wisdom traditions. For this was the fulcrum between past and future; this was the *turning point of time*. All that had come into time would rise out of time through the power of Christ. Although the third King had already died, nonetheless he had been brought to baptism in Christ through his belief in him. Not only was Theokeno healed, but the mysteries themselves were also given their future.[10] This is a day to ponder the presence of a Christianized Egypt in the spiritual stream of our time. What would that look like?

October 26: New moon 8° Libra (DT): Ancestors. The Teacher visits the place of the birth of his namesake and the shepherds who witnessed that event. He says, "No footstep of his holy parents should remain unblessed." This is a time to acknowledge our biological and spiritual ancestors, and to pour out our gratitude for them.

October 31: Pluto 10°29' Sagittarius conjunct Moon: John's disciples find Jesus near Megiddo (November 15, 30). Jesus is in the fields east of Megiddo teaching. Disciples of John the Baptist arrive and accompany Jesus into Megiddo where many lame, blind, dumb, deaf and other afflicted are gathered. Jesus cures them all:

> As they went away, Jesus began to speak to the crowds concerning John: "What did you go out into the wilderness to see? A reed shaken by the wind? What then did you go out to see? A man dressed in soft clothing? Behold, those who wear soft clothing are in kings' houses. What then did you go out to see? A prophet? Yes, I tell you, and more than a prophet. This is he of whom it is written, 'Behold, I send my messenger before your face, who will prepare your way before you.'" (Matt. 11:7–10 [ESV])

Jesus goes on to speak woe upon those towns that engage in acts counter to spiritual will, for they will lead humanity into the realm of shadows (Pluto). The next day He leaves Megiddo.

Pluto was at this degree in 2010 when the BP Deepwater Horizon rig exploded in the Gulf of Mexico, causing an unprecedented ecological disaster (April 20, 2010). Today Pluto remembers many healings and Jesus' words of praise for John. There we saw the lofty influence of Pluto–Phanes as minister of the Divine Love of the Father.

The reverse of this Divine Love is the subearthly force of Pluto–Hades, which works for the destruction of life. This aspect of Pluto was evident in the BP disaster in the gulf. It is interesting that Pluto, at this degree, finds Jesus in Megiddo (now know as the valley of Jezreel). This city is also known as Armageddon (derived from the Hebrew for *Har Megiddo*) and mentioned in Revelation 16:14–16. Historians believe that more battles were fought at this location than anywhere else on the Earth.

This is a day to pray that humanity be healed from blindness, deafness, dumbness, and disabling conditions. The body of our Mother is groaning in travail owing to human exploitation. The Mother is showing us that She can no longer endure the actions of the morally blind, deaf, dumb, and lame. They are leading her children into the valley of Armageddon. Pluto, at this degree, gives us images from the life of Christ that show there are disciples of John who accompany Christ into Megiddo, where healing takes place. We can all become disciples of John and work toward healing the Earth and humanity. John serves Sophia: the daughter of the Mother of everything living.

---

10 See Emmerich, *LJC*, vol. 3, pp. 542–543.

NOVEMBER

The Sun begins in Libra, and moves into Scorpio on the 17th. Neptune stations Direct on the 10th in Aquarius (the Water Carrier), retrograde since June. Mercury stations before moving Retrograde in Scorpio on the 25th (and stations Direct December, 15).

The full moon (Sun in Libra, Moon in Aries) is on the 10th. The day before, the almost full moon conjoins Jupiter in Aries, visible in the southeast in the deepening twilight. Jupiter will remain in our night sky for the rest of 2011. The Leonid meteor showers peak on the 17th to 18th; look to (you guessed it!) the constellation of Leo, where Mars shines. By the 19th, the Moon will have waned to half and will join Mars; Saturn will be present, too, but closer to the eastern horizon. View the meteors and the planets in the predawn hours. The Moon will journey toward Saturn over the next few days, conjoining on the 22nd. Saturn moves into Libra on the 23rd, and the Sun and Moon form a new moon in Scorpio on the 25th, with a partial solar eclipse.

November 1: Sun 13° Libra: Healing the blind (October 6, 30 and October 6, 31). According to Valentin Tomberg, Cain and Abel represent two thought streams—one stream (Abel) running vertically, and the other stream (Cain) running horizontally. The ascending vertical stream is more feminine in nature, connected to subtle spiritual guidance, and is too often killed by the horizontal stream, which is more overt and masculine. The masculine stream is too often filled with egoistic self-interest. The Cain side of human nature is often hostile toward the Abel side of human nature.[1]

World events make it clear that Cain continues to kill Abel. At the time of Christ, these streams manifested as two types of human beings. One type is born blind but has a sensitive capacity for hearing the spiritual Word (Homer is an example). The other type could see but is deaf to the spiritual Word: "You shall be a fugitive and a wanderer on the Earth" (Genesis 4:12). These eyewitnesses and ministers of the word, spoken of at the beginning of the Gospel of Luke, were united by Christ. The sheep (Abel) are those who hear the Word, and the goats (vagabond Cain) are those who subjectively see.

In the healing of the man born blind, Christ uses earth and saliva. This union of earth and water balanced the "I" between these two differing streams, thereby restoring equilibrium (Libra). Saliva is in the process of becoming a moral substance. In the future, hate will increasingly produce poisonous saliva, and love will increasingly produce healing saliva. Christ's saliva was filled with the healing power of love. The earth element in this healing represents the moral composition of the body and its effect on the Earth after death. A moral body serves the resurrection promise of the entire Earth, whereas a corrupt body serves Earth's degeneration. Together, earth and spittle—morality and love—heal. Today's conditions of human blindness and deafness tells us how far we are from the equilibrium of the center point, where these two streams are united. The man born blind incarnated specifically to develop the ears, so that he might hear the words of the Good Shepherd and, having heard these words, truly be able to see.

> For judgment I came into this world, that those who do not see may see, and those who see may become blind" (John 9:39 [ESV]).

These words ring through the world with escalating urgency. Virtual light can steal our sight (imagination), and virtual sound can steal our hearing (inspiration). A morally blind and deaf humanity is the intentional goal of the destructive beings working against what is moral (earth) and loving (saliva). We find the place of balance between these two streams of horizontal and vertical orientations (between sight and hearing) in our third eye. This is the cavity in the forehead that harbors "I" initiative; it is the seat of concentration and initiation of thought.

According to Valentin Tomberg, in Paradise human beings had one eye vertically above the other. Since the Fall, we have horizontally placed eyes. There is an inherent obligation with technological forces—the obligation to balance time spent

---
[1] Tomberg, *Christ and Sophia,* chapter 8.

SIDEREAL GEOCENTRIC LONGITUDES : NOVEMBER 2011 Gregorian at 0 hours UT

DAY	☉	☽	☊	☿	♀	♂	♃	♄	♅	♆	♇
1 TU	13 ♎ 19	22 ♐ 57	19 ♏ 56	2 ♏ 46	3 ♏ 24	29 ♋ 49	9 ♈ 59R	27 ♍ 29	6 ♓ 21R	3 ♒ 15R	10 ♐ 30
2 WE	14 19	6 ♑ 7	19 58	4 9	4 39	0 ♌ 21	9 51	27 36	6 19	3 15	10 32
3 TH	15 19	18 54	19 58R	5 30	5 53	0 53	9 43	27 43	6 18	3 15	10 33
4 FR	16 19	1 ♒ 22	19 57	6 51	7 8	1 24	9 35	27 50	6 16	3 15	10 35
5 SA	17 19	13 35	19 54	8 11	8 23	1 56	9 27	27 57	6 14	3 15	10 36
6 SU	18 19	25 38	19 50	9 29	9 37	2 27	9 19	28 4	6 13	3 14	10 37
7 MO	19 19	7 ♓ 34	19 45	10 47	10 52	2 58	9 11	28 11	6 11	3 14	10 39
8 TU	20 20	19 26	19 39	12 2	12 6	3 29	9 3	28 18	6 10	3 14	10 40
9 WE	21 20	1 ♈ 16	19 34	13 17	13 21	4 0	8 55	28 25	6 8	3 14	10 42
10 TH	22 20	13 8	19 29	14 29	14 35	4 30	8 47	28 32	6 7	3 14D	10 43
11 FR	23 20	25 2	19 26	15 40	15 50	5 1	8 40	28 39	6 5	3 14	10 45
12 SA	24 21	7 ♉ 1	19 24	16 48	17 4	5 31	8 32	28 46	6 4	3 14	10 47
13 SU	25 21	19 7	19 23	17 54	18 19	6 1	8 25	28 53	6 2	3 14	10 48
14 MO	26 21	1 ♊ 21	19 24D	18 57	19 33	6 31	8 17	29 0	6 1	3 15	10 50
15 TU	27 22	13 45	19 25	19 57	20 48	7 0	8 10	29 6	6 0	3 15	10 52
16 WE	28 22	26 23	19 26	20 53	22 2	7 30	8 3	29 13	5 59	3 15	10 53
17 TH	29 23	9 ♋ 17	19 28	21 46	23 17	7 59	7 56	29 20	5 58	3 15	10 55
18 FR	0 ♏ 23	22 30	19 29	22 34	24 31	8 28	7 49	29 26	5 56	3 15	10 57
19 SA	1 24	6 ♌ 4	19 29R	23 17	25 46	8 57	7 42	29 33	5 55	3 16	10 58
20 SU	2 24	20 1	19 28	23 54	27 0	9 26	7 35	29 40	5 54	3 16	11 0
21 MO	3 25	4 ♍ 20	19 26	24 25	28 15	9 54	7 29	29 46	5 53	3 16	11 2
22 TU	4 25	18 59	19 25	24 49	29 29	10 22	7 22	29 53	5 52	3 17	11 4
23 WE	5 26	3 ♎ 52	19 23	25 5	0 ♐ 44	10 50	7 16	29 59	5 52	3 17	11 6
24 TH	6 27	18 53	19 21	25 12	1 58	11 18	7 10	0 ♎ 6	5 51	3 18	11 7
25 FR	7 27	3 ♏ 53	19 20	25 11R	3 13	11 46	7 4	0 12	5 50	3 18	11 9
26 SA	8 28	18 43	19 20	24 59	4 27	12 13	6 58	0 18	5 49	3 19	11 11
27 SU	9 29	3 ♐ 16	19 20D	24 36	5 42	12 40	6 52	0 24	5 49	3 19	11 13
28 MO	10 29	17 26	19 21	24 2	6 56	13 7	6 47	0 31	5 48	3 20	11 15
29 TU	11 30	1 ♑ 10	19 22	23 18	8 11	13 33	6 41	0 37	5 47	3 21	11 17
30 WE	12 31	14 28	19 23	22 23	9 25	14 0	6 36	0 43	5 47	3 21	11 19

INGRESSES :

1 ♂ → ♌ 7:56	22 ♀ → ♐ 9:52
☽ → ♑ 12:45	☽ → ♎ 17:47
3 ☽ → ♒ 21:20	23 ♄ → ♎ 3:20
6 ☽ → ♓ 8:45	24 ☽ → ♏ 17:45
8 ☽ → ♈ 21:25	26 ☽ → ♐ 18:33
11 ☽ → ♉ 9:57	28 ☽ → ♑ 21:56
13 ☽ → ♊ 21:22	
16 ☽ → ♋ 6:47	
17 ☉ → ♏ 14:50	
18 ☽ → ♌ 13:20	
20 ☽ → ♍ 16:47	

ASPECTS & ECLIPSES :

1 ☿ □ ♆ 8:30	12 ☽ ☍ ☿ 21:21	21 ☽ ☍ ♅ 2:34
2 ☉ □ ☽ 16:37	☽ ☍ ♀ 22:14	22 ☽ ☌ ♄ 17:42
4 ☽ ☍ ♂ 0: 5	13 ☽ ☌ ☋ 0:32	23 ☽ ☍ ♃ 5:23
☽ ☌ ♆ 3:40	♀ ☌ ☊ 20:45	☽ ☌ P 23:17
5 ☽ N ☊ 12:28	14 ☿ ☌ ☊ 10:38	25 ☉ ☌ ☽ 6: 9
6 ☽ ☌ ♅ 21:13	☽ ☍ ♇ 18:25	☉ ● P 6:20
7 ♂ ☍ ♆ 12:35	18 ☉ □ ☽ 15: 8	26 ☽ ☌ ☊ 1: 0
8 ☽ ☌ A 12:46	☽ ☍ ♆ 19: 5	☽ ☌ ☿ 10: 1
☽ ☍ ♄ 18: 9	19 ☽ ☌ ♂ 5:11	27 ♀ □ ♅ 2:11
9 ☽ ☌ ♃ 15:18	☽ S ☊ 23: 3	☽ ☌ ♀ 4:27
10 ☉ ☍ ☽ 20:15	20 ☉ □ ♆ 20:42	☽ ☌ ♇ 13:24

SIDEREAL HELIOCENTRIC LONGITUDES : NOVEMBER 2011 Gregorian at 0 hours UT

DAY	Sid. Time	☿	♀	⊕	♂	♃	♄	♅	♆	♇	Vernal Point
1 TU	2:39:45	19 ♐ 52	1 ♐ 23	13 ♈ 19	23 ♊ 36	10 ♈ 39	25 ♍ 52	8 ♓ 3	5 ♒ 2	12 ♐ 0	5 ♓ 5'42"
2 WE	2:43:41	22 49	2 58	14 19	24 4	10 44	25 54	8 4	5 3	12 0	5 ♓ 5'42"
3 TH	2:47:38	25 48	4 33	15 19	24 32	10 50	25 56	8 4	5 3	12 0	5 ♓ 5'42"
4 FR	2:51:34	28 49	6 8	16 19	25 0	10 55	25 58	8 5	5 3	12 1	5 ♓ 5'41"
5 SA	2:55:31	1 ♑ 54	7 43	17 19	25 28	11 0	26 0	8 6	5 4	12 1	5 ♓ 5'41"
6 SU	2:59:27	5 2	9 18	18 19	25 56	11 6	26 2	8 6	5 4	12 1	5 ♓ 5'41"
7 MO	3: 3:24	8 13	10 53	19 19	26 24	11 11	26 4	8 7	5 4	12 2	5 ♓ 5'41"
8 TU	3: 7:20	11 29	12 28	20 19	26 51	11 17	26 6	8 8	5 5	12 2	5 ♓ 5'41"
9 WE	3:11:17	14 48	14 3	21 20	27 19	11 22	26 8	8 8	5 5	12 2	5 ♓ 5'41"
10 TH	3:15:14	18 12	15 38	22 20	27 47	11 28	26 10	8 9	5 5	12 3	5 ♓ 5'41"
11 FR	3:19:10	21 40	17 13	23 20	28 15	11 33	26 12	8 9	5 6	12 3	5 ♓ 5'40"
12 SA	3:23: 7	25 14	18 48	24 20	28 42	11 39	26 14	8 10	5 6	12 3	5 ♓ 5'40"
13 SU	3:27: 3	28 53	20 23	25 21	29 10	11 44	26 16	8 11	5 7	12 4	5 ♓ 5'40"
14 MO	3:31: 0	2 ♒ 37	21 58	26 21	29 37	11 50	26 18	8 11	5 7	12 4	5 ♓ 5'40"
15 TU	3:34:56	6 28	23 32	27 21	0 ♋ 5	11 55	26 20	8 12	5 7	12 4	5 ♓ 5'40"
16 WE	3:38:53	10 26	25 7	28 22	0 33	12 1	26 22	8 13	5 8	12 5	5 ♓ 5'40"
17 TH	3:42:49	14 30	26 42	29 22	1 0	12 6	26 23	8 13	5 8	12 5	5 ♓ 5'40"
18 FR	3:46:46	18 41	28 17	0 ♉ 23	1 28	12 12	26 25	8 14	5 8	12 5	5 ♓ 5'40"
19 SA	3:50:43	23 1	29 52	1 23	1 55	12 17	26 27	8 15	5 9	12 6	5 ♓ 5'39"
20 SU	3:54:39	27 28	1 ♑ 27	2 24	2 22	12 22	26 29	8 15	5 9	12 6	5 ♓ 5'39"
21 MO	3:58:36	2 ♓ 3	3 2	3 24	2 50	12 28	26 31	8 16	5 9	12 6	5 ♓ 5'39"
22 TU	4: 2:32	6 48	4 36	4 25	3 17	12 33	26 33	8 17	5 10	12 7	5 ♓ 5'39"
23 WE	4: 6:29	11 41	6 11	5 26	3 45	12 39	26 35	8 17	5 10	12 7	5 ♓ 5'39"
24 TH	4:10:25	16 43	7 46	6 26	4 12	12 44	26 37	8 18	5 10	12 7	5 ♓ 5'39"
25 FR	4:14:22	21 54	9 21	7 27	4 39	12 50	26 39	8 18	5 11	12 8	5 ♓ 5'39"
26 SA	4:18:18	27 14	10 56	8 28	5 6	12 55	26 41	8 19	5 11	12 8	5 ♓ 5'38"
27 SU	4:22:15	2 ♈ 43	12 31	9 28	5 34	13 1	26 43	8 20	5 12	12 8	5 ♓ 5'38"
28 MO	4:26:12	8 21	14 6	10 29	6 1	13 6	26 45	8 20	5 12	12 9	5 ♓ 5'38"
29 TU	4:30: 8	14 8	15 41	11 30	6 28	13 12	26 47	8 21	5 12	12 9	5 ♓ 5'38"
30 WE	4:34: 5	20 2	17 15	12 31	6 55	13 17	26 49	8 22	5 13	12 9	5 ♓ 5'38"

INGRESSES :

4 ☿ → ♑ 9:13
13 ☿ → ♒ 7:16
14 ♂ → ♋ 19:35
17 ⊕ → ♉ 14:56
19 ♀ → ♑ 2: 3
20 ☿ → ♓ 13:20
26 ☿ → ♈ 12:10

ASPECTS (HELIOCENTRIC +MOON(TYCHONIC)) :

1 ☽ ☍ ♂ 1:12	☿ □ ♃ 22:31	☿ ✶ ♇ 9:50	♀ △ ⊕ 16: 0	☿ □ ♂ 13:14
2 ☿ ☍ ♂ 12: 5	8 ☽ ☍ ♄ 13:33	♃ △ ♇ 19: 2	22 ☿ ☌ ♅ 7:22	☽ ☌ ♇ 14:57
3 ☿ □ ♄ 1: 9	9 ☽ ☌ ♃ 20:36	♀ □ ♄ 19:10	☽ ☌ ♄ 12:16	28 ☿ △ ♇ 15:50
♀ ✶ ♆ 7:32	11 ☿ S ☊ 12:52	18 ☽ ☍ ♆ 22:23	⊕ □ ♆ 17:48	☿ ☌ ♃ 20: 5
4 ☽ ☌ ♆ 7:12	☿ □ ⊕ 15:46	19 ⊕ ✶ ♂ 22:58	23 ☿ □ ♇ 2: 7	29 ☿ □ ♀ 8:40
5 ♀ □ ♅ 5:42	12 ☿ △ ♄ 6:43	20 ☽ ☍ ☿ 18:25	☽ ☍ ♃ 14: 7	☽ ☍ ♂ 9:48
6 ♂ □ ♄ 5:42	14 ☿ ☌ ♆ 15:39	♀ ☍ ♂ 19:49	24 ♀ ✶ ♅ 8: 4	♀ ☌ A 17:25
☿ ✶ ♅ 23:11	☽ ☍ ♇ 20:46	21 ☿ △ ♂ 4:23	25 ⊕ ✶ ♅ 20:34	30 ☽ ☌ ♀ 5:51
7 ☽ ☌ ♅ 1: 6	15 ☽ ☍ ♀ 21:17	☽ ☍ ♅ 6:29	☿ ☍ ♄ 21:32	☿ ☌ ☊ 14: 9
♀ △ ♃ 4:54	16 ☽ ☌ ♂ 8: 5	☿ ✶ ♀ 7:29	27 ♀ □ ♃ 8: 2	
♀ ☌ ♇ 17:23	☿ ✶ ♃ 9:38	☿ ✶ ⊕ 8:48	☿ ✶ ♆ 10:36	

with the virtual through time spent in nature, the arts, and all manner of sacred endeavors. Take a moment to sit in meditation with the chakra in the region of your brow. Feel its currents. Celebrate the gift of understanding. When Cain serves Abel, we have eyes to see and ears to hear. This is a day to see with our eyes shut and to hear in absolute silence. Meditate on the third eye.

November 10 (7-10-13): Full moon, 23° Libra (DT): A mother's courage. Fragment from the Oracle of the Solar Cross: A mother hears from her son that he will go into the desolate wilds with no supplies, barefoot, until he is born. Such are the challenges to a mother in this sign of balance, the Scales, to care for the child, yet support his or her growth, even though it risks the life that she gave the child.

November 12: ASPECT: Moon opposite Venus (18° Scorpio): Conversation with Nicodemus (April 9, 30). The Moon today remembers the nighttime conversation between Christ and Nicodemus, and Venus listens attentively to this karmic meeting. As we live in a world of days and nights, so, too, does the history of humankind have a day aspect and a night aspect. The day aspect comprises the actuality of that which *has* become, and the night aspect embraces the activity of what *is* becoming.

> For both the newly born Lazarus and the nighttime conversation of Jesus with Nicodemus belong to the "night side" of Christianity. They belong to the hidden core of being of Christianity, which is the mystery of "becoming," i.e., the essence itself of all miracles. For the essence of a miracle lies neither in might nor in mystery—neither in extraordinary power, nor in incomprehensibility—but in the reality of the moral world order working down into the reality of the mechanical, causal world order.[2]

At night we enter the angelic spheres (Moon) and visit with those with whom we interacted during the day, as well as with spiritual beings. Moral actions by day open us to spiritual teachings and meetings by night. Immoral deeds by day cause discordant reverberations in the night, obstructing communion with higher beings. As a result of our nightly communion with higher beings, miracles are born that reach into the daytime as gifts of grace. We are more alive when we are *becoming*, and most dead when we have already *become*. Night classes are the school of Sophia, where new miracles are becoming. Karmic communities are able to meet there. This is a good day to remember consciously the deep importance of right preparation for sleep. This is equally true for adults and for children. As we mature in our spiritual understanding, we come to realize that our day is best orchestrated as a preparation for our night.

November 15: ASPECT: Saturn conjunct Spica (DT): Spica, one of the five Royal Stars of Persia, on which the design of the heavens was understood to rest, comes at the very end of Virgo (29° and 6 minutes). This star exudes the power and wisdom of the divine feminine. Saturn hovers near here until August of 2012 and will not return here until 2041. In its negative functioning, Saturn could squelch the feminine here; in its positive functioning, Saturn could champion the truth of the boundless wisdom, all-merciful grace, beauty, and power of the divine feminine.

November 17: Sun 29° Libra: Start of the Forty Days (October 21, 29). Jesus has a conversation with Silent Mary (sister to Martha, Mary Magdalene, and Lazarus), whom he blessed. He then sets out for the wilderness.

> Here he started his forty-day fast and spent the night in prayer in a cave. Jesus knelt with outstretched arms and prayed to his heavenly Father for strength and courage in all the trials that awaited him.[3]

Silent Mary later died, as her gentle soul could not live to endure what she clairvoyantly beheld was to be the final destiny of Jesus Christ. One is left to wonder if this Mary's extreme inwardness of soul was the inversion of her sister Mary Magdalene's soul, and what part Silent Mary may have played, after her death, in Magdalene's conversions. This is a potent day for prayer and inner reflection.

---

2 Tomberg, *Lazarus, Come Forth!*, p. 120.

3 Powell, *Chron.*, p. 205.

ASPECT: Venus, 23° Scorpio, is directly opposite its position at the solar eclipse of 2009. It is also very close to what its heliocentric position will be at the Venus transit of 2012. As today's Sun remembers the beginning of the Forty Days following the Baptism of the True Light, Venus remembers the return of Pluto to its Baptism degree during the 2009 eclipse. Today's Venus is also where it was at the Raising of the Youth of Nain. The opposition to the eclipse, the heliocentric position of Venus at the Venus transit of 2012, the memory of the beginning of the Forty Days and the Raising of the Youth of Nain all tell of healing possibilities. May we find this!

November 17: Sun enters Scorpio: Patience becomes Insight, to penetrate the hidden (occult) mysteries.

November 19: Sun 1° Scorpio: Summons of Judas (October 24, 30). Venus and Sun had entered Scorpio just before Judas became a disciple. The twenty-five year old Judas had heard of the wealth and fame of Jesus and longed to satisfy his desires by becoming part of his group (Venus). Judas was introduced to Jesus by Bartholomew and Simon, saying, "Master, this is Judas of whom we have spoken." Jesus was most friendly toward Judas, but was filled with an indescribable sorrow. Judas bowed and said, "Master I pray that you may allow me to take part in your teaching." Jesus replied most gently with the prophetic words, "You may take a place, unless you would prefer to leave it to another."[4]

How these words ring through time! The ennobled Venus nature serves the true "I," while the lower, desire aspect of Venus, wants to be served. In the latter condition, the Judas principle is never far from the heart (Sun). This is a good day to reflect on any hidden agendas (Scorpio) we may harbor that are dangerous to our loyalties. As we enter into the constellation of Scorpio, we are mindful of how damaging hidden agendas can be. There is a bifurcating beast slinking through the world, searching in communities for the weak link. The beast delights in finding entry, and through that weak link can destroy communities, pitting one member against the other. This is what happened to Judas. He was the weak link in the circle of twelve, owing to the lower forces of his Venus nature working for self-gain. This is a day to review our loyalties. May we have the patience to curb our reactions and wait instead for understanding of the pain in our own hearts!

November 20: Sun 2° Scorpio: Conception of the Nathan Mary (October 24, 18 B.C.)

November 25: New moon and partial solar eclipse, 7° Scorpio (DT): Water and thirst. Fragment from the oracle of the Solar Cross: All life perishes from thirst. The water of a sacred well, blessed hundreds of years before by a wise man, lies deep in the earth, far from the surface. With much effort some lift the sacred water to the surface. We have many references to sacred water in the Moon transits of this year: the full moon of February 18 and the new moons of April 3, May 2, and July 30. Link with those times. Note how in the water sign of Scorpio, the water lies deep down, out of sight in a mysterious realm of darkness. Yet this water has been blessed and comes to serve the needs of those at the edge of death from thirst.

---

4 See Powell, *Christian Hermetic Astrology*, "The Sun Chronicle in the Life of the Messiah."

DECEMBER

The Sun begins the month in the Scorpion (Scorpio), and on the 2nd stands in front of the star Antares (15° Scorpio—Heart of the Scorpion and a Royal Star of Persia). The Sun moves into Sagittarius (the Archer) on the 17th. Uranus stations Direct on the 11th (retrograde since July), Mercury stations Direct in Scorpio on the 15th, and Jupiter stations Direct on the 26th (retrograde since September).

Approaching the full moon and total lunar eclipse on the 10th (Sun in Scorpio, Moon in Taurus), the Moon joins Jupiter in Aries on the 6th, visible in the south-southeast after sunset. The Geminids Meteor shower peaks on the 13th to 14th, but this may not be the best year for viewing with the waning Moon in Gemini. Still, considered the "most reliable" shower of the year, worth a peek!

Continuing her swift journey around the zodiac, the waning half Moon is visible on the 17th, in the south predawn hours below Mars in Leo. By the 20th, the Moon and Saturn in Libra are to the east-southeast in the dawn sky. The new moon in Sagittarius is on the 24th, and after this emerges a conjunction of the new crescent moon with Venus, as the evening star, low in the western sky on the 27th.

December 1: ASPECT: Venus conjunct Pluto at 11° Sagittarius (DT): Pluto showed its hand in relation to Venus's emphasis on karmic groups: in this aspect Yitzhak Rabin was assassinated on November 4, 1995.

Venus and Pluto were also conjunct at the conception of the Solomon Jesus, square to today's conjunction (12° Virgo). Venus listens to worlds above or worlds below, gathering karmic circles on Earth. When she listens to the worlds above, she brings peace into karmic groups. When she listens to worlds below, she brings ambition into karmic groups. Venus works out of love or out of hate, depending on the nature of the listener. In her purity she increases love in communities; in her ambitious jealousy she becomes divisive. Her consort today is Pluto, which reveals its influence as either Phanes, the Divine Love of the Father, or as Hades, the wrath of the god of the underworld. These two examples, the assassin and Jesus, exemplify two different relationships with both Pluto and Venus; the one is an inversion of the other. When Venus and Pluto come together in Sagittarius we are urged to tame the animal instincts of our lower nature. When Pluto was at this degree (December 10, 30), Jesus blessed the disciples and for the first time sent them into the world with flasks of oil, and Jesus taught them how to use it for anointing as well as for healing. The words from Matthew 9:36-10:16 are good to contemplate today. Do we act as healing influences in our communities?

December 4: Sun 17° Scorpio: First conversion of Mary Magdalene (November 8, 30). Jesus arrives at the mountain and delivers a powerful discourse: "Come! Come to me, all who are weary and laden with guilt! Come to me, O sinners! Do penance, believe, and share the kingdom with me!"[1]

Magdalene is deeply moved inwardly by these words and experiences her first conversion. Later that evening, at a banquet with the Pharisees, Magdalene enters the room to anoint Jesus' head. This is a sure sign that she recognizes him as a true King and as the Messiah. It is astonishing, given the times, that Magdalene walked uninvited into a room where men were gathered. Women of those times, as in many places today, were not allowed such privilege. The certainty of Magdalene is an example for us all. No matter where the old rules stultify, we are to walk in truth and without fear. This is a good day to contemplate where we may find ourselves limited or afraid before worn-out powers. Where do we fear to enter because of weariness and guilt? Whose hands are willing to carry our burdens so that we may be free to do penance?

ASPECT: Inferior conjunction of Mercury with the Sun, 17° Scorpio: Hidden dynamics (Scorpio) lie behind ordinary reality. At the start of the temptations, Mercury was coming into conjunction with the Sun. The messenger of the gods (Mercury) was approaching the heart of Jesus (Sun). Christ's task was to pass through the temptations without giving any attention to the tempters. Magdalene walked through the room to anoint Christ,

---

1 Powell, *Chron.*, p. 256.

SIDEREAL GEOCENTRIC LONGITUDES: DECEMBER 2011 Gregorian at 0 hours UT

DAY	☉	☽	☊	☿	♀	♂	♃	♄	⚷	♆	♇
1 TH	13 ♏ 32	27 ♉ 21	19 ♏ 23	21 ♏ 19R	10 ♐ 39	14 ♌ 26	6 ♈ 31R	0 ♎ 49	5 ♓ 46R	3 ♒ 22	11 ♐ 21
2 FR	14 33	9 ♊ 44	19 23	20 7	11 54	14 52	6 26	0 55	5 46	3 23	11 23
3 SA	15 33	22 9	19 23R	18 49	13 8	15 17	6 21	1 1	5 45	3 24	11 25
4 SU	16 34	4 ♋ 11	19 23	17 27	14 22	15 42	6 17	1 7	5 45	3 24	11 27
5 MO	17 35	16 5	19 23	16 4	15 37	16 7	6 13	1 12	5 45	3 25	11 29
6 TU	18 36	27 55	19 23	14 43	16 51	16 32	6 8	1 18	5 45	3 26	11 31
7 WE	19 37	9 ♌ 45	19 23D	13 27	18 5	16 57	6 4	1 24	5 44	3 27	11 33
8 TH	20 38	21 39	19 23	12 17	19 20	17 21	6 1	1 30	5 44	3 28	11 35
9 FR	21 39	3 ♉ 39	19 23	11 17	20 34	17 45	5 57	1 35	5 44	3 29	11 37
10 SA	22 40	15 48	19 23	10 27	21 48	18 8	5 54	1 41	5 44	3 30	11 39
11 SU	23 41	28 7	19 23R	9 47	23 2	18 31	5 51	1 46	5 44D	3 31	11 41
12 MO	24 42	10 ♊ 38	19 23	9 20	24 17	18 54	5 48	1 51	5 44	3 32	11 43
13 TU	25 42	23 21	19 22	9 3	25 31	19 17	5 45	1 57	5 44	3 33	11 45
14 WE	26 43	6 ♋ 18	19 21	8 57	26 45	19 39	5 42	2 2	5 44	3 34	11 47
15 TH	27 44	19 28	19 20	9 1D	27 59	20 1	5 40	2 7	5 45	3 35	11 49
16 FR	28 45	2 ♌ 52	19 19	9 15	29 13	20 22	5 38	2 12	5 45	3 37	11 51
17 SA	29 47	16 30	19 18	9 37	0 ♑ 27	20 44	5 36	2 17	5 45	3 38	11 53
18 SU	0 ♐ 48	0 ♍ 22	19 18	10 7	1 41	21 4	5 34	2 22	5 46	3 39	11 55
19 MO	1 49	14 28	19 18D	10 45	2 55	21 25	5 32	2 27	5 46	3 40	11 57
20 TU	2 50	28 46	19 19	11 28	4 9	21 45	5 31	2 32	5 46	3 42	12 0
21 WE	3 51	13 ♎ 13	19 20	12 17	5 23	22 5	5 30	2 37	5 47	3 43	12 2
22 TH	4 52	27 47	19 21	13 11	6 37	22 24	5 29	2 41	5 48	3 44	12 4
23 FR	5 53	12 ♏ 22	19 22	14 9	7 51	22 43	5 28	2 46	5 48	3 46	12 6
24 SA	6 54	26 51	19 22R	15 10	9 5	23 1	5 28	2 50	5 49	3 47	12 8
25 SU	7 55	11 ♐ 10	19 21	16 15	10 19	23 19	5 28	2 55	5 50	3 49	12 10
26 MO	8 57	25 13	19 19	17 23	11 33	23 37	5 27D	2 59	5 50	3 50	12 12
27 TU	9 58	8 ♑ 56	19 16	18 34	12 47	23 54	5 28	3 3	5 51	3 52	12 15
28 WE	10 59	22 16	19 13	19 47	14 1	24 11	5 28	3 7	5 52	3 53	12 17
29 TH	12 0	5 ♒ 14	19 9	21 2	15 14	24 27	5 28	3 11	5 53	3 55	12 19
30 FR	13 1	17 50	19 7	22 18	16 28	24 42	5 29	3 15	5 54	3 56	12 21
31 SA	14 2	0 ♓ 9	19 5	23 37	17 42	24 58	5 30	3 19	5 55	3 58	12 23

INGRESSES:

1 ☽→♒ 5:0	22 ☽→♏ 3:38			
3 ☽→♓ 15:37	24 ☽→♐ 5:14			
6 ☽→♈ 4:13	26 ☽→♑ 8:18			
8 ☽→♉ 16:43	28 ☽→♒ 14:13			
11 ☽→♊ 3:37	30 ☽→♓ 23:42			
13 ☽→♋ 12:22				
15 ☽→♌ 18:54				
16 ♀→♑ 15:11				
17 ☉→♐ 5:17				
☽→♍ 23:22				
20 ☽→♎ 2:3				

ASPECTS & ECLIPSES:

1 ☽☌♆ 11:26	☽☍♄ 6:55	17 ☽⚹☊ 4:53	☽☌☊ 11:34		
♀☌♇ 13:41	☽☌♃ 16:35	☽☌♂ 7:33	24 ☽☌☊ 18:6		
2 ☉□☽ 9:52	☉☌☊ 18:28	18 ☉□☽ 0:47	25 ☽☌♀ 1:41		
☽☍⚷ 10:1	9 ☽☍☿ 14:5	☽☌⚷ 9:13	27 ☽☌♀ 7:33		
☉□☿ 13:0	10 ☽☌♅ 7:1	♀□♄ 14:11	☿☌☊ 13:17		
☿☌♂ 14:33	☽⚸♈ 14:33	20 ☽☌♄ 6:18	28 ☽☌♆ 21:31		
☽♅☽ 18:33	☉☍☽ 14:36	☽☌♃ 11:13	29 ☉☌♇ 7:39		
4 ☽☌⚷ 3:9	12 ☽☍♆ 2:3	21 ♀□♃ 2:7	30 ☽⚸♅ 2:26		
☉⚸☿ 8:44	13 ☽☍♀ 4:27	22 ☽☌P 2:40	☽☍☌ 13:36		
☿□♂ 23:10	☉□☊ 5:42	☉□⚷ 22:4	31 ☽☌⚷ 11:26		
6 ☽☌♈ 1:3	16 ☽☌♆ 1:19	23 ☽☌☿ 3:9			

SIDEREAL HELIOCENTRIC LONGITUDES: DECEMBER 2011 Gregorian at 0 hours UT

DAY	Sid. Time	☿	♀	⊕	♂	♃	♄	⚷	♆	♇	Vernal Point
1 TH	4:38:1	26 ♈ 3	18 ♉ 50	13 ♉ 32	7 ♋ 22	13 ♈ 23	26 ♍ 51	8 ♓ 22	5 ♒ 13	12 ♐ 10	5 ♓ 5'38"
2 FR	4:41:58	2 ♉ 10	20 25	14 32	7 49	13 28	26 53	8 23	5 13	12 10	5 ♓ 5'38"
3 SA	4:45:54	8 22	22 0	15 33	8 17	13 34	26 55	8 24	5 14	12 10	5 ♓ 5'37"
4 SU	4:49:51	14 39	23 35	16 34	8 44	13 39	26 57	8 24	5 14	12 11	5 ♓ 5'37"
5 MO	4:53:47	20 57	25 10	17 35	9 11	13 44	26 58	8 25	5 14	12 11	5 ♓ 5'37"
6 TU	4:57:44	27 16	26 45	18 36	9 38	13 50	27 0	8 26	5 15	12 11	5 ♓ 5'37"
7 WE	5:1:41	3 ♊ 35	28 20	19 37	10 5	13 55	27 2	8 26	5 15	12 12	5 ♓ 5'37"
8 TH	5:5:37	9 52	29 55	20 37	10 32	14 1	27 4	8 27	5 15	12 12	5 ♓ 5'37"
9 FR	5:9:34	16 5	1 ♒ 30	21 38	10 59	14 6	27 6	8 27	5 16	12 12	5 ♓ 5'37"
10 SA	5:13:30	22 13	3 5	22 39	11 26	14 12	27 8	8 28	5 16	12 13	5 ♓ 5'36"
11 SU	5:17:27	28 15	4 40	23 40	11 52	14 17	27 10	8 29	5 17	12 13	5 ♓ 5'36"
12 MO	5:21:23	4 ♋ 9	6 15	24 41	12 19	14 23	27 12	8 29	5 17	12 13	5 ♓ 5'36"
13 TU	5:25:20	9 56	7 50	25 42	12 46	14 28	27 14	8 30	5 17	12 14	5 ♓ 5'36"
14 WE	5:29:16	15 34	9 25	26 43	13 13	14 34	27 16	8 31	5 18	12 14	5 ♓ 5'36"
15 TH	5:33:13	21 3	11 0	27 44	13 40	14 39	27 18	8 31	5 18	12 14	5 ♓ 5'36"
16 FR	5:37:10	26 22	12 35	28 45	14 7	14 45	27 20	8 32	5 18	12 15	5 ♓ 5'36"
17 SA	5:41:6	1 ♌ 32	14 11	29 46	14 33	14 50	27 22	8 33	5 19	12 15	5 ♓ 5'36"
18 SU	5:45:3	6 31	15 46	0 ♊ 47	15 0	14 55	27 24	8 33	5 19	12 15	5 ♓ 5'35"
19 MO	5:48:59	11 22	17 21	1 48	15 27	15 1	27 26	8 34	5 19	12 16	5 ♓ 5'35"
20 TU	5:52:56	16 3	18 56	2 49	15 54	15 6	27 28	8 35	5 20	12 16	5 ♓ 5'35"
21 WE	5:56:52	20 35	20 31	3 51	16 20	15 12	27 30	8 35	5 20	12 16	5 ♓ 5'35"
22 TH	6:0:49	24 58	22 7	4 52	16 47	15 17	27 32	8 36	5 21	12 17	5 ♓ 5'35"
23 FR	6:4:45	29 13	23 42	5 53	17 14	15 23	27 33	8 36	5 21	12 17	5 ♓ 5'35"
24 SA	6:8:42	3 ♍ 20	25 17	6 54	17 40	15 28	27 35	8 37	5 21	12 17	5 ♓ 5'35"
25 SU	6:12:39	7 20	26 52	7 55	18 7	15 34	27 37	8 38	5 22	12 18	5 ♓ 5'34"
26 MO	6:16:35	11 12	28 28	8 56	18 34	15 39	27 39	8 38	5 22	12 18	5 ♓ 5'34"
27 TU	6:20:32	14 58	0 ♓ 3	9 57	19 0	15 45	27 41	8 39	5 22	12 18	5 ♓ 5'34"
28 WE	6:24:28	18 38	1 38	10 59	19 27	15 50	27 43	8 40	5 23	12 19	5 ♓ 5'34"
29 TH	6:28:25	22 12	3 14	12 0	19 54	15 55	27 45	8 40	5 23	12 19	5 ♓ 5'34"
30 FR	6:32:21	25 40	4 49	13 1	20 20	16 1	27 47	8 41	5 23	12 19	5 ♓ 5'34"
31 SA	6:36:18	29 4	6 25	14 2	20 47	16 6	27 49	8 42	5 24	12 20	5 ♓ 5'34"

INGRESSES:

1 ☿→♉ 15:31	
6 ☿→♊ 10:22	
8 ♀→♒ 1:15	
11 ☿→♋ 7:4	
16 ☿→♌ 16:49	
17 ⊕→♊ 5:24	
23 ☿→♍ 4:30	
26 ♀→♓ 23:12	
31 ☿→♎ 6:41	

ASPECTS (HELIOCENTRIC + MOON(TYCHONIC)):

1 ☽☌♆ 14:59	6 ♀△♇ 3:58	☿□♃ 19:35	☿☍♆ 18:8	☿□⊕ 4:53	
2 ☿□♆ 11:51	7 △♆ 6:22	14 ☽☌♂ 13:6	♂♃ 18:34	☿☍⊕ 8:0	
☿⚹♂ 23:35	☽☌♃ 8:29	⊕△♇ 13:19	18 ☽☍⚷ 13:59	⊕□⚷ 16:56	
3 ☿⚹⚷ 0:4	8 ☽☌♀ 4:48	15 ☽☌♀ 4:48	19 ☿□♀ 4:33	☿□♇ 6:56	
♂△⚷ 6:25	☿☍⚷ 9:0	☽♅⚷ 11:16	☿△♃ 19:0	27 ☽☌♀ 18:41	
4 ☽☌⚷ 8:30	☿⚹♃ 16:14	♀⚹♀ 18:44	☽☌♀ 21:49	28 ☿⚹♂ 6:13	
☿☌⊕ 8:44	10 ☿□♄ 19:39	16 ☽☍♀ 4:20	20 ☿⚹♀ 23:31	29 ☽☌♆ 0:17	
5 ☿☌P 6:47	11 ☽☌♀ 9:15	☿♄ 4:27	21 ☽☌♃ 3:16	⊕☍♆ 7:39	
☿△⚷ 21:21	12 ☿⚹♅ 13:42	♀⚹♅ 13:42	☿☌♀ 20:31	30 ☽☌♀ 14:59	
☽☍♄ 22:9	☿△⚷ 17:58	☽♆♃ 19:25	22 ⊕△♆ 11:24	31 ☽☌♀ 14:17	
☿△♄ 22:59	13 ☿☌♂ 13:2	17 ♀⚹♃ 10:31	25 ☽☌♀ 1:54	☽☌⚷ 16:58	

giving attention only to him. We are to attend what we want to grow. Mahatma Gandhi's Saturn (19° Scorpio) was close to the Sun's position today. Gandhi represented this power: the power to focus on the good, overcoming all fear. He stands as one of the great leaders of the twentieth century.

December 6: Sun 19° Scorpio: Meeting with Maroni, the widow of Nain (November 10, 30). Today marks the place of the Sun when Jesus met Maroni (mother of the Youth of Nain) in the Valley of the Doves, south of Capernaum. She begged him to come and heal her twelve-year-old son. As he taught in the synagogue at the beginning of the Sabbath, a possessed man ran in, causing great commotion.[2]

Images we can work with are the Valley of the Doves, the widow, and the possessed man. The Holy Spirit (dove) can find us as we renew our relationship with the World "I" (mystical union), which grants us deliverance from possession by our lower nature (the Scorpion becomes the Eagle). As we begin to find Christ, as Maroni did, the dove of the Holy Spirit will lead us back to the Father, and we will be widows no longer. First we remember, then we awaken, then we are reborn.

December 10 (7-10-13): Full moon and lunar eclipse, 23° Scorpio (DT): See "The Excitement of the Polarities at 23° to 24° of the Fixed Signs" in this *Journal*. The eclipse can be experienced in all of Asia and Australia, seen as rising over Eastern Europe and setting over northwest North America. It occurs at the exact degree of the Venus eclipse of the Sun in 2004, readying us for the eclipse in 2012.

Sun 23° Scorpio: The Raising of the Youth of Nain (November 13, 30).[3]

December 14: Sun 27° Scorpio: First raising of the daughter of Jairus (November 18, 30). Jesus is approached by Jairus, the chief of the synagogue. Jairus pleaded with Jesus to come and heal his daughter Salome, who was on the point of death (Mark 5:21–24). Jesus agreed to go with Jairus, but on the way a messenger arrived to say that Salome was already dead. Jesus, in his mercy, performed the miracle of raising Salome from the dead. Because of her parents' attitude toward Jesus, she was led again to her illness and death two weeks later.[4] The Bible refers to "the dead" as unconscious ego desires carried over from a previous life. According to Robert Powell, reincarnation shapes the soul; this is the "mother aspect." Destiny, however, is carried over by the stars; this is the "father aspect." In the soul of Salome, the mother forces are shaping, and in her meeting with Christ the father aspect is brought as a gift of destiny. If we do not change our habits when grace awakens us to our enslavement to these unconscious instincts and drives and desires from another life, we will fall again—as Salome did. Hereditary patterns are unconsciously imitated until penetrated (Scorpio) by our individuality. As we do this, we find our willingness to be raised from the dead. We find Christ within. The Scorpion becomes the Eagle.

December 17: Sun enters Sagittarius: Control of Speech becomes Feeling for Truth. Blessed are the self-disciplined for they shall know the truth.

December 17: Sun 0°44' Sagittarius: Stilling the Storm (November 21, 30). In this miracle (Luke 8:22–25), Jesus and his disciples are crossing a lake. While they are sailing Jesus falls asleep and a great storm mounts, casting great waves and endangering the little boat. The disciples awaken Jesus saying: "Master, Master, we are perishing!" Jesus rises, lifts his hand and a great calm ensues. The disciples are amazed at his command over the elements. Powerful images are contained in this story.

In changing times, much will be asked of human beings who try to keep their destiny communities (the boat) intact. Astral forces of wind and etheric forces of water will surge from the depths of both individual and collective human nature. Change requires that we decide between fear and conviction. The nature of one's conviction will determine one's course of destiny. Unshakable belief in Christ and Sophia calms the storms in both the human and the earthly kingdoms.

---

2 Powell, *Chron.* p. 256.
3 See Tresemer's article on page 45 of this *Journal*.
4 See Powell, *Chron.* p. 258.

The eurythmy gesture "G" (Sagittarius) uses the force of the upper arms to push away the forces of darkness, to open the veiled secrets and the curtains of deception, with an *aim* to reveal the light of clarity and to understand the truth.[5]

Solutions to complex world dilemmas become possible as we part the curtains. This is a day to remember and rekindle our willingness to aim our arrows (Sagittarius) with conviction toward solutions, living beyond worldly possibilities. Storms of one sort or another always accompany change. It is rare that the nature of the change is perceived correctly as it is occurring. An example is this:

> People talk of mysterious manifestations; the whole divine revelation of spring, summer, autumn, and winter is mixed up. Chaos is setting in, and this comes not from Heaven but from the interior of the Earth. People think that these are merely climate changes, but this is not the case.[6]

This is a great contemplation on the connection between the Earth's actions and human thinking.

December 19: Sun conjunct the Galactic Center, 2° Sagittarius. The Archer's arrow aims at the Galactic Center: the heart of the Milky Way. This is opposite to where the Sun was at Pentecost. This is a seminal position—as it pertains to December of 2012.[7]

December 24: Christmas Eve and a new moon. This is a night of special opportunity for us to receive a gift, born from our striving over the past year and given as a promise of our new potential in the coming year. Every Christmas, the Christ spirit is born anew.

New moon, 7° Sagittarius (DT): Temptation! Fragment from the Oracle of the Solar Cross: An alluring voice speaks:

> I promise your grandest and most beautiful dreams will come true. All your needs will be satisfied and all your fantasies will be realized. You will become a famous teacher and leader, filling the needs of the world. And you shall have joy forever.

This voice is compelling and powerful. It adds, "All you have to do is kneel down and worship me—me and only me."

In this degree, one meets the echo of the first temptation of the Teacher. Are you susceptible to these promises? Or do you sense something else of importance in your life? As you look around at your life and the beautiful dreams that tempt, what lies behind them? That is, whom do you worship by having those dreams? What is your answer to this voice? Such is the end to 2011 and preparation for 2012.

December 25: Christmas Day. Joy arises in our souls as we find ourselves in the nadir of the year, celebrating the victory of the light over the darkness.

Sun 8° Sagittarius: The Second Temptation (November 28, 29). This is the temptation of *false* power, just as the first temptation can be seen as the temptation of the *false kingdom*.

> Circumstances are always influenced by the subconscious if the human being is not active. If we do not strive continually with respect to our subconscious, we succumb to some kind of inertia, which leads to a darkening of the subconscious. Thus, human beings can find themselves in complete darkness. "The pinnacle of the temple" (Luke 4:11) is the superconscious. The temptation [of casting oneself from the pinnacle of the temple] of Jesus Christ in the wilderness is that of believing in the wisdom of the subconscious."[8]

Christ's light leads us ever nearer to the pinnacle of the temple. May we remember the holiness of the radiant cross of light: the Sun in the heavens, and the Sun in our hearts!

December 26: Sun 9° Sagittarius: The Third Temptation (November 29, 29). This is the temptation of *false* glory.

> The temptation of "turning stones to bread" is that of "producing" the living and organic from the dead and material.

---

5 Paul and Powell, *Cosmic Dances of the Zodiac*, p. 74.
6 Tomberg, *Christ and Sophia*, pp. 399–400.
7 More on this will appear in the 2012 *Journal*.

8 Tomberg, *Starlight*, vol. 10.

For example, one does precisely this if one conceives of thinking as a mechanical process in the brain. That is, if one supposes that the brain produces thoughts just as the glands produce secretion. Thus, the third temptation has to do with materialism, just as the second temptation has to do with the force of moral irresponsibility, and the first temptation with the will to power." (Ibid.)

December 28 to 29: Sun conjunct Pluto 12°19' Sagittarius. The Sun was conjunct Pluto at the third temptation of Christ and at the raising of the daughter of Jairus. According to the Apocalypse Code by Robert Powell, one day in the life of Christ is equal to 29½ years in history. Applying this code, the time of the third temptation for humanity spans the years 1988 to 2018.[9] During this 29½-year period every Sun–Pluto conjunction is a heightened confrontation with the Prince of Darkness. When Pluto was at this degree John the Baptist was beheaded. This occurred during Herod's birthday celebration where his wife, Herodias, sent her daughter, Salome, to dance voluptuously before Herod. So entranced was Herod that he vowed to give her whatever she wished. Salome, prodded by her mother, asked for the head of John the Baptist on a platter. Mars at this time was close to the Pleiades (5° Taurus).

The Pleiades are the source of the Word and here the evil inspiration of negative Mars spirits acted in opposition to the Word. John was the one sent by God to reveal the Word bearer.[10] As the year ends with this conjunction, during the Holy Nights we may contemplate the lofty forces of our Father in heaven and his eternal guidance through his Sophia and his Son. Our true nourishment is from every word that issues from the mouth of God. Stones are stones and no matter the cunning of the virtual world dancing before us, we are not to be distracted by Salome, but rather stay faithful to the Word. It is just this faithfulness that raises us from the dead of material illusions.

December 30: Sun 14° Sagittarius: The healing of two possessed youths from Gergesa (December 5, 30). Jesus meets two possessed by ahrimanic demons inhabiting tombs beside a path. Because of the two possessed, none could pass owing to the demons' exceeding force. When they saw Jesus they cried out: "What have you to do with us, O Son of God?" (Matthew 8:29). Jesus cast out the demons into a nearby herd of swine, whereon the whole herd of swine rushed down a steep bank into the sea.

In this healing, the relationship of Ahriman to the element of water becomes clear. The perceptive demons recognize the Son of God and experienced him as a direct threat to their activity. The demons call out from the possessed, asking to be thrown into the herd of swine. Cleverly, as Ahriman stood before Christ, he wished to be cast into the swine so that through the people eating of the swine meat the demons would find more than just two bodies to possess. It was known in ancient wisdom that Ahriman could enter the human lymph system (the fluid system) through the pinworms in pork. This was the knowledge behind the Jewish prohibition against eating pork. Those laws were disregarded in this region. When the people of Gergesa heard of the death of their swine, they asked Jesus to leave. In the words of Judith von Halle:

> The fact that the Gergesenes finally urged the Lord to leave their district, expresses the tragic aspect which the Christ impulse already bore at the dawn of the new era, and must always bear whenever it encounters evil. People had then degenerated to such an extent that they could not properly value the benefits of His deed, but, happy to violate the laws, were more interested in the profit and loss attached to their herd of swine than in their own healing and wellbeing.[11]

As our year ends and we enter the year 2012, we can ask ourselves if we, too, are happy to violate the laws, preferring to cast out Christ rather than serve the flame of Love?

---

9 See Powell and Dann, *Christ & the Maya Calendar*, chapter 2.
10 See Powell's article on the Pleiades, pp. 31ff in this *Journal*.
11 See von Halle, *Illness and Healing*, pp. 132–138.

CORRECTION

In the *Journal for Star Wisdom 2010*, the song entitled "Epitaph: Though my soul may set in darkness" is on page 103. There it is stated that the music is by Josef Haydn and the words of the epitaph are attributed to Galileo.

> *Though my soul may set in darkness, it will rise in perfect light;*
> *I have loved the stars too fondly to be fearful of the night.*

These words are incorrectly attributed to Galileo's epitaph. This is a common error. The words are the last two lines of the poem "The Old Astronomer to his Pupil" by the English poet Sarah Williams (1837–1868). A slightly altered version of the words—"We have loved the stars too fondly to be fearful of the night"—appears on the crypt of astronomer John Brashear, and these words have become the motto for the Amateur Astronomers Association of Pittsburgh.

Galileo died in 1642, having been forced to abjure heliocentricity in 1633. He had begged to be buried in his family tomb in Santa Croce in Florence, but this request was denied. His friends wished to erect a monument over him; this, too, was refused. Pope Urban VIII said to the ambassador Niccolini that "it would be an evil example for the world if such honors were rendered to a man who had been brought before the Roman Inquisition for an opinion so false and erroneous; who had communicated it to many others, and who had given so great a scandal to Christendom." In accordance, therefore, with the wish of the Pope and the orders of the Inquisition, Galileo was buried ignobly, apart from his family, without fitting ceremony, without monument, without epitaph. Not until forty years after did Pierrozzi dare write an inscription to be placed above his bones; not until a further hundred years later did Nelli dare transfer his remains to a suitable position in Santa Croce, and erect a monument above them.

In a speech to the Pontifical Academy of Sciences in October 1992, Pope John Paul II stated that the Galileo affair—his condemnation in 1633 on "vehement suspicion of heresy" for holding to the Copernican heliocentric view that the Sun (and not the Earth) is at the center of the solar system—had created a myth of the supposed conflict between science and religion. In response, the *New York Times* reported that the Church had finally admitted that Galileo was right and that the Earth does revolve around the Sun. According to legend, these apocryphal words *"Eppur si muove"* ("And yet it does move," referring to the Earth) were muttered under his breath by Galileo as he rose from kneeling after making his abjuration of heliocentricity.

In 1737, almost a century after Galileo's death, in the same church that Michelangelo was interred in—the church of Santa Croce—Galileo's remains were transferred to a vault in the new monument designed by Giovanni Battista Foggini. The first part of the Latin epitaph on Galileo's tomb in the church of Santa Croce reads in English translation:

> *Galileo Galilei*
> *Notable citizen of Florence*
> *Most Eminent Restorer of Geometry, Astronomy and Philosophy*
> *Comparable to no one in his time.*

ABOUT THE CONTRIBUTORS

DANIEL ANDREEV (1906-1959) was born in Berlin. His father was the well-known Russian writer Leonid Andreev. His mother Alexandra Veligorsky died during childbirth. Daniel's father, overcome with grief, gave up Andreev to Alexandra's sister Elizabeth Dobrov, who lived in Moscow. It was a critical event in Daniel Andreev's life, for in contrast to many of the Russian intelligentsia at the time, the family maintained its Russian Orthodox faith. Daniel's childhood included contact with persons such as his godfather Maxim Gorky. Daniel was conscripted as a noncombatant in the Soviet Army in 1942, and after the war he returned to writing fiction and poetry. He was arrested in 1947, along with his wife and many of his relatives and friends, and sentenced to twenty-five years in prison, while his wife received twenty-five years of labor camp. All of his previous writings were destroyed. With the rise of Khrushchev, Andreev's case was reviewed and his sentence reduced to ten years. He was released to his waiting wife in 1957, his health ruined following a heart attack in prison. While in prison, he had written the first drafts of *The Rose of the World* and *Russian Gods* (a collection of poetry), as well as *The Iron Mystery*, a play in verse. Andreev spent the last two years of his life finishing these works. Andreev's wife Alla, realizing the negative reception the books would get from the Soviet authorities, hid them until the mid-1970s and did not publish them until Gorbachev and glasnost. The first edition of *The Rose of the World* (100,000 copies) quickly sold out, and since then several editions have been equally popular in Russia.

WILLIAM BENTO, Ph.D., has worked in the field of human development for more than thirty years. He is a recognized pioneer and a published author in psychosophy (soul wisdom) and astrosophy (star wisdom) and travels extensively as a speaker, teacher, and consultant. He currently resides in Citrus Heights, California. Dr. Bento is the Associate Dean of Academic Affairs at Rudolf Steiner College, Fair Oaks, California and works as a transpersonal clinical psychologist at the Center for Living Health in Gold River, California. His involvement in guiding social therapy seminars for Camphill Communities has been well received over the last two decades. He is coauthor of *Signs in the Heavens: A Message for Our Time* and author of *Lifting the Veil of Mental Illness: An Approach to Anthroposophical Psychology*. His forthcoming book is *Psychosophy: A Primer for an Extended Anthroposophical Psychology*, to be published by SteinerBooks.

KEVIN DANN, Ph.D., has taught history at SUNY Plattsburgh, the University of Vermont, and Rutgers University. His books include *Bright Colors Falsely Seen* (1998); *Across the Great Border Fault* (2000); *Lewis Creek Lost and Found* (2001); *A Short Story of American Destiny, 1909–2009* (2008); and (with Robert Powell) *Christ & the Maya Calendar: 2012 & the Coming of the Antichrist* (2009) and *The Astrological Revolution: Unveiling the Science of the Stars as a Science of Reincarnation and Karma* (2010).

WAIN FARRANTS discovered astrology (both tropical and sidereal) and Anthroposophy during his first years at the University of Toronto. After completing a B.Sc. in psychology and mathematics, he spent the next few years teaching math at a secondary school in Mochudi, Botswana. Later, he traveled to England and became a biodynamic gardener in a Camphill Community for disabled adults in the North York Moors National Park. After a few years there, he assumed responsibility for the Botton Village Bookshop. He has edited and coedited numerous books written by Karl König, Peter Roth, Baruch Urieli, Peter Tradowsky, and Andrea Damico Gibson. Wain has also contributed a number of articles to the *Christian Star Calendar*. He has considerable experience in a wide variety of orthodox, complementary medical, and alternative therapies, without which he would not have made his contribution to the *Journal*.

BRIAN GRAY trained as an architect, and, since 1981, he has been teaching at Rudolf Steiner College in Fair Oaks, California. He has taught classes to aspiring Waldorf school teachers on topics such as the creation of the world and cosmic warmth from a spiritual perspective, sacred architecture, and the constitution of the human being. He has also taught various aspects of Astrosophy as it relates to biography, life cycles, karma and reincarnation, and astro-geographia. A student of astrology since 1967, Brian has interpreted astrological charts for thousands of people and offers regular classes in observation of the stars and in Esoteric Christianity. He has discovered hidden astrological keys in several important works of literature, from the Parsifal story of the Grail Knights to parts of the Bible. Brian directs the Foundations in Anthroposophy Program at Rudolf Steiner College. At Easter 2011, he will help lead a tour of the Holy Land, Petra, and Turkey, exploring sacred sites and sacred architecture.

 CLAUDIA MCLAREN LAINSON is a teacher and Therapeutic Educator. She has been working in the field of Anthroposophy since 1982, when she founded her first Waldorf program in Boulder, Colorado. She lectures nationally on various topics related to spiritual science, human development, the evolution of consciousness and the emerging Christ and Sophia mysteries of the twenty-first century. Claudia is the founder of Windrose Farm and Academy near Boulder. Windrose is a biodynamic farm and academy for collaborative work in anthroposophic courses, therapeutic education, cosmic and sacred dance and nature-based educational programs. Claudia most recently founded the School for the Sophia Mysteries at Windrose.

 SALLY NURNEY has been interested in astrology all her life, beginning her research with her "Sun sign" in elementary school. After several years of travel and exploration, she arrived at The StarHouse in Boulder, Colorado, in 1997 and quickly transitioned to the Sidereal perspective of reading the stars. Along with her studies in the Path of the Ceremonial Arts, she has deepened her direct understanding of the stars through research with David Tresemer at The StarHouse and study with Brian Gray at the Rudolf Steiner College in Fair Oaks, California. She currently lives in the Rocky Mountain foothills near the StarHouse of Boulder.

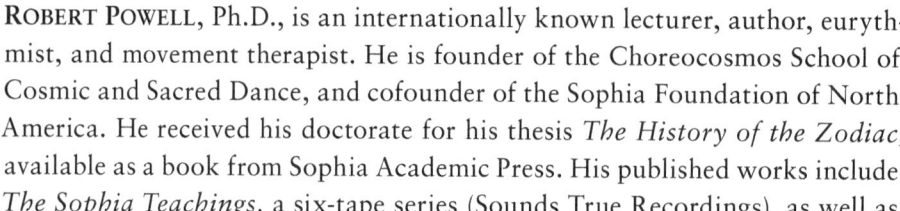
ROBERT POWELL, Ph.D., is an internationally known lecturer, author, eurythmist, and movement therapist. He is founder of the Choreocosmos School of Cosmic and Sacred Dance, and cofounder of the Sophia Foundation of North America. He received his doctorate for his thesis *The History of the Zodiac*, available as a book from Sophia Academic Press. His published works include *The Sophia Teachings*, a six-tape series (Sounds True Recordings), as well as *Elijah Come Again: A Prophet for Our Time*; *The Mystery, Biography, and Destiny of Mary Madgalene*; *Divine Sophia—Holy Wisdom*; *The Most Holy Trinosophia and the New Revelation of the Divine Feminine*; *Chronicle of the Living Christ*; *Christian Hermetic Astrology*; *The Christ Mystery*; *The Sign of the Son of Man in the Heavens*; *The Morning Meditation in Eurythmy*; and the yearly *Journal for Star Wisdom* (previously *Christian Star Calendar*). He translated the spiritual classic *Meditations on the Tarot* and co-translated Valentin Tomberg's *Lazarus, Come Forth!* Robert is also coauthor with Kevin Dann of *The Astrological Revolution: Unveiling the Science of the Stars as a Science of Reincarnation and Karma* and *Christ & the Maya Calendar: 2012 & the Coming of the Antichrist*; and coauthor with Lacquanna Paul of *Cosmic Dances of the Zodiac* and *Cosmic Dances of the Planets*. He teaches a gentle form of healing movement: the sacred dance of eurythmy, as well as the cosmic dances of the planets and signs of the zodiac. Through the Sophia Grail Circle, Robert facilitates sacred celebrations dedicated to the Divine Feminine. He offers workshops in Europe, Australia, and North America, and with Karen Rivers, cofounder of the Sophia Foundation, leads pilgrimages to the world's sacred sites: Turkey, 1996; the Holy Land, 1997; France, 1998; Britain, 2000; Italy, 2002; Greece, 2004; Egypt, 2006; India, 2008; Turkey, 2009; and the Grand Canyon, 2010. Visit www.sophiafoundation.org and and www.astrogeographia.org.

DAVID TRESEMER, Ph.D., has a doctorate in psychology. In 1990, he cofounded the StarHouse in Boulder, Colorado, for community gatherings and workshops (www.TheStarHouse.org) and cofounded, with his wife Lila, the Healing Dreams Retreat Centre in Australia (www.healingdreams.com.au). He has also founded the Star Wisdom website (www.StarWisdom.org), which offers readings from the Oracle of the Solar Crosses, an oracle relating to the heavenly imprint received on one's day of birth. Dr. Tresemer has written in many areas, including *The Scythe Book: Mowing Hay, Cutting Weeds, and Harvesting Small Grains with Hand Tools* and a book on mythic theater, *War in Heaven: Accessing Myth Through Drama*. With his wife, he also coauthored several plays produced in the U.S., including *My Magdalene* (winner of Moondance 2004, Best Script). With William Bento and Robert Schiappacasse, he wrote *Signs in the Heavens: A Message for Our Time*. He is also the author, with Robert Schiappacasse, of *Star Wisdom & Rudolf Steiner: A Life Seen through the Oracle of the Solar Cross*, and with his wife, the recent book, *One-Two-ONE: A Guidebook for Conscious Partnerships, Weddings, and Rededication Ceremonies*.

THE ASTROLOGICAL REVOLUTION
Unveiling the Science of the Stars as a Science of Reincarnation and Karma

Robert Powell and Kevin Dann

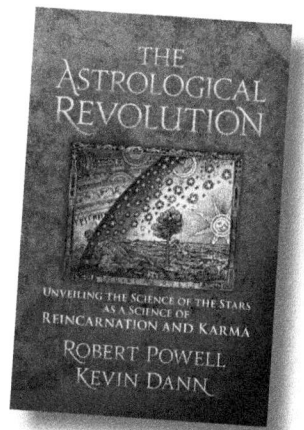

Humanity has for many centuries employed astrology to penetrate the mystery of the stars' relationship to human destiny. Based on decades of research into both astrological reincarnation and the history of astronomy/astrology, *The Astrological Revolution* unfolds this mystery. The reader is invited to call into question the basis of modern astrology. This basis, the tropical zodiac, emerged through Greek astronomers from what was originally a calendar dividing the year into twelve solar months. The fact that ninety-eight percent of Western astrologers use the tropical zodiac means that contemporary Western astrology is based on a calendar system that does not reflect the actual location of the planets against the background of the starry heavens. In other words, most astrologers in the West are practicing a form of astrology that no longer embodies the reality of the stars.

What is needed to bring astrology (which means the "science of the stars") back into alignment with the stars in the heavens? The first step in an astrological revolution that leads to true astrology is to recognize the sidereal zodiac (sidereal meaning "related to the stars"). In antiquity, the Babylonians, Egyptians, Greeks, Romans, and Hindus used the sidereal zodiac, and Hindu (Vedic) astrologers still use the sidereal zodiac. Based on recognition—through the newly discovered rules of astrological reincarnation, that the sidereal zodiac presents an authentic astrological zodiac—a new practice of astrology is possible. It offers tools to reestablish a wisdom-filled astrology for the modern world. This new astrology, based on the sidereal zodiac, is a modernized form of the classic sidereal astrology practiced by the three magi, who, prompted by the stars, journeyed to Bethlehem two millennia ago.

Drawing on specific biographical examples, *The Astrological Revolution* reveals new understandings of how the starry heavens work into human destiny. For instance, the book demonstrates the newly discovered rules of astrological reincarnation through the previous incarnations of composer Franz Schubert and his patron Joseph von Spaun—respectively, the Sultan of Morocco, Abu Yusuf Ya'qub, and his erstwhile enemy, Alfonso X, the Castilian King known as "El Sabio" (the Learned), along with their sidereal horoscopes. Rudolf Steiner's biography is also considered in relation to the sidereal zodiac and the rules of astrological reincarnation.

After reestablishing the sidereal zodiac as a basis for astrology that penetrates the mystery of the stars' relationship to human destiny, the reader is invited to discover the astrological significance of the totality of the vast sphere of stars surrounding the Earth. *The Astrological Revolution* points to the astrological significance of the entire celestial sphere, including all the stars and constellations beyond the twelve zodiacal signs. This discovery is revealed by studying the megastars, the most luminous stars of our galaxy, illustrating how megastars show up in an extraordinary way in Christ's healing miracles by aligning with the Sun at the time of those miraculous events. *The Astrological Revolution* thus offers a spiritual—yet scientific—path of building a new relationship to the stars.

www.steinerbooks.org | ISBN: 9781584200833 | 254 pages | paperback | $25.00

www.ingramcontent.com/pod-product-compliance
Lightning Source LLC
Chambersburg PA
CBHW081234170426
43198CB00017B/2759